READING McDOWELL

McDowell's path-breaking *Mind and World* was a brilliantly original, provocative, and rather cryptic book. *Reading McDowell* makes it much easier to grasp his intentions and strategies. It contains stimulating and fruitful exchanges between McDowell and some of the major figures of contemporary philosophy.

Richard Rorty, Stanford University

John McDowell's *Mind and World* is one of the most significant and widely discussed works of late twentieth-century philosophy. Smith brings together some first-class essays by some of the finest philosophers in the world, and McDowell's responses to his critics are illuminating. This book is an indispensable guide to McDowell's *Mind and World*; everyone with a serious interest in the subject will want to own a copy.

Tim Crane, University College London

John McDowell's *Mind and World* is widely acknowledged to be one of the most important contributions to philosophy in recent years. In this volume leading philosophers examine the nature and extent of McDowell's achievement in *Mind and World* and related writings.

The chapters, most of which were specially commissioned for this volume, are divided into five parts. The essays in part one consider *Mind and World*'s location in the modern philosophical tradition, particularly its relation to Kant's critical project. Parts two and three cover issues in epistemology and philosophy of mind, while in part four the focus turns to problems of rationality, realism and ethics. In the final part of the book McDowell responds to the contributors and further elaborates his own views. Together, the essays provide an indispensable resource for understanding McDowell's work and they offer an illuminating snapshot of the state of play in contemporary philosophy.

Contributors: J. M. Bernstein, Richard J. Bernstein, Robert Brandom, Rüdiger Bubner, Michael Friedman, Axel Honneth, Charles Larmore, Gregory McCulloch, John McDowell, Robert B. Pippin, Hilary Putnam, Barry Stroud, Charles Taylor, Crispin Wright.

Editor: Nicholas H. Smith is Senior Lecturer in the Department of Philosophy at Macquarie University, Sydney, Australia. He is the author of *Strong Hermeneutics* (Routledge, 1997) and *Charles Taylor* (2002).

READING McDOWELL

On Mind and World

Edited by Nicholas H. Smith

London and New York

First published 2002
by Routledge
11 New Fetter Lane, London EC4P 4EE

Simultaneously published in the USA and Canada
by Routledge
29 West 35th Street, New York, NY 10001

Routledge is an imprint of the Taylor & Francis Group

Selection and editorial matter © 2002 Nicholas H. Smith
Individual chapters © 2002 respective contributors

Typeset in Goudy by Taylor & Francis Books Ltd
Printed and bound in Great Britain by MPG Books Ltd, Bodmin

British Library Cataloguing in Publication Data
A catalogue record for this book is available from the British Library

Library of Congress Cataloging-in-Publication Data
A catalog record for this title has been requested

ISBN 0–415–21212–X (hbk)
ISBN 0–415–21213–8 (pbk)

CONTENTS

CONTENTS

CONTENTS

CONTRIBUTORS

J.M. Bernstein is University Distinguished Professor of Philosophy in the Graduate Faculty of the New School for Social Research, New York. He is the author of: *The Fate of Art: Aesthetic Alienation from Kant to Derrida and Adorno* (1992), *Recovering Ethical Life: Jürgen Habermas and the Future of Critical Theory* (1995), and, most recently, *Adorno: Disenchantment and Ethics* (2001). He is completing a work provisionally entitled *Against Voluptuous Bodies and Other Essays for a Late Modernism*.

Richard J. Bernstein is Vera List Professor of Philosophy at the New School for Social Research, New York. His books include *Beyond Objectivism and Relativism* (1983), *The New Constellation* (1991), *Hannah Arendt and the Jewish Question* (1996), *Freud and the Legacy of Moses* (1998), and *Radical Evil: A Philosophical Interrogation* (2002). His current research concerns a new interpretation of twentieth-century philosophy as The Pragmatic Century.

Robert Brandom is Distinguished Service Professor of Philosophy at the University of Pittsburgh. His books include *Making it Explicit: Reasoning, Representing and Discursive Commitment* (1994), *Articulating Reasons: An Introduction to Inferentialism* (2000), and *Tales of the Mighty Dead: Historical Essays in the Metaphysics of Intentionality* (2002).

Rüdiger Bubner is Professor of Philosophy at the University of Heidelberg. He is the author of several books, including *Handlung, Sprache und Vernunft* (1976), *Modern German Philosophy* (1981), *Ästhetische Erfahrung* (1989), and *Polis und Staat* (2002).

Michael Friedman is currently Ruth N. Halls Professor of Arts and Humanities at Indiana University and Frederick P. Rehmus Family Professor of Humanities at Stanford University. His publications include *Foundations of Space–Time Theories: Relativistic Physics and the Philosophy of Science* (1986), *Kant and the Exact Sciences* (1992), *Reconsidering Logical Positivism* (1999), *A Parting of the Ways: Carnap, Cassirer, and Heidegger* (2000), and *Dynamics Of Reason* (2001).

Axel Honneth is Professor of Philosophy at the Goethe University, Frankfurt. His books translated into English include *The Critique of Power* (1991), *The Struggle for Recognition* (1995), *The Fragmented World of the Social: Essays in Social and Political Philosophy* (1995), and *Suffering from Indeterminacy: An Attempt at a Reactualization of Hegel's Philosophy of Right* (2000).

Charles Larmore is Chester D. Tripp Professor in the Humanities at the University of Chicago. His books include *Patterns of Moral Complexity* (1987), *The Morals of Modernity* (1996), and *The Romantic Legacy* (1996). He is completing a book (in French) on the nature of the self, entitled *Les pratiques du moi*.

Gregory McCulloch was Professor of Philosophy at Birmingham University. Among his many publications are the following books: *The Game of the Name* (1989), *Using Sartre: An analytical introduction to early Sartrean themes* (1994), and *The Mind and its World* (1995).

John McDowell is a University Professor of Philosophy at the University of Pittsburgh; previously he was a Fellow of University College, Oxford. Apart from *Mind and World*, his works include a translation with notes of *Plato's Theaetetus* (1974) and a number of articles, many of which are collected in *Mind, Value, and Reality* and *Meaning, Knowledge, and Reality* (both 1998). He prepared Gareth Evans's *The Varieties of Reference* for publication (1982); and he co-edited, with Evans, *Truth and Meaning* (1976), and, with Philip Pettit, *Subject, Thought, and Context* (1986).

Robert B. Pippin is the Raymond W. and Martha Hilpert Gruner Distinguished Service Professor in the Committee on Social Thought, the Department of Philosophy, and the College at the University of Chicago. He is the author of several books, including *Hegel's Idealism: The Satisfactions of Self-Consciousness* (1989) and, most recently, *Henry James and Modern Moral Life* (2001).

Hilary Putnam is Cogan University Professor Emeritus at Harvard University. His books include *Reason, Truth and History* (1981), *Realism with a Human Face* (1990), *Renewing Philosophy* (1993), *Pragmatism* (1994), *Words and Life* (1995), and *The Threefold Cord: Mind, Body and World* (2001). His *The Collapse of the Fact/Value Dichotomy and Other Essays* will be published by Harvard University Press in 2002–2003.

Nicholas H. Smith is Senior Lecturer in Philosophy at Macquarie University, Sydney, Australia. He is the author of *Strong Hermeneutics: Contingency and Moral Identity* (1997) and *Charles Taylor: Meaning, Morals and Modernity* (2002).

Barry Stroud is Mills Professor of Metaphysics and Epistemology at the University of California, Berkeley. He is the author of *Hume* (1977), *The*

Significance of Philosophical Scepticism (1984), *The Quest for Reality* (1999), and two volumes of collected essays, *Understanding Human Knowledge* and *Meaning, Understanding, and Practice* (2000).

Charles Taylor is Emeritus Professor of Philosophy at McGill University. He has published several books, including *Hegel* (1975), *Sources of the Self* (1989), and *Philosophical Arguments* (1995). He is at present working on a book on modernity and secularism.

Crispin Wright, FBA, is Wardlaw Professor in the University of St Andrews, and a Leverhulme Research Professor (1998–2003). He is a regular Visiting Professor at Columbia and New York Universities. His books include *Wittgenstein on the Foundations of Mathematics* (1980), *Frege's Conception of Numbers as Objects* (1983), *Truth and Objectivity* (1992), *Realism, Meaning and Truth* (1993), and, with Bob Hale, *The Reason's Proper Study* (2001). His most recent book, *Rails to Infinity* (2001), collects together his writings on the central themes of Wittgenstein's *Philosophical Investigations*.

ACKNOWLEDGEMENTS

First, I would like to thank all the contributors to this volume for their contributions and their cooperation. I am particularly grateful to John McDowell for generously offering his set of responses.

A number of people kindly shared ideas with me about the book. I am grateful to them all, but Barry Lee and Phil Gerrans deserve a special mention. I am also grateful to Jim Conant and two anonymous referees for helpful comments. I'd like to express particularly warm thanks to Tim Crane, and to Tony Bruce and Muna Khogali at Routledge, for supporting the project. I am grateful to Maeve Cooke for helpful advice regarding the translation of Axel Honneth's paper. And I acknowledge the financial support of Macquarie University in the form of a research grant awarded in the second semester of 1999.

Two of the chapters have been published previously in journals: "Exorcising the Philosophical Tradition" by Michael Friedman first appeared in *Philosophical Review* 105: 427–467 (1996), and "Human Nature?" by Crispin Wright appeared in *European Journal of Philosophy* 4(2): 235–254 (1996). I thank the editors and publishers for permission to reprint this material.

Finally, on behalf of everyone involved with the book I would like to pay tribute to Greg McCulloch, who died while the book was in production.

INTRODUCTION

Nicholas H. Smith

Perhaps no book written in the past decade or so has generated more interest amongst professional philosophers than John McDowell's *Mind and World*. It has been and continues to be the subject of innumerable seminars, symposia, conferences, and research papers, not just in English but in several languages. It has become – in conjunction with McDowell's other writings – a key reference point in contemporary debates in epistemology, philosophy of mind, and meta-ethics. It has featured prominently in recent reassessments of Kant's legacy for philosophy. And it has stimulated renewed discussion, amongst philosophers in both Anglo-Saxon and European traditions, of the fundamental predicament of modern philosophy itself. Small wonder that *Mind and World* is already widely regarded as a classic.

My primary goal in compiling this collection of essays has been to enable readers to reach an informed, balanced judgment on the nature and extent of McDowell's achievement. I have sought to do this by bringing together high-quality readings of McDowell from a variety of philosophical perspectives, and by including a response from McDowell to these readings. While some of the essays deal exclusively with *Mind and World*, most cast their net more widely, either by addressing points that have arisen in the critical reception of McDowell's work, or by engaging with important material written by McDowell both before and after the publication of *Mind and World*. The two previously published critical notices of *Mind and World* included here (Crispin Wright's "Human Nature?" and Michael Friedman's "Exorcising the Philosophical Tradition") had a particularly strong impact on the reception of McDowell's book, as the references to them by some of the other contributors testify. Crispin Wright has also written a "Postscript" to "Human Nature?" especially for this volume. Among the other commissioned essays, those by the late Gregory McCulloch and by Axel Honneth deal as much with McDowell's previous writings in philosophy of mind and meta-ethics as they do with *Mind and World*, and Robert Pippin's piece considers McDowell's post-*Mind and World* writings on Kant and Sellars. The essays by Robert Brandom, Charles Taylor, and Hilary Putnam, while previously unpublished, were already written by the time I started collecting contributions. My good fortune in being able to include

1

them has helped me realize a secondary goal in undertaking this project. For I have been driven by the conviction that a volume such as this presents an opportunity not only for advancing our understanding of McDowell's work, but also for showing how a conversation is possible, amongst leading representatives of diverse philosophical traditions, about a subject-matter of deep concern to all.

I have divided the essays into five parts. The three essays that make up the first part thematize *Mind and World*'s location in the philosophical tradition, in particular its relation to Kant and post-Kantian idealism. Richard J. Bernstein reflects on the original way in which *Mind and World* follows through a Hegelian strategy for building on Kant's insights, a strategy – Bernstein points out – that is pursued in different forms by the American pragmatists, notably C.S. Peirce. The conceptual issues Bernstein draws attention to are explored more fully in later chapters. Michael Friedman's essay adopts a more critical perspective on the way McDowell situates himself in relation to the modern philosophical tradition. Friedman begins by challenging McDowell's interpretation of Kant, especially Kant's crucial distinction between sensibility and the understanding. He then outlines a genealogy of late twentieth-century analytic philosophy that leads back from Davidson – whose work provides the immediate background for *Mind and World* – to Quine, logical positivism, and from there to the Kantianism of the Marburg School. In view of this historical recontextualization, Friedman questions whether *Mind and World* really represents an advance on the position developed by Davidson – indeed, he suspects that the version of "absolute idealism" McDowell sketches there amounts to a regression. The contrast with Robert Pippin's chapter could not be more striking. While, like Friedman, Pippin is ultimately unconvinced by McDowell's alternative to Davidsonian coherentism, the source of Pippin's dissatisfaction is that McDowell is not "idealist" enough. The thrust of Pippin's argument is that McDowell's well-motivated idealism is spoiled by an adventitious desire to "re-enchant nature." The misplaced notion that nature requires an even partial re-enchantment embroils McDowell in difficulties – so Pippin argues – that Hegel, to his credit, managed to avoid. Pippin thus urges a radicalization (rather than a domestication) of the Hegelian spirit informing McDowell's work.

The second group of essays deals in different ways with the significance of McDowell's theory of experience for epistemology, broadly conceived. The focus of Barry Stroud's chapter is the notion of sense-experience or "impression" which, in McDowell's account, makes perceptual access to the world intelligible. Without such access the very idea of empirical knowledge is in jeopardy and yet, as Stroud notes, philosophers have had an extraordinarily difficult time making sense of it. Stroud then examines in some detail the justificatory or grounding role played by impressions in McDowell's theory, and he appraises McDowell's success in negotiating the epistemological "minefield" associated with "impression" talk. McDowell's concept of perceptual experience is also the central topic of Robert Brandom's chapter. Brandom begins with a reconstruction of what exactly is "empiricist" about McDowell's philosophy – an empiricism which is not, Brandom points out, incompatible with rationalist elements. He then strives to bring out the distinctive character of McDowell's concept of perceptual experience by contrasting it with two kindred notions, that of non-inferential knowledge on the one hand, and awareness of secondary qualities on the other. Against this contrast, the subtlety of McDowell's notion, but also its potential weaknesses, begin to emerge. Charles Taylor takes a broader perspective on McDowell's critique of classical epistemology. For Taylor, the epistemology McDowell criticizes incorporates a distinction between the "inner" and the "outer" that thinkers such as Heidegger and Merleau-Ponty have decisively undermined by showing that conceptual thought is always already embedded in a "background" of pre-conceptual ways of living and coping. While sympathetic to McDowell, Taylor is concerned that his model of empirical knowledge is in danger of losing sight of this background, the retrieval of which is crucial for overcoming the very picture of mind and world that in McDowell's own view "holds us captive." The chapter concludes with a consideration of how recent foundationalist epistemology distorts attempts at understanding other cultures.

If epistemology must be concerned with the justificatory relations that exist between experience and beliefs, as well as between beliefs themselves, then clearly it is going to merge with philosophy of mind. There are reasons, however, for wanting to keep the two domains of inquiry separate. One such reason, as Gregory McCulloch explains drawing on work published by McDowell prior to *Mind and World*, is that it helps to keep in view the mind's essential feature – intentionality. McCulloch shares McDowell's conviction that the great flaw in all Cartesian approaches to the mind – that is, approaches that build in a "Real Distinction" between mind and body – is that they make a mystery of how thought is able to be *about* objects at all. This is quite different from the capacity – naturally brought into question once the "Real Distinction" is in place – of the mind to know whether the objects that appear to it are external or not. To have one's mind directed at the world is one thing, to be able to justify beliefs about it is another. Because McCulloch takes the intelligibility of content, or thought about the world, to be primarily a phenomenological matter, he expresses reservations about McDowell's focus on justification in *Mind and World*. In its place he sketches an account of intentionality called "phenomenological externalism" that aspires to be more attuned with McDowell's earlier work. Crispin Wright, on the other hand, argues that a much more radical revision of the project undertaken in *Mind and World* is needed – if, indeed, it is salvageable at all. Wright gives two basic reasons. First, he draws attention to the violence McDowell's concept of experience seems to do to deeply embedded intuitions about the experience of animals and infants. If experience requires the involvement of conceptual capacities, as McDowell proposes, what are we to make of the apparent experiences of infants and non-human animals, beings in whom those capacities appear absent? This would only be a problem that needs solving, Wright continues, if there were no real alternatives to McDowell's notion of experience. But according to Wright's second line of attack, McDowell's arguments against those alternatives fall short; in Wright's view, they are either unconvincing or, at best, undeveloped. Hilary Putnam's contribution to the volume takes up a different issue raised by McDowell's thesis that perception involves the exercise of conceptual powers: its relation to the "direct realism" championed by McDowell in the philosophy of mind. Putnam regrets that direct realism plays no explicit role in the argument of *Mind and World*. He then reflects on some of the metaphysical issues that arise once direct realism is brought into the picture, issues that in Putnam's view call for a more serious engagement with functionalist theories than we find in *Mind and World*.

Of course, McDowell is well known as an advocate of realism not just in the philosophy of mind but in moral philosophy too. The essays in the fourth part consider some of the connections between the argument of *Mind and World* and McDowell's moral realism. A recurrent theme in this context is McDowell's conception of *reason*. Charles Larmore is impressed by McDowell's basic realist insight that reasons are there to be found in ethics as much as in science. He agrees with McDowell's thesis that moral knowledge is no less intelligible than any kind of valid normative claim, and he welcomes the idea, advanced by McDowell, that the acquisition and growth of such knowledge is impossible outside of some historical tradition. But far from bringing philosophy peace, Larmore sees this as opening up the further issue of the ontology of reasons, an issue that in Larmore's view can only be dealt with by constructive philosophy. It is McDowell's refusal to join in this endeavor – his "Wittgensteinian quietism" – that provides the central target of Larmore's critique. Rüdiger Bubner's essay presents a more up-beat appraisal of McDowell's Wittgensteinianism. For Bubner, this has to be understood in conjunction with McDowell's use of the notions of *Bildung* and "second nature" in *Mind and World*. Bubner's reflections on the historical significance of the term *Bildung*, and its potential for conflict with the Aristotelian idea of second nature, will be read with particular interest by those not so familiar with the German tradition to which these notions belong. The essay also contains more general remarks on agency and rationality from a hermeneutic perspective. Jay Bernstein begins his chapter by noting what he takes to be a commonality of purpose between McDowell's project in *Mind and World* and the work of Theodore Adorno: to achieve a "reconciliation" between reason and nature. But if we compare the two attempts at realizing this goal, Bernstein argues, we are bound to glimpse serious deficiencies in McDowell's approach. Some of these have to do with McDowell's philosophical method, which in Bernstein's view is insufficiently attuned to the disfigurements of modern social reality to be able to reconcile reason and nature properly. Bernstein finds other deficiencies in the details of McDowell's account of the "space of reasons," which for Bernstein are insensitive to the cognitive but non-conceptual grasp of things we have as subjects of experience. Bernstein argues provocatively that McDowell remains captive to the rationalized reason he seeks to escape from, and that consequently he is less well equipped than Adorno for tackling the central tasks of ethics in an age of disenchantment. Axel Honneth deals more directly with McDowell's moral realism. He begins by noting some convergences between McDowell's meta-ethical position and the "weak naturalism" recently elaborated by Jürgen Habermas. After reconstructing the epistemological background to McDowell's theory, he then explicates the philosophical motivation behind McDowell's central realist tenet – that we have a socialized perceptual access to a world of moral facts. While Honneth is not wholly unsympathetic to this view, he draws attention to the difficulty it seems to have in explaining how the rational reso-lution of conflicting moral perceptions is possible. For Honneth, morality must have a principle-oriented character that can come into play when everyday moral perceptions lose their authority. This suggests to Honneth, as it does to Habermas, that it is in virtue of the openness and inclusiveness of the proce-dures of moral argumentation – or in other words, of practical reason – rather than the attunement of perceptual faculties to the world of moral facts, that the demands of morality become progressively known to us.

McDowell responds to all the essays in the book in the chapter that makes up the fifth part.

I would like to add a couple of brief remarks about the structure of the book as a whole. First, my aim in partitioning the book the way I have is to give a general indication to the reader of the kind of approach, and main focus, of the chapters in each part. But the division should not be taken too rigidly. There is no sharp break between the historical, epistemological, metaphysical, and meta-ethical issues raised by McDowell's work, and this continuity is reflected in the essays collected here. Second, it may be worth drawing attention to a certain criss-crossing of themes explored in chapters located in different parts. For instance, McDowell's relation to the Kantian tradition is examined by Bubner, even though, for other reasons, I have placed his essay in the part entitled "Toward ethics." Robert Pippin's chapter raises issues about McDowell's meta-ethical stance, though, again on other grounds, I have put it in the part headed "Philosophy after Kant." To give one more example, the objection that McDowell does not properly accommodate pre-conceptual experience is taken up in various ways by Richard Bernstein, Charles Taylor, Crispin Wright, and Jay Bernstein, whose essays span all four parts (it is most explicitly dealt with by McDowell in his response to Wright). Such criss-crossing is a further reflection of the interweaving of topics in *Mind and World* itself.

Part I

PHILOSOPHY AFTER KANT

1

McDOWELL'S DOMESTICATED HEGELIANISM

Richard J. Bernstein

> It is central to absolute idealism to reject the idea that the
> conceptual realm has an outer boundary, and we have arrived at a
> point from which we could start to domesticate the rhetoric of
> that philosophy. Consider, for instance, this remark of Hegel's: "In
> thinking, I am *free*, because I am not in an *other*." This expresses
> exactly the image I have been using, in which the conceptual is
> unbounded; there is nothing outside it. The point is the same as
> the point of that remark of Wittgenstein's: "We – and our
> meaning – do not stop anywhere short of the fact."
>
> (*Mind and World*, p.44)

I suspect that many of John McDowell's "analytic," and former Oxford,
colleagues thought it was some sort of a joke when McDowell announced in the
Preface to *Mind and World* "that I would like to conceive this work ... as a prolegomenon to a reading of [Hegel's *Phenomenology of Spirit*]."[1] Hegel is a
philosopher that few "analytic" philosophers have taken seriously (or even read)
– a philosopher who is typically held up for ridicule, as someone who epitomizes
the intellectual vices that "analytic" philosophy has sought to overcome. Or as
McDowell himself more judiciously phrases it, Hegel is "someone we take
almost no notice of, in the philosophical tradition I was brought up in" (p.111).
McDowell's reference to Hegel is no joke. I want to show how profoundly
McDowell has been influenced by a *line of thinking* that is Hegelian, and that
McDowell's domesticated Hegelianism provides an essential clue for grasping
the overall strategy and direction of his thinking. One of the many attractive
features of McDowell's thought is that he shows just how outdated and provin-
cial the so-called "analytic–continental split" is for philosophy today. There is
good and bad philosophical thinking, and many of today's most creative
thinkers – like McDowell (and his colleague, Robert Brandom) – pay no attention to this artificial split; they incorporate ideas from what we have erroneously
labeled two different traditions.[2] One looks forward to the day (in the not too
distant future) when we glance back upon the ideological "culture wars"
between "analytic'" and "continental" philosophers with amusement, wondering
how these sometimes fruitless heated debates could be taken so seriously.

When I speak of McDowell's "domesticated Hegelianism," I mean something quite specific.[3] I am referring to his creative appropriation of a pattern of thinking that is exhibited in Hegel (at his best). Although such a line of thinking can be found in Hegel, its philosophic significance and justification are independent of its origin. And the reason why I use the adjective "domesticated" is because it is quite clear that McDowell also rejects large portions of Hegel that may strike some as "wild." McDowell is fond of using a variety of epithets to describe his philosophic orientation. We shall see that McDowell's "prolegomenon to a reading of the *Phenomenology*" is also a "minimal empiricism" or a "naturalized platonism" – epithets that would certainly upset and even shock many "straight" Hegelians. McDowell's explicit references to Hegel are few and scattered (although they are always crucial and revealing). He does not begin with reflecting on Hegel or commenting on his writings. Rather, McDowell begins where, it may be said, Hegel himself began – by reflecting on the achievements and limitations of Kant. McDowell uses the twentieth-century Kantian Wilfrid Sellars as a guide for his reading of Kant.[4]

Let me begin by giving a sketch of how I plan to approach McDowell. Kant's great philosophic achievement was his rich and textured articulation and probing of a number of interrelated philosophic distinctions: understanding and sensibility; concepts and intuitions; spontaneity and receptivity; phenomena and noumena; understanding (*Verstand*) and reason (*Vernunft*); appearance and the "thing-in-itself"; freedom and natural necessity. These (and other closely related distinctions) contributed to a radically new understanding of the nature and limits of knowledge and rationality. In this sense, Kant himself brought about a revolution in philosophy which was as dramatic and as consequential as Copernicus's revolution in astronomy. But the great achievement of Kant has also been the source for deep perplexities and philosophic anxieties. Why? Because Kant, at times, seems to reify these distinctions, to make them into rigid dichotomies that leave us with all sorts of aporiai. Virtually every philosopher since Kant, who has taken his achievement seriously, has sought to return to his provocative distinctions and dichotomies in order to modify, abandon or rethink them. The greatest of these was Hegel himself.[5] Indeed, there is a master strategy at work in Hegel. Viewed from one perspective, no other thinker of his stature sought to take Kant so seriously and "complete" his project.[6] But viewed from another perspective, no other thinker has been such a penetrating and sharp critic of Kant. These claims are compatible because Hegel does not abandon the Kantian distinctions, but rather seeks to show that when we think them through, we discover they are *not* rigid, fixed epistemological and/or metaphysical dichotomies. Rather, they turn out to be dynamic, changing, fluid distinctions which are to be comprehended within a larger whole or context. Thus Hegel's thinking and working through the Kantian distinctions leads to the rejection of all rigid distinctions and dichotomies (including perhaps the most fundamental distinction between the finite and the infinite). Using a Hegelian turn of phrase, the Kantian distinctions turn out to be distinctions which are no distinctions. Or stated in another way, Hegel seeks to draw out what he takes to be the "truth" (*Wahrheit*) implicit in the Kantian distinctions – a truth that turns out frequently to be the very opposite of what Kant presumably intended. We will see that this is just the strategy that McDowell himself develops in regard to the Kantian distinctions of understanding and sensibility, spontaneity and receptivity, concepts and intuitions, appearance and reality. This very strategy warrants McDowell's rejection of any vestiges of the "Myth of the Given," and enables him to argue there is no "outer boundary" to the conceptual realm; we are *not* (epistemologically or metaphysically) cut off from the world or reality as it exists "in itself." The essential relation that we, as thinking and knowing beings, have to the world is one of *openness* to the world with no fixed boundaries. There are not only causal constraints on what we can know, but also *rational constraints*. But let us now turn to the details of how this story unfolds.

Taking his cue from Sellars, McDowell sets himself against all varieties of the Myth of the Given. In the opening paragraph of "Empiricism and the Philosophy of Mind," Sellars makes the point that there is an innocent non-controversial sense of the "given" where the term is used to refer "merely to what is observed as being observed" and not inferred. This common variety sense of the "given" is not what is philosophically interesting or controversial. But Sellars also points out that "the phrase 'the given' as a piece of professional–epistemological shoptalk carries a substantial theoretical commitment."[7] The basic idea of givenness in this technical sense is closely associated with what Hegel calls immediacy. Although givenness has taken on many different forms in the history of philosophy, the Given is presumably not "contaminated" by any mediation, any form of inference. The Given is something that can be either directly known or known by acquaintance; it is an immediate intuition or a self-authenticating epistemic episode. This unmediated Given serves as a foundation for the edifice of knowledge. And this is why we might look upon Kant as initiating the modern critique of the "Myth of the Given" – a critique that is epitomized in Kant's remark "intuitions without concepts are blind." Now it is important to realize why the Myth of the Given *does not seem* to be a myth but rather some sort of basic truth, and why it is so attractive and seductive. To use a term that McDowell favors, there has been a pervasive philosophic "anxiety" that unless there is something Given, unless there is something that grounds knowledge in the way in which the Given presumably does, then the very possibility of empirical knowledge is threatened. We seem to be left with a bad free-floating conceptual realm that has not been tied down to the real world.

Kant's remark about intuitions and concepts is intimately related to his distinction between spontaneity and receptivity. As McDowell diagnoses our contemporary philosophic situation, there is a back and forth movement – a seesaw between two unacceptable extremes. He thinks that there is a "danger of falling into an interminable oscillation" – an oscillation between some version of the Myth of the Given where we deceive ourselves into thinking that empirical knowledge is grounded and epistemically justified by a Given that is not already conceptualized and some sort of frictionless coherentism (a position which he sometimes associates with Davidson). But McDowell thinks that we can dismount from this seesaw and that it is Kant (and Sellars) who begin to show us how this is to be done:

> The original Kantian thought was that empirical knowledge results from a co-operation between receptivity and spontaneity. (Here "spontaneity" can be simply a label for the involvement of conceptual capacities.) We can dismount from the seesaw if we can achieve a firm grip on this thought: receptivity does not make an even notionally separable contribution to the co-operation.
>
> (p.9)

We will soon see just how consequential this claim is for McDowell, but first we have to understand it. For everything depends on how we understand this "co-operation between receptivity and spontaneity."[8] We will set off on the *wrong* track if we think that receptivity can be sharply distinguished from spontaneity in such a manner that it is the source for non-conceptual "data," and that this receptivity is only conceptualized when spontaneity comes into play. This will lead us straight to the Myth of the Given. It is bad philosophy and bad Kant. Rather, we must grasp that conceptual capacities are "always already" drawn on in receptivity. In short, it is a fiction – a seductive misleading fiction – to think that there is some sort of "pure" receptivity that is free from all involvement of conceptual capacities. McDowell announces this theme early in his first lecture: he returns to it over and over again, explicating, amplifying, and defending it. He tells us:

> The relevant conceptual capacities are drawn on *in* receptivity. ... It is not that they are exercised *on* an extra-conceptual deliverance of receptivity. We should understand what Kant calls "intuition" – experiential intake – not as a bare getting of an extra-conceptual Given, but as a kind of occurrence or state that already has conceptual content. In experience one takes in, for instance sees, *that things are thus and so*. That is the sort of thing one can also, for instance, judge.
>
> (p.9)

McDowell restates and amplifies this theme at the beginning of his second lecture:

> In my first lecture I talked about a tendency to oscillate between a pair of unsatisfying positions: on the one side a coherentism that threatens to disconnect thought from reality, and on the other side a vain appeal

to the Given, in the sense of bare presences that are supposed to constitute the ultimate grounds of empirical judgements. I suggested that in order to escape the oscillation, we need to recognize that experiences themselves are states or occurrences that inextricably combine receptivity and spontaneity. We must not suppose that spontaneity first figures only in judgements in which we put a construction on experiences, with experiences conceived as deliverances of receptivity to whose constitution spontaneity makes no contribution. Experiences are indeed receptivity in operation; so they can satisfy the need for an external control on our freedom in empirical thinking. But conceptual capacities, capacities that belong to spontaneity, are already at work in experiences themselves, not just in judgements based on them; so experiences can intelligibly stand in rational relations to our exercises of the freedom that is implicit in the idea of spontaneity.

(p.24)

This is precisely the reading that Hegel gives to the Kantian distinctions of intuitions and concepts, receptivity and spontaneity. McDowell's statement of the relation of receptivity to spontaneity helps us to understand what Hegel means when he speaks of a distinction that is no distinction. Experience (Hegel's *Erfahrung*) is of such a character that it is "always already" constituted by conceptual capacities. There is no receptivity where spontaneity is not already at work.

But if this is what McDowell himself maintains, then one may wonder if he has really shown us how to dismount from the oscillating seesaw that he so trenchantly describes. If there is no escape from the Conceptual, then what is the difference that makes a difference between what McDowell is affirming and the type of coherentism that he objects to in Davidson? Put in another way, has not McDowell backed himself into a form of (linguistic) idealism in which he has failed to explain how empirical knowledge is tied down to an independent reality which is "outside" and "beyond" the Conceptual?

McDowell is perfectly aware that this is the sort of objection that will be raised against him. And it is in meeting (or rather undermining and defusing) this objection that we find some of his most subtle, perceptive, and original thinking. McDowell, like Wittgenstein, thinks that there is a picture here that holds us captive. It is a picture whereby we imagine that there *must* be something (a world of brute reality) that is "outside" and "exterior" to what is Conceptual. Unless we find some way to connect this brute reality with the exercise of our conceptual capacities, then (presumably) there is the danger of undermining not only the possibility of any empirical knowledge, but any knowledge whatsoever. For how can a conceptual realm that is not "tied down" to an external independent reality yield any *knowledge* of this reality? This is the picture that needs to be deconstructed, that needs to be undermined by a type of Wittgensteinian therapy. McDowell carries out this therapy by showing us

13

that the very idea of thinking that there is something "inside" the conceptual sphere and something "outside" it (that ties the conceptual sphere down) is a thoroughly confused and incoherent idea. We need to grasp and appreciate "The Unboundedness of the Conceptual."[9] McDowell's point, stated in a way that brings him into direct confrontation with Davidson (and many others), is that we do need to account for *rational constraints* on thinking and judging; it is not sufficient "to make do with nothing but causal constraints." Furthermore, we can affirm that there are rational constraints without falling back into the Myth of the Given. This sounds like a stunning trick. And we might well wonder how McDowell is going to pull it off. Let me first state what McDowell is affirming, and then unpack his meaning. McDowell writes:

> In the conception I am recommending, the need for external constraint is met by the fact that experiences are receptivity in operation. But that does not disqualify experiences from playing a role in justification, as the counterpart thought in the Myth of the Given does, because the claim is that experiences themselves are already equipped with conceptual content. This joint involvement of receptivity and spontaneity allows us to say that in experience one can take in how things are. How things are is independent of one's thinking .... By being taken in in experience, how things anyway are becomes available to exert the required rational control, originating outside one's thinking, on one's exercises of spontaneity .... In a particular experience in which one is not misled, what one takes in is *that things are thus and so*. *That things are thus and so* is the content of the experience, and it can also be the content of a judgement: it becomes the content of a judgement if the subject decides to take the experience at face value. So it is conceptual content. But *that things are thus and so* is also, if one is not misled, an aspect of the layout of the world: it is how things are. Thus the idea of conceptually structured operations of receptivity puts us in a position to speak of experience as openness to the layout of reality. Experience enables the layout of reality itself to exert a rational influence on what a subject thinks.
>
> (pp.25–26)

But still we may have a nagging feeling that this is just a fancy way of stating a "bad" idealism. This is how McDowell responds to such an accusation:

> Now it can seem that this refusal to locate perceptible reality outside the conceptual sphere must be a sort of idealism, in the sense in which to call a position "idealism" is to protest that it does not genuinely acknowledge how reality is independent of our thinking. If that were right, my affirmation of reality's independence would be disingenuous, mere lip-service. But though this objection is easy to understand, and

even to sympathize with, it is wrong. It reflects the conviction that we have to choose between a coherentist denial that thinking and judging are subject to rational constraint from outside, on the one hand, and an appeal to the Given as what imposes the constraint, on the other. If someone takes it that those are the only options, and if she has a firmer grip on the defects of unconstrained coherentism than she has on the uselessness of the Given, then anything short of believing in the Given will strike her as slighting the independence of reality. But the point of the third option, the option I am urging, is precisely that it enables us to acknowledge that independent reality exerts a rational control over our thinking, but without falling into the confusion between justification and exculpation that characterizes the appeal to the Given.

(pp.26–27)

It is at this point that McDowell cites a fertile remark by Wittgenstein: "When we say, and *mean*, that such-and-such is the case, we – and our meaning – do not stop anywhere short of the fact; but we mean: *this – is – so*" (p.27). Stating his point "in a style Wittgenstein would have been uncomfortable with," McDowell categorically asserts that "there is no ontological gap between the sort of thing one can mean, or generally the sort of thing one can think, and the sort of thing that can be the case. When one thinks truly, what one thinks *is* what is the case" (p.27).

Now let me try to state in my own words what McDowell is claiming, what his "third option" is. McDowell is perfectly aware that much of modern philosophy since Descartes has operated in a framework where we distinguish what is "out there" – what is presumably independently real – from what is somehow "in" our minds. This metaphor of what is "inside" and "outside" is deeply entrenched in our everyday language. Epistemology has been preoccupied with giving an account of the relation of mind and reality so that we can explain and justify knowledge. There have been many sophisticated ways of refining his basic picture (philosophers notoriously disagree about how to characterize "mind" and "reality" or the "world" outside us). But still, something like this picture has enormous pull on us. McDowell wants to show how deeply misleading this picture is, and how it ensnares us in all sorts of pseudo-problems. He rejects any form of the Myth of the Given, and any suggestion that we can account for empirical knowledge if and only if we acknowledge that there is some brute external independent reality "outside" our minds and our *conceptual capacities* – an external reality that presumably *grounds* this knowledge.

McDowell claims that if we have a proper understanding of the cooperation of spontaneity and receptivity, then we should have no anxiety about the claim that the Conceptual is unbounded. We are not somehow entrapped in a conceptual sphere that has nothing to do with a reality that is presumably "outside" it. Rather, it is our conceptual and judgmental capacities that *open us* to the world – a world that exercises a rational constraint on our knowledge. Of course, we can always be mistaken when we claim to know some aspect of the world, but it is an illusion to think that there is an "ontological gap" between what we mean, think, or know and the sorts of things that can be the case in the world that we encounter.

Even if we are prepared to accept McDowell's third option, we may ask what this has to do with Hegel. The simple answer is: everything! For this is precisely what Hegel shows in his *Phenomenology*. McDowell has creatively appropriated this Hegelian theme in order to articulate his third option. The specter of (bad) idealism that McDowell raises against himself – only to defuse it – is the standard objection raised against Hegel. And in both cases the plausibility of the objection presupposes a misleading picture whereby idealism is taken to be some sort of internal coherentism that is disconnected from an external independent reality. McDowell's remark about Hegel's absolute idealism, which I have already cited as an epigraph, not only exhibits McDowell's sensitivity and acuteness as a reader of Hegel, but it also illustrates why *Mind and World* can be understood as a "prolegomenon to a reading of the *Phenomenology*." McDowell grasps how misleading and distortive the standard charge of (bad) idealism is when raised against Hegel. Indeed, it is Hegel himself who has provided the most devastating critique of this (bad) idealism – one that presupposes that it is intelligible to speak about what is "inside" and "outside" the mind, or what is "inside" and "outside" the conceptual sphere. On the contrary, it is Hegel who has strongly argued for the thesis of the "unboundedness of the Conceptual" in the sense in which McDowell himself defends this claim. It is because the Conceptual is "always already" operative in receptivity, and because "perceptual reality" is not "outside the conceptual sphere," that we can speak of our openness to the world – *a world that is independent, but not "outside," of our conceptual capacities; our spontaneity opens us to a world which is independent of our thinking.*

But this is not all there is to McDowell's "domesticated Hegelianism." We find traces of Hegel in McDowell's reflections on nature, and in what he calls his "relaxed naturalism." In his fourth lecture, McDowell takes up a problem that arises from his critical discussion of Davidson and Evans. McDowell claims that even though they use different idioms, both Davidson and Evans "aim to accommodate the point of Kant's talk of spontaneity." Furthermore, neither of them is tempted by a vulgar "bald naturalism" that denies "that the spontaneity of the understanding is *sui generis* in the way suggested by the link to the idea of freedom" (p.67). But McDowell thinks that both Davidson and Evans have a blind spot – a "deep-rooted mental block" (p.69). This has to do with their tacit acceptance of a conception of nature, which although it may seem to be sheer common sense, is deeply flawed. This is what McDowell, following Max Weber, calls a "disenchanted" concept of nature, nature conceived as the realm of law where the kind of intelligibility that is proper to meaning is excluded.[10]

The crucial contrast that McDowell wants to draw "is between the internal organization of the space of reasons and the internal organization of nature" (p.71). Roughly speaking, what McDowell means by "nature as the realm of law" is the concept of nature that is presupposed by modern natural science. Without denigrating the contribution of this disenchanted conception of nature, McDowell argues that if we want to understand how spontaneity is related to nature, we must rethink the concept of nature itself. Although this part of McDowell's discussion is extremely sketchy and is filled with promissory notes, its importance cannot be underestimated. For ever since the rise of modern science, the disenchanted conception of nature has increasingly been taken for granted. It is, of course, true that there have been, and continue to be, disagreements about how such a disenchanted nature is to be properly characterized. But it is commonly assumed that to question this conception of nature would be to question the achievements of modern science – to bring us back to the "dark ages," lapsing back into "pre-scientific superstition" (p.85). McDowell certainly does not want to underestimate the intellectual advance achieved when the disenchanted concept of nature as the realm of law became secure. But he does want to argue that to *limit* our understanding of nature in this way is mistaken and invites us to think in terms of misleading dichotomies. For there is no place for spontaneity in such a disenchanted nature. Indeed, the sharp dichotomy that Kant makes between freedom and nature (and all the aporiai that result from this dichotomy) follow from Kant's "uncritical" acceptance of such a disenchanted concept of nature. McDowell's richer conception of nature is one that he develops by reflecting on Aristotle's *Ethics* (not his *Physics*). It is a concept of nature that takes the idea of a "second nature" seriously. We gain a glimpse of what McDowell intends when he says:

> The notion [of second nature] is all but explicit in Aristotle's account of how ethical character is formed. Since ethical character includes dispositions of the practical intellect, part of what happens when character is formed is that the practical intellect acquires a determinate shape. So practical wisdom is second nature to its possessors.
>
> (p.84)

But the point is not limited to ethics. As McDowell tells us:

> Moulding ethical character, which includes imposing a specific shape on the practical intellect, is a particular case of a general phenomenon: initiation into conceptual capacities, which include responsiveness to other rational demands besides those of ethics. Such initiation is a normal part of what it is for a human being to come to maturity, and that is why, although the structure of the space of reasons is alien to the layout of nature conceived as the realm of law, it does not take on the remoteness from the human that rampant platonism envisages. If we generalize the way Aristotle conceives the moulding of ethical character, we arrive at the notion of having one's eyes opened to reasons at large by acquiring a second nature. I cannot think of a good

short English expression for this, but it is what figures in German philosophy as *Bildung*.

(p.84)

The reason why this idea of second nature is so attractive to McDowell is because it points the way to integrating the space of reasons (spontaneity) into a concept of nature. But this cannot be accomplished if we restrict ourselves to the concept of a disenchanted nature – a concept of nature that does not "embrace the space of reasons." McDowell gives an eloquent, and indeed moving, description of the task for a philosophical reconciliation that he envisages in a passage that displays not only his sensitivity to the history of philosophy, but the ease with which he transgresses the "boundaries" between "analytic" and "continental" philosophy:

> We need to recapture the Aristotelian idea that a normal mature human being is a rational animal, but without losing the Kantian idea that rationality operates freely in its own sphere. The Kantian idea is reflected in the contrast between the organization of the space of reasons and the structure of the realm of natural law. Modern naturalism is forgetful of second nature; if we try to preserve the Kantian thought that reason is autonomous within the framework of that kind of naturalism, we disconnect our rationality from our animal being, which is what gives us our foothold in nature .... We need to see ourselves as animals whose natural being is permeated with rationality, even though rationality is appropriately conceived in Kantian terms.
>
> (p.85)[11]

The language and the letter of this passage are McDowell, but the spirit that breathes through it is Hegel. It is Hegel who sought to bring about the reconciliation that McDowell calls for. It is Hegel who assigns *Bildung* a central place in his understanding of human nature. It is Hegel who explores in depth the concept of a second nature (including its historical dimensions). Indeed, it is Hegel himself who looks to Aristotle and Kant to effect a reconciliation of Nature and Spirit. Although Hegel realizes the importance of distinguishing a limited conception of disenchanted nature from the realm of spontaneity, thinking, and reason, he rejects the idea that there is a rigid ontological gap between Nature and Spirit. I do not want to deny that there are many unresolved difficulties in Hegel's attempt to reconcile Nature and Spirit, but it is clear that he seeks to establish this reconciliation. In McDowell's terms, Hegel seeks to rethink nature as the "realm of law" in a manner that is compatible with recognizing the *sui generis* character of spontaneity.

As I suggested in the previous note, it is unfortunate that McDowell, who has such a sensitive and sophisticated understanding of the history of philosophy, is not better acquainted with the American pragmatic tradition, especially the work of Charles Sanders Peirce. He might then have realized how much he shares in common with Peirce. Peirce is also a thinker who began his philosophical journey with reflections on Kant, and was sympathetic with the Hegelian interpretation and critique of Kant. Furthermore, in a series of papers published in 1868–1869, Peirce developed one of the most forceful critiques of the Myth of the Given. Peirce anticipates virtually every argument that Sellars and McDowell have developed against the Myth of the Given.[12] Peirce was also concerned to dismount from the oscillating seesaw between the Myth of the Given and unconstrained coherentism. Indeed, his strategy for "dismounting" bears a strong resemblance to the strategy that McDowell employs. Just as McDowell makes a sharp distinction between exculpations and justifications, Peirce makes a categorical distinction between Secondness (brute exculpations) and Thirdness (justifications). Peirce also maintains that "experience" (in the sense in which McDowell uses the expression) is "receptivity in operation." This becomes especially clear in Peirce's analysis of perceptual judgments. McDowell would agree with Peirce's claim that "our very precepts are the results of cognitive elaboration." Peirce stresses that the "logical space of reasons" is essentially normative. Norms are embedded in our practices. Just as McDowell interprets his "unbounded" thesis to mean that we have access to a reality that is independent (but not "outside") of our thinking, so does Peirce. Peirce tells us "reality is independent, not necessarily of thought in general, but only of what you or I or any finite number of men may think about it." Peirce, who was a practising experimental scientist, argues strongly against a "disenchanted" and mechanistic conception of nature. He sought to develop a conception of nature that brings out the continuity of physical and biological nature with the "second nature" exhibited by rational beings. I cite these significant points of agreement to illustrate how much the pragmatism of Peirce (what Peirce called his "pragmaticism") anticipates, and is in agreement with, the letter and spirit of McDowell's claims.

In showing the deep affinities between one strain in Hegel's thinking and McDowell's, I am not suggesting that there is nothing original about McDowell, that it all can be found in Hegel. McDowell's creative appropriation of Hegel in order to make (what appears to be) a very un-Hegelian defense of "naturalized platonism" and a "minimal empiricism" is at once brilliant and thought-provoking. McDowell has not only opened the possibility of a fresh way of reading and interpreting Hegel, but he shows that his reading of Hegel enables us to confront some of the deepest philosophic perplexities. In short, McDowell shows us how a sensitive reading of Hegel (and not only Hegel, but also Aristotle, Kant, Sellars, and Wittgenstein – as well as his contemporaries Davidson and Evans) enables us to come to grips with our philosophic anxieties and problems.

In this essay I have refrained from criticizing McDowell. Rather, I have attempted to show a way to gain a deeper grasp of what I take to be the primary thrust and direction of his thinking, and to situate his own project with reference to Hegel. But I also think that this perspective enables us to see the types of problems that McDowell still has to confront in carrying out his project, and in satisfying some of the promissory notes that he has issued. One deep problem concerns making fully explicit the distinction between what may be called "sapience" and "sentience." If we accept the claim that spontaneity is "always already" at work in receptivity, and that perceptual awareness is already characterized by our conceptual capacities, then we need to give a proper account of what we share with (brute) animals who lack our conceptual capacities. Ordinarily, we have no hesitancy in referring to the feelings and sensations of animals, and we frequently use the same language to characterize both. For example, we have no hesitancy to say that animals experience pain. But given McDowell's strong claims about how spontaneity is implicated in our experience, we must realize that the word "experience" has a very different meaning when we say that (brute) animals experience pain. McDowell is certainly aware of this problem and he struggles nobly with it. But I am not persuaded that he has yet shown us how to deal adequately with this problem. And there is the closely related problem of how we are to characterize the "experience" of infants *before* they have learned any language or have shown any ability to master the normative aspects of the employment of concepts. Furthermore, McDowell himself realizes how sketchy his understanding of second nature is, and how the reconciliation that he wants to effect between nature as the realm of law and nature as encompassing spontaneity is little more than a promise. There are many obstacles and problems that need to be confronted if such a reconciliation is to be successful and persuasive. We need a deep analysis of causality, and where it fits in relation to a disenchanted concept of nature and the spontaneity of reason. We need to know how to answer those who claim that ultimately a science based on the disenchanted concept of nature will (or may) prove sufficient to fully account for what McDowell wants to single out as spontaneity. And there are other problems looming on the horizon. The idea of a "second nature" is not only restricted to Aristotle and Hegel. It has played an important role in the development of Western Marxism and also the tradition of hermeneutics. Both of these traditions take seriously the historical development of "second nature" – the way in which "second nature" changes and develops in the course of history. McDowell whets our intellectual appetite when he concludes his Lectures with some very suggestive remarks about tradition (remarks that echo another thinker indebted to Hegel, Hans-Georg Gadamer):

> The feature of language that really matters is rather this: that a natural language, the sort of language into which human beings are first initiated, serves as a repository of tradition, a store of historically accumulated wisdom about what is a reason for what. The tradition is subject to reflective modification by each generation that inherits it. Indeed, a standing obligation to engage in critical reflection is itself part of the inheritance .... But if an individual human being is to

realize her potential of taking place in that succession, which is the same thing as acquiring a mind, the capacity to think and act intentionally, at all, the first thing that needs to happen is for her to be initiated into a tradition as it stands.

(p.126)

So while there are many knotty and difficult problems that McDowell still has to confront to carry out the type of reconciliation that he envisages, it is nevertheless an extremely impressive achievement to have accomplished and condensed as much as he does in the 126 pages that comprise his Lectures.

Notes

1 McDowell makes this remark in acknowledging his intellectual debt to his colleague, Robert Brandom. McDowell singles out the importance for him of Brandom's "eye-opening seminar on Hegel's *Phenomenology of Spirit*, which I attended in 1990" (p.ix). *Mind and World* is based on the John Locke Lectures that McDowell delivered in Oxford in 1991. All page references in the text are to *Mind and World*.

2 In my book *Praxis and Action* published in 1971, I wrote:

> The opening section of the *Phenomenology*, "Consciousness," which deals with "sense certainty," "perception," and "understanding," is rarely read and discussed by contemporary philosophers. This is a pity because these sections can be read as a perceptive and incisive commentary and critique of a dialectical development in epistemology which has been repeated in contemporary analytic philosophy. The stages in contemporary epistemological investigations which have moved from phenomenalism with its foundation in "sense data" to the emphasis on the "thing language" as an epistemological foundation, to the realization of the importance of "theoretical constructs" and finally the "new" concern with total "conceptual frameworks" or "language games" closely parallels the development that Hegel sketches for us in the opening sections of the *Phenomenology*. One can find analogues in the development of epistemology during the past fifty years for the difficulties that Hegel locates at each dialectical stage. I do not mean to suggest that Hegel was prophetic, but rather that he had a genuine insight into a dialectical progression of epistemological positions, which has repeated itself in a linguistic mode during our time.
> (*Praxis and Action*, Philadelphia: University of Pennsylvania Press, 1971, p.24)

Although this was written more than twenty years prior to the publication of *Mind and World*, I would certainly now single out McDowell as a contemporary philosopher who has a deep understanding and appreciation of this dialectical movement in Hegel's *Phenomenology*.

3 For a very different reading of the influence of Hegel on McDowell, see Sally Sedgwick, "McDowell's Hegelianism," *European Journal of Philosophy* 5: 1 (1997).

4 One should also mention the extent to which McDowell has also been influenced by the reading of Kant by one of his own teachers, P. F. Strawson. Like Strawson in *The Bounds of Sense* (London: Methuen, 1966), McDowell is very skeptical of Kant's claims about transcendental philosophy. He plays down this aspect of Kant's philosophy. Indeed, McDowell remarks that "Strawson's Kant is more Hegel than Kant" (p.111).

McDowell begins his Woodbridge Lectures, "Having the World in View: Sellars, Kant, and Intentionality," by declaring that in "Empiricism and the Philosophy of Mind" Wilfrid Sellars offers "the outlines of a deeply Kantian way of thinking about intentionality about how thought and language are directed to the world." He tells us that it was Sellars's belief that "no one comes closer than Kant to showing us how to find intentionality unproblematic, and that this means rethinking (and even correcting) Kant for ourselves." McDowell shares this belief with Sellars, and suggests that "coming to terms with Sellars's sustained attempt to be a Kantian is a fine way to begin appreciating Kant" and thereby "to become philosophically comfortable with intentionality" (The Woodbridge Lectures 1997: "Having the World in View: Sellars, Kant, and Intentionality," *Journal of Philosophy* 95(9) (September 1998)). The Hegelian thrust of McDowell's thinking is even more pronounced and explicit in these lectures. In his concluding remarks of the Woodbridge Lectures McDowell says: "The fate of Sellars's reading [of Kant] suggests that the thought Hegel tries to capture with the image of Reason as subject to no external constraint ... is already Kant's own thought" (p.490).

5 The list of philosophers who can be said to "begin" with a rethinking of the Kantian distinctions includes not only Fichte and Schelling, but also Peirce and Dewey, as well as Strawson, Sellars, Putnam, Brandom, Habermas, and Rawls (and many others).

6 See Robert B. Pippin, *Hegel's Idealism: The Satisfactions of Self-Consciousness* (Cambridge: Cambridge University Press, 1989).

7 Wilfrid Sellars, *Empiricism and the Philosophy of Mind* (Cambridge, MA: Harvard University Press, 1997), p.13. In order to distinguish the technical sense of "given" from its non-controversial sense, I have – following McDowell – capitalized the term when I use it in its technical epistemological meaning.

8 For both McDowell and Sellars, the great hero who slew the dragon of the Myth of the Given is Kant (even though both claim that Kant himself did not escape the vestiges of the Myth). And when they claim that Kant is the hero, they emphasize how Kant argued that there is no knowledge whatsoever that does not involve our conceptual capacities, the spontaneity of the understanding. But neither Sellars nor McDowell does full justice to the reading of Kant whereby he is not only the hero of the story but the great villain. For there are many passages in the *Critique of Pure Reason* and the *Prolegomena* that can easily lead one to think that empirical sensible intuitions are the Given which serve as the foundation for all knowledge.

9 This is the title of the second lecture of *Mind and World*.

10 McDowell appropriates insights, themes, and strategies from Kant, Aristotle, Hegel, Sellars, Gadamer, and many other philosophers. But he thinks of his overall project as "genuinely Wittgensteinian in spirit." And by this he means that, like Wittgenstein, he is engaged in a form of philosophic therapy that requires a *proper* diagnosis of philosophical anxieties. He takes to heart the Wittgensteinian claim that "The real discovery is the one that makes me capable of stopping doing philosophy when I want to" (*Philosophical Investigations*, p.133). Consequently, McDowell thinks of his project not as advancing new philosophic theories or engaging in "constructive philosophy" but rather as attempting to show us how we can loosen the grip of our philosophic anxieties. Concerning "modern naturalism" he tells us:

> What I suggest is that our philosophical anxieties are due to the intelligible grip on our thinking of a modern naturalism, and we can work at loosening that grip. It is a way of making this suggestion vivid to picture a frame of mind in which we have definitely shrugged off the influences on our thinking that lead to philosophical anxieties, even if we do not suppose we could ever have such a frame of mind as a permanent and stable possession. Even so, this identification

of a source for our apparent difficulties can be one of our resources for over-coming recurrences of the philosophical impulse: recurrences that we know there will be.

(pp.177–178)

He does not say that bald naturalism is a *false* doctrine or that it is a *mistaken* theory, but rather he disparages bald naturalism because it does not provide an adequate diagnosis and response to a deep philosophical anxiety – an anxiety that can be alle-viated only if we rethink our conception of nature:

If we can rethink our conception of nature so as to make room for spontaneity, even though we deny that spontaneity is capturable by the resources of bald naturalism, we shall by the same token be rethinking our conception of what it takes for a position to deserve to be called "naturalism."

(p.77)

McDowell's Wittgensteinian approach to naturalism is even more evident in his reply to Rorty's criticism. McDowell seeks to distinguish good and bad ways of "opting out" of philosophic problems. The trouble with bald naturalism is that it opts out by simply denying a genuine philosophic perplexity. Bald naturalists think that the talk of "logical space of reasons" and "spontaneity" is some sort of illusion that can be ignored:

Opting out in the sense I disparage is not just discarding the apparent problems, but doing so without, as I do, granting force to the distinctive intuition that – in a certain context – makes it seem as if they are genuine: the intuition that the conceptual apparatus that centers on the idea of the objective purport belongs in a logical space of reasons that is *sui generis*, by comparison with the logical space in which the natural sciences function.

(John McDowell, "Reply to Commentators,"
Philosophy and Phenomenological Research 58(2): 421 (1998))

11 There are many problems and perplexities concerning the type of "enriched," "relaxed" naturalism that McDowell advocates. I have indicated some of these diffi-culties in my Patrick Romanell Lecture, "Whatever Happened to Naturalism?" *The Proceedings and Addresses of the American Philosophical Association* 69: 57–76 (1995). In this respect, as in another that I shall comment upon in a moment, McDowell might have learned from Peirce. McDowell wants to show that the concept of spon-taneity that is *sui generis* in his demanding sense can be reconciled with a concept of nature if we rethink what we mean by nature so that it encompasses "second nature." But this project of reconciliation (if it is not to be the artificial joining of two incom-patible concepts of nature) demands that we also rethink the disenchanted concept of nature – what McDowell calls "the natural as the realm of law." But McDowell does not indicate how this is to be done. Peirce, long before McDowell, also seeks to integrate spontaneity into an enriched concept of nature. But Peirce fully realized that if this is to be accomplished, it requires rethinking the disenchanted concept of nature that has been uncritically accepted as an unquestioned presupposition of natural science. And unlike McDowell, Peirce sought to develop a type of evolu-tionary naturalism in which there is genuine continuity in the realm of nature. In short – to use McDowell's terminology – the integrated naturalism that McDowell seeks not only requires the achievement of a "firm hold on a naturalism of second nature" (p.86), but a rethinking of what McDowell calls "nature as the realm of law." This project of genuine integration is Peirce's project in his evolutionary naturalism.

RICHARD J. BERNSTEIN

The issue confronting McDowell can be stated in another way that parallels the Sellarsian problem of "joining" the manifest image and the scientific image into a single coherent synoptic vision of man-in-the-world. Sellars notes that the problem arises because these two images are not just different, but *rival* images. So, too, in an analogous fashion, we can say that nature conceived of as what McDowell calls the "realm of law" and nature that encompasses "second nature" are *rival* concepts of nature. One way of construing the basic claim of the "bald naturalist" is that nature conceived of as the "realm of law" is sufficient to describe and explain all of reality (including what McDowell singles out as spontaneity). Consequently, it is not adequate to claim that bald naturalism is inadequate. McDowell must also show how the clash of the competing rival concepts of nature can be resolved. He asserts that they can, but he has not shown in detail how this is to be accomplished. This is what Peirce attempted to do when he argued that there is a continuity from inanimate inorganic nature to human nature – a human nature that encompasses man's "second nature."

12 See "Questions Concerning Certain Faculties Claimed for Man," "Some Consequences of Four Incapacities," and "Grounds of Validity of the Laws of Logic: Further Consequences of Four Incapacities." These papers are included in volume 5 of the *Collected Papers of Charles S. Peirce*, ed. Charles Hartshorne and Paul Weiss (Cambridge, MA: Harvard University Press, 1931–1935). For a discussion of these and related matters in Peirce, and their relevance to Sellars's "Empiricism and the Philosophy of Mind," see my article "Peirce's Theory of Perception" in *Studies in the Philosophy of Charles Sanders Peirce* (Amherst, MA: University of Massachusetts Press, 1964).

2

EXORCISING THE
PHILOSOPHICAL TRADITION[1]

Michael Friedman

One of the most interesting aspects of McDowell's very interesting book is the way in which it locates the problems of late twentieth-century Anglo-American philosophy within the historical development of the Western philosophical tradition.[2] Beginning with an opposition between Coherentism and the Myth of the Given exemplified in the recent work of Donald Davidson,[3] McDowell proceeds to frame his discussion in terms of the Kantian distinction between concepts and intuitions, understanding and sensibility, spontaneity and receptivity. McDowell's basic idea is that we can satisfactorily overcome the opposition between Coherentism and the Myth of the Given only by recognizing, with Kant, that concepts and intuitions, understanding and sensibility, must be integrated together in every cognitive act or process – even in the mere intake of experiential content characteristic of sense perception. There is thus no room, according to McDowell, for either unconceptualized sensory input standing in no rational relation to conceptual thought ("intuitions without concepts are blind") or purely intellectual thought operating independently of all rational constraint from sense experience ("thoughts without content are empty").

McDowell characterizes the understanding, the sphere of conceptual thought, as the "space of reasons" (p.5).[4] The understanding, for McDowell, is thus constituted by rational or inferential relations ("relations such as implication or probabilification" (p.7)), and it counts as a faculty of spontaneity in virtue of the Kantian linkage between rational necessitation and freedom. The understanding is active rather than passive because of our freedom – and accompanying responsibility – rationally to examine and to revise all elements in our perpetually evolving conception of the world (pp.12–13). However, if the understanding can thus generate a conception of a truly independent empirical world, there must also be some rational constraint from sense experience. The operations of spontaneity cannot be entirely free, on pain of "degenerat[ing] into moves in a self-contained game" (p.5) or "a frictionless spinning in a void" (p.11). This is precisely the threat posed by Coherentism, and the opposing Myth of the Given then tries to alleviate this threat by invoking bare (unconceptualized) sensory presences somehow acting on the understanding from outside the conceptual sphere. But the problem here, as Davidson, in particular, has made especially clear, is that the relation between sense experience and conceptual thought can now not be conceived of as a rational one – as a genuine relation of justification. As Davidson himself puts the point, "nothing can count as a reason for holding a belief except another belief."[5]

This last formulation leads Davidson himself to a "coherence theory of truth and knowledge": specifically, to the view that sense experience – the impact of the world on our senses – plays a causal role in the generation of belief rather than a justificatory role.[6] And precisely this consequence is the basis for McDowell's objection to Davidson. Since "Davidson's picture depicts our empirical thinking as engaged in with no rational constraint, but only causal influence, from outside," it does indeed pose the Coherentist threat of "spontaneity as frictionless, the very thing that makes the idea of the Given attractive" (p.14). For McDowell, the only way to overcome *this* threat is to maintain that sense experience itself – the causal impact of the world on our senses – already has conceptual content: "In experience one takes in, for instance sees, *that things are thus and so*. That is the sort of thing one can also, for instance, judge" (p.9).[7] This does not mean, however, that sense experience, for McDowell, just is a form of belief or judgment. For the impact of the world on our senses is an expression of our receptivity rather than our spontaneity. In sense experience the world strikes us, independently of our control, as it were, as thus and so: we are passively presented with the world's appearing to be thus and so rather than actively judging (perhaps after reflectively deciding whether to accept this appearance or not) that the world is in fact thus and so (pp.10–11).

McDowell thus interprets the Kantian insistence on a necessary integration of concepts and intuitions, understanding and sensibility, as the claim that "experiences themselves are states or occurrences that inextricably combine receptivity and spontaneity" (p.24). In virtue of possessing conceptual content – and thereby being capable of entering into truly rational relations with the active operations of judgment – passive episodes of sensory receptivity belong to the conceptual sphere, to the space of reasons. The space of reasons is not acted on by sensory experience from the outside and is in this sense absolutely "unbounded" (Lecture II).[8] Precisely in virtue of their passive or receptive character, however, sense experiences also yield the desired rational constraint on the operations of spontaneity from an independent empirical world – the constraint that the Myth of the Given vainly attempted to achieve through bare (unconceptualized) sensory presences. Conceptually structured sensory experiences – which are thereby taken in or passively received precisely *as* impacts of the objective empirical world on our senses – do not lead to the Coherentist image of confinement but rather to the opposite image of "openness to reality":

> That things are thus and so is the conceptual content of an experience,
> but if the subject of the experience is not misled, that very same thing,

that things are thus and so, is also a perceptible fact, an aspect of the perceptible world.

(p.26)

Of course our judgments can be false, our sense experiences can mislead. But there is no "distance from the world" – no necessary confinement within a self-enclosed conceptual sphere – "implicit in the very idea of [conceptual] thought" (p.27). Only in this way, according to McDowell, can we finally overcome the fruitless dialectical opposition between Coherentism and the Myth of the Given. Only in this way can the Kantian interweaving of thought and intuition become, at the same time, a genuine interweaving of mind and world.

Yet McDowell does not stop here, for he also asks himself why the simple and attractive picture of sense experience that he recommends – the picture of sense experience as possessing conceptual content yet nonetheless belonging to our receptivity rather than to our spontaneity – has not even been entertained as a possibility. It is not entertained by Davidson, who, as we have seen, moves directly from the idea that sensory experiences are not beliefs to the conclusion that they can only have a causal *as opposed to* a rational or justificatory relation to beliefs. Nor is McDowell's picture entertained in the contrasting approach of Gareth Evans – according to which sensory experiences indeed possess (representational or propositional) content, but a content that is nonetheless explicitly segregated from the conceptual content proper to beliefs and judgments.[9] Since Davidson and Evans do not even entertain McDowell's simple and attractive picture of sense experience as a possibility (and are therefore, according to McDowell, saddled with an interminable oscillation between Coherentism and the Myth of the Given), there must be a fundamental philosophical difficulty standing in the way of appreciating it –"one whose roots must lie deep" (p.67). And it is in attempting to uncover the roots of this philosophical difficulty that McDowell's argument takes a most unexpected and intriguing turn.

McDowell's diagnosis of the difficulty in question is that the scientific revolution of the sixteenth and seventeenth centuries resulted in a "disenchantment" of sensible nature. In particular, nature became identified as the "realm of law" and was thereby deprived of the meaningful relations constituting the space of reasons definitive of conceptual thought. It thus became difficult or impossible to see how sensory intake – which surely belongs to our nature as perceiving organisms – could be integrated with conceptual thought at all. Therefore, we can truly become comfortable with the idea of a Kantian interweaving of concepts and intuitions, according to McDowell, only when we overcome the opposition between the realm of law and the space of reasons – the dualism of reason and nature – as well.[10] In this way, McDowell unexpectedly traces the roots of the problem about the relation between mind and nature exemplified in the opposition between Coherentism and the Myth of the Given (the epistemological problem of how conceptual thought can apply to or refer to sensible nature) to a version of the traditional mind–body problem (the ontological problem of how minds – and therefore conceptual thinking – can be located in or exist in sensible nature). Whereas in the pre-modern, Aristotelian–Scholastic natural philosophy nature was characterized and explained in teleological and intentional terms, the scientific revolution aimed to purge such elements from nature as the object of natural science once and for all. But it has thereby become difficult or impossible to find a place for human intentionality – and thus for the space of reasons definitive of rational conceptual thought – in nature conceived of in this way. Rationality as such threatens to be "extruded" from nature, and this is the true source, according to McDowell, of the epistemological problem for which the idea of a Kantian interweaving of concepts and intuitions is the correct response.[11]

In responding to the ontological problem about the relation of mind and world – the threat that rationality as such might be extruded from nature – we should, according to McDowell, avoid two traditional strategies. We should avoid a "bald naturalism" that seeks to incorporate the space of reasons into the realm of law through some kind of philosophical reduction or construction – a reconstruction of reason from within the domain of nature as the object of modern natural science (p.73). Equally, however, we should avoid a "rampant platonism" that pictures the space of reasons as existing somehow independently of empirical nature – as "autonomous in that it is constituted independently of anything specifically human" (pp.77–78). The true solution, rather, is to appreciate an Aristotelian insight into our "second nature" as rational animals (pp.78–84). The space of reasons definitive of conceptual thought is not to be dualistically set over and against our animal nature. On the contrary, initiation into the space of reasons is simply a normal part of the maturation of adult human beings – rational animals who thereby acquire a second nature in which natural or animal processes such as sensory perception (belonging, as it were, to our "first nature") become infused with conceptual meaning. And it follows that nature as the object of modern natural science – nature conceived of as a meaningless realm of law – is not the *whole* of nature. Nature as such also includes human nature – rational animals whose initiation into the space of reasons gives the latter a "foothold in the realm of law" (p.84) that avoids both bald naturalism and rampant platonism.

A satisfactory resolution of the opposition between Coherentism and the Myth of the Given, as it arises in such contemporary writers as Davidson and Evans, thus takes us back to Kant, to the scientific revolution, and finally to Aristotle. It is important to note, however, that McDowell's use of this historical framework is intended to dissolve rather than to solve the original problem. McDowell aims ultimately at a Wittgensteinian "quietism" (p.93) in which constructive philosophy is replaced by an "exorcism" of the philosophical anxieties that gave birth to the problem in the first place (pp.142, 147, 176, 183–184). In particular, as we have just seen, the fundamental Aristotelian insight into our second nature as rational animals is not to be viewed as (the beginnings of) a naturalistic reconstruction of reason from within the realm of law. Such a project would indeed call for constructive philosophy; but this is not what McDowell is aiming at.[12] On the contrary, McDowell's appeals to Kant and to Aristotle are simply intended to make us comfortable with a "relaxed naturalism" (p.89) or "naturalized platonism" (p.91) in which we are relieved from the philosophical anxieties engendered by the opposition between the space of reasons and the realm of law. Without the anxieties there is no need for reduction and thus no need for constructive philosophy at all. We thereby attain rather "the discovery that gives philosophy peace" (p.86, from *Philosophical Investigations* §133).

McDowell's work is intended, therefore, to contribute towards a transcendence or overcoming of the philosophical tradition – an exorcism of the dualistic oppositions that have given rise to the traditional "problems of philosophy." Yet what is novel in his approach is a self-consciously sympathetic use of the philosophical tradition to achieve this end. According to McDowell, the tradition itself contains not only the fruitless dualistic oppositions we should aim at exorcising, but also the insights that make this possible.[13] The kind of exorcism at which McDowell aims thus requires an internal engagement with the tradition rather than the merely external "debunking" characteristic of Richard Rorty's work (p.142, note 17). In this way, McDowell's style of exorcism contrasts not only with Rorty's approach but also with that taken by Wittgenstein himself, for Wittgenstein's own "quietism" involves no explicit engagement with the philosophical tradition at all.

* * *

I am very much in sympathy with the idea that an internal engagement with the philosophical tradition can greatly illuminate our current intellectual predicament. I have my doubts, however, whether McDowell's particular framework puts the historical developments in their proper perspective. And I can begin to bring this out in a preliminary way by noting several striking oddities in McDowell's story from a historical point of view. First, McDowell portrays the opposition between Coherentism and the Myth of the Given as resting, in the end, on a disenchantment of nature resulting from the scientific revolution. It is this that prevents us from appreciating the idea (as interpreted by McDowell) of a Kantian interweaving of concepts and intuitions, understanding and sensibility. Yet Kant developed his own characteristic conception of the interdependence of understanding and sensibility precisely in order fully to accommodate the new idea of nature represented by the scientific revolution; so it is prima facie odd to be told that it is the latter that has prevented a proper appreciation of the former. Second, the entire problematic of Coherentism – as a distinctive and explicit philosophical issue – only developed much later. It developed for the first time, in fact, in the context of post-Kantian absolute idealism – a movement based fundamentally on a thoroughgoing rejection of Kant's own conception of the relationship between concepts and intuitions, understanding and sensibility.[14] Moreover, after several intervening twists and turns, the problem re-emerged once again in the philosophy of logical positivism – which, for rather different reasons, also rejected Kant's original conception. Prima facie, then, it would seem that the emergence of the problematic of Coherentism had more to do with a rejection of Kant than with an acceptance of the idea of nature resulting from the scientific revolution. Finally, the kind of constructively oriented bald naturalism to which McDowell opposes his own relaxed naturalism of second nature is an even more recent development arising in the context of contemporary post-Quinean philosophy. The project of thus reconstructing reason from within the realm of law – on pain of rampant platonism – was not felt as philosophically urgent before these particular post-Quinean developments. So, once again, it would seem that the route from the scientific revolution, through Kant, to the kind of problematic for which bald naturalism and rampant platonism are possible (if ultimately unsatisfactory) responses is considerably more complex than McDowell's account suggests.

My doubts about McDowell's framework do not simply concern its historical fidelity, however. For McDowell's resolution of the opposition between Coherentism and the Myth of the Given is supposed to be a form of direct realism according to which we can be unproblematically presented in perception with "a worldly state of affairs itself" (p.143). We are directly and immediately in contact with the world as it is in itself, as it were, and it is this image of "openness to reality" that allows us to escape from the fruitless dialectical opposition with which we started. McDowell develops and articulates this image by appealing to the Kantian conception of the understanding and the fundamental transformation of this conception in post-Kantian German idealism, and also by contrasting his own position with the "coherence theory of truth and knowledge" recently developed by Donald Davidson. Yet, because he presents a seriously misleading picture of the Kantian conception of the understanding and its relation to post-Kantian German idealism, and because he fails to appreciate the way in which Davidson's position evolves from the earlier opposition between Coherentism and the Myth of the Given in the philosophy of logical positivism, McDowell's own framework ends up being much closer to idealism and Coherentism than he intends. Or so I shall argue.

* * *

Let us first consider Kant's relation to the scientific revolution. A central philosophical preoccupation framing this revolution was the ancient debate between Plato and Aristotle over the rational intelligibility of sensible nature. Because of the obvious instability and imperfection of sensible nature, Plato had denied that the proper objects of rational knowledge, the forms, could be perfectly or exactly instantiated there. A primary example of this phenomenon, of course, was the lack of fit between precise and exact mathematical forms and sensible natural objects; and, on this basis, Plato denied that sensible natural objects could be rationally or mathematically understood. Aristotle agreed that sensible natural objects (at least in the sublunary realm) could not be mathematically understood, but he held, nonetheless, that they could be rationally understood in terms of a fundamentally different ideal of intelligibility – the hylomorphic and teleological scheme exhibited most clearly in the growth and maturation of biological organisms. It was on this basis that Aristotle articulated the dualistic cosmological vision that was to dominate Western natural philosophy until the scientific revolution. Mathematical understanding, in the form of mathematical astronomy, is indeed appropriate to the superlunary realm of perfect and essentially unchanging heavenly bodies. In the imperfect and chaotic sublunary realm, however, mathematics must yield to teleology – whereby the four sublunary elements tend naturally to their natural places.

One of the guiding thoughts of the scientific revolution and the philosophy associated with it (a thought which is perfectly explicit in the work of Galileo, for example) was that this dualistic Aristotelian cosmology is to be definitively overturned in favor of a unified and fundamentally mathematical account of the whole of nature. The mathematical ideal of intelligibility already permeating astronomy must be extended to the apparently chaotic sublunary realm as well – where, in particular, it should entirely replace the teleological ideal of understanding articulated by Aristotle. Physics must therefore be radically transformed so that inertial motion replaces the idea of natural place, and the result is that the same mathematical order reigns in both celestial and terrestrial regions. Indeed, the very distinction between celestial and terrestrial regions is thereby destroyed once and for all. The Earth is now another planet or heavenly body moving according to the same mathematical laws as all other bodies in an infinite, essentially geometrical universe. It is no wonder, then, that this vision of a fundamentally mathematical physical cosmology dominated, in one form or another, the natural philosophies of Descartes, Spinoza, Leibniz, and Kant.

From Kant's point of view, however, his rationalist predecessors were still unable to account for the *application* of pure mathematics to empirically given nature – they had still not overcome the Platonic gap between sensible nature itself and the ideal precision of our new mathematical models of nature. And it is precisely in order to overcome this gap that Kant introduces his revolutionary new doctrines of a priori sensibility, on the one hand, and of the necessary interweaving of understanding and sensibility, on the other. This stands out most clearly in the *Prolegomena to any Future Metaphysics*, where the two sections corresponding to the Transcendental Aesthetic and Transcendental Analytic of the first *Critique* are entitled "How is Pure Mathematics Possible?" and "How is Pure Natural Science Possible?" respectively. The first question is answered by appealing to the a priori structure of our sensibility – the pure intuitions of space and time. The second question is answered by appealing to the a priori structure of our understanding – the pure concepts or categories arising from the logical forms of judgment. More precisely, the second question, which concerns the possibility of mathematical physics, is answered by appealing to the fundamentally original and characteristically Kantian idea that pure concepts or categories have objective meaning only when applied to the spatio-temporal world of sense. (This, for Kant, is the meaning of the slogan "thoughts without content are empty.") It is in this way that Kant closes the Platonic gap between mathematical reason and sensible nature, for it now follows that sensible nature can become an object of empirical knowledge only when it is organized or framed by the a priori mathematical structures arising from the necessary interaction between our spatio-temporal intuition and our pure faculty of thought.

Kant himself thus integrates conceptual thought and sense experience through the idea that pure conceptual thought – as represented most clearly by pure logic – only has objective meaning when applied to or "schematized" in terms of the independent (spatio-temporal) structures supplied by pure intuition. It is in this way, and in this way alone, that pure conceptual thought acquires "relation to an object" – relation, that is, to empirical objects perceptually given in space and time ("appearances").[15] For Kant, our sensible experience is necessarily governed by and framed within a "space of reasons" consisting, essentially, of logical and mathematical relations; and there can be no question, therefore, of an epistemological gap between such rational relations on the one side and our sensible experience on the other. Nor can there be an ontological gap between nature as the object of modern mathematical science and the "space of reasons" arising from the necessary interaction of pure understanding and a priori sensibility – there can be no threat of anything like rampant platonism from Kant's own point of view. Since nature as the object of modern mathematical science is first made possible or constituted by the a priori rational structures that Kant has articulated, one cannot distance the latter from nature without making nature itself impossible. To be sure, there is, for Kant, a problem of how the freedom required by morality is compatible with nature as the object of modern mathematical science. But the freedom required by morality should not be confused with the "spontaneity" characterizing the understanding. Indeed, the difference between these two marks precisely the distinction between the faculty of understanding and the faculty of reason for Kant. The understanding, which necessarily operates in cooperation with sensibility, secures the foundations for the modern idea of nature by injecting the a priori rationality of mathematics and logic into sensible experience. The faculty of reason, by contrast, can operate entirely independently of sensibility, and its product – the moral law – is thus wholly free of all empirical contamination.[16]

* * *

It is characteristic of post-Kantian absolute idealism (and, indeed, characteristic of virtually all post-Kantian philosophy) to reject Kant's dualistic conception of our rational faculties as divided between pure sensibility on the one side and pure understanding on the other. And this means, accordingly, that Kant's way of drawing a distinction between the faculties of reason and understanding must also be rejected, since, as we have just seen, the difference between these two faculties, for Kant, is simply that the latter must operate in cooperation with sensibility (on pain of emptiness) whereas the former can operate entirely independently of sensibility. Moreover, it is also characteristic of post-Kantian absolute idealism to take the Kantian faculty of reason rather than the Kantian faculty of understanding as the model for rationality as such – and, indeed, to take the rational freedom required by morality as the model for all rationality.[17] The combined effect of these two moves is then a tendency to distance rational thought from sensible experience and to minimize the empiricist elements in Kant's own conception. For, on the one hand, the Kantian bridge between rational thought and sensory perception – pure intuition and its schematism by the understanding – has now been self-consciously rejected. And, on the other hand, our new conception of rational thought is now modeled on the Kantian faculty of reason – a faculty requiring no cooperation from an independent faculty of pure sensibility. So it is not surprising, then, when post-Kantian idealism eventually leads to explicitly Coherentist conceptions of the objects of rational knowledge (see note 14 above).

Yet McDowell views his own version of the Kantian conception of a necessary interweaving of understanding and sensibility as resting, in the end, on the further articulation of Kantian thought in post-Kantian absolute idealism. His intention is to "domesticate the rhetoric" of post-Kantian absolute idealism so that it actually stands revealed as a kind of direct realism aimed at "protect[ing] a commonsense respect for the independence of the ordinary world" (p.44). And the basis for this reading of the situation is that post-Kantian idealism involves the rejection of the Kantian opposition between appearances and things in themselves. For Kant, what receptivity supplies are appearances or objects of experience, and Kant maintains, in addition, that we are *immediately* related to these objects of experience. Nevertheless, so the argument goes, Kant spoils his insight by embedding this empirical realism in a "transcendental story" according to which appearances are the transcendental products of a non-empirical interaction between our sensibility and things in themselves, and this makes the empirical objectivity of appearances seem "second rate" (pp.40–45).[18] Therefore, when the post-Kantian idealists reject the opposition between appearances and things in themselves, they simultaneously open the way for a fully robust direct realism with respect to what Kant calls appearances – with respect to the objects we experience in the ordinary empirical world. We thereby open the way for the conception McDowell himself recommends, according to which receptivity can actually supply us with "a worldly state of affairs itself."

McDowell does not point out, however, that the post-Kantian rejection of the opposition between appearances and things in themselves is, at the same time, a rejection of the Kantian distinction between concepts and intuitions, understanding and sensibility, as well. Indeed, these are just two aspects of the same distinction, for Kant, since the idea of a thing in itself arises by *abstracting* the concepts of pure understanding from their necessary application to sensibility. The idea of a noumenon or thing in itself is the idea of an object thought through pure understanding alone, independently of sensibility; and such an idea, for precisely this reason, can only be a "problematic concept."[19] Thus only the doctrine that sensibility is a distinct and independent faculty of the mind allows room, by contrast, for the idea of ("problematic") objects thought through pure understanding alone. Giving up the opposition between appearances and things in themselves therefore means giving up the notion of a distinct and independent faculty of intuition as well. It is entirely natural, then, if post-Kantian absolute idealism views the objects of rational knowledge as manifestations of an absolute rational freedom entirely unconstrained by anything outside itself.

Now McDowell is sensitive to the circumstance that his own conception might appear vulnerable to the charge of idealism, and he devotes Lecture II, on "The Unboundedness of the Conceptual" (the conclusion of which is the above discussion of absolute idealism), to answering this charge. McDowell's conception might appear to be a version of idealism – and thus of Coherentism – because it pictures the sphere of the conceptual as absolutely unbounded. Since sense experience is itself permeated by spontaneity, the understanding does not rationally respond to anything outside the conceptual sphere. And this much, in fact, McDowell does share in common with even the "undomesticated" rhetoric of absolute idealism. But, and this is the key point in McDowell's rejection of Coherentism, the spontaneity of the understanding is not entirely unconstrained. On the contrary, it is necessarily constrained by the deliverances of receptivity, with respect to which, despite their thoroughly conceptual character, we are nonetheless passive rather than active: there is a difference between its appearing to us that such and such is the case in experience (concerning which we have no free choice) and our actively judging that such and such is the case in thought (concerning which we have free choice). Therefore, although the empirical world indeed consists of *thinkable* contents belonging to the space of reasons, it is thus independent of the free and spontaneous *activity* of thought. And this should be all we need, according to McDowell, to exorcise the specter of idealism in favor of the direct realism of common sense (pp.25–29).[20]

McDowell himself makes it perfectly clear, however, that the bare idea of passive receptivity is not yet the idea of constraint from an independent objective world. This is because we are equally passive with respect to "impressions of inner sense" that do not provide access to an independent objective world existing beyond themselves.[21] Only "impressions of outer sense" have this latter property – a property in virtue of which they count as "glimpses" of an independent objective world. Hence, the distinction between passive experience (concerning which we are simply "struck" one way or another, as it were) and active judgment (concerning which we have free choice) is not at all the same as the distinction between that which expresses constraint by an independent objective world and that which does not. The crucial question, in this regard, concerns rather how we distinguish between "inner" and "outer" sense. And McDowell's idea here, if I understand him correctly, is that passively received impressions become experiences of an objective world (and thus impressions of outer sense) only by being *taken as such* by the active faculty of understanding: by being subject, that is, to the perpetually revisable procedure through which the understanding integrates such impressions into an evolving world-conception (pp.29–40).[22] Relation to an independent objective world is thus not secured by the idea of receptivity, but rather by the spontaneous conceptual activities of the understanding as it rationally evolves an integrated picture of this world. Hence, given McDowell's own conception of what impressions of outer sense amount to, I do not see, in the end, how he has fully rebutted the charge of idealism. I do not see why his conception itself is not finally a version of Coherentism.[23]

* * *

McDowell's attempt to assimilate post-Kantian absolute idealism is at least partly responsible, I believe, for an important ambiguity in his notion of the understanding, of the space of reasons definitive of conceptual thought. On the one hand, as we have been just emphasizing, the understanding is the faculty of empirical thinking: it centrally involves the continual revision of our conception of the empirical world in light of the deliverances of sense experience. As such, in harmony with Kant's own characterization of the understanding, it is responsible for both our common sense conception of the empirical world and the perpetual refinement of that conception by empirical science. On the other hand, however, McDowell also characterizes the understanding as "our capacity to recognize and bring into being the kind of intelligibility proper to meaning" (p.71). Accordingly, after stating that the understanding is "the faculty that enables us to recognize and create the kind of intelligibility that is a matter of placement in the space of reasons" (p.79), McDowell characterizes the space of reasons as "the structure in which we place things when we find meaning in them" (p.88), and as "the rational structure within which meaning comes into view" (p.92).[24] A paradigmatic object of the understanding, in this sense, is "a text or an utterance or some other kind of action" (p.72), and the understanding therefore emerges as the faculty whose characteristic function is precisely the recognition (and creation) of specifically *intentional* phenomena.

This last characterization of the understanding and the space of reasons frames McDowell's explanation of the conflict he discerns between the latter and the realm of law. Whereas the pre-modern world-view considered nature as "filled with meaning" (p.71) – as if nature itself were a kind of text – the scientific revolution, by self-consciously eliminating all intentional notions from natural science, portrayed nature as a sequence of mere "law-governed happenings" (p.133) and thus as "empty of meaning and value" (p.181).[25] We end up with a fundamentally different ideal of intelligibility – placement in the realm of law – as the "rightly entrenched view of the kind of understanding aimed at by properly scientific investigation" (p.181). But, if the kind of intelligibility correlative to the understanding and the space of reasons is thus entirely distinct from the kind of intelligibility aimed at by properly scientific investigation, we have a puzzle: how can the understanding in this sense *also* be responsible for our evolving conception of the empirical world expressed in common sense and in science – which conception includes the mere law-governed happenings constituting the realm of law?

McDowell himself is of course aware of this puzzle, and he uses it, in fact, to motivate his own solution to the conflict he discerns between the space of reasons and the realm of law:

> I have urged that conceptual capacities, capacities for the kind of understanding whose correlate is the kind of intelligibility that is proper to meaning, are operative also in our perception of the world apart from human beings. The question is how we can take this view without offering to reinstate the idea that the movement of the planets, or the fall of a sparrow, is rightly approached in the sort of way we approach a text or an utterance or some other kind of action.
>
> (p.72)

And an exposition of his Aristotelian "relaxed" naturalism of second nature then follows. Similarly, after explaining that Kant aimed to secure the particular type of intelligibility characterizing the realm of law against Hume's skeptical doubts, McDowell points out that "[f]or Kant, the ordinary empirical world, which includes nature as the realm of law, is not external to the conceptual", so that "[t]he understanding – the very capacity that we bring to bear on texts – must be involved in our taking in of mere meaningless happenings" (p.97). Again, it was "Kant's lack of a pregnant notion of second nature" (p.97) that prevented him from being entirely successful in bridging the gap between these two realms.

Hence, it is the idea of a naturalism of second nature that is supposed to overcome the dualism of reason and nature and thereby solve our puzzle. This idea is supposed to show us how we can maintain that the ordinary empirical world (including the scientific refinement thereof) is internal to the conceptual realm without lapsing into the pre-modern conception of this world as itself "filled with meaning." As we have seen, according to McDowell's naturalism of second nature, human beings belong to nature as perceiving animals and thus have a "foothold in the realm of law." Nevertheless, as rational animals, human beings also acquire a second nature through a purely natural process of maturation and initiation in which meaning – and thus the rational structure of the space of reasons – comes into view. This removes the threat of rampant platonism, according to which "the rational structure within which meaning comes into view is independent of anything merely human" (p.92), and the way is now open to "claim both that the notion of spontaneity functions in a conceptual framework that is alien to the structure of the realm of law, and that it is needed for describing the actualizations of natural powers as such" (p.88). In particular, "experiences are actualizations of our sentient nature in which conceptual capacities are inextricably implicated" (pp.89–90); and, in this way, "we can keep nature as it were partially enchanted, but without lapsing into pre-scientific superstition or a rampant platonism" (p.85).

I see how McDowell's naturalism of second nature removes the threat of rampant platonism, but it is not yet clear to me how the threat of something akin to pre-scientific superstition – according to which nature itself must be viewed as a kind of text – is also removed. According to McDowell's naturalism of second nature, if I understand it correctly, nature is subject to only a "partial re-enchantment" (p.88), in that nature as the realm of law is now revealed as *part* of a larger nature that also includes the second nature produced by human maturation and initiation. As a consequence, even though "we cannot capture what it is to possess and employ the understanding ... in terms of concepts that place things in the realm of law" (p.89), it does not follow that we cannot locate the understanding in nature as such – for we can now locate the understanding in "re-enchanted" human nature. I am still puzzled, however, for the issue about pre-scientific superstition concerns the *objects* of the understanding. Suppose we grant to McDowell that the understanding comfortably resides in our human second nature produced by maturation and initiation. Nevertheless, one important object of the understanding is the *nonhuman* part of nature belonging to the realm of law. And if we persist in characterizing the understanding as "our capacity to recognize and bring into being the kind of intelligibility proper to meaning," it is still not clear how the very same understanding can also produce the modern scientific intelligibility appropriate to "mere meaningless happenings."

Kant's own conception of the understanding is not subject to this difficulty. For Kant, the understanding is not the faculty through which meaning and intentionality are revealed: it is emphatically not "the very capacity that we bring to bear on texts." The understanding is rather precisely the faculty responsible for the intelligibility of the realm of law. Kant's own "space of reasons," as emphasized above, is constituted by the logical and mathematical relations resulting from the necessary application of pure understanding to pure sensibility, and, as such, it makes nature – considered precisely as the object of modern mathematical science – first possible. This is why there can be no question of an opposition between the "space of reasons" and the realm of law for Kant himself.[26] For Kant, meaning and intentionality (or "meaning and value") are then the province of the distinct faculties of reason (the faculty of ends) and judgment (the faculty of purposiveness). And here we are indeed faced with a conflict – a conflict, in Kantian terms, between the realm of nature and the realm of freedom. This conflict is resolved, for Kant, in the solution to the Antinomy of Teleological Judgment articulated in the third *Critique*: both the idea of universal mechanism of nature fostered by the understanding and the idea of teleological purposiveness of nature due to the faculty of judgment are purely *regulative* ideals functioning to guide our reason towards the forever unattainable goals of a complete science of nature and a fully realized moral order.

Now post-Kantian absolute idealism, as discussed above, rejects the fundamental Kantian distinction between the faculties of understanding and sensibility. Accordingly, it also rejects the Kantian distinctions among the three "higher" rational faculties of understanding, judgment, and reason. Indeed, it is characteristic of post-Kantian idealism to take the faculty of reason as its model for rationality as such and, on this basis, to take the articulation of "meaning and value" as the central task of our rationality. But this then suggests, in the idealist tradition in question, that (non-human) nature itself must also be reconceived, so that, in particular, purposiveness (and thus intentionality) is now objectively – and not just regulatively – located in (non-human) nature itself. We are thereby led to the philosophies of nature of Schelling and Hegel and, in the end, to the idea that even (non-human) nature itself is a manifestation of self-realizing spirit. We end up, that is, with something considerably stronger than the "partial re-enchantment of nature" envisioned by McDowell.[27]

* * *

I suggested above that the kind of problematic for which bald naturalism and rampant platonism are possible (if ultimately unsatisfactory) responses does not in fact arise in the immediate aftermath of the scientific revolution. One way to begin to see this is to note that, as McDowell himself intimates, the problematic in question is not *identical* to the traditional mind–body problem. The space of reasons definitive of conceptual thought is not the human mind; it is rather a "rational structure within which meaning comes into view" (p.92) or a "normative structure within which meaning comes into view" (p.93). Accordingly, the threat of rampant platonism is not the threat of mind–body dualism, but rather the threat of an "autonomous" and "inhuman" normative structure to which, nonetheless, "human minds must somehow be able to latch on" (p.77). Indeed, it is for precisely this reason that McDowell explains that "I mean the label 'platonism' in something like the sense it bears in the philosophy of mathematics" (p.77, note 7). Hence, the threat that human intentionality might be extruded from nature does not immediately imply that "platonistic" normative structures must be extruded as well. On the contrary, as we saw above, a central guiding idea of the scientific revolution was that one such normative structure – that of pure mathematics – actually pervades sensible nature much more thoroughly than was ever imagined before.[28]

Moreover, if we look for an example of a real historical tradition within which something like McDowell's rampant platonism does in fact arise, the closest we can come, I believe, is a second important strand in post-Kantian thought: the "pure logic [*reine Logik*]" tradition associated with Bolzano, Herbart, Lotze, and Meinong – and then, especially, with the extended polemic against psychologism of Gottlob Frege and Edmund Husserl. The thinkers in this tradition tended to follow Kant in emphasizing the importance of mathematics, mathematical physics, and the exercise of pure thought expressed in the logical forms of judgment – which exercise is conceived in terms of normative principles prescribing how we ought to think and reason rather than descriptive principles governing how we in fact think and reason. At the same time, however, the thinkers in this tradition refused to follow Kant in his dualism of concepts and intuitions, understanding and sensibility. Thus, whereas these thinkers rejected the speculative ambitions of post-Kantian absolute idealism in favor of a return to the scientific preoccupations of Kant himself, they were nonetheless in basic agreement with the stress placed by absolute idealism on the independence and autonomy of pure thought. For precisely this reason, however, they were unable to view the Kantian "space of reasons" definitive of logico-mathematical thinking as essentially spatio-temporal and thus as immanent in sensible nature itself. The Kantian "space of reasons" thereby took on a characteristically "platonistic" autonomy in this tradition,[29] and, accordingly, it indeed became difficult to see how pure thought could after all apply to or refer to an independently existing sensible nature.

The "logical idealism" formulated within the Marburg School of neo-Kantianism represented by Hermann Cohen, Paul Natorp, and Ernst Cassirer was of particular importance in this regard. Pure thought, according to the Marburg School, successively generates a sequence of logico-mathematical structures of ever increasing richness and complexity – a sequence that is clearly discernible in the actual historical evolution of the exact sciences. In pure mathematics, for example, we find a succession of more and more sophisticated conceptions of space and thus of geometry. But in empirical natural science – in mathematical physics – we also find a succession of logico-mathematical structures as we describe nature itself by an ever richer sequence of mathematical models. The difference between empirical natural science and the purely formal mathematical sciences, then, is simply that in empirical natural science the relevant sequence of logico-mathematical structures is subject to *perpetual revision* and so never actually terminates. Indeed, the empirical natural world, on this conception, is simply the never completed "X" towards which our sequence of logico-mathematical models of nature is converging.

Now the logical idealism of the Marburg School exerted a profound influence on the epistemology of early twentieth-century logical positivism. Indeed, Rudolf Carnap's *Der logische Aufbau der Welt* was a self-conscious attempt to synthesize the insights of the Marburg School into the "experience constituting" role of logico-mathematical structure with the complementary emphasis of radical empiricist "positivism" on the fundamental role of the experiential "given" as the necessary basis of all empirical knowledge.[30] Accordingly, the constitutional system of the *Aufbau* represents empirical knowledge as a sequence of logico-mathematical relational structures defined purely formally (progressing up the type-hierarchy of *Principia Mathematica*) – a sequence that is erected, however, on an empirically given basis of "elementary experiences." In this way, Carnap hoped, we can accommodate the neo-Kantian emphasis on pure thought to the unavoidable need for empirical content. And we can do this, moreover, without any reliance whatsoever on Kantian pure intuition.

This last point brings us to a decisive question, however, for how is it now possible even to develop pure mathematics without Kantian pure intuition? The answer, of course, was given by the logicism articulated by Frege and Bertrand Russell. Pure mathematics is simply a branch of logic, and it is thereby seen to be a product of pure thought alone independently of all intuitive content: pure mathematics is analytic a priori rather than synthetic a priori. But this just pushes the question back to the nature and character of logic or pure thought itself – a question that becomes especially pressing in view of the vast increase in mathematical power and complexity of the logic developed by Frege and Russell. How is pure thought or pure logic in this sense now possible? For the logical positivists, the answer to this new question was definitively given by Ludwig Wittgenstein's *Tractatus Logico-Philosophicus*. Pure thought or pure logic (in the new sense) is built into the most general representational possibilities of *language*. It expresses the logical syntax or logical grammar of our language, as it were, and it is in precisely this sense that logic (and therefore mathematics) is analytic. We thus end up with what is now known as the linguistic doctrine of logico-mathematical truth – a doctrine which is intended, among other things, to mitigate the "platonistic" tendencies of the *reine Logik* tradition.[31]

Yet we thereby end up with a new fundamental difficulty about empirical content as well. For the constitutional system of the *Aufbau* now stands revealed as a system of linguistic syntactic items – a system of terms and sentences. To be sure, some of these terms and sentences are non-logical in the technical sense. The term for the "basic relation" between elementary experiences, for example, is not definable in the purely logical vocabulary of *Principia Mathematica*. But what attaches this primitive non-logical term to actual given experience? How does this term itself acquire empirical content? These questions were the subject of the celebrated protocol–sentence debate within the Vienna Circle.[32] The so-called "right wing" of the Circle, represented by Moritz Schlick and Friedrich Waismann, insisted that something extra-linguistic – actual given experience – must be somehow associated with language by particular acts of ostension. Otherwise, they argued, we have definitively renounced empiricism in favor of the coherence theory of truth. The so-called "left wing" of the Circle, represented by Otto Neurath and (under Neurath's influence) Carnap himself, maintained, on the contrary, that the very idea of an association between language and something extra-linguistic is "metaphysical" and thus unintelligible. The only intelligible relations we can consider in epistemology are logical and hence intra-linguistic. Therefore, all talk of an extra-linguistic given must be purged once and for all from a logically purified empiricism. It is evident, then, that we are here confronted with an especially acute form of the dialectical opposition between Coherentism and the Myth of the Given. And it is this crucial episode within the development of logical positivism, I believe, that constitutes the immediate historical background to the way in which the dialectical opposition in question has resurfaced, in recent years, in Davidson's work.[33]

* * *

A central idea of the *reine Logik* tradition – including the philosophy of logical positivism – is that logical considerations are entirely distinct from psychological considerations: logic gives normative rules governing how we ought to think and reason rather than a descriptive account of how we in fact think and reason. And it is precisely this distinction which, in the context of a rejection of Kant's own account of the spatio-temporal *schematism* of the understanding, generates a "platonistic" threat of an unbridgeable gulf between the space of reasons definitive of conceptual thought on the one side and actual human thinking on the other.[34] Moreover, as indicated above, one of the main attractions of the linguistic doctrine of logical truth is that it promises to retain the sharp distinction between the logical and the psychological without creating such a "platonistic" gulf. The logical structure constituting the space of reasons does not subsist in an autonomous ontological realm but rather in the meaning relations of our language. This logical structure acquires its normative force, therefore, not in virtue of some peculiar supernatural ideality, but rather because it expresses purely analytic truths – which, as such, have no ontological import whatsoever.[35]

A fundamental question arises at this point, however. Is the language within which logical relations are supposed to subsist an ideal, purely formal language – of the kind discussed in Frege, the *Tractatus*, and Carnap's *Logical Syntax of Language* – or is it rather the actual natural language we speak? It would seem that the former alternative is needed for maintaining a sharp distinction between the logical and the psychological, whereas the import of the latter alternative is precisely to blur this distinction. And the strategy of W. V. Quine's critique and eventual rejection of the linguistic doctrine of logical truth, accordingly, is to force us away from a consideration of ideal languages and towards the consideration of natural language. In particular, Quine exploits technical problems that have arisen in the study of formal languages to argue that no satisfactory demarcation of logical or analytic truth from empirical or synthetic truth can be provided there.[36] He then asks for the "empirical meaning" of the notion of logical or analytic truth in actual linguistic behavior and concludes that no satisfactory demarcation can be found here either. The upshot is that the central distinction between meaning relations and merely synthetic relations on which the linguistic doctrine of logical truth rests has no reality in actual linguistic behavior and thus stands revealed as philosophically bankrupt.[37]

41

From the present point of view, it is the first step of Quine's argument that is the truly fundamental one. For it is precisely by forcing us away from formal languages and towards the consideration of real natural languages that Quine turns the distinction between logical and non-logical relations into a psychological question and, in this sense, collapses the problem of normative structures of rationality into the mind–body problem. Quine's skepticism about the reality of meaning relations in actual human behavior then threatens indeed to extrude the space of reasons from nature once and for all. And this is why I suggested above that McDowell's problematic of an opposition between reason and nature really first arises in the context of contemporary post-Quinean naturalism. For it is in this context alone that the threat of an extrusion of human intentionality from nature as the object of modern natural science threatens a corresponding extrusion of normative structures of rationality as such. It is in this context alone that a preoccupation with the scientific study of nature characteristic of the modern period can make rational normative structures as such appear "spooky."[38]

And it is in this context, accordingly, that Quine himself removes normative rational structures from nature by the doctrine of the indeterminacy of translation. What Quine calls "the whole truth about nature" – the totality of truths of physical natural science – is insufficient, according to this doctrine, to determine the choice of radically incompatible translation manuals between different languages and thus to fix the meanings of (non-observational) sentences of any single language.[39] In the context of Quine's tough-minded physicalist naturalism there are therefore no "facts of the matter" about meanings at all. And it follows, by the identification of rational relations with meaning relations characteristic of the linguistic doctrine of logical truth against which Quine's polemic is directed, that there can equally be no rational relations in the traditional sense at all. On the contrary, the project of Quine's naturalized epistemology is precisely to *reconstrue* all putatively rational relations formerly located in the space of reasons in frankly physical and behavioral terms: empirical evidence is replaced by sensory stimulation, evidential relations more generally are replaced by conditioned associations, and so on. In the end, therefore, Quine's own naturalism amounts to a thoroughgoing rejection of the distinction between the normative realm of logic and the purely descriptive realm of empirical human psychology. In the context of the gulf between nature and reason arising from his attack on the linguistic doctrine of logical or analytic truth, Quine has definitively rejected the traditional philosophical conception of normative structures of rationality on behalf of empirical science.

From this point of view, Davidson's philosophy of "radical interpretation" appears as an attempt to salvage such a philosophical conception of rationality from the force of Quine's attack. Starting from Quine's problematic of radical translation, and agreeing fundamentally with the doctrine of indeterminacy of meaning in terms of physical natural fact, Davidson adds an essentially new element – the principle of charity. Recognizing explicitly that no physical or behavioral facts of the Quinean type – no facts about sensory stimulation, conditioned associations, and so on – are enough to fix translation sufficiently to explain the possibility of meaningful communication, we introduce an additional postulate as a realization of our "constitutive ideal of rationality": we require that translation is to proceed so as to make most sentences held true by the speaker actually true by the lights of the interpreter. This yields substantially more determinacy than was possible for Quine; for, in essence, it extends the constraint Quine had imposed on a fragment of the language (observation sentences and logical particles) to the whole of the language. It is in this way, and in this way alone, Davidson urges, that we can make meaningful linguistic understanding intelligible.[40]

It is in this way, too, that we can rescue notions like rationality, evidence, reasons to believe, and so on, from the aftermath of Quine's critique. To be sure, Quine has indeed shown that these notions "have no echo in physical theory." But this means, for Davidson, that what he calls "psychology" is not and cannot be reduced to or constructed out of physical natural science. On the contrary, what Davidson calls "psychology" is an essentially autonomous normative discipline – governed by the principle of charity as a realization of the constitutive ideal of rationality – which, as such, is not characterizable in terms of exceptionless laws of nature like those found in physics. Thus, according to Davidson's "anomalous monism," although causal relations in psychology must, like all causal relations, be supported, in the end, by truly universal natural laws, this means only that each psychological event must be token–token identical with some physical event (i.e., an event described in the language of physics wherein alone truly universal natural laws are possible). So Davidson's anomalous monism rests on the principle of charity, understood as a realization of the constitutive ideal of rationality, and it is this principle, in turn, therefore, which, for Davidson, bridges the gulf between reason and nature.[41] In the context of Quine's problematic of radical translation, his attack on the analytic–synthetic distinction, and his doctrine of the indeterminacy of meaning in terms of physical natural fact, we can nonetheless save something significant in the traditional philosophical ideal of normative structures of rationality.[42]

Davidson's application of the constitutive ideal of rationality – as realized by the principle of charity – is the basis for his "coherence theory of truth and knowledge" as well. In particular, it follows that in any coherent and therefore interpretable set of beliefs most elements thereof must be true. Indeed, general truth in the sense of the principle of charity is a condition for any system of noises produced by putatively rational creatures counting as expressions of belief at all. But this means, first, that Coherentism, properly understood, is perfectly compatible with the demand for empirical content – the demand that a coherent system of beliefs reflects an independent empirical world known through the senses. For, in applying the principle of charity, the interpreter necessarily insures that the system of beliefs in question is mostly true of the objects in the environment with which the speaker is causally interacting. So there is no possibility, from this point of view, of radical skepticism with respect to the external world. And it also means, second, that the idea of non-intertranslatable or incommensurable languages or "conceptual schemes" is entirely incoherent. For any putative system of beliefs must be fully translatable into our language, and in a way, moreover, that leaves it in fundamental agreement with our system of beliefs – otherwise this putative system is no system of beliefs at all. There is equally no possibility, therefore, of linguistic or conceptual relativism.

* * *

Now it is precisely Davidson's philosophy of radical interpretation that sets the stage for McDowell's own argument. And it is this context, I believe, that explains both why McDowell traces his problem of reason versus nature to the scientific revolution and why he characterizes the understanding as the faculty for recognizing (and creating) "meaning and value." As we have seen, both of these ideas are fundamentally misguided from the point of view of a Kantian conception of the understanding. In the context of Davidson's post-Quinean philosophy of radical interpretation, however, the problem of rationality as such has become an explicitly psychological problem – so that, in particular, problems about integrating human intentionality into nature pose problems for integrating reason as such into nature as well. For Davidson, rationality then reappears in the guise of constraints on our interpretation of one another – and thus, explicitly, as a "rational structure within which meaning comes into view."[43] Here we see a peculiar convergence between the way in which Davidson reintroduces the concept of rationality as the foundation for the interpretation of human intentionality, on the one hand, and the way in which post-Kantian idealism collapses the Kantian faculty of understanding into the faculties of reason and judgment, on the other. And it is clear, I believe, that this peculiar convergence has exerted a profound influence on McDowell.

Yet, although McDowell's entire argument is thus framed within the context of Davidson's post-Quinean philosophy of radical interpretation, the starting point for his argument is a rejection of Davidson's "coherence theory of truth and knowledge." In full agreement with Davidson about the necessary autonomy of the space of reasons with respect to the domain of physical natural fact (the realm of law), McDowell is not at all satisfied with the way in which Davidson himself bridges the resulting gap. According to Davidson's anomalous monism, the conceptual–psychological domain revealed in radical interpretation is related by way of token–token identities to the Quinean, purely naturalistic domain of physical natural fact. For only so can causal relations within psychology – such as, for example, the causal relations that relate expressions of belief to objects in the immediate physical environment via sensory stimulation – be properly grounded in the laws of physics. But then, McDowell objects, occurrences of sensory stimulation, considered as physical natural events belonging to the realm of law, cannot, as such, be *rationally* related to our expressions of belief: they cannot, as elements of the realm of law, also belong to the space of reasons. Davidson himself has no other alternative but to hold that the relation of sense experience to our beliefs is causal *as opposed to* rational, and Davidson's "coherence theory" thus rests, in the end, on an inadequate conception of the relationship between the space of reasons and the realm of law.[44]

For McDowell, by contrast, it is the idea of a naturalism of second nature that bridges the gap between the space of reasons and the realm of law. It is this idea that replaces Davidson's anomalous monism. There is no need, according to McDowell, to view the conceptual–psychological domain of the space of reasons as resting on the purely naturalistic domain of physical natural fact in virtue of an injection or imposition of our constitutive ideal of rationality onto a realm of law devoid of all rational meaning. For this would force us to relate the domain of the conceptual to something wholly outside this domain by means of purely external (causal as opposed to rational) relations. What is needed, rather, is to recognize that initiation into the space of reasons is simply a normal part of the maturation process of adult human beings as they are educated into their linguistic and cultural tradition. When one has undergone such an initiation or education (for which McDowell adopts the traditional German concept of *Bildung*) one is then *inside* the space of reasons, and one sees everything – including the sensible natural world – from within this point of view. In this way, the realm of law gives birth, as it were, to a second nature constituted by human intentionality – a second nature (the realm of the conceptual) which is now absolutely unbounded. So the way is now open to view occurrences of sensory stimulation themselves – causal impacts of the world on our senses – as, at the same time and as such, elements of the space of reasons bearing rational relations of justification to the judgments based upon them.

In Davidson's picture the world that our beliefs and judgments are about is, at least in principle, characterizable wholly independently of the conceptual–psychological domain of human intentionality. Indeed, the causal (as opposed to rational) relations between our thinking and the world must ultimately be supported by the entirely non-intentional characterization of the world as the domain of physical natural fact. In this sense, experience relates thought to an independent objective reality across an outer boundary; and it is precisely such a boundary that McDowell himself is most concerned to erase:

> [W]e must not picture an outer boundary around the sphere of the conceptual, with a reality outside the boundary impinging inward on the system. Any impingements across such a boundary could only be causal, and not rational; that is Davidson's perfectly correct point, and he urges that we should settle for holding that in experience the world exerts a merely causal influence on our thinking. But I am trying to describe a way of maintaining that in experience the world exerts a rational influence on our thinking. And that requires us to delete the outer boundary from the picture. The impressions on our senses that

keep the dynamic system in motion are already equipped with conceptual content. The facts that are made manifest to us in those impressions, or at least seem to be, are not beyond an outer boundary that encloses the conceptual sphere, and the impingements of the world on our sensibility are not inward crossings of such a boundary.

(p.34)

This is the full force, for McDowell, of the idea that the domain of the conceptual is absolutely unbounded.

But now who is closer to idealism and Coherentism – Davidson or McDowell himself? Despite his repeated disavowals,[45] it seems clear from the present context especially that the answer must be McDowell himself. Davidson, in virtue of the residual Quinean naturalism and physicalism expressed in his anomalous monism, has a robust conception of the independence of the reality to which we are (causally) related in sense experience. And it is precisely the thesis that the mediation between belief and reality established in sense experience is causal as opposed to rational that permits Davidson to maintain that we are nonetheless, from an epistemic point of view, *immediately* related to the external objects of our beliefs.[46] Thus, by rejecting Davidson's use of anomalous monism here and insisting on the absolute unboundedness of the conceptual, McDowell has given up Davidson's robust conception of the independence of reality as well. All that remains of this independence, for McDowell, is the contrast between the active judging characteristic of spontaneity and the passive intake characteristic of receptivity. Yet, as I argued above, this contrast alone is far too weak. For, according to McDowell himself, we need the additional idea of impressions of specifically outer sense, and this idea, in turn, refers simply to passive manifestations of conceptualization that are *taken* as impressions of an independent reality by the understanding.[47] Are we not here very close indeed to the traditional idealist doctrine that the world to which our thought relates is a creature of our own conceptualization?

We can further elucidate the sense in which McDowell's own position is actually more idealistic than Davidson's by contrasting Davidson's response to the threat of linguistic and conceptual relativism via the principle of charity with McDowell's use of the idea of a "fusion of horizons" derived from Hans-Georg Gadamer (p.36, note 11). For Gadamer, unlike Davidson, shared cultural and linguistic traditions are what mediate our understanding of one another. And for Gadamer, again unlike Davidson, such cultural and linguistic traditions can certainly be conceptually divergent from one another. What saves us from relativism, nonetheless, is the possibility of a fusion of such divergent horizons – whereby members of one cultural tradition can learn, and thus be initiated into, a divergent cultural tradition.[48] McDowell, as one might expect, is very sympathetic to Gadamer's emphasis on the central place of cultural and linguistic traditions. Indeed, in the context of an explicit reference to Gadamer, he asserts that "languages and traditions can figure not as 'tertia' that would threaten to make our grip on the world philosophically problematic, but as constitutive of our unproblematic openness to the world" (p.155) and, in the same vein, "[t]he Gadamerian note that the lectures end on is that understanding is placing what is understood within a horizon constituted by tradition" (p.184).[49] One might wonder, accordingly, how McDowell himself would respond to the threat of cultural or linguistic relativism. Are we not faced, in particular, with the threat that there is not one space of reasons but many different ones – each adapted to its own cultural tradition and each constituting its own "world"?

When McDowell first introduces the idea of a fusion of horizons he is considering the case of an initially opaque and thus alien thinker:

> Of course we can initially find another thinker opaque. It may take work to make the conceptual contents of someone else's engagements with the world available to us. And in the meantime the world she engages with is surely already within our view. I have said nothing that threatens that obvious fact.
>
> (p.34)

In what sense, however, is the world *with which the alien thinker is engaged* open to our view? For Davidson, as we have seen, the principle of charity guarantees that there is only one such world. Indeed, for Davidson, the purely objective and non-intentional realm of physical natural fact must ultimately underlie the causal relations between expressions of belief and the external world to which the principle of charity is applied. For McDowell, by contrast, the realm of the conceptual is absolutely unbounded, and we are especially to eschew, in particular, all talk of impingements across an outer boundary enclosing the conceptual sphere. If the conceptual contents of an alien thinker's engagements with the world are not yet available to us, therefore, how can the world corresponding to these conceptual contents be so?[50] Are we not faced – *before* a fusion of horizons – simply with two different conceptual systems together with two different "worlds" constituted by these systems?[51]

Now McDowell, in this connection, expresses considerable sympathy for "linguistic idealist" interpretations of Wittgenstein's later philosophy. Yet they are not finally satisfactory, he thinks, because there is nothing in Wittgenstein to parallel Kant's transcendental subject – there is nothing, that is, "to do the constituting of the harmony [between mind and world]" (p.159). In light of the above, however, it would seem that there is indeed something to do the constituting of the harmony between mind and world – not a Kantian transcendental subject, of course, but rather empirically given linguistic cultural traditions (which are "constitutive of our unproblematic openness to the world"). And it should be obvious that, in this kind of "linguistic idealism," Wittgenstein is not exorcising the philosophical tradition but rather continuing it. Or perhaps we should say that it is not Wittgenstein, but McDowell himself, in the guise of

Wittgenstein's representative, who is thus continuing the philosophical tradition (and, in particular, the tradition of post-Kantian German idealism of which Gadamer is a worthy recent representative). For it is characteristic of Wittgenstein's own method, as I noted at the beginning, to deliberately step back from any explicit engagement with the philosophical tradition at all and to concentrate, instead, on particularistic and self-consciously non-theoretical investigations of imaginary "language-games." It is this method of exploring the limits of our language *from within* that is then Wittgenstein's replacement for traditional philosophy. In light of the historical–philosophical tangles produced by McDowell's attempt to bring Wittgensteinian "quietism" into some kind of explicit relation with the philosophical tradition nonetheless, one can only conclude, in the end, that Wittgensteinian quietism may itself only make sense in the context of Wittgensteinian philosophical method.

Notes

1   I am indebted to extensive comments from both John McDowell and Donald Davidson on an earlier draft of this chapter which helped me to clear up misunderstandings and infelicities in my exposition of their views. (Any such problems that remain are of course my responsibility alone.) I would also like to thank Graciela De Pierris for very useful discussion of the issues as well as patient and careful reading of earlier drafts, and to thank Paul Franks for helping me to present a somewhat more balanced picture of the relationship between Kant and post-Kantian idealism. Finally, I am indebted to the editors of *The Philosophical Review*, and to Mark Wilson, for valuable feedback.
2   John McDowell, *Mind and World* (Cambridge, MA: Harvard University Press, 1994) – which is a version of the John Locke Lectures delivered in 1991. Page numbers in brackets are to this volume.
3   Donald Davidson, "On the Very Idea of a Conceptual Scheme," in *Inquiries into Truth and Interpretation* (Oxford: Clarendon Press, 1984), and "A Coherence Theory of Truth and Knowledge," in *Truth and Interpretation*, ed. E. LePore (Oxford: Blackwell, 1986). The idea of the Myth of the Given is of course taken from Wilfrid Sellars, "Empiricism and the Philosophy of Mind," in *Minnesota Studies in the Philosophy of Science*, vol. 1, ed. H. Feigl and M. Scriven (Minneapolis: University of Minnesota Press, 1956).
4   This terminology derives from §36 of Sellars, op. cit., which argues that

> in characterizing an episode or state as that of *knowing*, we are not giving an empirical description of that episode or state; we are placing it in the logical space of reasons, of justifying and being able to justify what one says.

Sellars derives the notion of "logical space," in turn, from Wittgenstein's *Tractatus*. There its connection with the notion of "logical manifoldness [*logische Mannigfaltigkeit*]" links it to Riemann's generalized notion of "n-fold extended manifold" and thus to the *geometrical* notion of space.
5   "A Coherence Theory of Truth and Knowledge," p.310 (cited by McDowell (p.14)).
6   Davidson, op. cit., p.311:

> The relation between a sensation and a belief cannot be logical, since sensations are not beliefs or other propositional attitudes. What then is the relation?

The answer is, I think, obvious: the relation is causal. Sensations cause some beliefs and in *this* sense are the basis or ground of those beliefs. But a causal explanation of a belief does not show how or why the belief is justified.

7 In the terms of Davidson's remarks cited in note 6 above, then, for McDowell sensations *are* propositional attitudes.

8 Thus, the contrast between spontaneity and receptivity is not at all the same as that between the conceptual and the non-conceptual. For McDowell, both active judgments and passive experiences belong to the conceptual sphere in virtue of possessing conceptual content (expressible in a that-clause) and thus being at least *possible* objects of active thought. At the same time, however, it is precisely this possibility of active thought that is definitive of the conceptual sphere:

> We would not be able to suppose that the capacities that are in play in experience are conceptual if they were manifested only in experience, only in operations of receptivity. They would not be recognizable as conceptual capacities at all unless they could also be exercised in active thinking, that is, in ways that do provide a good fit for the idea of spontaneity. Minimally, it must be possible to decide whether or not to judge that things are as one's experience represents them to be.
>
> (p.11)

9 McDowell devotes Lecture III, on "Non-conceptual Content," to an examination of Evans's views on the relationship between the "perceptual system" and the "conceptual system" expressed in The Varieties of Reference, ed. J. McDowell (Oxford: Oxford University Press, 1982). The perceptual system (which we share with the lower animals) yields outputs having propositional content – expressible in a that-clause – then taken up by the conceptual system (which is distinctive of our human rationality). McDowell objects that this is essentially a version of the Myth of the Given, since it again makes it impossible to see how the relation between perception and conceptualization can itself be rational (pp.51–55). Evans himself characterizes the relation between the internal states that the perceptual system yields as outputs and the conceptual system (for which these states count as inputs) by stating that "[j]udgements are then based upon (reliably caused by) these internal states" (op. cit., p.227).

10 As McDowell states:

> [I]t can seem impossible to reconcile the fact that sentience belongs to our nature with the thought that spontaneity might permeate our perceptual experience itself, the workings of our sensibility. How could the operations of a bit of mere nature be structured by spontaneity, the freedom that empowers us to take charge of our active thinking? If we see no possibility here, we are forced to suppose intuitions must be constituted independently of the understanding, by the senses responding naturally to the world's impacts on them. And then we are in the space of options that Davidson and Evans locate themselves in.
>
> (p.70)

Here we are meant to recall Davidson's insistence that the action of sensibility is *merely* causal and Evans's characterization of the perceptual system as what we have in common with the lower animals (note 9 above). McDowell (p.71, note 3) refers to chap. 1 of Charles Taylor, *Hegel* (Cambridge: Cambridge University Press, 1975), for the contrast between the pre-modern view of nature as "filled with meaning" and the modern conception (as articulated by Max Weber) of "disenchanted" nature.

11 According to McDowell:

> Animals are, as such, natural beings, and a familiar modern conception of
> nature tends to extrude rationality from nature. The effect is that reason is sepa-
> rated from our animal nature, as if being rational placed us partly outside the
> animal kingdom. Specifically, the understanding is distanced from sensibility.
> And that is the source of our philosophical impasse. In order to escape it, we
> need to bring understanding and sensibility, reason and nature, back together.
> (p.108)

12 In this connection, McDowell explicitly opposes communitarian or "social pragmatist" interpretations of Wittgenstein, according to which meaning is to be
reconstructed out of social interactions (of "ratification" and so on) within a speech
community (pp.92–95).

13 "Moves in the language of traditional philosophy can be aimed at having the right
not to worry about its problems, rather than at solving those problems" (p.155, note
30).

14 The problematic of Coherentism first developed explicitly, of course, in the work of
British absolute idealists like Bradley, Bosanquet, and Joachim around the turn of the
twentieth century. As we will see below, McDowell himself expresses considerable
sympathy for German absolute idealism. Indeed, one of his fundamental ideas is that
it took the insights of Hegel to complete and to consolidate Kant's salutary conception of the necessary interdependence between understanding and sensibility. In this
sense, McDowell's own interpretation of this interdependence is intended, in the
end, to be more Hegelian than Kantian (p.111) (in the Preface McDowell characterizes his work "as a prolegomenon to a reading of the *Phenomenology [of Spirit]*"
(p.ix)).

15 However, pure or "unschematized" categories possess a kind of meaning nonetheless,
in that they have *thinkable* but not *knowable* content. And this is crucial, in fact, in
properly understanding the sense in which pure categories like causality can also
acquire "objective reality" independently of intuition – from a *practical* but not a
theoretical point of view – through their application in morality.

16 McDowell mentions Kant's contrast between the realm of freedom and the realm of
nature as a model for his own contrast between the space of reasons and the realm of
law (p.71, note 2). However, if we take the Kantian *understanding* as our model for
the space of reasons, McDowell is here glossing over the crucial Kantian distinction
between understanding and reason. The Kantian contrast between the realm of
freedom and the realm of nature is developed in the *Critique of Judgment* – and, in
particular, in the Antinomy of Teleological Judgment where mechanism and teleology are opposed. This last opposition, too, is indeed closely related to problems
arising from the scientific revolution; but it involves, in Kant's own terms, the relationship between reason and the understanding (between which the faculty of
judgment is supposed to mediate) rather than between the understanding and sensibility (between which the faculty of imagination or "schematism" is supposed to
mediate).

17 This does not mean, of course, that the post-Kantians adopt the Kantian conception
of reason entirely unchanged. On the contrary, Kant's moral philosophy, in particular, is subject to searching criticism, the result of which is the addition of a
fundamentally historical dimension that is not present (at least explicitly) in Kant
himself. In this way, Kant's conception of reason is also eventually "historicized."
(Here I am especially indebted to comments from Paul Franks.)

18 Here, as McDowell makes clear, he is following P. F. Strawson's interpretation of
Kant in *The Bounds of Sense* (London: Methuen, 1966). I myself am rather in agree-

ment with an opposing trend in recent Kant scholarship that has challenged this "two-worlds" account of Kant's transcendental idealism: see, for example, G. Bird, *Kant's Theory of Knowledge* (London: Routledge, 1962), H. Allison, *Kant's Transcendental Idealism* (New Haven, CT: Yale University Press, 1983), H. E. Matthews, "Strawson on Transcendental Idealism," in *Kant on Pure Reason*, ed. R. Walker (Oxford: Oxford University Press, 1982).

19 See especially the chapter on phenomena and noumena in the *Critique of Pure Reason*:

> If I remove all thought (via categories) from an empirical cognition, then no cognition of any object at all remains over. For nothing at all is thought through mere intuition, and the circumstance that this affection of sensibility is in me constitutes no relation at all of this kind of representation to any object. By contrast, however, if I leave aside all intuition, then the form of thought – i.e., the manner of determining an object for the manifold of a possible intuition – still remains over. Therefore, the categories thus extend further than sensible intuition, for they think objects in general, without attending to the particular manner (of sensibility) in which they may be given. But they do not thereby determine a larger sphere of objects, since one cannot assume that such can be given without presupposing another mode of intuition than the sensible as possible – which we are in no way justified in doing.
>
> (A253–254/B309)

This passage seems to me to count decisively against the "two-worlds" interpretation of Kant's distinction (note 18).

20 "The fact that experience is passive, a matter of receptivity in action, should assure us that we have all the external constraint we can reasonably want. The constraint comes from outside *thinking*, but not from outside what is *thinkable*" (p.28).

21 As McDowell explains, "the objects of 'inner sense' are internal accusatives to the awareness that 'inner experiences' constitute; they have no existence independently of that awareness" (p.21). Thus:

> [T]he impressions of "inner sense" must be, like the impressions of "outer sense", passive occurrences in which conceptual capacities are drawn into operation. But if we are to respect the point about internal accusatives, we cannot conceive these passive operations of conceptual capacities exactly on the model of the impressions of "outer sense". We cannot suppose that these operations of conceptual capacities constitute awareness of circumstances that obtain in any case, and that impress themselves on a subject as they do because of some suitable relation to her sensibility.
>
> (p.22)

22 As McDowell says:

> In "outer experience", a subject is passively saddled with conceptual contents, drawing into operation capacities seamlessly integrated into a conceptual repertoire that she employs in the continuing activity of adjusting her world-view, so as to enable it to pass the scrutiny of its rational credentials. It is this integration that makes it possible for us to conceive experience as awareness, or at least seeming awareness, of a reality independent of experience.
>
> (p.31)

23 "[C]onceptual contents that are passively received in experience ... are about the world, as it appears or makes itself manifest to the experiencing subject, or at least seems to do so. That ought not to activate a phobia of idealism" (p.39). The problem I am emphasizing, however, is not simply that the world in question is the world as it appears to the experiencing subject. It is rather that the very idea of experience of the world – the idea, that is, of impressions of outer sense – is itself a product of spontaneity: the impressions in question *become* expressions of constraint by an independent world precisely through the integrative activities of the understanding. In this way, the crucial notion of *independence* is, in the end, given a purely coherence-theoretic reading. For Kant himself, by contrast, the distinction between inner sense and outer sense belongs to *sensibility*: it rests on the difference between the pure intuition of time and the pure intuition of space. And on this basis Kant develops what he calls a "Refutation of Idealism," according to which our knowledge of the temporal order of our own inner states is ultimately parasitic upon our knowledge of the *spatio*-temporal order of external objects.

24 Similarly, McDowell speaks of "possession of meaning, the kind of intelligibility that is constituted by placement in the space of reasons" (pp.92–93).

25 In this connection we should not forget that the philosophical conception accompanying the scientific revolution also made it difficult to find a place for less than fully intentional living organisms in "nature" – and thus made even the place of *biology* among the "natural sciences" highly problematic (cf. note 28 below).

26 This is the heart of Kant's reply to *Humean* naturalism. There is an unfortunate tendency to identify the modern view of nature with a Humean conception and to generate an opposition between reason and nature on *this* basis. Thus Taylor, in contrasting the pre-modern view with the modern one (see note 10 above), characterizes the latter as "the 'modern' view of a world of ultimately contingent correlations, to be patiently mapped by empirical observation" (op. cit., p.4), as "a view of the world not as a locus of meanings, but rather of contingent, de facto correlations" (p.8), and states that the new conception of the scientific revolution "was mechanistic, atomistic, homogenizing, and of course saw the shape of things as contingent" (p.10). Kant's opposing view is that nature as the object of natural science is infused with *rational necessity* (but not, of course, with "meaning and value").

27 Taylor, in explaining the background and motivations of Hegel's idealism, puts the point this way:

> If I am to remain a spiritual being and yet not be opposed to nature in my interchange with it, then this interchange must be a communion in which I enter into relation with some spiritual being or force. But this is to say that spirituality, tending to realize spiritual goals, is of the essence of nature. Underlying natural reality is a spiritual principle striving to realize itself.
>
> (op. cit., p.39)

A few pages later, in describing how Schelling's philosophy of nature gives an ontological foundation to Schiller's aesthetics, Taylor explains that "[art] is therefore the point at which spontaneity and receptivity, freedom and nature are one. And this meeting point is, as it were, foreordained in the ontological fact that nature and consciousness have ultimately the same source, subjectivity" (p.42). In order to preserve the idea that nature as the realm of law consists of "mere meaningless happenings," McDowell presumably wants to "domesticate" this rhetoric as well. Until he shows us how to do this, however, his own conception of the relationship between the understanding in his sense and non-human nature belonging to the realm of law will, I believe, remain fundamentally obscure.

28 As we will see below, in the context of post-Quinean naturalism the idea of rational normative structure is "psychologized" so as to become thoroughly entangled with the question of human intentionality. In this context, the question of autonomous norms of rationality is indeed inextricably linked to the mind–body problem (cf. Davidson's "anomalous monism"). My point here is simply that the scientific revolution itself does not immediately supply such a context. It is also worth noting that the rejection of teleological and intentional notions characteristic of the scientific revolution extended much further than specifically *human* intentionality – it extended to biological phenomena in general, including animals and even plants (cf. Kant's famous expression of skepticism concerning a Newton capable of explaining a blade of grass in the Antinomy of Teleological Judgment). And this means that even the purely animal "perceptual system" introduced by Evans (note 9 above) – which is rejected by McDowell in favor of an inclusion of perception within the spontaneity definitive of specifically *human* intentionality – would also be extruded from nature according to the scientific revolution.

29 Frege's "third realm" has often been taken to be exemplary of this kind of "platonism." However, such a reading of Frege has recently been subject to critical reassessment. See, for example, the exchange between Tyler Burge, "Frege on Knowing the Third Realm," *Mind* 101: 633–650 (1992), and Thomas Ricketts, "Logic and Truth in Frege," *The Aristotelian Society, Supplementary Volume* 70: 121–140 (1996).

30 See §75 of the *Aufbau*:

> The merit of having discovered the necessary basis of the constitutional system thereby belongs to two entirely different, and often mutually hostile, philosophical tendencies. *Positivism* has stressed that the sole *material* for cognition lies in the undigested experiential *given*; here are to be sought the *basic elements* of the constitutional system. *Transcendental idealism*, however, especially the neo-Kantian tendency (Rickert, Cassirer, Bauch), has rightly emphasized that these basic elements do not suffice; *order-posits* must be added, our "basic relations".

Carnap's *basic elements* are initially undifferentiated "elementary experiences" – which are linked to one another by a *basic relation* of "remembrance of part similarity." Carnap then uses the formal–logical structure of this basic relation to define all further concepts of his constitutional system – including the concepts that characterize and differentiate the basic elements themselves.

31 W. V. Quine traces what he dubs the linguistic doctrine of logical truth to the assimilation of Wittgenstein's *Tractatus* within the Vienna Circle and holds that this doctrine reached its maturity in the work of Carnap; Quine then encapsulates this "Viennese" teaching as follows: "Metaphysics was meaningless through misuse of language; logic was certain through tautologous use of language." See "Carnap and Logical Truth," in *The Philosophy of Rudolf Carnap*, ed. P. Schilpp (La Salle, IL: Open Court, 1963), pp.385–386. In the *Tractatus* itself, however, the notion of logical truth – through the idea that there is only *one* logical structure for any possible language – still retains a Kantian "transcendental" cast characteristic of the *reine Logik* tradition. And it is this *Tractarian* conception, of course, which then serves as the primary focus for Wittgenstein's critique of "platonistic" conceptions of meaning in the *Philosophical Investigations* (a critique that is taken by McDowell as a model for his own rejection of rampant platonism (pp.92–95)). In Carnap's *Logical Syntax of Language*, by contrast, the logical "absolutism" of the *Tractatus* is explicitly discarded in favor of syntactic pluralism. And it is this Carnapian conception of language which, as explained in the text below, then fuels both the protocol–sentence debate and Quine's eventual rejection of the linguistic doctrine of logical truth.

32 For this debate, with particular attention to Neurath's role, see Thomas Uebel, *Overcoming Logical Positivism from Within* (Amsterdam: Rodopi, 1992).

33 Davidson himself explicitly makes the connection in "Empirical Content," reprinted in E. LePore, ed., op. cit. Sellars, by contrast, is not so explicit, but he does refer, in §59 of "Empiricism and the Philosophy of Mind," to Carnap's "Psychologie in physikalischer Sprache" – an important text of the protocol–sentence debate which Davidson also cites in footnote 39 of "Empirical Content."

34 What Kant calls "transcendental logic" is just as distinct from empirical human psychology as is the pure thought of the *reine Logik* tradition. For Kant, however, the entire point of the schematism of the understanding is that pure thought can have content only by functioning as the a priori presupposition of *empirical* thinking (including, in particular, empirical psychological thinking). Kant's "space of reason" is thus necessarily spatio-temporal; and this is why, as emphasized above, there can be no possibility of a "platonistic" gulf for Kant himself.

35 The distinction between the logical and the psychological also seems to be central in Sellars's contrast between "placing [an episode or state] in the logical space of reasons" and "giving an empirical description of that episode or state" (note 4 above). Sellars wants to avoid a regress threatening his view that knowledge of "This is green" presupposes knowledge that utterances of "This is green" are reliable indicators of the presence of green objects in standard conditions of perception. And the point of his contrast is precisely to distinguish the logical relation of presupposition from empirical relations of temporal and psychological priority (op. cit., §§36–37). This is not to say, however, that Sellars also accepts the idea, characteristic of logical positivism, that "logical" relations are to be explained through the concept of analyticity.

36 These technical problems include, first, the need for special existential axioms (reducibility, infinity, choice) in the wake of the discovery of the paradoxes, and, second, the metamathematical results of Gödel and Tarski, which threaten Carnap's attempt to preserve the analyticity of logico-mathematical truth in the face of the first problem. Quine discusses this crucial second set of problems in §VII of "Carnap and Logical Truth" (note 31 above).

37 Quine of course distinguishes logical truth in the narrower sense, restricted to first-order logic, from analytic truth in the wider sense, which is to include the results of substituting synonymous terms into logical truths in the narrower sense and also, in Carnap's hands, set theory and higher mathematics. And Quine holds, in addition, that logical truth in the narrower sense is at least relatively determinate in translation on a behavioral basis. Quine makes it perfectly clear, however, that the maxim of preserving elementary logical truth is simply an instance of the maxim of preserving *obvious* truth in general, and thus gives no aid and comfort to the linguistic doctrine of logical truth: it applies equally to "There have been black dogs," for example. In the end, therefore, the *obviousness* of elementary logical truth collapses into that of "stimulus analytic" truth in general. See W. V. Quine, *Word and Object* (Cambridge, MA: The MIT Press, 1960), §§12–14. Essentially the same idea is found in §III of "Carnap and Logical Truth."

38 McDowell explains that, when "one finds a spookiness in norms if they are conceived platonistically," "[t]his reflects looking at norms from nature's side of the duality of norm and nature; nature is equated with the realm of law, and that poses the familiar threat of disenchantment" (p.94). Within the *reine Logik* tradition, as we have seen, normative structures definitive of the Kantian "space of reasons" are indeed separated from the spatio-temporal realm. This, however, has nothing to do with the disenchantment of nature – the extrusion of "meaning and value" – effected by the scientific revolution; it is due, rather, to a rejection of Kant's own doctrine of the schematism of the understanding (cf. note 34 above). Only when the

normative structure of the space of reasons is "psychologized" does the disenchantment of nature effected by the scientific revolution become relevant here.

39 W. V. Quine, "Reply to Chomsky," in *Words and Objections*, ed. D. Davidson and J. Hintikka (Dordrecht: Reidel, 1969), p.303.

40 Davidson himself tends to minimize his divergence from Quine. For example, he often compares the indeterminacy of translation with that of different scales of measurement – for a recent instance, see "Three Varieties of Knowledge," in *A. J. Ayer Memorial Essays*, ed. A. Griffiths (Cambridge: Cambridge University Press, 1991), p.161. I myself doubt whether this particular comparison can capture the full force of Quine's "no fact of the matter" rhetoric, and, in any case, I have here chosen to emphasize the starkly physicalistic side of Quine in order better to bring out what I take to be Davidson's genuinely novel contribution: the attempt to show how our "constitutive ideal of rationality" can survive in a post-Quinean context (cf. note 42 below).

41 In "Three Varieties of Knowledge" (note 40 above), p.162, Davidson explains the source of anomalous monism as follows:

> [Mental concepts], at least in so far as they are intentional in nature, require the interpreter to consider how best to render the creature being interpreted intelli-
> gible, that is, as a creature endowed with reason. As a consequence, an interpreter must separate meaning from opinion in part on normative grounds, by deciding what, from his point of view, maximizes intelligibility. In this endeavor, the interpreter has, of course, no other standards of rationality to fall back on than his own. When we try to understand the world as physicists, we necessarily employ our own norms, but we do not aim to discover rationality in the phenomena.

Here, McDowell's gulf between reason and nature is clearly evident in the contrast between the standpoint of the radical interpreter and that of the physicist.

42 Here see especially Davidson's revealingly entitled paper "Psychology as Philosophy," reprinted, with appended discussion, in *Essays on Actions and Events* (Oxford: Oxford University Press, 1980), p.241:

> [T]here is no way psychology can avoid consideration of the nature of ratio-
> nality, of coherence, of consistency. At one end of the spectrum, logic and rational decision theory are psychological theories from which the obviously empirical has been drained. At the other end, there is some form of behaviourism better imagined than described. Psychology, if it deals with propo-
> sitional attitudes, hovers in between. This branch of the subject cannot be divorced from such questions as what constitutes a good argument, a valid infer-
> ence, a rational plan, or a good reason for acting. These questions also belong to the traditional concerns of philosophy, which is my excuse for my title.

(This quotation comes from the appended discussion. The idea that notions of ratio-
nality "have no echo in physical theory" occurs on p.231 of the paper.) Davidson, like Quine, thus rejects the distinction between the normative realm of logic and the descriptive realm of psychology. For Davidson, however, psychology has itself become an explicitly normative discipline.

43 Such rational constraints include, paradigmatically, logic and rational decision theory – both considered explicitly as "psychological theories" (note 42 above). Note how strange it is from a traditional point of view – for a Kant or for a Frege – to characterize *logic* as a "psychological theory."

44 As McDowell states:

[I]mpressions of sense are manifestations of sentient life and hence natural phenomena. [Anomalous monism] ensures that it cannot be as the natural phenomena they are that impressions are characterizable in terms of spontaneity. Their place in nature is their location in the quite different structure of the realm of law. So actualizations of a natural capacity of sensibility, considered as such, can only be intuitions on a dualistic conception: products of disenchanted nature operating independently of spontaneity.

(p.76)

For McDowell, then, it is only by recognizing that impressions of sense belong to our second nature – and thus do *not* belong to the realm of law – that such a dualistic conception of concepts and intuitions can be definitively overcome. From Davidson's own point of view, however, there is nothing in anomalous monism itself to prevent events of sensory stimulation from having *both* physical and rational–intentional properties. Davidson's own motivation for maintaining that the relation of sensory stimulation to belief is causal but *not* rational is rather to avoid "epistemic intermediaries" between belief and the world; see note 46 below.

45 Indeed, immediately following the last quotation, McDowell continues: "My point is to insist that we can effect this deletion of the outer boundary without falling into idealism, without slighting the independence of reality" (p.34).

46 See "A Coherence Theory of Truth and Knowledge," p.312: "[W]e should allow no intermediaries between our beliefs and their objects in the world. Of course there are causal intermediaries. What we must guard against are *epistemic* intermediaries" (my emphasis). In this connection, McDowell's portrayal of Davidson as the arch Coherentist becomes especially misleading. Thus, for example, McDowell chides Davidson for using "confinement imagery" in the very paragraph from "A Coherence Theory" from which I have just quoted (p.16). However, when Davidson here states that "we can't get outside our skins to find out what is causing the internal happenings of which we our aware," he is arguing against *Quine's* reliance on sense-data-like sensory stimulations, not expounding his own view: he is here *rejecting* "internal happenings of which we are aware." Moreover, McDowell then proceeds to criticize Davidson's appeal to the principle of charity for "start[ing] with the body of beliefs to which we are supposed to be confined" and then seeking "to make the confinement imagery unthreatening by reassuring us that those beliefs are mostly true" – so that Davidson is here responding only to "a shallow skepticism, in which, taking it for granted that one has a body of beliefs, one worries about their credentials" (p.17). The point of the principle of charity, however, is that a system of noises does not count as a body of beliefs in the first place unless it is interpretable as mostly true – true of independent objects in the external environment to which one is (epistemically) immediately related. It is perhaps not surprising, then, that Davidson explicitly retracts the Coherentist label in "Afterthoughts, 1987" to a reprinting of "A Coherence Theory" in *Reading Rorty*, ed. A. Malichowski (Oxford: Blackwell, 1990).

47 As McDowell says:

To reject the [Myth of the Given] ... is to refuse to conceive experience's demands on a system of beliefs as imposed from outside the activity of adjusting the system, by something constituted independently of the current state of the evolving system, or a state into which the system might evolve. The required adjustments to the system depend on what we take experience to reveal to us, and we can capture that only in terms of the concepts and conceptions that figure in the evolving system. What we take experience to tell us is already part of the system, not an external constraint on it.

(pp.135–136)

48 See *Truth and Method*, Part Three, III, 3:

> Certainly, those brought up in a determinate linguistic and cultural tradition
> see the world differently from those belonging to other traditions. Certainly, the
> historical "worlds" that dissolve into one another in the course of history are
> different from one another and from the present world. Nevertheless, it is
> always a human world – i.e., a linguistically constituted world – that, in what-
> ever tradition, presents itself. As linguistically constituted, every such world is
> open of itself for every possible insight and thus for every possible extension of
> its own world-picture – and correspondingly accessible for others.

49 This last passage initiates a section (pp.184–186) devoted to defending Gadamer's
    ideas on the importance of shared cultural and linguistic traditions for mediating our
    understanding of one another against Davidson's more individualistic conception of
    radical interpretation.
50 Recall that for McDowell there is no distinction at all between the conceptual
    contents of experience and – at least when the subject is not misled – the perceptual
    facts in the world corresponding to that experience (p.26, quoted above).
51 According to McDowell:

> When the specific character of [an alien's] thinking starts to come into view for
> us, we are not filling in blanks in a pre-existing sideways-on picture of how her
> thought bears on the world, but coming to share with her a standpoint *within* a
> system of concepts, a standpoint from which we can join her in directing a
> shared attention at the world, without needing to break out through a boundary
> that encloses a system of concepts.
>
> (pp.35–36)

After a fusion of horizons, however, we (along with the alien) have *changed* our
system of concepts – in the terms of Gadamer's remarks cited in note 48 above, our
initial horizon has undergone an "extension of its own world-picture." And we have
thereby changed, apparently, the "world" corresponding to our system of concepts as
well (note 50). So the possibility of fusion does nothing to diffuse the threat of
idealism.

3

LEAVING NATURE BEHIND

Or two cheers for "subjectivism"*

Robert B. Pippin

Custom is almost a second nature.
(Plutarch, *Rules for the Preservation of Health*, 18)

I

1. It is not difficult to imagine quite a credible narrative of the history of philosophy that concentrated mostly on the concept of nature and the various uses to which appeals to nature have been put. For many scholars, the idea that everything in the cosmos was intelligible in itself, that "what it was to be" anything was accessible to human reason as such, marked the origin of a distinctly philosophical approach, and "What is it?" or "What is its nature?" remained the question constantly close to the heart of the philosophic enterprise. All of this could be imagined while conceding that the variations in such appeals are very wide, and the links between such uses sometimes difficult to make out.

Almost always, though, some great *opposition* is at stake and the use of the term is meant to distinguish and contrast. In the everyday sense, the contrast is between the familiar, what happens for the most part, what is expectable and normal, and what is uniquely unexpected, out of the ordinary, strange, "the unnatural." In early philosophical uses, the important contrasts are between "by nature" and "by art," between *physis* and *techne*, and between nature and custom, *physis* and *nomos*. It is with Lucretius, and *De rerum natura*, that what would eventually become the great issue in modernity first appeared with clarity, even if in an undeveloped form: the claim that *everything* is natural, and natural in pretty much the same sense, and so *all* bound by the "bond of nature" (*foedus naturae*), including the unusual, the freakish, and even the instituting of, and changes in, human customs and laws. And it is quite important that this most comprehensive appeal should be so immediately associated with the idea of being bound, since this sets out the contrast with our common sense experience quite well – that we do not seem to ourselves bound, but to be able to evaluate and settle on claims about the empirical world and to initiate action as we deem best, not in the way that bees build hives or bloodhounds sniff out trails or water flows downhill.

I mention the range, complexity, and importance of the theme of nature as a way of appreciating the ambition and impressive scope of John McDowell's *Mind and World*.[1] McDowell believes that a specific understanding of the realm of nature, due largely to modern natural science, has had philosophy in its grip for some time, and this in a way that then creates the appearance of unavoidable and largely unanswerable problems: how could meaning be possible? how could we be responsive to, and act on, reasons, given that we are the natural beings we are? These become such critical questions, and their topics begin to look "spooky," or only possible because of non-natural capacities, when natural being is understood as it is by modern natural science, where all intelligibility, understanding, and explanation are tied to subsumption under scientific law, and so to notions of causal necessity. This take on the problem is, broadly speaking, post-Kantian (in the sense of Kant's Third Antinomy, and his dialectic between mechanism and teleology), but McDowell's response is not. For him, we don't need Kant's noumenalism, however that is interpreted,[2] nor do we have to rest content with an "I don't know how freedom is possible but as agents we are simply stuck with the assumption" approach, the practical point of view business. Likewise he does not plead for the various anti-dualist positions popular in recent years: functionalism, anomalous monism, dual aspect and emergent property theories, supervenience logics, and so forth.[3] (He is not optimistic about "social pragmatist" approaches either, as we shall see.) None of these, he claims, addresses the root problem: our starting point, nature as the realm of law, that is, the domain of that explicable by subsumption under causal law, and as long as we don't address our unbalanced and narrow commitment to that starting point (the realm of nature as *exhausted* by that notion of explicability), such answers will always seem the unsatisfying hedges that they are. We don't then need a better solution to the post-Kantian problem – how the organic, evolution-produced, biological entities that we are could mean anything or *really* respond to reasons. What we need instead is an "exorcism," a way of freeing ourselves from "the starting point" assumption about nature that makes it seem, prima facie, that such capacities are simply impossible (p.147). We need to understand that the dispositions and potentialities we come naturally equipped with can be "actualized" in adult human beings by a process of socialization and education that goes far beyond anything that might be explicable by reference to the natural events and properties of the biological world, even while it involves nothing non- or supernatural. It is not our nature simply to come to occupy, in response to biological imperatives, an evolved niche in our environment; it is our nature to orient *ourselves* in a world by exercising, perfecting, and critically revising our unique capacity for reasoning, for justifying claims about the world, and for explaining and justifying our actions to each other (pp.115–116). Adopting and maintaining such normative stances is just the opposite of "unnatural." It is how we go on as the kind of beings we are. Everything of importance in McDowell's exorcism and, let us say, his "pacifying" of the mind–world tension thus comes down to his ability to convince us that human nature can be said to be a realization of a "second nature," still natural, even if second. (It is second because essentially acquired, not the simple, untended maturation of biological properties. There is something of the sense of this natural-yet-cultivated second nature, or tended growth, in the modern notion of culture, another translation for the word McDowell leans heavily on, *Bildung*.)

I want to raise several questions about that attempt, most of them reactions to the many fascinating things McDowell says about the post-Kantian legacy in modern philosophy in general; more specifically, reactions to the way the terms of his account open onto a set of issues in the modern German philosophical tradition.[4] My main question will be whether we gain that much, free ourselves from that much, if we can come to see our capacity for normative stances as "second-nature natural." I want to offer some suggestions that we are better off leaving nature out of the picture altogether, and that doing so begs no questions. This will involve a limited defense of what McDowell, in a sweeping indictment, calls "subjectivism."

Although the historical issues are too unwieldy to be treated here, the theme that I want to pursue amounts to one way of understanding the difference between Hegel on the one hand, and Schiller, Schelling, and even the Kant of the third *Critique* on the other, at a crucial period in modern philosophy. The last three all still felt the force of the question *what must nature be like* for meaning in nature – conceptually informed sensibility and practical reasons having a grip, for example, but also purposive life, organic wholes – to be possible? This is the question McDowell wants to avoid, as he sometimes puts it, with a "reminder" about, or a pointing toward, a "partially enchanted nature."[5] But ultimately Hegel did not feel the force of this question. There is of course a *Philosophy of Nature* in his *Encyclopedia*, but as anyone who has slogged through it knows, there is a lot there that seems to turn no other wheel elsewhere in what Hegel says, and very little in the *Philosophy of Spirit* seems to depend on it or refer back to it. Said very crudely, the developmental "direction" of Hegel's system (a systematic account of forms of intelligibility, ever better explanatory adequacy) is "away" from nature and "towards" "spirit," *Geist*; his "logic" concerns more the inadequacy of *appeals* to nature as *explicans*. And so he rejects as misguided such "how possible" questions, questions it seems to me that McDowell, despite the "quietism," is still grappling with (even if not answering) by appealing to the possibility of second nature.[6] It is not that McDowell wants to reanimate a romantic or Schellingean philosophy of nature, but even his "reminder" remains tied to the problem of nature, and I want to propose the non-metaphysical character of the *Natur–Geist* distinction in Hegel as a better way of leaving first nature behind.[7]

2. How do philosophical exorcisms work? McDowell is candid at the end of his book in admitting that it is unlikely that the considerations he advances will themselves, alone, free us from the grip of this distorting picture (p.177 – for one thing, it is unlikely in the extreme that the origin of this hold was lack of

attention to a neglected alternative). His procedure in working at loosening the grip of modern naturalism has, broadly conceived, two steps, or two kinds of moves. One step is the demonstration that our starting point has created unsolvable and unacceptable *aporiai,* especially in epistemology. We end up, he thinks, oscillating between various versions of the Myth of the Given on the one hand, wherein our putatively decisive, guiding contact with the physical world cannot, paradoxically, be said to play any real normative role in a knowledge claim (we try to understand how such claims could be constrained from "outside" the conceivings we seem able to control and direct; and we fail), and, on the other hand, we give up the idea of exogenous normative constraints or normative foundations, and end up with a coherentism in epistemology that looks like a "frictionless" spinning in the void, normatively unconstrained by the way the world is. Appreciating that these are dead-ends should then motivate us to search for the assumptions that are causing things to go so wrong. McDowell's second step is the crucial one, when he diagnoses the origin of such aporetic symptoms and reaches the fundamental claim of his book: that that origin is an unjustified presumption, a distorting picture of the fundamental situation, basically a restricted conception of nature ("the realm of law"). We can "free" ourselves from this conception, or begin to work at freeing ourselves from it, by appreciating a naturalism that could encompass both a "first" and a "second" nature naturalism. Once we accomplish that, the problem, and the anxiety, dissolve (or begin to dissolve).

Such an exorcism rests on three turning points in McDowell's book. There is first the epistemological dilemma sketched in the first two lectures, oriented from Kantian issues and presented in a way designed to disabuse us eventually of the assumptions about nature which generate the dilemma. Second, there is the presentation and defense of the idea of second nature itself. And third, there are various issues introduced by McDowell's invocation of a Wittgensteinian "quietism," or a case for a diagnostic and non-revisionary version of philosophy, as against a constructive or positive role. I will concentrate here on the first two issues, although the last is likely the most important to him and it will turn up periodically.

3. McDowell's starting point is Kant's famous claim in the *Critique of Pure Reason* that "thoughts without content are empty; intuitions without concepts are blind."[8] Contentful human experience requires the cooperation and relation between both faculties. But the statement of the principle already exhibits its paradoxical quality. If intuitions without concepts are blind, how could the application of concepts ever be said to be guided by the intuitive content of a sensory manifold? There wouldn't be any content unless already conceptualized, and if that is so, what could possibly guide the application of the concept? The other side of the dilemma is harder to state but no less real. To explain how concepts without intuitions are empty, Kant has to distinguish between formal logic – where of course concepts are not meaningless and have a certain sort of determinacy – and transcendental logic, where Kant must defend his principle

about emptiness and the need to add or supply conceptual content, but still allow for the possibility of synthetic a priori knowledge, independent of experienced content. He argues that concepts do not just "acquire" intuitive content from experience. That is, pure concepts must be able to have content that is intuitive even if not empirically derived. Since he must hold to this distinction, even while he insists that a "pure content" is possible for pure concepts, the doctrine of a "pure formal intuition" must supply such a possibility. McDowell underplays the latter issue, preferring to see much of that a priorist strand in Kant as a kind of bald subjectivism, motivated by a sense of nature's complete disenchantment. That issue will return in a couple of ways below. But it is the former paradox that McDowell is most eager to avoid.[9]

He does so by means of a partly Sellarsian strategy: denying that the concept–intuition distinction is congruent with the spontaneity–passivity distinction. (It is partial because Sellars himself also defends a theoretical role for something like "sheer receptivity.") Our sensory contact with the world is through and through "already conceptual," even if still basically receptive, and even if not a product of a fully spontaneous synthesis or judgment. It can thereby stand as a possible reason for a cognitive judgment about the way things are, and so play a justificatory role in the normative claim of empirical knowledge. If we don't get this point right, such sensory contact will be conceived in too immediate a way (the Myth of the Given) and can then play only a causal and "exculpatory" role, not a justifying one; or we will make Davidson's error and read such conceptuality as evidence of no real guidance "from without," and opt for a radical coherentism – the frictionless, or empirically unconstrained "spinning" that McDowell charges that Davidson leaves us with.

We are, McDowell suggests, so impressed by the fact that sensory looks and feels and smells and so forth are real natural events, occurring in space and time in the same way that fires start and lives end, that we feel constrained to treat such events as our modern notion of nature teaches us to, and that leaves us only with some causal story about how our conscious states got to be the way they are, and no room to introduce the normative language of knowledge claims. We are also impressed, overly impressed according to McDowell, with the accomplishments of higher-order, perceiving animals, and so think that our perceivings must be possible like *that*, apart from any complex conceiving or spontaneous mental activity unique to human animals.

Before we get to the diagnostic issue, McDowell needs to make clear just what it is for. Here a variety of locutions are introduced: conceptual capacities to be "operative" not only in judgments, but "already in the transactions in nature that are constituted by the world's impacts on the receptive capacities of a suitable subject" (p.xx). This is to be distinguished from the claim that conceptual capacities are exercised "*on* non-conceptual deliverances of sensibility" (p.39, my emphasis). For McDowell, by contrast, such deliverances are *always already* conceptual, or: "capacities that belong to spontaneity are in play

Kinesis for
of conception

in actualizations of receptivity" (p.66). "In play" in *what* sense, then, if not in an assertoric judgment?[10]

4. Consider that Kant, for example, had a devil of a time trying to find the right way to put this point, and it might be useful to remind ourselves of the nature of his difficulty.[11] The first *Critique* spoke of a "synthesis of apprehension *in* intuition" but only, apparently, as a component or moment of a full judgmental synthesis, including reproduction and recognition.[12] There was also an obscure notion of a "figurative" synthesis (*synthesis speciosa*) to be distinguished from an "intellectual" synthesis,[13] and that looks like an attempt to invoke the imagination to make the point McDowell is after. And there is a dense, infamous footnote in the second edition that, whatever else is being claimed, appears to assert that any manifold conforming to the intuitional constraints of sensibility already requires a minimal conceptualization, that *intuitional* unity itself "presupposes a synthesis which does not belong to the senses."[14] But neither passage offers much concrete help with the "in play in *what* sense?" question; they just give rise to the question in different ways.

In the *Prolegomena*,[15] Kant goes much farther in insisting on the conceptual character of our first "take" on how things are, and he uses language that seems compatible with some of what McDowell wants. There he claims that there is a difference between "*judgments of perception*," which only have subjective validity (but which clearly do involve the exercise of conceptual capacities, if only problematically), and "judgments of experience," which claim objective validity, and that "all our judgments are at first merely judgments of perception," and can upon reflection "become" judgments of experience. Judgments of perception might thus, following Gerold Prauss's interpretation, be considered mere "seeming" judgments, first takes on the world, first "looks" prior to cognitive commitment, awaiting some sort of objectifying reassurance. The first take, "it seems to me that the sun warms the stone," could become, upon reflection, a cognitive commitment, "the sun warms the stone"; or "impressions of the sun are regularly followed in my experience by impressions of the stone's warmth" could become "the sun causes the stone to become warm."[16]

Now McDowell, in his "Introduction" to *Mind and World* (p.xvii), makes clear that he does not want to rest a theory of empirical knowledge on "appearings" or seemings. His ambition is a more common sense one; or, he wants empirical claims to be answerable to the world, not to appearances or impressions, and he certainly does not want some phenomenalist picture in which experience is constructed from subjective states. But Kant too is not treating judgments of perception as subjective states out of which experience is built (they are indeed first takes on the way *the world* seems, as *it* first presents itself to me), and much of the language McDowell later introduces suggests this Kantian direction. An early distinction that McDowell makes sounds like Kant in the *Prolegomena*: "How one's experience represents things to be is not under one's control, but it is up to one whether one accepts the appearance or rejects it" (p.11). He wants, in his account of sensory contact, an account of "the world, as it appears or makes itself manifest to an experiencing subject, or at least seems to do so" (p.39). "A judgment of experience does not introduce a new kind of content, but simply endorses the conceptual content, or some of it, that is already possessed by the experience on which it is grounded" (pp.48–49). This first "seeming glimpse of the world" (p.54) already involves the exercise of conceptual capacities because "having things appear to one a certain way is already itself a mode of actual operation of conceptual faculties" (p.62).[17]

5. Although for McDowell, as we shall see, there is a parallel practical issue that forces the question of nature on us (how do any claims of reason come to have a grip on us, move us, as the natural beings we are, to act?), it is clear in his numerous replies to critics, and in his Woodbridge Lectures, that it is the concern about perception as an originally intentional natural state and about the role it must be able to play in a knowledge claim that bears most of the burden in the whole enchantment argument. McDowell's concern is about the *immediate* "world-directedness," intentionality, or "objective purport" of perceptual states, something that requires, he argues, a normative context in a special sense if we are to get that world-directedness right. It is this requirement that any Fichtean talk of a merely *self*-constrained spontaneity, and Hegelian talk of social bases of normativity, threaten to miss.[18] McDowell is clearly convinced that, for the individual observer, a kind of object-relatedness *happens* in perception, as part of a "transaction *in* nature," all in a way that requires we most definitely cannot "leave nature out of it."[19] Any such strategy will not allay our philosophic distress about the possibility of such a pre-judgmental, but conceptual state.

That "normative context" is conceptual structure and discrimination, or the way in which perceptual takes on the world are conceptually normative, if in a special sense. For the way in which claims are embedded in perception is not the way claims are actually made in judgments. Any immediately experienced, conceptually determinate state is not itself the result of a judgment (that would require a non-conceptual manifold and the merry-go-round would start again), but presents us with a conceptually contentful "item" that is an element in what it would be to have so discriminated judgmentally (as in a "this-cube perception" and not "there is a cube here").

But I don't see that, having traced the issue to this level, we have yet met up necessarily with the problem of nature and second nature. Even if this sort of relatedness claim is normative in a *special* sense, it still of course means at least having already understood, mastered, the proper conceptual role of "cube," all in such a way that having *such* a perception "wrung out of one" is recognizable *to* one, and so must be understood as the product in some way of a discriminating activity. But if we are proceeding in a roughly Kantian context, then such concepts are "predicates of possible judgments," and understanding the content of the concept means having mastered its role, understanding how it can and cannot be combined with other possible concepts. And it is not much of a leap from here to claim that the discriminatory capacity essential for and operative in objective purport thus already requires and draws on a general claim-making competency, the *content* of which derives from the proprieties and prohibitions of a predicate's possible use in judgment. This sort of discrimination, even if problematic, cannot be said to have been simply "wrung out of one." It would be a long story, but not an unfamiliar one, then to see such proprieties and so forth (i.e., norms) as essentially social, and some of them as not "due to experience" at all, but "due to us," if Kant's worry about a priori knowledge has any purchase. The presence of a perceptible cube does not then just "wring out of us" this-cube perceptions; the possibility of that content requires a receptiveness that is also already actively, even if provisionally, *discriminating.* If normatively constrained, then (the longer story would go) it would be *socially* informed and socially constrained. It is that activity, training, and sociality (a historical and social, not a natural result) that make possible such determinate intentionality and the more we emphasize this, the more the question of answerability shifts from answerability "to the world" to "to each other." Or at least those two issues begin to seem inseparable, even if distinct.

McDowell is right that in such first takes, I assume no "responsibility" for such content; it just seems that — . But how is it that such a first take is going to play a role in what we ultimately determine that there is? If such a "look" counts as a reason to say there is such an object *because* it was wrung out of us involuntarily, then its sheer "wrungness" looks like a non-conceptual consideration, close to causal considerations, the "guiding from without" that McDowell wants to avoid; an exculpation.[20] If the determination that there is a cube here is reasonable because such a first take coheres with other takes and perceptions and with what others are willing to say, all "according to a rule," then the question of normative propriety will lead us back to some form of social normativity again, and the "take" (*even with respect to its content*) will be parasitic on that capacity, not on "nature." Or it could so depend on such a capacity, understood as so constituted; that would be one sort of explanation, and that is all I am claiming. No re-enchanted nature need apply.[21] Moreover, without something like a *theory* of second nature, something more than a reminder about such acquisitions, it is not hard to imagine all sorts of bald naturalists nodding in agreement, convinced that the "training up" of "neural nets" can handle second-nature considerations just fine.

6. Put a different, much more general way, the relevant image for our "always already engaged" conceptual and practical capacities in the German idealist tradition is *legislative power*, not empirical discrimination and deliberative judgment, and the force of this image of legislative power makes it very difficult to integrate what McDowell says about the overall effect of *Bildung* – that it simply "opens our eyes" and allows us to "see the reasons that are always there whether we notice them or not" – with the Kantian and even Hegelian elements he has also imported.[22] And I mean that those elements which McDowell would want to call "subjectivist," given the starting points common to McDowell and the idealists, cast reasonable doubt, raise appropriate questions, about McDowell's

position. The point is not a historical one. One can see this more clearly in considering the manner of his invocation of the notion of second nature.

7. The transition to that topic might be introduced this way. The most complex, and potentially the richest idea in *Mind and World* (and in the later Woodbridge Lectures) is the notion that one can regard sensible intuitions as always already conceptually shaped, even though still genuinely receptive. If we can hold onto this somewhat slippery idea, we can reject mythological Givens and still find a way of explaining how the world "has its own say" in how we take it up and eventually make judgments about it. But, as noted above, the "conceptually shaped" part of that claim has already altered what it could mean for "the world to exercise constraint." "Conceptually shaped" means shaped in one form rather than another, and if our conceptual array is not *all* as it is because everywhere and in all decisive senses it is responsive to experiences of the world, then we would seem inevitably pushed away from a comprehensive empirical interpretation of "constrained by the world" (although, again, not away from the notion of constraint altogether). What *counts* as constraint, and the notion of a collective *self*-constraint (what we allow each other to claim as justified), look to loom larger. After all, if the world is said to be *doing* all the constraining, we start sliding back toward foundationalisms, and mythic Givens. McDowell wants to resist what he regards as quite an understandable move at this point, were it the case that all meaning had been expelled from nature; namely relying heavily on the social dimension of normativity, socially "made" criteria about what is appropriate or not, justified or not, within some social practice, all in order to "reintroduce" such meaning. This is a kind of "subjectivism," an intersubjective kind, which he wants to resist, together with all other forms of meaning-making subjectivism. Again, we (supposedly) resist *his* option – that our "conceptual capacities" are "operative also in our perception of the world apart from human beings" (p.72) – because we do not think nature, or our nature, could embody such meaning. We can avoid *that* anxiety – and so the social pragmatist and all subjectivist temptation – if we are just reminded that second natures are possible, and that with the right acquisition of such a second nature our normative response to the world will not be a species of the subjectivist or "social pragmatist" genus. We will simply have our "eyes opened" to what is and what ought to be.

II

8. How does this occur, so that we end up "resonating" to reason in the space of reasons? Much of McDowell's discussion, in *Mind and World* and elsewhere, is oriented from a very important and valuable negative answer; that is, an account of what such a resonating *is not*. It involves a compelling interpretation of Aristotle on the acquisition of second natures. The basic point is that we should not understand the proper exercise of practical reason to be in some way based on some known fact about nature, neither a teleological fact about how

natures perfect themselves and flourish, nor some Hobbesian fact about passions, fears, and interests, which then functions as what we appeal to in order to justify what we decide to do (pp.78–81). As he points out, there will always be some gap between any claim about what members of my species do, how they come to flourish, what they must avoid to stay healthy, and so forth, and what reasons bear on what I must face at some moment, as an individual. Such facts do not on their own give *me* a reason to do anything; I can always acknowledge them, but count as a more compelling reason for me free-riding, deceiving, malingering, taking a risky gamble, or whatever.[23] Likewise, we should not take this to mean that the formative powers of second-nature training only habituate our dispositional and emotional characters to be inclined to obey, to submit to, what *phronesis* or practical wisdom dictates. We will not get Aristotle or the point right, McDowell argues (especially not Aristotle's puzzling indifference to ethical justification, or his insistence that he is only writing for people already properly brought up), unless we take full measure of the fact that practical reason itself is formed, shaped, wholly dependent (even in its self-correcting aspects) on a proper formation within an ethical community.[24] Its exercise and authority, not just our willingness to submit, can thus only be understood within and as a "natural" product of such a community. A practically wise man does not know something about nature that helps him see what to do or to justify his actions, and he has not merely been made malleable to what practical reason demands. His rational nature itself has come to be formed in a certain way, or it is not what it would have been had he been improperly or otherwise brought up. It is *because* it has thus been shaped that *different aspects of the practical landscape look different to him, have a different salience*, all in such a way that he has, just by virtue of how he understands what is happening, reasons to act that he would not otherwise have.

Taking such a full measure means we will be able to resist what I have already indicated McDowell's account (enthusiastically) leaves out in his appropriation of the German tradition (and what I want to claim cannot be omitted) – what he calls "subjectivism" in ethics. We are tempted, he thinks (especially if we are some species of Kantians), toward a number of bad alternatives by virtue of having come to think that *all* there really is are the objects of the modern sciences. If the exercise of practical reason must always occur in a way naturally explicable, can only be conceived as having some grip in a way continuous with the kind of emotional and responsive being one is by nature, and if we think of that nature as disenchanted, the realm of law, etc., we will then face the obvious alternatives of pointing to what our natural (first-nature) psychology *can* handle as motivating such a grip – passions, self-interest, contingently acquired desires, and the like. Or we might take the opposite tack, and insist on the radically non-natural status of the faculty of practical reason altogether, insisting that it owes nothing to our empirical natures and instead issues commands based on its own authority alone. Meaning in McDowell's extended sense would then be understood as made by subjects and projected onto a disenchanted nature. For a variety of reasons, McDowell argues that in the latter scenario we could never explain how such a conception of practical reason could ever have a grip on us; that is, ever produce reasons for me to act.

On almost all the major points here, I think McDowell is right, and, along the way, he has also managed to state with great economy the nature of a deep, persistent, fundamental worry in the German tradition after Kant, from Schiller to Hegel to Nietzsche to Heidegger. It was first made noticeable by Schiller's "rigorism" critique of Kant, but Hegel's early critique of the "positivity" of the Christian religion, and his use of the same notion to criticize Kant (his insistence that we must find a way to understand how the demands of reason could be said to be "embodied", *verkörpert*), surfaces with surprising regularity afterward with respect to all sorts of ideals.[25]

But any response to such a worry should, I think, once again leave nature out of it and accept and work within a basic distinction between spirit and nature, *Geist* and *Natur*. These are, in other words, all images, and are not meant to invite us to ask how a rational consideration can literally become part of nature, in some way not explicable by subsumption under natural law. The problem concerns a kind of historical achievement – an achievement that has now, in the modern world, become much harder than it ever was, perhaps even impossible. The question is: how does a claim of reason, or a commitment to an ideal or goal, become part of the fabric of some form of life? How is the achievement of a genuinely common mindedness (something quite different from a codified, explicit belief system, or subjective commitments to ideals) possible? How could there be a common mindedness such that our reactions to conduct that is objectionable have become so intimate and such a part of that fabric that the conduct being the sort of conduct it is counts *thereby* as reason enough to condemn it? But to understand this, we don't need to know anything about growth, organic life, cultivated nature, and so forth. We need to understand "the labor of the Concept" in time.[26]

In Hegel's *Encyclopedia* presentation such a line between appeals to nature and appeals to intention, practical reasons and purposiveness, is not a sharp one. There is a kind of overlap of the sort that interests McDowell, but it has a human meaning for Hegel only as an "expression" of a historical spirit. In his "Anthropology" (the first part of his "Philosophy of Subjective Spirit") he is concerned to preserve and understand properly (in their relation to other sorts of accounts) certain kinds of explanation that must partially appeal to the natural conditionedness of human life. We know, for example, that a person's outlook, the way the person thinks about everything, is some sort of a function of the person's natural age; we know that diet and climate are not irrelevant to cultural practices; we know that the body, especially the face, can carry and convey a meaning like no linguistic event; and we know that in our erotic life, we are hardly projecting a subjective meaning onto a disenchanted machine. And Hegel has his own way of accounting for the "place" of such appeals, but that way does not require any second *nature*. The plot for his narrative concerns attempts by human spirit to free itself from a self-understanding tied to nature, and these anthropological elements are understood as initial, very limited successes.[27]

9. McDowell's invocation of a kind of natural development and training of our conceptual–discriminatory and judgmental–evaluative capacities, by contrast, soon does invoke the teleological language of "actualizations of our nature" (p.76). In the same vein, he writes that "our mode of living [with its educated exercise of spontaneity] is our way of actualizing ourselves as animals" (p.78). Moreover, there is a lot of talk about appropriate upbringing and "proper" training. This latter is either window-dressing, that is philosophically idle ("proper" just to any old community, by its lights; the Taliban, for example, in which case "proper" doesn't distinguish much). Or it is substantive, in which case, while participants need not base what they do on a knowledge of what is naturally proper, somebody, McDowell for example, had better be able to defend the idea of "by nature proper/improper" for the claim to have any philosophical purchase. If all that comes down to is producing something like "critical reasoning skills," and that is "proper" because it "can open a human being's eyes" to "the demands of reason," it would be nice to have some examples of the latter with which to reassure ourselves about the direction this is heading.

The former, developmental, teleological language also seems relatively idle. It is all very well to claim (and it is a fine way to put it) that "certain bodily goings-on are our spontaneity in action, not just effects of it," and that this "is central to a proper understanding of the self as a bodily presence in the world" (p.90, note 5), but there doesn't seem to be a lot for "nature" to do in any concrete account of the various possible realizations of such spontaneity-in-body. Given the unbelievable variety in human culture, it seems safe to say that first nature radically underdetermines, even while it conditions, any second nature. And while Aristotle's hylomorphism might help us see here how one might in general avoid dualism (the soul just is the being-at-work of the body), there is no reason I can see not just to stop there with the Stagirite, and not buy into his or any other account of species-specific and determinate forms of natural actualization (small cities, patriarchy, natural slaves, slow gait, deep voice, and so on). If the point is simply that given the various biological and neurological capacities we are endowed with by nature and evolution, human beings have (do as a matter of natural fact have) the capacity to make, sustain, hold themselves to and pass on in historical memory various kinds of normative institutions, and can form the characters such institutions require, and can create practices that allow for developing and revising the various claims for institutional authority inherent in such institutions, what is then gained by declaring so insistently that all of this must be understood as a "realization of second nature"?[28] To adopt Rortyan rhetoric, it sounds more like an attempt at an exaggerated compliment than a substantive point. Unless we need to claim, as some objection, something brutally obvious, say that some such possible realizations are in themselves grossly unnatural – that is, unless we are talking about institutional practices that try to educate human beings to perform like ants or beavers, and so on, and I take it that we are not – then "second nature" just means "*deeply* habitual," a historically achieved result (not naturally achieved, in any sense of "due *to* nature"), the observance of which eventually becomes largely unreflective. A culture (*Bildung*) in this sense, while it is something we must have the requisite natural, enabling capacities to build and sustain, *is only* something that we build and sustain. "Subjectivism" then, directing us as it does toward the historical dissatisfactions and tensions responsible for the institutional change we effect, seems unproblematic enough and to be directing us properly toward history not nature as the domain where accounts of human practices are to be based. In Hegel's somewhat puzzling language, while "*Geist*" is not non-natural or immaterial, it *is* "a product of itself."[29]

The notion of practical reason gaining some purchase in our lives, having its distinctive grip, thus plays a role in McDowell's theory parallel to his claims about a sensibility in which conceptual capacities can be activated. We need both, he thinks, in order to avoid the bad alternatives and *aporiai* that stem from the implications of accepting the modern notion of nature, and, he thinks, only a "partially re-enchanted" nature, this second nature, will allow us to maintain consistently both such a purchase and such an activation. But defending a "partially enchanted" nature seems quite a high price. A "*gezauberte Natur*" after all is a "nature made magical" and there seems no good reason to be driven that far. What one wants to object to in bald naturalism is not so much what gets counted as "occurring in nature or not," but what gets counted as a sufficient explanation, and there is no necessary connection between the latter and the former issue. There are some philosophers who obviously think there is, and who are convinced that a naturalist ontology has to mean that it will "one day" be possible to explain naturalistically, perhaps through evolutionary neurobiology, why Germans voted for Hitler and why the Yankees won the pennant, but surely the right response to them is "I won't hold my breath," and not a rush to enchant nature.[30]

In sum, if the space of reasons, as a historically constituted human practice, is autonomous, *sui generis*, not explicable in first-nature terms, not supernatural, subject to revision and critical correction, then what is going wrong with what McDowell calls "subjectivism" just seems to be some distorting implications of the "projection" metaphor. This would of course include the possible inference that, since such subjectivity is unconstrained by the world or by a direct perception of what ought to be done, it is unconstrained period. It is thus understandable that that charge was the first blast in German romanticism and in the German counter-enlightenment led by Jacobi. However, such implications stem from limited interpretations of such subjectivity, and not from the basic point about subjectivity as source.[31]

The more direct, obvious, erroneous implication of the projection image is that such normative commitments are viewed as "up to" individuals conceived in isolation from the world or from their tradition and community, as noumenal beings, rational choosers, or projective responders. The error is to think either that such commitments can be adopted and abandoned as the straightforward result of, as objects of, reflection and imposed on a blank content or a formless life, or that lacking anything in the metaphysical world to make the projections true, we decided that there is no way to evaluate subjective stances at all.[32] But we can take on all those points – the rejection of dogmatic empiricism as well as a transcendentalism that separates concept and content, the subjective stance from its occasion in the social world, and concepts from their historical and social authority – and still insist on the autonomy and revisability of rationality, without needing to wave that "red flag" of a "partially enchanted" nature.

Notes

*   I am indebted to Charles Larmore, Terry Pinkard, and Nicholas Smith for comments on an earlier draft.

1   See McDowell, *Mind and World* (Cambridge, MA: Harvard University Press, 1994), paperback edition with "Introduction," 1996. Page references to *Mind and World* are given in the text.

2   That is, McDowell's point holds whether the noumena–phenomena distinction is understood as a metaphysical dualism, a veil of perception phenomenalism, or a purely methodological, "dual aspect" theory (i.e., in line with the rejection of the "two-world" interpretation, a rejection and methodological reinterpretation pioneered by Graham Bird in Anglophone criticism and Gerold Prauss in the German literature). All of them make the Kantian assumption McDowell is out to free us from, the assumption about the realm of nature itself, and that is what is important for his claim. For a good discussion of the Kantian counter-attack, see Sally Sedgwick, "Hegel, McDowell, and Recent Defenses of Kant," *Journal of the British Society for Phenomenology* 31(3): 229–247 (October 2000).

3   Strictly speaking, the objection (especially to Davidson) is not to the ontology dimension of anomalous monism (see *Mind and World*, p.75ff.). McDowell shares the intuition behind attempts to render the space of reasons *sui generis* and autonomous. But to conceive it as simply autonomous, with nature conceived wholly as the realm of law, will lead, he thinks, inevitably to a frictionless coherentism. We thus need in effect some overlap between what is possible naturally and our responsiveness to reasons, and Davidson's position does not allow that. Similar sorts of objections, I assume, would be raised against supervenience theories (where the "base," nature, effectively and exclusively determines the truth conditions for any supervening property talk, and such a nature is, again, conceived entirely as exemplification of scientific law).

     In "Two Sorts of Naturalism," in *Mind, Value, and Reality* (Cambridge, MA: Harvard University Press, 1998), pp.167–197, McDowell is comfortable admitting the possibility of "looking for a scientific explanation of the place of, say, ethical discourse in disenchanted nature" (p.187). He is there interested only in showing that such a "counterpart" account of the causes of and results of ethical discourse is not a competitor with the actual exercise of ethical logos. This sounds more Davidsonian in spirit than the passages in *Mind and World*.

4   Perhaps the most important image in the book is a Hegelian one, the "unboundedness of the conceptual," so relied on in Lecture II. As McDowell also writes in Lecture IV: "the way to correct what is unsatisfactory in Kant's thinking about the supersensible is rather to embrace the Hegelian image in which the conceptual is unbounded on the outside" (p.83).

5 There are several articles that discuss the relation between McDowell's position and the German idealist and romantic traditions. Besides the essay by Michael Friedman included in this volume, see Graham Bird, "McDowell's Kant: Mind and World," *Philosophy* 71: 219–243 (1996); Andrew Bowie, "John McDowell's *Mind and World* and Early Romantic Epistemology," *Revue Internationale de Philosophie* 3: 515–554 (1996); Sally Sedgwick, "McDowell's Hegelianism," *European Journal of Philosophy* 5(1): 21–38 (April 1997), and her "Hegel, McDowell, and Recent Defenses of Kant," op. cit.; and Robert Stern, "Going Beyond the Kantian Philosophy: On McDowell's Hegelian Critique of Kant," *European Journal of Philosophy* 7(2): 247–269 (August 1999).

6 I realize that by McDowell's lights, I seem to be asking for exactly what he wants to foreclose, a "*theory* of second nature," which McDowell writes "would be a refusal to take the reminder [of second nature] as I intend it" ("Comments on Hans-Peter Krüger's Paper," in *Philosophical Explanations* 2: 123 (May 1998). But McDowell himself seems to present a good deal of theory in explaining the relevance for perception and action of a second-nature reminder, and I do not understand how the various transcendental questions he raises could be addressed by such a reminder alone. I am indebted to Nick Smith for comments on this issue.

7 Strictly speaking, nothing is ever "left behind" in Hegel's synthetic account, but "*aufgehoben*," or preserved, even while transcended. In this case, the logic of appropriate explanations of nature is not external to and imposed on the natural world, and Hegel has to show how. Hegel's radical insistence on the inseparability of thought and content is at work here as elsewhere. And the concepts required for an account of *Geist* require nothing "unnatural," even if natural accounts are themselves insufficient.

8 Kant, *Critique of Pure Reason*, tr. Norman Kemp-Smith (London: Macmillan, 1929), A51/B75.

9 McDowell does not deal with Kant's category theory in *Mind and World*. There is a hint of the interpretation he prefers in "Having the World in View: Sellars, Kant, and Intentionality," "Lecture II: The Logical Form of an Intuition," *Journal of Philosophy* 95(9): 451–470 (September 1998). There the dependence of experience on a prior categorial structure is glossed: "we can make sense of objects coming into view in intuitions only because we can see how objects fit into a view of the world" (p.465). I find this, and the argument behind it in Lecture II, persuasive, but will concentrate here on *Mind and World*.

10 That is, any interpretation must keep faith with Kant's principle: "the senses do not err – not because they always judge rightly, but because they do not judge at all" (*Critique of Pure Reason*, A293/B350).

11 On the important difference between epistemological issues raised by this issue and "transcendental" ones (i.e., the very possibility of objective purport) see McDowell's "Comments on Hans-Peter Krüger's Paper," p.121.

12 *Critique of Pure Reason*, A99.

13 Ibid., B151.

14 Ibid., B160n. See McDowell's gloss in "The Logical Form of an Intuition," p.456, note 6, and the discussion in my *Hegel's Idealism: The Satisfactions of Self-Consciousness* (Cambridge: Cambridge University Press, 1989), pp.24–32.

15 See Kant, *Prolegomena*, tr. Paul Carus (Chicago: Open Court, 1902), section 18.

16 Gerold Prauss, *Erscheinung bei Kant. Ein Problem der Kritik der reinen Vernunft* (Berlin: de Gruyter, 1971). Prauss also makes extensive use of a *Prolegomena* metaphor that resonates with many of McDowell's interests: that it is necessary "to spell out appearances" first, in order to be able to "read them as experience" (*Prolegomena*, section 30). There are a number of similarities between Prauss's view and McDowell's, but Prauss does not attend much to the dimension of "seeming" judgments that (rightly) so interests McDowell – that character of being impressed *on* the perceiver, of being

immediately (in some sense) how things just seem ("wrung out of one"), and Prauss is content enough with the problematic, "judgmental" quality of such "*Wahrnehmungsurteile*."

17 There is a great deal more detail about what is involved in such conceptual-but-not-fully-judgmental sensory takes on the world in the Woodbridge Lectures, much of it extremely helpful, but beyond the scope of one essay. See "Lecture II: The Logical Form of an Intuition," op. cit., pp.440–441. What McDowell is doing is essentially re-parsing the Kantian notion of immediacy, away from "conceptually unmediated" and toward something like "involuntary" just seeming so, not yet subject to our judgmental affirmation, and so forth. This allows him to account for how such sensory takes "contain" claims in ways quite different from the way judgments make claims. See especially ibid., pp.458–459.

18 McDowell's claim is that there would be nothing for a "context of justification" to be *about* if we could not account for this objective purport independently of it. This emerges frequently in his exchanges with Brandom in Enrique Villanueva, ed., *Perception* (*Philosophical Issues*, vol. 7, Atascadero, CA: Ridgeview, 1996), and in the shorter exchange published in *Philosophy and Phenomenological Research* 58(2): 369–374, 403–409 (June 1998), and is no doubt how he would reply to Michael Williams's suggestions in the latter's "Exorcism and Enchantment", *Philosophical Quarterly* 46(182): 99–109 (January 1996).

19 McDowell's condition on what the nature of rational constraint in perception amounts to is one of the most important elements in his response to Brandom. See Bob Brandom, "Perception and Constraint: McDowell's *Mind and World*," and McDowell's "Reply to Gibson, Byrne, and Brandom," in *Perception*, op. cit., where McDowell writes: "Brandom's less demanding reading of the constraint does not yield anything genuinely recognizable as the rational vulnerability of thinking to the world" (pp.293–294). He means, as the next paragraph makes clear, recognizable for the subject, even as he also admits that this subject cannot be detached from the languages and traditions into which the subject has been initiated. Throughout his discussion and replies, if what it amounts to for conceptual capacities to be "in play" in the looks or takes "wrung out" of one by contact with the world are (and are for the experiencer) what it *would be* for a judgment to have been made, and this capacity is itself rich with "tradition" and so sociality (what it would be to judge is a matter of what else I would be committed to backing up etc.), then I do not see the need to drag nature into the discussion. I should note again: sometimes McDowell gives the impression that *he* means to say:

> I don't have any particular stake in a possible appeal to nature, but anybody who *was* dead set on orienting all possible explanation from what was "naturally possible" would not find himself fated to be a reductionist if he could appreciate second nature. If he doesn't start off with naturalist assumptions in the first place, I've nothing in particular to say to him.

See his "Comments on Hans-Peter Krüger's Paper," op. cit., pp.122–123.

20 See Michael Williams, "Exorcism and Enchantment," op. cit., p.106.

21 Or, Sellars could be right about the possibility of what he calls "noumenal science." He distinguishes between "the conceptual framework of which nature was the cause," and the "freely elaborated conceptual frameworks with which we now challenge Nature," but notes that the latter is "free" only because the reality about which it ultimately theorizes is in principle unobservable and incapable of effecting within experience a causal alteration in our theories. So the framework is only "free" *relative* to the objects it is about, and is in itself a (noumenal) causal system. Where McDowell thinks the Paralogisms leave open the possibility that the I is an

embodied, natural (second-nature) subject, Sellars thinks they leave open that the I is a "system of scientific objects, the true counterparts of Kant's things-in-themselves." See Sellars, "Metaphysics and the Concept of a Person," in *The Logical Way of Doing Things*, ed. Karel Lambert (New Haven, CT: Yale University Press, 1969), pp.248–252. McDowell states his criticism of Sellars on this general point at the end of "The Logical Form of an Intuition" (op. cit., p.467), but his remarks there still seem to me open to the Sellarsian rejoinder that McDowell has not taken full enough account of the fact that Sellars wants the "sheer receptivity" guidance "from below the line" to be an object of such a numenal science, purely theoretical and postulated, and not to be confused with the "guiding" constituents of experience as experienced.

22 We cannot of course legislate arbitrarily; the *quid iuris* question must still be addressed.

23 See McDowell, "Two Sorts of Naturalism," op. cit., section 3.

24 See ibid., p.184, note 33.

25 See, for example, Kierkegaard on the difficulty, the impossibility, of truly becoming a Christian; Marx on alienation; Nietzsche's way of raising the problem of whether truth could be "incorporated," *einverleibt*; and Heidegger's accounts of "falling" and inauthenticity.

26 For more on the subjectivism issues, and an especially clear statement of why his rejection of "projectivist" versions does not commit him to a straightforward realism, see "Projection and Truth in Ethics," in *Mind, Value, and Reality*, op. cit., pp.151–166, especially p.159. See also "A Sensible Subjectivism?" by David Wiggins in his *Needs, Values, Truth* (Oxford: Basil Blackwell, 1987), pp.185–214; and for a valuable account of the empirical/philosophical distinction at stake in this problem, see Jonathan Lear, "Transcendental Anthropology," in his *Open-Minded: Working Out the Logic of the Soul* (Cambridge, MA: Harvard University Press, 1998), pp.247–281.

27 For a fuller discussion of this point see my "Naturalness and Mindedness: Hegel's Compatibilism," *European Journal of Philosophy* 7(2): 194–212 (1999).

28 Given how little content there is in McDowell's own appeals to second nature, perhaps this all simply *is* his position, and second nature *is* only an image, the point being to disabuse us of the notion of taking up or discarding norms as the result of reflection or choice. Historically acquired forms of life are (but are only) like nature in *that* sense.

29 Hegel kept flirting of course with the idea that one might understand nature as "dormant" or implicit or "sleeping" *Geist*, as if nature had a *conatus*, striving to be *Geist*, but he also succumbed to his better side, as in the *Lectures on Fine Art*, where *Natur* is called simply "spiritless," *geistlos*. See G. W. F. Hegel, *Aesthetics. Lectures on Fine Art*, vol. one, tr. T. M. Knox (Oxford: Clarendon Press, 1975), p.12.

30 This is in effect what McDowell says in his *Précis* for *Perception, Philosophical Issues*, vol. 7, in response to Fodor, op. cit., p.238. But he takes himself to be entitled to it only by having defended an enchanted nature, whereas I think the radical reductionist and eliminativist position begs the question of "explanation" at the start.

31 Of course, we are also going to need a different sort of argument about the ineliminability of such a domain, something other than an appeal to the proper realization of our nature. That appeal will have to be one to some sort of practical unavoidability and it will not be easy. That is, we cannot content ourselves with just noting the *physis–nomos* distinction in the way Michael Williams does in "Exorcism and Enchantment," op. cit., p.104. From even well before Lucretius, it was possible to claim that what *looks* like *nomos* is really *physis* again (the rule of the stronger, and so forth); the nature of its "self-regulating" potential is not easy to make out, and the basis for insisting on the autonomy of a kind of explanation, *without* an enchanted

nature ontology, presents difficult problems. There is a hint of this sort of strategy in McDowell himself when he distinguishes between the "forms of intelligibility" proper to explanations in nature, and forms that belong in the space of reasons. But that seems to him due to the difference between first and second nature. See Rorty's comments in "The Very Idea of Human Answerability to the World: John McDowell's version of Empiricism," in Richard Rorty, *Truth and Progress, Philosophical Papers*, vol. 3 (Cambridge: Cambridge University Press, 1998), p.144.

32 See again the valuable points made by McDowell in "Projection and Truth in Ethics," op. cit., especially on the "earned vs. unearned truth" distinction.

Part II

EPISTEMOLOGY

4

SENSE-EXPERIENCE AND THE GROUNDING OF THOUGHT

Barry Stroud

John McDowell's *Mind and World* seeks to expose and thereby to exorcise a line of thinking that leads to a philosophical challenge to the possibility of thought. Theories meant to answer the challenge cannot succeed; the defects of each drive us to an opposed theory, and then back, in endless oscillation. The key to the exorcism is to see how and why we are not forced to choose among the unsatisfactory theories. To be liberated in this way would not be to answer the philosophical question. Ideally, the challenge will simply disappear, or will lose whatever point it had seemed to have.

The troubling reflections start from the idea that thought has a subject-matter, or is about something, only if certain conditions are fulfilled. One such requirement is found in the idea of truth. A belief or judgment to the effect that things are thus and so is *correctly* or *incorrectly* held according to whether or not things are thus and so. Thinking is in that way "answerable" (p.xii)[1] to the way things are – and so to something independent of thought – for its being correctly or incorrectly executed. But it is the "cognitive predicament" (p.xii) of human beings to confront the world by means of sense-experience, so McDowell holds that reflection on thought's answerability to the world must begin for us with an understanding of our access to "the empirical world" (p.xii). This is where we can easily fall into the quandary he wants to show how to avoid. For "how can we understand the idea that our thinking is answerable to the empirical world, if not by way of the idea that our thinking is answerable to experience?" (p.xii). But to be answerable to experience our thought must be subject to a "verdict" from experience, something that indicates whether our beliefs or judgments have been adopted correctly or incorrectly, or at least reasonably or unreasonably. And there are obstacles in the way of seeing how such a verdict from "the tribunal of experience" (p.xii) is even possible.

Human sense-experience is a matter of impingements by the world on beings who possess certain sensory capacities. Such impingements are events in nature; something that is impinged upon is affected in a certain way. That is a causal connection, describable in terms of scientific laws of nature. But to understand two things as connected in accordance with a law of nature is not to understand one of those things as making the other reasonable in any way, or as justifying

79

or supporting it. It is to see that one thing happens because something else happens, but not to see that one thing is correctly or incorrectly executed, or is warranted or justified in the light of something else. Understanding sensory impacts in this way makes it impossible to see them as constituting a tribunal "standing in judgement over our beliefs" (p.xiii). The idea that mere impingements on our sensory surfaces can "ground" our beliefs and make them reasonable is nothing more than a myth: the Myth of the Given. But with no experiential "grounding," thought will not be answerable to anything independent of thought, and so will degenerate into a series of "moves in a self-contained game" (p.5), "a frictionless spinning in a void" (p.11). We are left with a familiar kind of philosophical anxiety: how is thought about the world possible at all?

McDowell's way of avoiding this quandary is to explain how and why there is no tension between sense impressions' being occurrences in nature and their grounding one's beliefs. The liberation comes from seeing how certain happenings in nature can nonetheless support or make reasonable beliefs about the way things are. Mature human beings possess concepts which they employ in thinking about the world. Impacts by the world on the receptive capacities of such beings are not mere impacts describable only in terms of scientific laws of nature. They are typically cases of a person's perceiving that things are thus and so in the world. A suitably equipped subject "takes in, for instance, sees, *that things are thus and so*" (p.9). That things are thus and so is also something one can think, or judge, or believe. Having an experience of seeing that things are thus and so can therefore make it highly reasonable (to put it mildly) to believe that things are thus and so. That belief gets a very favorable verdict from that experience.

Of course, one can be misled into thinking that one takes in that things are thus and so when they are not. Human beings are not infallible, even in perception. But the key to McDowell's exorcism is to reveal how, when one is not misled, one perceives how things are. That is why, as he points out, it does not matter much that one can be misled. Actually being misled can matter a great deal; it can even be fatal. But the general possibility of being misled is no obstacle to an understanding of the possibility of thought. The perceptual access one has to the way things are when one is not misled is what supports or warrants one's belief to the effect that things are that way. Not only has one's thought been correctly executed; one also has good reason to believe that it has. When sense-experience is understood as "openness to the layout of reality" (p.26) in this way we can see how an independent reality can "exert a rational influence on what a subject thinks" (p.26).

This insistence that in sense-experience we can take in the way things are, or that things are thus and so, is obviously crucial to McDowell's way of bypassing the philosophical quandary. He is admirably clear and forthright about its importance, and explicitly sets himself against the widespread tendency "to conclude that even a non-misleading experience cannot genuinely be a case of openness to reality" (p.111). If, even when things go as well as they can, there is a difference, and hence a gap, between what we perceive to be so and what is so, we could never have "the fact itself impressing itself on a perceiver" (pp.112–113). And for McDowell that "strains our hold on the very idea of a glimpse of reality" (p.112). It would leave inexplicable how thinking can be answerable to anything independent of itself.

McDowell is surely right to insist that in experience we can see that things are thus and so. The history of philosophy (if nothing else) should have convinced us by now that no conception of perception which offers us at best only something less than what is so in the independent world could explain how we can have any reason to believe anything about such a world. Most of *Mind and World* is taken up with the diagnostic task of explaining how and why such a conception of experience has come to seem unavailable, and with doing what is needed to bring it clearly and convincingly into view. It is not easy, as McDowell is fully aware; a trouble-free conception of sense-experience has certainly eluded a great many impressive philosophers.

I will not take up McDowell's rich exploration of the ground that must be cleared in order to put the otherwise inevitable quandary behind us. I find his account extremely illuminating, and promising of even greater riches. Rather I want to ruminate on the conception of sense-experience that will ensure what he is right to insist is needed – perceptual access to the way things are. Does even McDowell avoid all danger in this traditional minefield?

To suppose that mere impacts from the world, conceived as such, could justify or make reasonable any beliefs they might happen to generate is to fall victim to the Myth of the Given. McDowell accordingly stresses that we must start from the idea that "the world's impressions on our senses are already possessed of conceptual content" (p.18). So what is needed is "a notion of experience as an actualization of conceptual capacities in sensory consciousness."[2] This means that anyone who receives sense impressions has certain conceptual capacities. Where there are no such capacities, there is no experience of the way things are. Creatures with sensory capacities but without conceptual capacities of the kinds human beings so conspicuously possess do not really have experience as McDowell conceives of it. They might be perceptually sensitive to various features of their environment, but they do not have experience of the world.

To have the requisite conceptual capacities is to be capable of activities of thinking which are "responsibly undertaken by a subject who is in control of the activity,"[3] and so "is responsive to rational relations, which link the contents of judgements of experience with other judgeable contents" (p.12). In perception, what one perceives to be so is, after a certain point, not directly under one's control. But the capacities brought into play in passive perceptual experience must be available to the subject in fully active, and so non-perceptual, thinking. Impacts by the world on the sensory capacities of a person with such conceptual capacities are sense impressions with conceptual content.

That things are thus and so is the conceptual content of an experience, but if the subject of the experience is not misled, that very same thing, *that things are thus and so*, is also a perceptible fact, an aspect of the perceptible world.

(p.26)

This looks like just the conclusion we want.

That conclusion would seem to be secured by the idea that having a sense-experience or impression, at least when things go well, is simply a matter of seeing or otherwise perceiving that things are thus and so. The experience of seeing that something or other is so certainly involves receiving an impact from the world on the senses. And no one could see that *p* without understanding the thought that *p*, and so having the conceptual capacities required for understanding that thought. So seeing that *p* is "an actualization of conceptual capacities in sensory consciousness." Impressions for McDowell are also what can give us reasons to believe something about the empirical world. And seeing that *p* can certainly give a person reason to believe that *p*. The justification of the person's belief can be traced back to that person's experience of seeing that *p*. If that experience is an impression, our beliefs would be answerable to our impressions, and so answerable to experience, by our sometimes seeing or otherwise perceiving that things are thus and so.

This is what McDowell wants his conception of experience to deliver, but he says many things about impressions which suggest that he does not regard them as simply cases of seeing that things are thus and so in the independent world. Or if that is how he thinks of them, he does not think it is enough to explain in the right way how they ground empirical beliefs. I would like to understand why not.

One indication that he thinks something is missing is his dissatisfaction with the views of Donald Davidson, whom he describes as not merely committed to the idea that "experience cannot count as a reason for holding a belief" (p.14), but even suffering from "a block that prevents [him] from seeing any possibilities in this direction" (p.18). But there seems to be nothing to prevent Davidson from accepting a view of impressions as cases of seeing that *p*. He has famously argued that a certain physical movement's occurring in a suitably equipped person can be a case of that person's acting with a certain intention,[4] and that the utterance of a certain sound by a person equipped with certain conceptual capacities can be a case of that person's expressing a certain belief.[5] It is hard to see why he could not also accept the idea that the world's having a certain impact on a person adept in the use of the relevant concepts can be a case of that person's seeing that it is raining. And how could Davidson, or anyone, deny that seeing that it is raining can give one good reason to believe that it is raining? Looking and seeing what is going on is the best way to get a reasonable belief about the weather.

It is true that some things Davidson says appear to conflict with the idea that sense-experience can give one reason to believe something. He speaks of sense impressions or sensations as causes of certain effects in perceivers, and denies that as such they can provide reasons for believing something. In a sentence McDowell puts a lot of weight on, Davidson says: "Nothing can count as a reason for holding a belief except another belief."[6] The sentence is unfortunate, first, in its apparent implication that one can have a reason for holding a belief only if one also holds a different belief. That would mean that seeing that it is raining could not be one's reason for believing that it is raining, since there is not "another belief" involved – only the proposition that it is raining. But since what matters for the reasonableness of a belief is not the proposition believed but the reasonableness of the person's believing it, it is possible for one's having a certain attitude toward a proposition (e.g., seeing that p) to justify or give one reason to hold a different attitude toward that same proposition (e.g., believing that p).

Putting too much weight on the unfortunate sentence also obscures Davidson's reason for denying that sense impressions or sensations can give one reasons to believe something: sense impressions understood as mere impacts from the world have no content. That is something McDowell himself insists on. He says he has no objection to what Davidson expresses in the unfortunate sentence if it means "nothing can count as a reason for holding a belief except something else that is also in the space of concepts" (pp.140, 143). But if that is what it means, it does not conflict with the view that seeing that p, which is receiving an impact from the world by a person possessing the relevant concepts, can give one reason to believe that p.

McDowell nonetheless thinks Davidson is not in a position to explain in the right way how experience can give one reason to believe things about the world. One thing he finds lacking is any account of that "external constraint" that is essential for thought's having any bearing on an independent reality. We must acknowledge a role in perception for what McDowell calls "receptivity," as well as for those essential conceptual capacities that come from the side of "spontaneity." But in understanding that "external constraint" "we must not suppose that receptivity makes an even notionally separable contribution to its co-operation with spontaneity" (p.51). To suppose that it does, or could, leads directly to the Myth of the Given, and hence to the fatal oscillation.

The idea of an impression as a seeing that p appears to fulfill this condition. Seeing that p occurs only when there is an impact by the world on a perceiver equipped with conceptual capacities sufficient for grasping the thought that p. Only then is there "receptivity" in perception. An impact on an organism that lacks those capacities, or in whom they are inoperative, is not a case of seeing that p; it is in that respect a different kind of impact. But the difference between the two kinds of impact lies only in the absence or presence of those conceptual capacities that are essential to seeing that p. So receptivity does not make a contribution to seeing that p that is "even notionally separable" from the contribution of the conceptual capacities characteristic of spontaneity. It is nonetheless required for seeing that p, and so required for such an experience to give one reason to believe that p.

As McDowell thinks of reasons to believe, an impression gives one reason to believe something only if it is, or provides, *the person's* reason for believing what the person does. It is not enough for an experience simply to render a person's belief reasonable, even to a very high degree. This is the point behind his criticism of Gareth Evans's and Christopher Peacocke's appeal to states or experiences with what they call "non-conceptual content" that is not "available" to the subject at the time (pp.50–55, 162–166). Even if something square is present, for example, whenever a person is in a certain sensory state and believes that something square is present, it does not follow that that sensory state is the person's reason for holding that belief (pp.163–164). Since the belief would be true whenever it was held in those circumstances, it could perhaps be said to be highly reasonable for anyone in that state to hold it then. But for McDowell that belief would not be "based on" the sensory state in the required way. The so-called sensory experience that gave rise to it would fall beyond the reach of the conceptual capacities involved in spontaneity, and in that sense would be "blind" (p.54). It would not even count as an experience. Experience involves awareness, and that requires possession and deployment of conceptual capacities that can be exercised in "active, self-conscious thinking" (p.55).

The idea of impressions as seeings that p also appears to fulfill this requirement. No one could have an experience of seeing that p without the conceptual resources for understanding the thought that p. The experience therefore has "conceptual content"; it is not "blind." Someone who sees that p is aware that p, or "takes in" that p. The content of that experience is therefore "available" to the person to be rationally linked with other "judgeable contents." Having that experience could be said to be the person's reason, or what gives the person reason, to believe what he or she does.

But I think that for McDowell this still does not explain how what he calls an impression can count as a person's reason for holding a belief about the world. Appealing only to seeings that p, even if we call them experiences, does not do justice to that cooperation of receptivity and spontaneity that he sees as essential to experience. A person who sees that it is raining judges or believes or accepts or otherwise puts it forward as true that it is raining. That judgment or belief or assertion is a judgment about the independent world, so for McDowell its justification must eventually be traced back to an impression that grounds it. "When we trace the ground for an empirical judgement, the last step takes us to experiences" (p.10). But tracing the justification back only to what I have called the experience of seeing that it is raining would trace it back only to something that still involves judgment or belief about the independent world. To see that p is to judge that p. And for McDowell that judgment, like all empirical judgments, will be justified only if it is grounded in an experience which is an impression.

In receiving a sense impression, the perceiver is passive. It is true that one receives an impression with content only if the conceptual capacities that are present and operative in it are "integrated into a rationally organized network of capacities for active adjustment of one's thinking to the deliverances of experience" (p.29). But those "deliverances of experience" are not themselves results of the "active, self-conscious thinking" characteristic of exercises of what McDowell calls spontaneity. That is a form of "freedom," and requires assessment, decision, and judgment. But "in experience, one finds oneself saddled with content. One's conceptual capacities have already been brought into play, in the content's being available to one, before one has any choice in the matter" (p.10).

This is perhaps what leads McDowell to speak of impressions as "appearances" or "appearings." Having a sense-experience is "having things appear to one in a certain way" (p.62). Those appearances are "rationally linked" to the rest of our thought through "the way appearances can constitute reasons for judgements about objective reality – indeed, do constitute reasons for judgements in suitable circumstances" (p.62). In such circumstances, an empirical judgment is "satisfactorily grounded in how things appear to one" (p.62).

Speaking of impressions as "appearances," and distinguishing them from the judgments one makes on the basis of them, is perhaps a way of drawing attention to the passivity of perception as contrasted with the "freedom" that is essential to "active thinking." But how is that contrast to be drawn? McDowell expresses it this way:

> Minimally, it must be possible to decide whether or not to judge that things are as one's experience represents them to be. How one's experience represents things to be is not under one's control, but it is up to one whether one accepts the appearance or rejects it.
>
> (p.11)

This strongly suggests that whenever one receives an impression one is presented with an "appearance" that "represents" things to be a certain way, but one can decide not to accept or judge that things are in fact that way. Withholding one's assent from the "appearance" would not be to see that things are that way. Seeing that p involves judging that p, but having an impression that merely "represents" things to be such that p does not. So although in seeing that p there would be an experience that grounds the judgment that p, seeing that p would not itself be that grounding experience. On this view, having an impression would be part of, but it would not be the same as, seeing that p. Impressions would be restricted to "appearances" which involve acceptance or endorsement of nothing beyond "how one's experience represents things to be," and so nothing about the independent world.

Do we always have an impression of something less than that things are thus and so every time we see that things are thus and so? One reason to think so might be the possibility of the empirical judgment's being false even when made on the basis of an impression. An object can fail to be square even though a very sharp-sighted person who looks at it carefully judges that it is square. In such a case, the person does not see that the object is square, since it is not square, but the person certainly sees something, or has some kind of impression. We know from the tortuous history of the philosophy of perception that it is very tempting to conclude that a perceiver must have the same kind of impression when the object is in fact square and when it is not but only looks that way. The content of the impression in either case implies nothing about the independent world. The perceiver judges on the basis of that impression, either truly or falsely, that the object is square.

This cannot be how McDowell thinks of impressions as "appearances." This view really would rule out the possibility of "the fact itself impressing itself on a perceiver" (pp.112–113). I think it is fatal even to the prospect of any reasonable belief about the world. But McDowell has convincingly shown that it can be avoided. The general possibility of an empirical judgment's being false does not imply that whenever a person has an impression that grounds that judgment it is an impression that is non-committal about the judgment's truth.[7] So there is no reason here for thinking that impressions are always of something less than the truth of the empirical judgments we make on the basis of them.

Another reason for thinking of "appearances" as non-committal in that way might be the thought that in the passive receptivity of perception alone we merely "receive," and do not make or accept any judgment at all. As an illustration of the way an experience can ground a belief McDowell says that an ordinary person asked why she holds a belief to the effect that an object within her field of view is square could give the unsurprising reply "Because it looks that way." He says that gives a reason for holding the belief (p.165). Now when she *says* "Because it looks square" she is presumably expressing the belief that it looks square (to her). And the content of that belief, together with an assumption about conditions' being normal – or at least the absence of information to the contrary – could be given as a reason for believing that the object (probably) is square. But that traces the justification of the original belief back only to a belief or judgment about how things look. For McDowell there must be an *experience* which is the believer's reason, not just a judgment or belief.

Perhaps in saying "Because it looks square" the person is referring to such an experience. Its looking that way to her is certainly an experience she might have. But if she has such an experience, it must be true that that object looks square to her, and if that is the way it looks to her, she must be aware that that object looks square to her. Experience involves awareness. But for her to be aware that that object looks square to her is for her to accept or endorse as true the proposition "That object looks square (to me)." She is aware that that proposition is true. So it cannot be that in receiving an impression that is an appearance there is no acceptance or judgment at all.

McDowell might seem to be denying this when he says "Its appearing to me that things are thus and so is not obviously to be equated with my believing something" (p.140). But that denies only that sensory appearings and believings are the same thing. He is right that they are not; it is possible to believe something without anything appearing to me in perception at all. The question is whether things could perceptually appear to me to be a certain way without my believing anything at all. McDowell says that in sense-experience "one finds oneself saddled with content ... [which is] available to one, before one has any choice in the matter" (p.10). But to be "saddled" with a certain content in perception is not simply for that content to be "available" to be entertained or contemplated, as it is in the unasserted antecedent of a conditional proposition, for instance. To take in some content in perception is to have accepted or endorsed that content, or to find oneself accepting or endorsing it.

"Believe" is perhaps not the best word to capture the attitude of acceptance or endorsement involved in perception, especially if it suggests actively making up one's mind (p.60). The word "judgment" seems even less apt, with its connotation of deliberation and decision. But there is awareness or acceptance of some kind in perceptual experience, not mere entertainment of content. Even to be aware that things appear to be thus and so is to take in or acknowledge that they appear to be that way. It is not to remain neutral on the question of how things appear to you to be.

So the passivity and absence of choice in perception, which is the mark of receptivity and "external constraint," cannot be equated with the absence of all judgment or assent. In being "saddled" with content one is "saddled" with assent to or affirmation of that content, or at least of some content or other. When the content of one's impression is things' appearing to be thus and so, it looks as if the impression that grounds the judgment involved in accepting that content must be the very impression in the receiving of which that judgment is made. There is nothing else that could serve as its ground. To insist that its ground must be found elsewhere, because a judgment can be adequately grounded only if it is based on an impression that does not involve making that very judgment, would lead to a skeptical regress; no judgment would be grounded. But if an experience involving a judgment can ground that very judgment in the case of minimally committal "appearances," what reason is there to deny that an empirical judgment about the independent world can be grounded by an experience that involves making that very judgment?

Someone who is asked why she believes that a certain object in her view is square might also give the unsurprising reply "Because I see that it is square." That is an even better reason for her to believe that it is square than that it looks square to her. It involves judging or asserting that the object is square. That judgment is part of the experience of seeing that the object is square. Must its justification be traced back to an "appearance" whose content implies nothing about the way things are in the independent world?

There is no question that we sometimes – even fairly often – have impressions that are minimally committal in that way. If I know or believe that two lines in a familiar configuration are the same length, although they now appear to me not to be, I will not judge or believe that those lines are unequal. I do not go beyond the appearance in what I accept. It is in that sense "up to me" to judge that the lines are unequal when I see what I see, and in such a case I do not make that judgment. But when I do judge that two lines that I see are unequal, that judgment is also "up to me" in the same sense, even if it is something I cannot help believing at the time, and something I never reject. Sticking by it or not is "up to me"; the judgment is revisable, even if never revised. If I come to see or suspect that it is not true, or that I do not see that it is true, I can settle for its appearing to me that the lines are unequal. Or if I stick by the original judgment and it is, unknown to me, false, then I did not see that the lines are unequal, even though I thought I did. Since in that case I had an impression with some content or other – but not that the lines are unequal – it could again be said that I had an experience of the lines appearing to me to be unequal. But none of this shows that I have such an experience every time I see that two lines are unequal in length.

The fact that judgments made in perceptual experience are revisable in the light of reflection or further experience can make it seem that continued acceptance of a perceptual judgment about the independent world cannot be based solely on the original experience that gave rise to it; further reflection or experience serves to support it as well. And this can make it tempting to suppose that the content of that original experience in itself must have implied nothing about the independent world, and its acceptance was direct and unrevisable. But yielding to this temptation is another way of falling into that "highest common factor" view of perception and reasonable belief that McDowell has rightly rejected.

That view also assumes that what is accepted in "appearances" is known or endorsed in some direct way, and is unrevisable. But that is not so. One's acceptance of how things appear to be is also revisable, just as one's beliefs about what is so are. Closer scrutiny or further reflection can reveal to me that two lines that I see do not really appear to be the same length, although I thought earlier that they did. Finding them to appear equal or not is "up to me" in the same sense as finding them to be equal or not is. As far as I can see, to acknowledge this revisability of perceptual judgments is not to deny the presence of an "external constraint" on thought or the receptivity involved in perception.

So although I find McDowell certainly right to stress that sense impressions have content, because of the conceptual capacities of the perceiver, and right to see those impressions as giving the perceiver reason to believe something, I am less than certain of how he thinks of those impressions, and of how he thinks they provide such reasons. If all impressions are "appearances," but even seeing that things are thus and so in the independent world counts as receiving an "appearance," there is no difficulty. We can get reason to believe that p by seeing that p. And if all impressions are "appearances" whose contents always fall short of implying anything about the independent world, the "openness to reality" that McDowell rightly demands of a satisfactory account of experience is lost. No one could ever see that things are thus and so; the most anyone could be aware of in perception alone would be things' appearing to be thus and so.

"The fact itself" would never be impressed on a perceiver. That threatens even the possibility of reasonable belief about an independent world. How could "appearances," so understood, ever give one reason to believe anything about what is not an "appearance"?

McDowell nonetheless puts his problem of how experience can give rational support to empirical judgments as that of accounting for "the way appearances can constitute reasons for judgements about objective reality" (p.62). His answer appeals to "rational relations" between experiences and the judgments about the world that we make on the basis of them (p.52), and he appears to think of those relations as holding between the *contents* of the experiences and the beliefs (p.166). "Because it looks square," he says, is "easily recognized" as giving a reason to believe "It is square" (p.165); it is the person's reason for believing that the object is square. But is it recognized as a reason because we discern a certain "rational linkage" between the *content* of the experience and the *content* of the belief?

I think the content of an experience alone cannot give a person reason, or be a person's reason, to believe something. The content of an experience is typically expressed in a proposition, and propositions are not reasons, nor do they make other propositions reasonable. Propositions are true or false, not reasonable or unreasonable, justified or unjustified. Even if one proposition implies another, it does not justify, support, warrant, or make reasonable that other proposition. What is justified or reasonable or supported or warranted is a person's accepting a certain proposition, or rejecting it, or taking some other attitude toward its truth.

It is true that when asked for the reason for believing something a person can simply cite a proposition. A detective who is asked "Why do you believe this suspect didn't do it?" could answer "Because he was in Cleveland that night." But in giving that as her reason the speaker indicates that the proposition she cites is something she believes. Her believing that proposition – in fact, her believing it for good reason – is required for her having that reason to believe that the suspect didn't do it. If she had no idea that the suspect was in Cleveland, even if it were true, she would not have the reason she has for believing that he didn't do it. And even if it were not true, she would still have good reason for believing he didn't do it if she had good reason to believe that the suspect was in Cleveland.

The same holds for experiences. It is not simply the content of a person's experience that gives the reason to believe something; it is the person's experiencing, or being aware of, or accepting, or somehow "taking in" that content. Taking in that a certain object looks square can give you reason to believe that the object is square. That cannot be because "It looks square" is always reason to believe "It is square." If you already know that an object is not square, the experience of its looking square does not give you reason to believe that it is. In the right circumstances, an object's looking square could even be excellent reason to believe that it is spherical. Whether the way something looks is a reason to believe that it is that way or not depends on what else is true in the situation, and on what else you have reason to believe.

Can we say, then, that there is a "rational relation" holding for the most part, or other things being equal, between "It looks square" and "It is square"? It is probably true that, for the most part, or normally, anyone to whom an object looks square has reason to believe that the object is square. That is an observation about how often, or under what circumstances, having a certain perceptual experience gives a person reason to hold a certain belief, or under what circumstances having a certain attitude gives one reason to hold a different attitude. Some such connections hold in all circumstances. Seeing that an object is square always gives one reason to believe that it is square.

For present purposes the crucial question about any "rational relations" between "It looks F" and "It is F," however they are understood, is whether they also run in the opposite direction. Does seeing that an object is square require having an impression of its looking square? Must the justification of all empirical judgments be traced back to "appearances" understood as minimally committal in that way? I find I do not know McDowell's answer to this question. I cannot see how or why he could possibly say "Yes." Yet he seems reluctant to hold that seeing that p, which involves judging that p, is the kind of experience that could count in the right way as grounding a person's belief that p. He insists that thought will have a bearing on reality only if it is ultimately grounded in something "outside thought," in the sense of outside thinking or judging. But why can seeing that p not serve as that ground? It is something "outside," or beyond, thinking. It is *seeing*, and not merely thinking or judging, that p.

More recently McDowell has invoked the chicken sexers of philosophical legend to illustrate what he regards as a condition any satisfactory account of perceptual experience must meet.[8] As he describes them, those experts declare a chick with which they are presented "Male" or "Female" without knowing how they do it, and even without claiming that the two sexes look different to them. The best chicken sexers get it right most of the time; truth is what counts. What he finds unacceptable is the idea that this could be the way things are in general, for all perceptual experience and all concepts. Even those chicken sexers, he thinks, will presumably acknowledge that they recognize something as a *chick* because it looks like a chick.

It is no doubt implausible to suppose that speakers know nothing about what features they rely on in applying *any* of their concepts to anything. The richness and variety of the concepts one would have to have in order to have any concepts at all are probably enough to rule that out. But McDowell appears to require that a satisfactory account of visual perceptual experience should show how the way things look to us is what we rely on in judging, on the basis of experience, how things are. Taken with complete generality, for all concepts applied in experience, that would lead to a regress; no concepts at all could be applied in experience. But if there is no regress because it is conceded that the concept "looks F" can be directly recognized to apply, and not on the basis of its looking as if it looks F, why must the concept "is F" be thought to be justifiably applicable only on some such indirect basis? A perceiver often has no reason for applying a certain concept beyond the fact that the perceiver sees that it applies to the item to which the perceiver applies it. "'How do I know that this color is red'? – It would be an answer to say: 'I have learnt English.'"[9]

Notes

1 All page references in the text are to the paperback edition of *Mind and World* (Cambridge, MA: Harvard University Press, 1996).
2 "Précis of *Mind and World*," *Philosophy and Phenomenological Research* (1998), p.367.
3 Ibid.
4 See, for example, Donald Davidson, "Agency," in his *Essays on Actions and Events* (Oxford: Oxford University Press, 1980).
5 See, for example, Donald Davidson, "Radical Interpretation," in his *Inquiries into Truth and Interpretation* (Oxford: Oxford University Press, 1984).
6 Quoted by McDowell in *Mind and World*, p.14.
7 See, for example, *Mind and World*, pp.112–113 and references there to his "Criteria, Defeasibility, and Knowledge" and "Singular Thought and the Extent of Inner Space," both in McDowell, *Meaning, Knowledge and Reality* (Cambridge, MA: Harvard University Press, 1998).
8 See "In Conversation: Donald Davidson: The McDowell Discussion," Philosophy International, London, 1997 (videotape).
9 L. Wittgenstein, *Philosophical Investigations*, tr. G. E. M. Anscombe (Oxford: Blackwell, 1953), §381.

5

NON-INFERENTIAL KNOWLEDGE, PERCEPTUAL EXPERIENCE, AND SECONDARY QUALITIES

Placing McDowell's empiricism*

Robert Brandom

Empiricism can be a view in epistemology: without perceptual experience, we can have no knowledge of contingent matters of fact. Empiricism can be a view in semantics: propositional or more generally conceptual content is unintelligible apart from its relation to perceptual experience. Empiricism can be a view in the philosophy of mind: "experience must constitute a tribunal, mediating the way our thinking is answerable to how things are, as it must be if we are to make sense of it as thinking at all."[1] McDowell is an empiricist in all these senses. In this essay I want to highlight certain features of his concept of experience, first by showing how he avoids some pitfalls that notoriously ensnare traditional attempts to work out empiricist intuitions, and second by comparing and contrasting it with two other ways of construing perceptual experience – one wider than McDowell's and one narrower than his – that also avoid the classical difficulties.

I

McDowell's empiricism is distinguishable from classical versions in at least two fundamental ways. First, with Kant and Sellars, McDowell understands experience as a thoroughly *conceptual* achievement. Thus he insists that anything that does not have concepts does not have perceptual experience either. Because he does, McDowell counts also as endorsing the fundamental *rationalist* insight: that to be aware of something in the sense in which such awareness can serve as evidence for beliefs amounting to knowledge is to bring it under a concept. This principle dictates that one must already have concepts in order to have experience in the sense he is addressing – a sense that in view of its fealty to the rationalist principle deserves to be seen as a successor of Leibniz's notion of apperception.

McDowell also insists that anything that does not have perceptual experience does not have concepts either. That is, he endorses the view I called semantic empiricism above. Concept use and perceptual experience are two aspects of *one* achievement. This view was emphatically not a feature of traditional rationalism. In his synthesis of these themes of classical rationalism and classical empiricism, as in so many other respects, McDowell is a Kantian.

Second, for McDowell perceptual experience is generally (though not in every case) immediately and essentially revelatory of empirical facts. That is, it is essential to McDowell's concept of perceptual experience that the fact that things are thus and so can *be* the content of a perceptual experience. When things go well, the fact itself is visible to us. It *is* the content we experience. The perceiving mind includes what it perceives.

Because he understands perceptual experience as requiring the grasp of concepts, McDowell avoids the Myth of the Given, which afflicts all classical versions of epistemological empiricism. The Myth of the Given is the claim that there is some kind of experience the having of which does not presuppose grasp of concepts, such that merely *having* the experience counts as *knowing* something, or can serve as *evidence* for beliefs, judgments, claims, and so on, that such a non-conceptual experience can *rationally ground*, and not just causally occasion, belief. In "Empiricism and the Philosophy of Mind,"[2] Sellars shows to McDowell's satisfaction (and to mine) that the project of making intelligible a concept of experience that is in this way amphibious between the non-conceptual world and our conceptually structured thought is a hopeless one. By contrast, McDowell is clear in taking perceptual experiences to have the same sort of content that perceptual *judgments* have – and hence to be conceptually structured.

Since McDowell also takes concept use to be a *linguistic* achievement (in line with Sellars's doctrine that to grasp a concept is to master the use of a word), he takes it that we learn to have perceptual experiences only when we come to have a language. Thus perceptual experience is *not* something we share with non-linguistic animals such as cats and chimpanzees. No doubt there is some sort of broadly perceptual attunement to things that we *do* share with our primate and mammalian cousins. We might call it "sentience." But it will not qualify as *experience*, according to McDowell's rationalist usage. We might call the capacity for experience in this sense "sapience." As a consequence, McDowell insists that we cannot understand what we have, perceptual experiences, by construing it as the result of starting with what we share with our sentient but not sapient animal relatives, and then *adding* something (say, the ability to use concepts). For what we would need to "add" is not itself intelligible apart from the notion of perceptual experience.[3]

Other thinkers who are careful to avoid the Myth of the Given do so by placing the interface between non-conceptual causal stimuli and conceptual response at the point where environing stimuli cause perceptual *judgments*. That is, they avoid the Myth by seeing nothing non-judgmental that could serve to *justify* perceptual judgments, rather than just to *cause* them. Davidson notoriously takes this line, endorsing the slogan that nothing but a belief can justify another belief. I would argue that Sellars himself has a view of this shape.[4] And it is the line I take in my book.[5] McDowell, however, construes perceptual experiences as not involving the sort of *endorsement* characteristic of judging or believing: perceptual experiences have judgeable, believable contents, but they are not judgments or beliefs. When a perceiver *does* advance from perceptual experience to judgment or belief, however, the experience can serve to justify the resulting commitment.

I said above that the second feature that distinguishes McDowell's view of perceptual experience from those appealed to by empiricists of a more traditional stripe is his view that in favored cases, when perception is veridical, the content of perceptual experience just *is* the fact perceived. McDowell endorses the Fregean approach, which construes *facts* as *true thoughts* – "thoughts" not in the psychological sense of thinkings, but in the semantic sense of the *contents* that are thought, or better, thinkable. The obvious pitfall in the vicinity of such a view is the need to deal with the fact that we make perceptual *mistakes*. That is, we sometimes cannot tell the difference between the case in which we are having a perceptual experience whose content is a fact and cases where there is no such fact to be perceived. Traditionally, the explanatory strategy for addressing such phenomena had the shape of a *two-factor theory*: one starts with a notion of perceptual experience as what is *common* to the veridical and the non-veridical cases, and then distinguishes them by *adding* something external to the experience: the truth of the claim, that is the actual existence of the fact in question. Epistemologically, this strategy sets the theorist up for the Argument from Illusion, and hence for a skeptical conclusion. McDowell's objection to the two-factor strategy is not epistemological, however, but semantic. It is not that it makes the notion of perceptual *knowledge* unintelligible (though it does that, too). It is that it makes unintelligible the notion of *objective purport* – our experiences (and therefore, our thoughts) so much as *seeming* to be about the perceptible world. He thinks that constraint can only be met by an account that is entitled to endorse what is perhaps his favorite quote from Wittgenstein: "When we say, and *mean*, that such-and-such is the case, we – and our meaning – do not stop anywhere short of the fact; but we mean: *this-is-so*."[6] McDowell's perceptual realism is his way of explaining how this can be so. Extending the doctrine of semantic empiricism, he thinks that if we can't make this feature of our thought and talk intelligible for perceptual experience, then we can't make it intelligible for *any* claims or beliefs.

On his view, the *only* thing a veridical perceptual experience and a corresponding hallucination have in common is that their subject can't tell them apart. There is no *experience* in common. We just are not infallible about the contents of our experiences, and can confuse being in the state of having one for being in the state of having another – for instance, by responding to each by endorsing the same perceptual judgment. Once again, he insists, we cannot understand veridical experience by construing it as the result of starting with a notion of what is common to the state that prompts a veridical perceptual judgment and the state that prompts a corresponding mistaken perceptual judgment, and then *adding* something (say, the truth of the claim in question).[7]

The various features of McDowell's view that I have focused on are related. The revelation of perceptible fact in perceptual experience is "immediate" in the sense that the conceptual abilities required (by the first condition above) are exercised *passively* in perception. They are the very same conceptual abilities exercised actively in, say, making a judgment as the result of an inference, but differ in that the application of concepts in perceptual experience is wrung from us involuntarily by the perceptible fact. The way in which concepts are brought passively into play falls short of judgment or belief, however. The content is presented to the potential knower as a *candidate* for endorsement. But an act of judgment is required to endorse it. So what is wrung from us by the facts is not *judgments*, but only *petitions* for judgments.

II

I want to situate McDowell's notion of perceptual experience by placing it with respect to two other notions, one broader than his and one narrower. The broader notion is *non-inferential knowledge acquired in response to environing stimuli*. The narrower notion is *immediate awareness of secondary qualities*.

I said above that thinkers such as Davidson, who reject the Myth of the Given, have typically rejected also the idea of any conceptually structured intermediary between causal stimuli and full-blown observational judgments. McDowell thinks that we need to postulate perceptual experiences, which are such intermediaries – though we must be clear that they are intermediaries only in the straightforward causal sense of being brought about by environing stimuli and bringing about observational judgments, not in the sense of the sort of epistemological intermediaries that give rise to the picture of a "veil of ideas." His view is clearly coherent, and is not subject to the objections Davidson forwards against epistemological intermediaries as classically conceived. But we might still ask what explanatory ground is gained by countenancing perceptual experiences, since we can avoid the Myth of the Given without them. One part of McDowell's answer is that his notion of experience lets us distinguish cases of genuine perception from other cases of responsively acquired non-inferential knowledge. I want to sketch an account of this broader class, and then say why McDowell thinks we must also distinguish a privileged species within this genus.

Quine suggests[8] that what distinguishes specifically *observational* knowledge is that observation reports are reliably keyed to environing stimuli in a way that is widely shared within some community – so that members of that community almost always agree about what to say when concurrently stimulated in the same way. This suggests that we think of there being two elements one needs to master in order to be able to make a certain kind of observation report, two distinguishable sorts of practical know-how involved. First, one must have acquired a *reliable differential responsive disposition*: a disposition reliably to respond differentially to some kind of stimulus. Which stimuli we can come differentially to respond to depends on how we are wired up and trained. Humans lack the appropriate physiology to respond differentially to different radio frequencies, for instance, without technological aids. Blind mammals cannot respond differentially to colors. These capacities are something we can share with non-conceptual creatures such as pigeons – or as far as that goes, with photocells and thermostats. Second, one must have the capacity to produce *conceptually articulated* responses: to respond to red things not just by pecking at one button or closing one circuit rather than another, but by *claiming* that there is something red present. I think we should understand this latter capacity as the ability to take up a certain kind of stance in the space of reasons: to make a move in what Sellars calls "the game of giving and asking for reasons" of a sort that can both serve as and stand in need of reasons. A parrot could be taught to respond to red things by uttering the *noise* "That's red," but it would not be *saying* or *claiming* that anything was red. I think we can understand what it is lacking as the ability to tell what it would be committing itself to by such a claim, and what would entitle it to that commitment – that is, what follows from the claim that something is red (for instance, that it is colored and spatially extended) and what would be evidence for it (for instance, that it is scarlet) or against it (for instance, that it is green). But nothing in what follows depends on this particular way of understanding the dimension of endorsement that distinguishes observational reports from mere differential responses.

If it turns out that I can reliably differentially respond to a certain sort of state of affairs by non-inferentially reporting the presence of a state of affairs of that sort, and if I know that I am reliable in this way, then I think that true reports of this kind deserve to be called observationally acquired *knowledge*. This is in some ways a fairly radical view – though, I think, a defensible one. For one consequence of thinking of observation this way is that there is no particular line to be drawn between what is in principle observable and what is not. The only constraints are what a reporter can be trained under some circumstances reliably to differentiate, and what concepts the reporter can then key the application of to those responsive dispositions. Thus a properly trained physicist, who can respond systematically differently to differently shaped tracks in a cloud chamber will, if responding by non-inferentially reporting the presence of mu mesons, count as genuinely *observing* those subatomic particles. The physicist may start out by reporting the presence of hooked vapor trails and *inferring* the presence of mu mesons, but if the physicist then learns to eliminate the intermediate response and respond directly to the trails by reporting mu mesons, the physicist will be observing them. "Standard conditions" for observing mu mesons will include the presence of the cloud chamber, just as standard conditions for observing the colors of things include the presence of adequate light of the right kind. And the community for whom "mu meson" is an observation predicate will be much smaller and more highly specialized than the community for whom "red" is one. But these are differences of degree, rather than kind.

Again, it may be that if challenged about a non-inferential report of a mu meson, our physicist would *retreat* to an inferential justification, invoking the shape of the vapor trail that prompted the report. But we need not understand that retreat as signifying that the original report was, after all, the product of an *inference*. Rather, the claim of the presence of a mu meson, which was non-inferentially elicited as a direct response to a causal chain that included (in the favored cases) both mu mesons and vapor trails (but which was a report of mu mesons and not vapor trails – or retinal irradiations – because of the inferential role of the *concept* that was applied in it), can be justified inferentially after the fact by appealing to a *safer* non-inferential report, regarding the shape of the visible vapor trail. This report is safer in the dual sense that, first, the physicist is more reliable reporting the shapes of vapor trails than the presence of mu mesons (since the latter are more distal in the causal chain of reliably covarying events that culminate in the report, so there is more room for things to go wrong) and, second, the capacity reliably to report the presence of vapor trails of various shapes is much more widely shared among various reporters than is the capacity reliably to report the presence of mu mesons (even in the presence of a cloud chamber). The practice of justifying a challenged report by retreating to a safer one, from which the original claim can then be derived inferentially, should not (certainly *need* not) be taken to indicate that the original report was itself covertly the product of a process of inference.

As I would use the terms, following out the rationalist principle that I take McDowell also to endorse, to be aware of something (in the sense relevant to assessments of sapience) is just to apply a concept to it – that is, to make a judgment or undertake a doxastic commitment regarding it. Awareness deserves to be called "immediate" just in case it is not the product of a process of inference. Thus, beliefs acquired non-inferentially, by the exercise of reliable dispositions to respond differentially to stimuli of a certain sort by making corresponding reports ("corresponding" in the sense that what is reported is some element of the causal chain of reliably covarying events that culminates in the report in question), embody *immediate awareness* of the items reported. The first contrasting view (null hypothesis) with respect to which I want to place McDowell's view is then that this is the *only* sense of "immediate awareness" we need in order to understand our perceptual knowledge of the world around us.

If we press this picture of observation as consisting just in the exercise of reliable differential responsive dispositions to apply concepts,[9] even more *outré* examples present themselves. Suppose that at least some people can be conditioned to discriminate male from female newly hatched chicks, just by being corrected until they become reliable. They have no idea what features of the chicks they are presented with they are responding differentially to, but they not only become reliable, they also come to *know* that they are reliable. When they non-inferentially respond to a chick by classifying it as male, if they are correct, I think they have observational knowledge of that fact. (And I think McDowell is prepared to agree.) This can be so even if it is later discovered (I'm told that this is true) that the chicken sexers are wrong in thinking that they are discriminating the chicks *visually* – that in fact, although they are not aware of it, the discrimination is being done on an *olfactory* basis. According to this way of thinking about observation, what sense is in play can *only* be discriminated by discovering what sorts of alterations of conditions degrade or improve the performance of the reliable reporters. If altering light levels does not change their reliability, but blocking their noses does, then they are working on the basis of scent, not of sight.[10]

McDowell thinks that although there can be cases of what is in a broad sense *observational* knowledge like this, they must be sharply distinguished from cases of genuine *perceptual* knowledge, for instance being able to see shapes or colors. That is, he rejects the suggestion that the latter be assimilated to the former. When we see colors and shapes, we have perceptual *experiences* corresponding to the judgments we go on to make or the beliefs we go on to form. The chicken sexers in my example do not have perceptual experiences of chicks as male or female. They just respond *blindly*, though they have learned to trust those blind responses. There is for them no *appearance* of the chicks *as* male or female.

Put another way, McDowell is committed to there being *two kinds* of beliefs acquired non-inferentially by the exercise of reliable dispositions to respond differentially to stimuli by reporting elements of the causal chain that culminates in the report. In genuine perception, the belief is the result of *endorsing* the content of a perceptual *experience*. In the other sort (what might be called "mere observation") the belief is acquired blindly, that is in the absence of a perceptual experience with the same content. Under the right circumstances, one just finds oneself with the belief in question. But this sort of belief formation is not a case of facts becoming visible (or more generally, perceptible) to us. Although these beliefs are non-inferentially elicited from the believer by environmental stimuli, the warrant for those beliefs is in an important sense inferential. The believer's justification for beliefs of this sort depends on drawing conclusions from an antecedent claim of reliability. In this respect, the believer is in no different position than a third-person observer would be.

There is certainly an intuitive appeal to this distinction. But I worry whether its appeal is *merely* intuitive, or whether there is important explanatory work for the distinction to do. After all, we have lots of residually Cartesian intuitions. This worry is a pragmatic one, in the spirit of Quine's query in "Two Dogmas of Empiricism" concerning what features of our linguistic practice – the way we actually use language – reflect or are explained by the distinction of claims into analytic and synthetic. Intuitions that are quite possibly (I'm inclined to say *necessarily*) infected by prior theoretical commitments are not to the point here. Once properly trained, we just find ourselves responding to visible red things by calling them red. And in this usage, "visible" need mean no more than "in standard conditions for visual observation", that is in good light, on an unoccluded sight line to the observer, and so on.

Once we have relinquished the Myth of the Given, we must be careful not to assimilate the making of such non-inferential judgments to the identification of something by criteria. I may apply the concept "white oak" to a tree because I have noticed the characteristic bilateral, symmetrical, roundly lobed leaves. It makes sense to ask how I knew that it was a white oak, and an answer can be given. But in the case of red things, there is no set of features I am noticing, from which I conclude that they are red. I can just tell red things by looking at them. If there weren't some features like this, there couldn't be any empirical knowledge of the sort exemplified by my white oak judgment either. I can say that the patch looks red, in a sense of "looks" that is no more committive than that involved in saying I can tell red things by looking at them. That is the only sense in which the world need *appear* to me *as* anything.

In "Empiricism and the Philosophy of Mind," Sellars offers a recipe for introducing "looks" or "appears" talk, wherever there is a non-inferential reporting practice. Whenever a reporter suspects her own reliability under certain conditions of observation, she can *express* her usually reliable disposition to report something as being φ, but *withhold* her *endorsement* of that claim, by saying only that it *looks* (or *appears*) φ. The chicken sexers are certainly able to introduce "looks" and "appears" talk in this way. But McDowell's claim is then that there is an important difference between such uses of these locutions and their use to report perceptual experiences. He thinks that the capacity to have perceptual experiences is different from, and more fundamental than, the capacity to make non-inferential observations of mu mesons in cloud chambers and of the sexes of chickens. Unless we could have perceptual experiences, we could not make any observations at all – even though not all observations of a state of affairs involve perceptual experiences of those states of affairs. That is, the capacity to become non-inferentially informed about the world by learning *blindly* to respond differentially to it depends upon a more basic capacity for states of affairs to become immediately apparent in perception. Thus it is important to McDowell to distinguish a notion of conceptually structured perception that is *narrower* than the merely responsive notion of conceptually structured observation I have sketched.

I asked above, in a pragmatic spirit, about what explanatory work such a distinction does for us. McDowell has a response, of course. It is that without the notion of conceptually articulated perceptual experience that distinguishes genuine perception from merely responsively acquired non-inferential belief, we cannot understand the empirical content of *any* of our claims. For without that notion, we are doomed to embrace one horn of the dilemma from which *Mind and World* sets out to free us. In McDowell's view, the picture of observation I have been suggesting may be all we need substitutes mere *causal* constraint by the world for the genuinely *rational* constraint that is required for us to make intelligible to ourselves the idea of our beliefs as *about* the world without us. For that notion of aboutness requires that our beliefs answer *rationally* for their correctness to the facts they purport to present, not merely that they are causally occasioned by them. This way of working out semantic empiricism presents deep and important issues, which I cannot pursue here. (I have addressed some of them in a preliminary fashion elsewhere.[11])

Rather than press that set of global philosophical issues, I focus here on the distinction McDowell is obliged to draw between genuine perception and what I have been calling "mere observation" to raise a much more local and limited issue. What sort of a fact is it that in some cases where we non-inferentially acquire a true belief by exercising a reliable disposition non-inferentially to respond to the fact in question by acquiring the belief there is a perceptual experience present, while in others there is not? How would we go about settling the question of whether the physicist has genuine perceptual experiences of mu mesons? Is there any way in principle to tell other than asking? And if we do ask, is there any chance that the physicist is wrong, because the physicist has been taught a bad theory? Could I think I was having perceptual experiences of mu mesons or the maleness of chickens when I was not, or vice versa? Do we know just by having a perceptual experience what sensory modality it corresponds to (so that the – supposed – fact that the chicken sexers get this wrong is decisive evidence that they do not have genuine perceptual experiences)? The answers to questions such as these determine just how classically Cartesian McDowell's notion of perceptual experience is – and so, from my point of view, just how suspicious we should be of it. I do not assert that his answers to these questions will be Cartesian ones. I don't know how to answer them, and do not find much help in *Mind and World*.

III

Putting things in terms of how the world appears to us raises a danger of getting McDowell wrong in the other direction, however. For a natural response to the sort of distinction of cases on which I am claiming McDowell insists – at least for philosophers familiar with the empiricist tradition McDowell is extending – is to think that what sets off mere observation of the sort epitomized by the mu meson and chicken sexing cases from genuine perception is that the physicist and the chicken sexer are not reporting their awareness of any *secondary qualities*. Being a mu meson or a male chick are primary qualities, and so not directly or immediately experienceable in the sense in which secondary qualities such as *red* are. For traditional empiricism took it that our awareness of the perceptible world is, as it were, *painted* in secondary qualities: qualities that nothing outside the mind can literally have, purely experiential properties more or less reliably induced in minds as the effects of external bodies.[12] These secondary qualities correlate with, and so *represent*, features of perceptible objects. But since they are merely the effects those features have on suitably prepared and situated minds, they do not *present* properties literally exhibited by the objects themselves. Phenomena of this sort, the secondary qualities of things, are all that is directly or immediately perceivable. Coming to know about anything else is the result of making *inferences* from the occurrence of the experiences of secondary qualities they occasion in us.

Following Gareth Evans, McDowell has endorsed a pragmatic account of the distinction between secondary and primary qualities. (By calling it "pragmatic" I mean to indicate that it defines the distinction in terms of differences in the *use* of expressions for – predicates used to attribute the occurrence of – secondary and primary qualities.) According to this way of understanding things, to take φ to express a secondary quality concept, is to take it that one cannot count as having mastered the use of "φ" talk[13] unless one has also mastered the use of "looks-φ" talk. This criterion distinguishes predicates such as "red," which express secondary qualities, from those such as "square," which express primary qualities. For one does not count as fully understanding the concept *red* unless one knows what it is for things to *look* red; while a blind geometer *can* count as fully understanding the concept *square* even if the geometer cannot discriminate one by looking at it. According to the minimally committive account of observation sketched above, one can learn "looks-φ" talk just in case one has mastered the *non*-inferential circumstances of appropriate application of the concept φ – that is, just in case one has both mastered the inferential role of the concept, and been trained into the reliable differential responsive dispositions that key its non-inferential application to the apparent presence of the reported state of affairs.[14]

Since McDowell's "minimal empiricism"[15] seeks to rehabilitate what was right in the appeals to experience that motivated classical empiricism, it is tempting to understand his distinction between genuine perceptual experience and mere non-inferential observation of environing circumstances in terms of the role of secondary qualities in the former. Perceptual experience, the thought would run, is always experience immediately *of* secondary qualities. That is what is missing in the mu meson and chicken sexing cases. (Not that there are not secondary qualities involved in those cases, but rather that what is reported in those cases is not the occurrence of secondary qualities.) But this would be to misunderstand McDowell's position. For he thinks we can have perceptual experience of some *primary* qualities, not just *secondary* ones. Thus shapes, for instance, can be visible and tangible – genuinely the subjects of perceptual experience. Where there are perceptual experiences, there are appearances, which can be reported by the use of "looks" talk. And since McDowell admits that a certain attenuated form of "looks" talk applies even to *mere* observation, without corresponding perceptual experiences, it should be marked that in these cases it will be "looks" talk in the stronger sense. But the existence of perceptual experiences that are being reported by such "looks" talk does not require that the mastery of such talk is an essential feature of mastery of the concepts being applied. Talk of perceptual experiences is not a way of talking about secondary qualities. All immediate awareness of secondary qualities involves perceptual experiences, but not necessarily vice versa.

Here it is important to keep in mind a distinction between two different ways in which one might understand the Evans–McDowell characterization of secondary qualities in terms of "looks" talk. I claimed above that Sellars gives us a recipe for introducing a use of "looks-φ" (or, more generally, "appears-φ") corresponding to any predicate φ that has a non-inferential reporting use. According to this understanding, there is no problem with the physicist talking about things looking like mu mesons, or the chicken sexer talking about things looking like (or appearing to be) male chicks. If the Evans–McDowell criterion for being a secondary quality concept is combined with this understanding of the use of "looks" (or "appears"), then what results is the notion of concepts that are *essentially observable* – in the sense that in order fully to master the concept, one must have mastered its *non*-inferential circumstances of application. *Red* is pretty clearly like this, and *mu meson* is pretty clearly not like this. But just as we can introduce a use for "looks to be a mu meson," we could also introduce another concept, which is just like *mu meson* except that mastery of the non-inferential use of the expression, and of the corresponding "looks" locution, *is* required for certification as having mastered that concept. And similarly for any merely observational property. This fact may suggest that the notion of *essentially observable concept* should not be identified with the classical notion of *secondary quality concept*.

In fact, this is McDowell's view. For this reason, he does not understand the appeal to "looks" in the definition of secondary qualities in the minimal Sellarsian sense identified above. For in this sense, there could be experience of secondary qualities where there are no corresponding perceptual experiences in his sense. And he is committed to perceptual experiences being *necessary*, though not sufficient, for awareness of secondary qualities. McDowell understands the responsive use of "looks-φ" locutions as genuine *reports* – not, as on the minimal Sellarsian line rehearsed above, merely expressions of dispositions to make endorsements one is not in fact making. What "looks" claims report (at least in the central cases) is just perceptual experiences.

I have situated McDowell's notion of perceptual experience between a broader notion and a narrower one – between the concept of knowledge non-inferentially acquired by applying concepts as the result of reliable differential responsive dispositions, and the concept of immediate awareness of secondary qualities. As I pointed out above, McDowell denies that the broader concept of merely non-inferential knowledge is independent of that of perceptual experience: if we could not have perceptual experiences, then we could not know things non-inferentially at all. (Indeed, he thinks we could not know *anything* at all.) I would like to end this discussion with a question, his answer to which I have not been able to determine from McDowell's writings: could there be perceptual experience, for McDowell, if there were no secondary qualities? That is, could anyone have perceptual experiences of primary qualities if they could not also have perceptual experiences of secondary qualities? If not, why not? If so, what would it be like? And once again, what sort of questions are these? How ought one to go about addressing them? Is it a matter for introspection, or for empirical investigation? If purely philosophical argumentation is needed, what are the criteria of adequacy according to which we should assess the answers?

IV

In closing, I would like to add a further query. If we look at the end of *Mind and World*, we see that we can have non-inferential knowledge of *normative* facts: of meanings, for instance, and of how it is appropriate to act. Coming to be able to make such non-inferential judgments is part of being brought up properly, part of acquiring our second nature. Along something like the same lines, in his earlier writings, McDowell has urged (in opposition to Davidson's interpretational view) that fully competent speakers of a language do not *infer* the meanings of others' utterances from the noises they make, rather they directly or immediately *hear* those meanings. Coming to speak the language is coming to be able to *perceive* the meanings of the remarks of other speakers of it. The connection I have in mind between these claims is that claims about what someone means are normative claims. They have consequences concerning what that someone has *committed* themselves to, what they are *responsible* for, what it would take for their claim to be *correct*, and so on. So McDowell's view is that *normative* facts are non-inferentially knowable.

It has always seemed to me to be one of the great advantages of the account of observational knowledge in terms of reliable differential responsive dispositions to apply concepts non-inferentially that it makes perfect sense of these claims. If I have mastered the use of some normative vocabulary (whether pertaining to meanings, or to how it is proper to behave non-linguistically), and if I can be trained reliably to apply it non-inferentially, as a differential response to the occurrence of normatively specified states of affairs, then I can have observational knowledge of those normative states of affairs: I can *see* (or at least *perceive*[16]) what it is appropriate to do or say. Normative concepts are no worse off than concepts like *mu meson* in terms of their capacity to acquire observational uses. So here is my final question for McDowell: is this *mere* non-inferential knowledge? Or are the normative statuses also perceptually experienceable, for McDowell? I don't think he commits himself on this, any more than he does on the question of whether secondary qualities are necessary for experience. Indeed, one could ask further: are there (can there be) secondary qualities corresponding to essentially normative states of affairs that are non-inferentially knowable?

I think that these are important questions in their own right. It seems to me a virtue of McDowell's writings about sensory experience that they bring such questions into view. I am also inclined to think that I do not fully understand McDowell's concept of perceptual experience until I know how it bears on this sort of question. McDowell does not address himself to these questions, and I do not know what he would say about them if he did. I do suspect[17] that his response will be in the form of deflection: interesting questions though these be, the project of Mind and World does not require that they be addressed. For the project of that work is heavily diagnostic and lightly therapeutic, but not at all theoretical. Its task is not, as its author understands it, to present a theory of content, or of perceptual experience. It is rather to make evident to its readers the common presuppositions powering an oscillation between two equally unsatisfactory ways of talking about the role of experience in empirical thought. It aims further at giving us some instruction in how we might talk once we have freed ourselves from attachment to those fatal philosophical assumptions that structure so much of the tradition by which we have been shaped. Doing that does not, the claim would be, require taking a stand on every potentially controversial issue that could arise in the vicinity once we have thrown off the fetters in which commitment to defective (though after Mind and World intelligibly and forgiveably tempting) ways of thinking about nature and the relation between causal and rational constraint have bound us.

The response I am putting in McDowell's mouth has considerable force. But in the end, I do not find it satisfactory. It seems to me that the therapeutic dimension of the enterprise of Mind and World involves a commitment to there being at least some satisfactory way of extending the things he has said about observation, perception, and sensory experience so as to answer the sort of questions our following out of his remarks has raised. For instance, he is committed to there being a distinction between two sorts of non-inferentially acquired knowledge of states of affairs: in one kind there is an experience of that state of affairs, and in the other not. But, we should ask, does this distinction manifest itself in any way or explain anything outside the confines of the theory? (Compare Quine's corresponding question about the analytic/synthetic distinction.) Or is it real only in the way the question of whether Socinianism is a heresy once had to be taken seriously, because until it was settled we wouldn't know who the true Pope is? I think the issue of whether the ways McDowell has recommended we talk about perceptual experience can be extended so as to afford sensible answers to the sorts of questions I have argued his discussion implicitly raises delineates a fair dimension along which the adequacy of his story should be appraised.

McDowell's bold and ingenious rehabilitation of the empiricists' concept of experience requires us to make conceptual distinctions far subtler than any the tradition worried about. He also gives us the conceptual raw materials to make those distinctions clear. This is all pure advance. I have sought here to rehearse some of these distinctions, and to use them to invite McDowell to commit himself in the terms he has provided on issues that he has not yet formally addressed.

Notes

* An abbreviated version of this chapter has appeared in Hungarian translation in the Proceedings of a Conference on *Mind and World* held at the Janus Pannonius University in Pecs, Hungary, in May 1998.

1 *Mind and World* (Cambridge, MA: Harvard University Press, 1994), p.xii (from the Introduction, added in the paperback edition of 1996).

2 Originally published in 1956, this classic essay has recently been reprinted, with an Introduction by Richard Rorty and a section-by-section Study Guide by Robert Brandom (Cambridge, MA: Harvard University Press, 1997).

3 In this respect he parts company with the picture I present in *Making It Explicit* (Cambridge, MA: Harvard University Press, 1994), as he makes clear in his comments on the book in "Brandom on Inference and Representation," *Philosophy and Phenomenological Research* 57(1): 157ff. (March 1997).

4 What he calls "sense impressions" are *causal* antecedents of perceptual judgments, but do not serve to *justify* them.

5 *Making It Explicit*. See especially the first half of chap. four.

6 *Philosophical Investigations* §95.

7 On this point, see his "Knowledge and the Internal," and my companion piece "Knowledge and the Social Articulation of the Space of Reasons," both in *Philosophy and Phenomenological Research* 55(4) (December 1995).

8 In "Epistemology Naturalized," in *Ontological Relativity and Other Essays* (New York: Columbia University Press, 1969).

9 I develop and defend such an account in chap. four of *Making It Explicit*.

10 I owe this way of thinking about the difference between sensory modalities in terms of conditions of reliability to Lionel Shapiro.

11 "Perception and Rational Constraint," in Enrique Villaneuva (ed.), *Perception* (*Philosophical Issues*, vol. 7, Atascadero, CA: Ridgeview 1996), pp.241–260. Abbreviated version published in *Philosophy and Phenomenological Research* 58(2): 369–374 (June 1998).

12 Berkeley is the paradigmatic defender of such a view, but as an implicit theme, this way of thinking about secondary qualities was pervasive in pre-Kantian empiricism.

13 Sellars glosses grasping a concept as mastering the use of a word.

14 McDowell will insist that a richer notion of mastering "looks" (or, more generally, "appears") talk – one that involves the reporting of perceptual experiences, not just the conceptually structured exercise of reliable differential responsive dispositions – should be brought to bear in defining secondary qualities. But this qualification does not make a difference for the use I am making here of the Evans–McDowell characterization of secondary qualities.

15 His characterization, in the Introduction to the paperback edition of *Mind and World*.

16 Perhaps not "see" or "hear," since these terms are committive as regards sense *modality* – commitments to be cashed out, as I indicated above, in terms of the nature of the conditions that degrade or improve reliability. Notice that in this sense it *is* appropriate to talk about *hearing* the meaning of someone's oral utterance, and seeing the meaning of their written remark.

17 Based on our conversations on the matter in connection with our Joint Seminar on Perception (University of Pittsburgh, Spring 1998).

6

FOUNDATIONALISM AND THE INNER–OUTER DISTINCTION

Charles Taylor

I

I hardly know where to begin in commenting on John McDowell's rich and interesting *Mind and World*. Of course, everything I say stands against a background of massive agreement with the main line of his thinking, and excitement and admiration for his formulations. *"Ein Bild hielt uns gefangen"*[1] indeed, and it was and is a powerful one, which seeps into not only our philosophical thought, but many other domains of our culture. It is a picture of the mind in the world, a dualist one in which, as McDowell shows, the understanding of the world is dominated by a certain modern conception of natural law. This helps to generate a conception of what valid knowing is, which is no small matter in our culture, one of whose underpinnings and most prestigious achievements is science.

We might call this conception the "Inside/Outside" (I/O) one, although this is not McDowell's expression, and I'm not sure he'd agree with this revision. A crucial feature of this view is that it portrays our understanding of the world as taking place in a zone, surrounded by and (hopefully) in interaction with a world, which is thus seen as playing the role of Outside to its Inside. This deep and powerful image raises the issue of the boundary. Inside and outside have to interact; this is indeed implicit in the very idea of knowledge: what goes on in the inner zone is meant to be in some way at least partly modeled on what exists outside. But how are we to conceive this interaction?

According to the laws of the world, naturalistically conceived, this interaction would have to be understood like the proceedings in disenchanted inanimate nature. Things "impress" themselves on the senses, "surface irradiations" take place. But what we understand as taking place inside should function according to the laws of a "space of reasons"; they stand as justifications or as rational challenges to each other, they establish relations of validation and refutation. For the last three centuries, the events at the boundary – variously referred to as "ideas," "impressions," "sense data," "surface irradiations" – have been caught in a kind of conceptual crossfire, at once causal imprintings within disenchanted nature, and reasons within a rationally evolving view of things. But the theories which were developed out of this dominant image never succeeded in giving a coherent account of this double existence, in explaining how being one of these things enabled being the other, or even how the two facets could properly coexist.

It is now fashionable in virtually all philosophical milieux to be extremely impatient with this way of thinking, and to claim to have transcended or "deconstructed" it. But McDowell is rightly unconvinced by the loud cries of victory arising on all sides. It is all too easy to think one has laid the problems to rest, even escaped the image, while remaining prisoner of its assumptions at a deeper level.

One "way out" would be to reconstruct the inner zone on the same explanatory principles as disenchanted nature. This is the path of much contemporary cognitive psychology, particularly those strands which have invested deeply in the computer model of the mind. This way of thought is, of course, deeply indebted to the classical dualism, because it has simply taken one of the terms defined by that dualism and universalized it at the expense of the other. For its adepts, this seems a magnificent solution, but for those like McDowell who are unconvinced by the reductive reconstructions of mind, it is just another avatar of the problem: the prisoners of the dominant image have just moved to another cell.

Another popular line, championed by Richard Rorty, is to pour scorn on the hopeless intellectual shifts by which philosophers of the dominant image have unsuccessfully tried to resolve its difficulties, and to call for the abandonment of this whole field of endeavor. This stance is often accompanied (though not much by Rorty) by an (I think invalid) appeal to Wittgenstein and his notorious refusal to engage in positive philosophizing. McDowell rightly sees that this line won't do. The I/O image is too powerfully embedded in our beliefs and (scientific, technical, freedom-oriented) way of life. Just repudiating it won't release us. We need to think through the philosophical motivations which generate I/O and give an alternative interpretation of them, since if left alone, these motivations retain their power to regenerate I/O in ever new forms.

Of course, the aim of this activity is not to resolve the puzzles arising within I/O, and in particular not the one concerning the two natures of the input, on their own terms. The point is rather to delegitimate these terms. But it is possible to misrepresent this activity as simply another attempt to wrestle with the old dilemmas. Hence McDowell must come across to Rorty as still a prisoner of the I/O image. While ironically, on McDowell's side (and mine), it is Rorty who in his refusal to face the deep motivations and give an alternative account of them seems to be perpetuating the imprisonment.

II

Exposing the motivations, offering an alternative account: both these things McDowell does admirably. I'd like to offer some comments on both of these, and also some further remarks on the importance of this whole debate. The background to my comments is the continued existence of an interesting diversity of approach in the camp of those who really offer a way out of the I/O prison. One line of thinking has arisen largely within "analytic" philosophy, fed by the work of Wittgenstein, Strawson, and others. The other is "continental" in origin, the major names being Heidegger and Merleau-Ponty. Both find a common starting point in Kant. Despite this, for a long time, contacts were very rare, but this is fortunately ceasing to be so. McDowell's argument draws heavily on Hegel and Gadamer, for instance, who were long seen as simply of relevance to the other tradition. A "fusion of horizons" seems imminent.

But it is not yet complete. There remain interesting differences still. Since my thinking on these matters has been mainly shaped by Heidegger and Merleau-Ponty, I will play the "continental" foil to what is still "analytic" in McDowell's account. Hopefully some interesting points may come to light.

First, I would like to add a codicil or two to McDowell's account of the motivations for the epistemological imbroglio, an account with which I am in substantial agreement. Critical reasoning is something we do, an activity, in the realm of spontaneity and freedom. But, as far as knowledge of the world is concerned, it is meant to be responsive to the way things are. Spontaneity has to be merged somehow with receptivity. But it is hard to see how this can be, if we conceive of spontaneity as a kind of limitless freedom, which at the point of contact has to hit a world under adamantine, post-Galilean "laws of nature." The schizophrenic nature of boundary events, inexplicably partaking of both nature and freedom, is an inevitable consequence of this way of seeing things.

But there are also other reasons. The standard notion of the impression, or sense datum, or minimal input is overdetermined. For it is also generated by the demands of the foundationalist enterprise. Miles Burnyeat has, I believe, an interesting point about the novelty of Descartes's invocation of skepticism in, say, the First Meditation, in relation to his ancient sources.[2] Through this, he manages to parlay a doubt about our everyday certainties into a certainty about the nature of doubt. Instead of remaining in the incurable uncertainty that rehearsing the sources of error was meant to bring on, the solvent of doubt is made to hit one irreducible kernel, namely, our experience of the world. Perhaps I am not really sitting before the fire, clothed, but it is clear that I think that I am so situated. The nature of this item of experience is quite clear and indubitable. Modern phenomenology has argued that Descartes didn't have the right to help himself to this clear delimitation of doubt, but the rights and wrongs are not to my purpose here. What is relevant is the role of this distinctly demarcated "idée adventice" in Descartes's foundationalist strategy.

Doubt reaches its limit at the existence of a mental item which purports to be about the external world, and presents a determinate content. The issue of skepticism can therefore be exactly stated; we can be certain about the nature of doubt. The issue is, do these purported contents really hold of the external world, or do these ideas lie? A case in which the latter unhappy condition might hold would be where a malign spirit had set out to fool us. But now this, and any other such systematic cause of error, can be ruled out by our demonstrating that we are the product of a benign, veracious Creator.

How convincing the argument is doesn't concern me; what is important is that the foundationalist argument required the stabilization of doubt in a clearly defined issue. We can't be left reeling under the cumulative effect of all the possible sources of error, where the ancients abandon us, with the injunction to cease the fruitless quest for certain knowledge. The reasons for doubt have to be shown to come down to a single clear issue, which we can then hope to handle. This requires the invention of the strange boundary event, whose dual nature causes all the trouble that McDowell so well demonstrates.

On one hand, it has to be about the world, present a unit of information, be a small item of knowledge, and hence belong to the space of reasons; on the other, it has to be prior to all interpretation, its having the content it has must be a brute fact, not in any way the result of thought or reasoning activity on our part. This latter feature emerges in the argument in the Sixth Meditation about possible sources of error, like the round tower which looks square in the distance. In order that this mistake, even though the result of a general feature of appearances-at-a-distance, not be laid at God's door, thus refuting the thesis of his goodness and veracity, we have to argue that the erroneous conclusion here results from some (in this case sloppy, unfocussed) inference on our part. For this, we are responsible, and we ought to have been more careful. What God stands surety for are the genuine cases of interpretation-free appearance. The system starts from these.

I have been discussing the motives for believing in this notion of a brute input within Descartes's philosophy. But it is clear that we can detach it from his idiosyncratic arguments, and see how it has to figure in all foundationalist epistemologies. The aim of foundationalism is to peel back all the layers of inference and interpretation, and get back to something genuinely prior to them all, a brute Given: then to build back up, checking all the links in the interpretive chain. Foundationalism involves the double move, stripping down to the unchallengeable, and building back up. Unless at some point we hit bedrock, if interpretation goes on for ever ("all the way down," in Dreyfus's apt expression),[3] the foundationalist project is ruined.

My thesis is that an important motive behind the I/O picture, which generates all the aporiai of the sense datum, is the foundationalist project itself. It is not just that the picture of the mind in disenchanted nature generates the notion of the brute input, a site for insoluble philosophical problems, as an unfortunate side-effect. I think this is true; that is, indeed, one motive. But it is also true that the foundationalist drive generates this unfortunate notion for its own purposes.

What takes place is a kind of ontologizing of proper method. The right way to deal with puzzles and build a reliable body of knowledge is to break the issue down into sub-questions, identify the chains of inference, dig down to an inference-free starting point, and then build by a reliable method. Once this comes to seem the all-purpose nostrum for thinking, then one has an overwhelming motivation to believe that that is how the mind actually works in taking in the world. Because if not, one has to draw the devastating conclusion that the only reliable method is inapplicable in the most important context of all, where we build our knowledge of the world.

Hence the notion of the brute input, under different names, goes marching on. Locke argues for something of this sort in his metaphor of building materials. We start with simple ideas, as builders start with their given materials. Construction is not an activity which can go on "all the way down." It has to start somewhere with things we just find lying around. And so must it be with knowledge.

Again, the vogue in cognitive psychology for AI-inspired models of the mind was powered by the same double set of motives: on the one hand ontological – the mind is set in disenchanted nature, it is a product of the brain which is itself a piece of this nature, therefore it must work fundamentally like a machine; on the other hand methodological – what is thinking anyway? It is building chains of inference from minimal starting points. These starting points are givens. And so that's how the mind must work.

III

The above point was meant as an addition to McDowell's account, which remains valid, I think, whether or not the view I've been propounding is true.

But I now want to turn to a more serious difference between the two traditions. And here I'm genuinely not sure whether we're dealing with a disagreement, or just a shift in emphasis.

The difference arises within an important common aim. McDowell makes clear that he wants to break out of the I/O image. In Lecture II, section 2, of *Mind and World*, he speaks of "experience as openness to the layout of reality"; "*that things are thus and so*, is also a perceptible fact, an aspect of the perceptible world" (p.26). And elsewhere, he approves the Hegelian idea that reasoning is not limited from the outside.

Now in Heidegger and Merleau-Ponty, this point is made through an account of what it is to "be in the world," or "*être au monde*," and these accounts are rather rich, detailed, and multi-facetted.[4] Is this just a matter of one tradition tending to give a lot of vivid particulars, to add to philosophical argument a power of literary description? Is the difference in this sense merely "rhetorical"?

This might be so, but one thing gives me pause. There is a dimension of these two accounts, to which there seems nothing corresponding in McDowell's story. More ominously, where he discusses Evans's position in Lecture III, what he rejects in it seems to be precisely an attempt to formulate this dimension (as I interpret Evans).

Heidegger, Merleau-Ponty, and (I think) Evans portray human conceptual thinking as embedded in an ordinary way of living and moving around in the world, and dealing with things, which is in an important sense pre-conceptual; what Dreyfus calls "everyday coping." Dealing with things pre-conceptually can't involve rational, critical reflection on world or action; it doesn't exhibit Kantian "spontaneity" at its fullest. But at the same time this interaction can't be understood just in the terms of stripped down, post-Galilean nature. We can't understand the causal processes here the way we understand them in inanimate nature. There is something in nature between full spontaneity and mere mechanism.

Living with things involves a certain kind of understanding (which we might also call "pre-understanding"). That is, things figure for us in their meaning or relevance for our purposes, desires, activities. As I navigate my way along the path up the hill, my mind totally absorbed anticipating the difficult conversation I'm going to have at my destination, I treat the different features of the terrain as obstacles, supports, openings, invitations to tread more warily, or run freely, etc. Even when I'm not thinking of them these things have those relevances for me; I know my way about among them.

This is non-conceptual; or put another way, language isn't playing any direct role. Through language, we (humans) have the capacity to focus on things, to pick an X out as an X; we pick it out as something which (correctly) bears a description "X," and this puts our identification in the domain of potential critique (is this really an X? Is the vocabulary to which X belongs the appropriate one for this domain/purpose? And so forth). At some point, because of some breakdown, or just through intrinsic interest, I may come to focus on some aspects of this navigational know-how. I may begin to classify things as "obstacles" or "facilitations," and this will change the way I live in the world. But in all sorts of ways, I live in the world and deal with it, without having done this.

Ordinary coping isn't conceptual. But at the same time, it can't be understood in just inanimate–causal terms. This denial can be understood in two ways. Maximally, it runs athwart a common ambition of, for example, much cognitive psychology, which aims precisely to give one day a reductive account in machine terms. I would also bet my money that the denial will turn out right in this strong sense, and that the reductive ambition is ultimately a fantasy. But for our purposes, we just need to focus on a minimal sense: that in the absence of this promised but far distant mechanistic account, our only way of making sense of animals, and of our own pre-conceptual goings-on, is through something like pre-understanding. That is, we have to see the world impinging on these beings in relevance terms; or alternatively put, we see them as agents.

We find it impossible not to extend this courtesy to animals, as I have just indicated, and McDowell certainly agrees (p.182). But in our case, the reasons are stronger. When we focus on some feature of our dealing with the world and bring it to speech, it doesn't come across as just like a discovery of some unsuspected fact, like, for example, the change in landscape at a turn in the road, or being informed that what we do bears some fancy technical name (M. Jourdain speaking prose). When I finally allow myself to recognize that what has been making me uncomfortable in this conversation is that I'm feeling jealous, I feel that in a sense I wasn't totally ignorant of this before. I knew it without knowing it. It has a kind of intermediate status between known and quite unknown. It was a kind of proto-knowledge, an environment propitious for the transformation that conceptual focus brings, even though there may also have been resistances.

Now I said above that the Heidegger/Merleau-Ponty thesis is that our conceptual thinking is "embedded" in everyday coping. The point of this image can be taken in two bites, as it were. The first is that coping is prior and pervasive ("*zunächst and zumeist*"). We start off just as coping infants, and only later are inducted in speech. And even as adults, much of our lives consists in this coping. This couldn't be otherwise. In order to focus on something, we have to keep going – as I was on the path, while thinking of the difficult conversation; or as the person is in the laboratory, walking around, picking up the retort, while thinking hard about the theoretical issues (or maybe, what's for lunch).

But the second bite goes deeper. It's the point usually expressed with the term "background." The mass of coping is an essential support to the episodes of conceptual focus in our lives, not just in the infrastructural sense that something has to be carrying our mind around from library to laboratory and back. More fundamentally, the background understanding we need to make the sense we do of the pieces of thinking we engage in resides in our ordinary coping.

I walk up the path, and enter the field and notice: the goldenrod is out. A particulate take on the world, rather of the kind that boundary events are supposed to be on the I/O; except that under the pressure of foundationalism, they sometimes are forced to be more basic – yellow here now – and only build up to goldenrod as a later inference. One of the errors of classical epistemology was to see in this kind of take the building blocks of our knowledge of the world. We put it together bit by bit out of such pieces. So foundationalism had to believe.

One of the reasons that Kant is a crucial figure in the overcoming of the I/O – here I heartily agree with McDowell – is that he put paid to this picture. We can't build our view of the world out of percepts like "the goldenrod is out," or even "yellow here now," because nothing would count as such a percept unless it already had its place in a world. Minimally, nothing could be a percept without a surrounding sense of myself as perceiving agent, moving in some surroundings, of which this bit of yellow is a feature. If we try to think all this orientation away, then we get something which is close to unthinkable as an experience, "less even than a dream," as Kant puts it.[5] What would it be like just to experience yellow, never mind whether it's somewhere in the world out there or just in my head? A very dissociated experience, not a very promising building block for a world-view.

Our understanding of the world is holistic from the start. There is no such thing as the single, independent percept. Something has this status only within a wider context which is understood, taken for granted, but for the most part not focussed on. Moreover, it couldn't all be focussed on, not just because it is very widely ramifying, but because it doesn't consist of some definite number of pieces. We can bring this out by reflecting that the number of ways in which the taken-for-granted background could in specific circumstances fail is not delimitable.

Invoking this undelimitable background was a favorite argumentative gambit of Wittgenstein in both the *Philosophical Investigations* and *On Certainty*. He shows, for instance, that understanding an ostensive definition is not just a matter of fixing a particular; there is a whole surrounding understanding of what kind of thing is being discussed (the shape or the color), of this being a way of teaching meaning, and the like. In our ordinary investigations, we take for granted a continuing world; so that our whole proceedings would be radically undercut by the "discovery," if one could make it, that the universe started five minutes ago. But that can't be taken to mean that there is a definite list of things that we have ruled out, including among others that the universe started five minutes ago.

Now this indefinitely extending background understanding is sustained and evolved through our ordinary coping. My recognition that the goldenrod is out is sustained by a context being in place, for example, that I'm now entering a field, and it's August. And I'm not focussing on all this. I know where I am, because I walked here, and when I am because I've been living the summer, but these are not reflective inferences; they are just part of the understanding I have in everyday coping. I might indeed take a more reflective stance, and theorize the existence of goldenrod in certain geographical locations of the Earth's surface in a certain season etc.; just as I might lay out the environment I normally walk about in by drawing a map. But this wouldn't end the embedding of reflective knowledge in ordinary coping. The map becomes useless, indeed ceases to be a map in any meaningful sense for me, unless I can use it to help me get around. Theoretical knowledge has to be situated in relation to everyday coping to be the knowledge that it is.

In this way, embedding is inescapable; and that in the stronger sense: that all exercises of reflective, conceptual thought only have the content they have situated in a context of background understanding which underlies and is generated in everyday coping.

But then the enriched description of our predicament in Heidegger and Merleau-Ponty, the analyses of "*In-der-Welt-Sein*" and "*être au monde*," seem more than literary elaborations of the basic point that experience is open, that the kind of boundary supposed by the I/O doesn't exist. They are meant to explain, as McDowell's argument is, how it can be that the places at which our view is shaped by the world, in perception, are not just causal impingings, but are sites of the persuasive acquisition of belief. But they argue that one can never give a persuasive account of this, if one focusses just on belief formation at the conceptual level.

We are able to form conceptual beliefs guided by our surroundings, because we live in a pre-conceptual engagement with these which involves understanding. Transactions in this space are not causal processes among neutral elements, but the sensing of and response to relevance. The very idea of an inner zone with an external boundary can't get started here, because our living things in a certain relevance can't be situated "within" the agent; it is in the interaction itself. The understanding and know-how by which I climb the path and continue to know where I am is not "within" me in a kind of picture. That fate awaits it if and when I make the step to map-drawing. But now it resides in my negotiating the path. The understanding is in the interaction; it can't be drawn on outside of this, in the absence of the relevant surroundings. To think it can be detached is to construe it on the model of explicit, conceptual, language- or map-based knowledge, which is of course what the whole I/O tradition, from Descartes through Locke to contemporary AI-modellers, has been intent on doing. But just that is the move which re-creates the boundary, and makes the process of perceptual knowledge unintelligible.

All this places me in some uncertainty in relation to McDowell's argument. It would seem that we can't achieve a goal we both cherish, that is, giving an account of perception such that it lays to rest the temptations to go for the I/O with all its aporiai, unless we allow for a way of being in the world which is between inanimate–causal interaction and full-fledged conceptual–critical thinking. But some things McDowell says seem to show reluctance to allow for this, in particular his critique of the passage from Evans quoted in Lecture III, section 2 (pp.47–48), which I interpret (perhaps erroneously) as an attempt to allow for precisely such an intermediate way of being; as well as some of the things he says about the relation between ourselves and animals.

Another way of getting at a possible difference might be this: McDowell's response to Evans is to argue that the operations of a pre-conceptual "information-system" (Evans's term) would produce their results "independently of spontaneity" (p.49). Perhaps we have to probe this latter term more. "Spontaneity" could be reserved for full-fledged conceptual, self-reflective thinking, a restriction which would suit its Kantian origins. But it figures in another way in McDowell's argument, or so it seems to me. It seems also to designate the dimension of interpretation taken on by the agent in virtue of which a perceptual state can be a persuasive reason to believe something. Or put in other terms, it seems to designate the antonym to brute causal impingings on the organism, understood in terms of bare post-Galilean naturalism (without allowance for "second nature"). Or in other terms again, it might designate whatever it is in perception which enables it to participate in the space of reasons.

Now we have to hold these two senses apart: the strong Kantian sense, turning crucially on conceptual, reflective thought; and the weaker sense, which turns on participating in the space of reasons. To elide the two would be disastrous, going along with the most questionable side of Kant (on which judgment McDowell agrees with me), in which he paints freedom as a full-blown, reflective, self-possessing, radical emancipation from nature. And it could also render impossible an escape from the I/O, if the above Heidegger- and Merleau-Ponty-derived arguments are valid. Since by these, even obvious card-carrying members of the space of reasons like theoretical propositions depend for their meaning and persuasiveness on their anonymous dumb cousins in the implicit realm of pre-understanding.

IV

Last, I want to make a comment about the deleterious consequences of the I/O. The point is particular, even picky, but I preface it with a more general observation.

It has often been noticed how foundationalism leads, by recoil, to skepticism, relativism, and various forms of non-realism. Once the foundationalist arguments for establishing truth are seen to fail, we are left with the image of the self-enclosed subject, out of contact with the transcendent world. And this easily generates theses of the unknowable (for example, *Dingen an sich*), of the privacy of thought (the Private Language argument), or of relativism. More particularly in this last case, the picture of each mind acceding to the world from behind the screen of its own percepts, or grasping it in moulds of its own making, seems to offer no way of rational arbitration of disputes. How can the protagonists base their arguments on commonly available elements, when each is encased within his or her own picture?

The conception of the knowing agent at grips with the world opens quite different possibilities. There may be (and obviously are) differences, alternative takes on, and construals of reality, which may even be systematic and far-reaching. Some of these will be, all may be, wrong. But any such take or construal is within the context of a basic engagement with and understanding of the world, a contact with it which cannot be broken off short of death. It is impossible to be totally wrong. Even if, after climbing the path, I think myself to be in the wrong field, I have situated myself in the right county, I know the way back home, etc. The reality of contact with the real world is the inescapable fact of human (or animal) life, and can only be imagined away by erroneous philosophical argument. As Merleau-Ponty put it: "*Se demander si le monde est réel, ce n'est pas entendre ce qu'on dit.*"[6] And it is in virtue of this contact with a common world that we always have something to say to each other, something to point to in disputes about reality.

We can see that this picture yields a kind of "principle of charity": my interlocutor can't be totally wrong, and nor can I, because we are inescapably in contact with reality. But this is rather different from Davidson's. The argument is quite different. This one is ontologically based: human beings are in contact with the real. Davidson's is epistemological: the condition of my understanding you is that I construe you as making sense most of the time. We might think that the basis doesn't count; what matters is the conclusion. But in fact, the two principles have a fatefully different impact on the important issues of intercultural difference.

This becomes evident if you hang out where I do a lot of the time, in that murky, marginal intellectual territory, on the marshy borderline between philosophy, social science, and political argument. Here precisely, a big issue is what one makes of intercultural differences, and one of the offshoots of the I/O is a kind of facile relativism, a too quick and precipitate abandonment of the very ideal of arbitration in reason, or even, in some versions, of mutual understanding. These positions have multiple motivations; there are also moral and political reasons. But I/O plays a big role in their intellectual legitimation, as do such in the end unconvincing repudiations of I/O as Rorty's.

Now in this domain, I believe that Davidson's arguments against the scheme–content distinction, which are powered in part by his principle of charity, have done a lot of damage. Properly understood, Davidson's point has no relevance to the intercultural case; improperly understood it can be a license for ethnocentrism; or just for dodging the issues.

To make part of the latter point first, Davidson's principle of charity requires that I, the observer/theorist, must make sense of him, the subject studied, in the sense of finding most of what he does, thinks, and says intelligible; else I can't be treating him as a rational agent, and there is nothing to understand, in the relevant sense, at all. Now the problem just is that the standing ethnocentric temptation is to make too quick sense of the stranger, that is, sense in one's own terms. The lesser breeds are without the law, because they have nothing we recognize as law. The step to branding them as lawless and outlaw is as easy as it is invalid and fateful. So the *conquistadores* had an easy way of understanding the strange and disturbing practices of the Aztecs, including human sacrifice. While we worship God, these people worship the Devil.

Now Davidson would certainly be right to protest at this abuse of his point. Nothing in his argument says that other people have to be totally intelligible, and certainly not at first meeting. And nothing in the argument licenses insensitivity to differences. But the defense just shows how the argument is irrelevant to this case.

What the argument through the (Davidsonian) principle of charity shows is that total unintelligibility of another culture is not an option. For to experience another group as unintelligible over some range of their practices, we have to find them quite understandable over other (very substantial) ranges. We have to be able to understand them as framing intentions, carrying out actions, trying to communicate orders, truths, etc. If we imagine even this away, then we no longer have the basis which allows us to recognize them as agents. But then there's nothing left to be puzzled about. Concerning non-agents, there is no question about what they're up to, and hence no possibility of being baffled on this score.

116

But then the relevance to the intercultural case disappears. What the argument from charity ruled out is the total unintelligibility of beings we nevertheless recognize as agents. (Note that it doesn't rule out the existence of such beings, only our ability to see that they're agents. They may indeed exist, only we'll never know.) The argument does nothing to exclude our encountering partial unintelligibility; which is indeed what we do meet with regularly in the intercultural case.

So far, so good. But by the same token, the argument does nothing to show that talking about different schemes is not a good and useful way of proceeding in the intercultural case; indeed, an indispensable way. For the use of the scheme concept only undercuts itself when what is supposed is total mutual unintelligibility; and this by hypothesis is not what we face here. All the sadder then, when failure to make this distinction licenses numberless half-baked thinkers in evading all issues of intercultural comparison and assessment, on the pretext that the illegitimacy of the scheme–content distinction shows that pursuing these questions must be misguided.

There are, however, other Davidsonian arguments, which users of "scheme" have to meet. In particular, the question is what one puts over against "scheme" in the statement of the distinction. The term "content" is certainly very bad. It belongs to the very idea of a scheme, in the sense one is tempted to use it in intercultural studies, that it indicate some systematic way in which people are interpreting or understanding their world. Different schemes are uncombinable such ways of understanding the same things.

"But what things?" runs the objection. How can you point to the things in question? If you use the language of the target society to get at them, then all distinction between scheme and content disappears. But what else can you use? Well, let's say our language, that of us, the observer/scientists, about this target area. But then we still won't have got at the "content" we share in common, which would have to be somehow identifiable independently of both schemes.

The point is well taken; and needs to be kept in mind in order to avoid certain easy pitfalls, such as thinking that one has a neutral, universal categorization of the structures or functions of all societies, for example, "political system," "family," "religion," etc., which provides the ultimately correct description for what all the different fumbling, cultural languages are aiming at; as it were, the noumena to their phenomenal tongues. But the notion of two schemes, one target area, remains valid and, indeed, indispensable.

Let's go back to the case of the *conquistadores* and the Aztecs. We might say that one thing the *conquistadores* had right was that they recognized that all that ripping out of hearts in some way corresponded in Spanish society to the Church and the Mass, and that sort of thing. That is, the right insight, yielding a good starting point for an eventual fusion of horizons, involves identifying what something in the puzzling life of an alien people can usefully be contrasted with in ours. An example will show what is at stake here. A few years ago a wildly reductivistic American social scientist produced a theory of Aztec sacrifice in which it was explained "materialistically" in terms of their need for protein. On this view the right point of comparison in Spanish society would be their slaughterhouses rather than their churches. Needless to say, from such a starting point, one gets nowhere.

The fruitful supposition is that what went on atop those pyramids reflected a very different construal of an X which overlaps with what Christian faith and practice is a construal of in Spain. This is where thinking, enquiry, can usefully start. It has one very powerful – and in principle challengeable – presupposition: that we share the same humanness, and that therefore we can ultimately find our feet in Aztec sacrifice, because it's a way of dealing with a human condition we share. Once this is accepted, then the notion of two schemes, same X, becomes inescapable. Only we have to be careful what we put in the place of the "X."

In a general proposition, we might say it is a dimension, or aspect, of the human condition. In the particular case, it is much more dangerous to specify. "Religion" would be an obvious candidate word. But the danger is precisely that we happily take on board everything which this word means in our world, and slide back toward the ethnocentric reading of the *conquistadores*. So we perhaps retreat to something vaguer, like "numinous." But even this carries its dangers.

The point is to beware of labels here. This is the lesson to be learnt from attacks on the scheme–content distinction. But that the Mass and Aztec sacrifice belong to rival construals of a dimension of the human condition for which we have no stable, culture-transcendent name, is a thought we cannot let go of, unless we want to relegate these people to the kind of unintelligibility that members of a different species would have for us. If rejecting the distinction means letting this go, it is hardly an innocent step.

But refusing to take this step, recognizing that they share in the realities of the same human condition, is precisely adopting the other, ontological, non-Davidsonian "principle of charity." We can see now how much the two pull in different directions. The one, properly understood, tells us nothing relevant to intercultural understanding, and improperly taken discredits the terms in which we can make a serious try at this understanding, when it doesn't recover for ethnocentrism the badge of innocence. The other, ontological variant is directly relevant, and indeed underpins the efforts to achieve a fusion of horizons. The arguments against the scheme–content distinction largely reflect the epistemological variant; their impact in the social field has been, largely through confusion, to undermine and discredit the ontological variant.

These confusions, and the troubles they wreak, represent another way in which we continue to suffer from the dominance of the classical epistemological tradition, and the I/O model. The very idea of grounding a principle of charity epistemologically reflects this dominance. The arguments against speaking of a plurality of schemes need to undergo a serious overhaul before they can be unproblematically reinvoked in discussion.

Notes

1   Ludwig Wittgenstein, *Philosophical Investigations* (Oxford: Blackwell, 1953), §115.
2   See Miles Burnyeat, "Idealism and Greek Philosophy," in G. Vesey (ed.), *Idealism Past and Present* (New York: Cambridge University Press, 1982).
3   See Hubert Dreyfus, *Being in the World* (Cambridge, MA: MIT Press, 1988).
4   See Martin Heidegger, *Sein und Zeit* (Tübingen: Niemeyer, 1927), Maurice Merleau-Ponty, *Phénoménologie de la Perception* (Paris: Gallimard, 1945).
5   Kant, *Critique of Pure Reason*, A112.
6   Maurice Merleau-Ponty, *Phénoménologie de la Perception*, p. 396.

Part III

PHILOSOPHY OF MIND

7

PHENOMENOLOGICAL
EXTERNALISM

Gregory McCulloch

Introduction

Among other things, John McDowell's *Mind and World* develops the anti-
Cartesian philosophy of his work on singular thought. This philosophy involves
a radical rejection of Descartes's Real Distinction between mind and body:

> The point of the conception of singular thought that I have been
> recommending is that it treats the Cartesian fear of loss [of the world]
> ... not by trying to bridge a gulf between intentionality and objects ...
> but by fundamentally undermining the picture of mind that generates
> the Cartesian divide.[1]

The main target is not Descartes's immaterialism: it is the losing of the world,
which can be a feature of materialisms too.

Now in Descartes's hands, the idea that our thinking as such is – God and
whatever He brings in His train set aside – absolutely independent of what it
supposedly concerns, led to the conclusion that empirical enquiry needs an
intellectual warrant, trading on God's good nature. But Descartes's argument
that the warrant is needed found far more favor than his – or anyone else's –
proposals about how to get it. So the Real Distinction, as made graphic by the
malicious demon scenario of the *First Meditation*, has come down as a threat to
empirical knowledge. However, a pervasive if somewhat under-remarked theme
of McDowell's work is that this preoccupation with the *epistemology* is superfi-
cial, since knowledge – along with unwarranted opinion, with which it is
contrasted – presupposes that we can direct our minds at, think about, the
empirical world.[2] And *this itself* is supposed to be ruled out by the Real
Distinction. It's not (just) that we can't *know* about the world; it's that we can't
have *any* sort of opinion about it, so that no substance can be given to the idea
of harmony between the mind and its world. The Real Distinction, and in
particular Descartes's way of grounding it in his view of the subjective, rules out
the very possibility of intentionality:

Ironically, when reverence for the authority of phenomenology is carried to the length of making the fact that internal configurations are indistinguishable from the subject's point of view suffice to establish that those configurations are through and through the same, the upshot is to put at risk the most conspicuous phenomenological fact there is. The threat which the Cartesian picture poses to our hold on the world comes out dramatically in this: that within the Cartesian picture there is a serious question about how it can be that experience, conceived from its own point of view, is not blank or blind, but purports to be revelatory of the world we live in.[3]

Moreover,

it seems plausible that if we conceive propositional attitudes on the same [Cartesian] principles, as occupants of the same autonomous inner realm, we make it no less problematic how it can be that they have a representational bearing on the world.[4]

I think that McDowell is absolutely right, and what follows is largely my account both of why he is right, and of how his anti-Cartesian philosophy helps. But along the way I air some small reservations. I am unpersuaded by McDowell's appeal in *Mind and World* to the notion of *justification* in building his anti-Cartesian conception of intentionality, and say why in the second section. Before that, in the next section, I say in my own way why the Real Distinction cannot deliver intentionality. And in the third section I say what is better about McDowell-style anti-Cartesian philosophy, outlining a view I call *phenomenological externalism*.

Intentionality and the Real Distinction

Why should the Real Distinction rule out intentionality? Consider the *Demonic Dilemma*:

Intentionality belongs either on the mind side of the Distinction, or on the world side (it can't be on both, or the Distinction isn't Real). Then if, on the one hand, intentionality is on the mind side of the Distinction, it is all used up, signed and sealed, regardless of whether "its" world gets into the equation: hence the putative demon possibility that the "right" world never does anyway. The idea that the mind's activity (supposedly thinking) is intentionally directed at something in particular is a sham: world, demon, it makes no difference to it as it is in itself, and the mind's activity simply co-exists alongside whatever is beyond in sublime indifference.

But if, on the other hand, intentionality is on the world side of the Distinction, then the mind isn't as part of its nature directed at anything

HAVERFORD COLLEGE
BOOKSTORE

WELCOME TO THE BOOKSTORE!!
HOURS: MON-FRI 10-4:30 SAT 11-2:30

1 TEXT BOOKS   @ 26.95   26.95
                                ========
  SUB TOTAL   26.95
  TAX   0.00
                                ========
  TOTAL   26.95

  DATE   TIME   TRANSACTION
_____
10/27/03 04:26PM HC #481929

_____
Townsend, Joseph B.
ID# 002428

Current BOOKSTORE charges: $334.22

anyway, and hence is not, in itself, directed at "its" world: where there is demon rather than world, there is no world-directedness either.

It just doesn't help to suggest that intentionality *must* therefore be *a relation* that somehow straddles the Real Distinction. On a straightforward understanding, a relation can only obtain if the relata (mind, world) exist, so where there is demon rather than world, world-directedness does not obtain: and this is the second horn of the Dilemma. So suppose the relation to hold even when the world-relatum does not exist. This is the first horn: mind retains its (sham) "intentional" properties quite independently of what, if anything, lies beyond at the other end of the relation. Given the Real Distinction, there could *at best* be two absolutely distinct realms related by blind cause and effect, with potential harmony – prearranged, causally underpinned or otherwise – unprovided for.

This is all we could have "at best" because there remain questions about cause itself. If it is on the world side of the Distinction, it cannot underpin intentionality-as-a-mental-feature, and there is also a problem about the mind's internal economy. If it is on the mind side, then it has no capacity to relate mind and world. These are two aspects of Descartes's interaction problem. But even if cause does somehow straddle the Distinction without obliterating it, it is an important point that cause *itself* cannot provide the potential harmony between the mind and its world demanded by intentionality. The necessary potential harmony requires that, say, cats be the appropriate occasion for cat-thoughts, in a sense of "appropriate" richer than that delivered by mere reliable causation. Otherwise intentionality is everywhere reliable cause is: smoke is intentionally directed at fire. And for this reason it is *no help at all* simply to say that the mind involves *mental representations* which are intentionally directed at whatever reliably causes them. Even if this is part of the right answer – where empirical thought is concerned anyway – we won't have begun accounting for intentionality until the idea of *what it is to be a mental representation* has been explained. And in the present context, doing that is the same as saying what it is for the mind to be directed at, potentially in harmony with, its world.

The depth of the problem here is obscured so long as the traditional Idea idea, of intrinsically contentful items such as pictures that wear their interpretation on their sleeve or "resemble" their objects, is still, perhaps tacitly, operative. For then intentionality/being a mental representation can seem to be *both* a mental feature *and also* an intelligible link with the world – an (at worst) potential fit. But once this view of the mind's way of fitting its objects is seen to be hopeless, as of course it is, the problematic nature of intentionality – in the context of the Real Distinction – should immediately surface. It is indeed a very striking feature of contemporary philosophy of mind that official rejection of the Idea idea is widespread, part of nearly everyone's stock-in-trade, while talk of mental representations – as sentences of Mentalese, or mental models, or neural nets, or other things again – is nearly as common. But combining orthodox rejection of the Idea idea with *unredeemed* talk of mental representations involves simple failure to appreciate the depth of the problems left over when the Idea idea is seen to fail. Mental representations cannot *simply* be the reliable effects of what they are intentionally directed at, even if they are *at least* that. The big question is: what more is involved in their being *mental representations* in addition to being *reliable effects*?

Nor, as remarked, is the fundamental problem Descartes's 'immaterialism.' The real problem comes from supposing that world-directed thinking can exist whether or not it has a world of the appropriate kind to be directed at, and someone who believes that the mind is the brain could (but need not) suppose that. Indeed, I think Jerry Fodor, an intrepid materialistic Cartesian, moves over the years from one horn of the Dilemma to the other (much more on him in the third section). In *Psychosemantics*, for example, narrow content is taken to be the important psychological notion.[5] Being both narrow *and* content, it is supposed to be world-independent and yet somehow directed-at: and this is spiked by the first horn. In *The Elm and the Expert*, on the other hand, Fodor more or less abandons narrow content and even takes to calling himself an externalist.[6] But he interprets externalism as the view that "semantics is not part of psychology," and glosses this further as "The content of your thoughts ... does not supervene on your mental processes."[7] And this entails that the mind is not, of itself, directed at anything (the mind's processes are not, of themselves, directed at anything): and this is spiked by the second horn.

I contend that the Demonic Dilemma is fatal to any view, immaterialist or materialist, which accommodates the Real Distinction. This is because any credible account of the mind must incorporate an intelligible conception of intentionality. Descartes was quite right to hold that directedness-at or intentionality is as much a feature of *known* or *given* consciousness as, say, sensations of pain. In this sense, as I shall put it, content – that in virtue of which the mind is directed at its world – is itself a *phenomenological* notion. So denying that our minds have intentional properties is in the same boat as denying that we feel sensations: you may as well just deny outright the existence of our minds. In sum, there can be no minds like ours without intentionality (just as there can be no minds like ours without sensations), and no intentionality with the Real Distinction. Hence the Real Distinction is incoherent. Put otherwise, a central task of post-Cartesian philosophy is to build an intelligible conception of intentionality in the face of the joint failure of the Idea idea and the Real Distinction. Or again, as McDowell puts it in *Mind and World*: "philosophy must not be allowed to make a mystery out of thought's bearing on its object" (p.138) and:

> Although reality is independent of our thinking, it is not to be pictured as outside an outer boundary that encloses the conceptual sphere. *That things are thus and so* is the conceptual content of an experience, but if the subject of the experience is not misled, that very same thing, *that*

things are thus and so, is also a perceptible fact, an aspect of the perceptible world.

(p.26)

We can thus fruitfully see much of his work on content as involving positive suggestions on how to avoid the Demonic Dilemma, on how to build an intelligible conception of intentionality. But before getting to the positive business, I want to air my small reservations.

McDowell and justification

McDowell approaches "thought's bearing on its object" by considering the idea of *justification*. According to McDowell, justification can only be understood as a relation between conceptually structured items – think of entailment or probabilification – so either the world is conceptually structured or it cannot justify our beliefs. But, McDowell continues, justification by our experience of the world is required not just for knowledge to be possible, but if we are to make anything of the idea of intentionality:

> We could not begin to suppose that we understood how pointing to a bit of the Given could justify the use of a concept in judgement ... unless we took this possibility of warrant to be constitutive of the concept's being what it is.

(p.6)

He underscores the point in the new Introduction:

> To make sense of the idea of a mental state's or episode's being directed towards the world ... we need to put the state or episode in a normative context. ... [T]hinking that aims at judgement, or at the fixation of belief, is answerable to the world ... for whether or not it is correctly executed. ... That is what I mean by a "minimal empiricism": the idea that experience must constitute a tribunal, mediating the way our thinking is answerable to how things are, as it must be if we are to make sense of it as thinking at all.

(pp.xi–xii)

This position is set against two views, traditional empiricism and Davidsonian coherentism, which according to McDowell share the root defect of conceiving the impact of world on mind in at best merely causal terms, leaving no room for the normative idea of justification, and hence ruling out not just knowledge but intentionality. And as indicated above, there is something in this: bare reliable cause cannot itself be what makes intentionality what it is, even if we restrict attention to empirical thought. All the same, I wonder if justification is the

127

right idea to work with, and I can best develop my unease by first putting the point in a brief albeit partly incoherent way: it is at least arguable that *the possibility of justification is neither necessary nor sufficient for intentionality*.

To see why justification is arguably not necessary, consider the following remark on the coherentism that leaves thinking a "frictionless spinning in the void" (p.11):

> It can seem that if we reject the Given, we merely reopen ourselves to the threat to which the idea of the Given is a response, the threat that our picture does not accommodate any external constraint on our activity in empirical thought and judgement. ... If our activity in empirical thought and judgement is to be recognizable as bearing on reality at all, there must be external constraint.
>
> (pp.8–9)

What is undeniable is that intentionality does require "external constraint": it doesn't make sense to say that thinking is about, directed at, the world, if the world cannot appropriately constrain or influence it. That is the fundamental problem with the Real Distinction. However, the Given would supply *some* external constraint. As McDowell acknowledges, "constraint from outside is exerted at the outer boundary ... in what we are committed to depicting as a brute impact from the exterior" (p.8). But he objects that the most this can yield is exculpation – one *cannot be blamed* for succumbing to the brute impact – whereas what intentionality requires, we have seen him claim, is justification. And here I think we should ask why. True, if there is no justification in the offing, there will be no empirical knowledge. But that is not supposed to be the issue. Rather, *intentionality* is meant to be under threat from the Given, and I cannot quite see why. After all, exculpation is a minimally normative relation. Trees aren't exculpated for dropping their leaves, since the relevant kind of assessment of them was never an issue. Exculpation only gets into the frame when the rest of the normative apparatus does. So, why can't it help to determine that an episode is about cats that the subject of the episode can't be blamed for cat-appropriate responses, though in the same circumstances the subject could be blamed for, say, daffodil-appropriate responses? That is, there is already in place a minimal answerability to the world once the notion of exculpation is in play, something that goes beyond the brutely causal in so far as it only applies when other normative notions do. So, for instance, if P justifies Q and one finds oneself blamelessly holding P, one would have at least conditional justification for moving to Q: all that would be missing would be the ultimate warrant from the world which the Given does not provide. But it would provide exculpation. So to repeat: if exculpation is all we are Given, then knowledge goes; but if all intentionality requires is minimal normative constraint, why is exculpation not enough?

Maybe the intended answer is that the notion of exculpation only applies once normativity has been earned, and given the Given there will be no normativity between what passes for the mind and its world (McDowell's actual wording is "Now *perhaps* this picture secures that we cannot be blamed for what happens at [the] outer boundary" (p.8, emphasis added)). But this threatens to beg the question, sending us back empty-handed to the notion of ultimate justification. So it seems that something else is needed to show that even a minimally normative notion like exculpation is unavailable in the presence of the Given. Failing that, we are left with the suggestion that exculpation may be enough for intentionality to be in the picture.

This point can be underlined using McDowell's own remarks about what made Cartesian skepticism such a new departure. The background to Cartesian skepticism – the Real Distinction – results in the loss of the world, since it cannot accommodate intentionality. By contrast,

> ancient scepticism did not call our possession of a world into question; its upshot was, less dramatically, to drive a wedge between living in the world and (what is made to seem dispensable) knowing about it.[8]

Moreover, it is clear that although rejection of the Real Distinction stifles radical Cartesian skepticism at birth,[9] there remain other ways of attacking knowledge which resemble somewhat the strategies employed by the ancients: one might argue, for example, that what we *ordinarily call* justification for a belief can always be undermined.[10] But were such arguments to succeed, and knowledge go missing, we should still be unable to help finding ourselves (blamelessly!) thinking one thing rather than another. Might we not then rest content with exculpation and mere possession of the world, secure at least of our "subjectivity as a mode of being in the world"?[11] Put otherwise, what McDowell seems to need, but not to provide, is an argument to show that "the ancient option of giving up the claim that knowledge is one of the ties that relate us to the world"[12] is no option at all.

So much for the necessity of justification to intentionality. What of its sufficiency? In discussing Davidson's coherentism, McDowell considers the reportedly Davidsonian idea that "if one were a brain in a vat, it would be correct to interpret one's beliefs as being largely true beliefs about the brain's electronic environment" (pp.16–17). McDowell complains that this "gives us a dizzying sense that our grip on what it is that we believe is not as firm as we thought" (p.17), and he amplifies in a footnote, saying that the fundamental problem with the idea is that

> we ring changes on the actual environment (as seen by the interpreter and brought into the interpretation) without changing how things strike the believer, even while the interpretation is supposed to capture how the believer is in touch with her world. This strikes me as making it impossible to claim that the argument traffics in any genuine idea of

being in touch with something in particular. The objects that the interpreter sees the subject's beliefs as being about become, as it were, merely noumenal so far as the subject is concerned.

(p.17, note 14)

McDowell's immediate target is a possible use of the claim that vat-brains have beliefs about their electronic environment to square another Davidsonian claim – that beliefs are by and large true – with the worry that we might be radically deceived vat-brains. And McDowell's comments come in the course of his attempt to draw unsatisfactory conclusions from Davidson's coherentism. Nevertheless, McDowell clearly means to deny for his own part that vat-brains have beliefs about their electronic environments, or indeed anything.[13] And I agree that this is indeed the correct line to take.[14] But oddly enough, there is some doubt about whether McDowell is entitled to take it on the basis of his stated views.

Consider first this (uncharitable) gloss of what he means in the footnote: the vat-brain takes itself to have experiences as of cats and the like, when really it is experiencing electronic impulses. So it is systematically wrong about what its empirical thinking is about; indeed, so wrong that it isn't really thinking about anything at all. This would be uncharitable because, as McDowell remarks (p.17, note 14), the supposed contents of the vat-brain's reflective or second-order thinking would be sensitive to the supposed contents of its first-order states: if its "cat" thoughts and experiences are really *electronic impulse* thoughts and experiences, then the vat-brain equally takes itself to have thoughts and experiences as of electronic impulses, and there is no systematic mistake. A less careless gloss of what McDowell means in the quoted passage would be that the nature of the vat-brain's *experiences as of electronic impulses* is not appropriate to their supposed content, since *ex hypothesi* they strike the vat-brain just as our experiences as of cats strike us. One might even try to see here the operation of McDowell's idea that intentionality requires justification, since the background thought could be that experiences subjectively indistinguishable from experiences as of cats cannot justify thinking about electronic impulses.

However, this would not capture McDowell's background thought either, despite his use of the phrase "without changing how things strike the believer." For McDowell, experience is conceptual through and through – there is no residual non-conceptual cattiness in our experiences as of cats, once their content has been bracketed. Much less do we host intrinsically intentional cat-pictures which, in the vat-brain's unfortunate case, are reliably caused by electronic impulses. So in the only sense of "how things strike the believer" McDowell allows, the supposed vat-brain experiences really would strike the vat-brain as experiences as of electronic impulses, and so presumably could serve to justify its supposed beliefs about them too. Thus if it is wrong to suppose that the vat-brain's states are really "in touch with" electronic impulses, it cannot be because they are not justified. Hence justification is not sufficient for intentionality.

Of course, that is a left-handed way of making the conclusion, since McDowell's real point is that the vat-brain hasn't got any beliefs about electronic impulses, so that the question of their justification cannot arise. But what is the argument? It cannot be that if we allow, for *reductio*, that the vat-brain's states are electronic impulse beliefs, they wouldn't be justifiable by the appropriate experiences and hence would not be beliefs after all: because if they *are* beliefs they *are* justified, at least by McDowell's lights.

In sum, McDowell's focus on justification does not seem to engage with the issue of intentionality in the right way. It is not clear what is supposed to rule out minimal normativity in the face of the Given (or to show that exculpation isn't normative enough). And it is not clear what drives McDowell's doubt about whether the vat-brain story "traffics in any genuine idea of being in touch with something in particular." Rather than pursue these matters any further, however, I shall now go back to the roots of McDowell's anti-Cartesian philosophy to see if anything more illuminating on the topic of intentionality can be developed. I ought to add that I should be surprised – or much worse – if McDowell turns out to be unsympathetic to the view I am about to describe. More, it may well be compatible with what he says about the relevance of the notion of justification to the matter of intentionality, my reservations notwithstanding. But anyway I am satisfied that what is to follow is an illuminating way to present the credentials of McDowell-type approaches to intentionality.

Phenomenological externalism

I begin with externalism – another pervasive feature of McDowell's work – as an approach to intentionality. There are externalisms and externalisms, however, and the version I want to recommend is, as remarked, *phenomenological externalism*. This can be unoriginally sloganized as "The mind ain't in the head," and it embraces the claims

(1) Content ain't in the head

and

(2) Content is in the mind.

Claim (1) is an expression of *content* externalism, and I shall just assume it has been established using appropriate Twin-Earth arguments.[15] Claim (2) records the idea, canvassed in the preceding section, that content or intentionality is a genuine feature of the mind as such, as given to consciousness. Phenomenological externalism is an attempt to cash out intentionality, *construed as a genuine mental feature*, in terms of real (e.g., ontic, causal, nomic) relations between thinkers and bits of the world. A crucial implication is a denial of the

Real Distinction: intentionality is mental, but can only be understood in terms of (ontic, causal, nomic) world-involvingness, so that our thinking is *not* as such absolutely independent of what it supposedly concerns in the way made graphic by the malicious demon scenario. Phenomenological externalism thus offers a significant move forward on the matter of intentionality, since it dissolves the Demonic Dilemma by denying the absolute distinction on which it is based. But why *phenomenological* externalism? Everything, we shall see, hangs on what one must mean by the "in" in (2).[16]

We need to start with approaches which attempt to embrace externalistic morals while accommodating central Cartesian claims. A very important example is Jerry Fodor's combination of what he calls a denotational (in *Psychosemantics*) or externalistic (in *The Elm and the Expert*) account of content with a "narrow" computational construal of mental processes. He says:

> My philosophical project ... has been to understand the relation between a venerable, old idea borrowed from what philosophers call "folk psychology", and a trendy new idea borrowed mainly from Alan Turing. The old idea is that mental states are characteristically intentional. ... The new idea is that mental processes are characteristically computational. My problem lies in the apparent difficulty of getting these ideas to fit together.[17]

Fodor accepts that intentionality has to be addressed in terms of content externalism, so an acute problem arises with his additional aim to count appropriate Twin-Earth *Doppelgänger* as cognitively equivalent, despite the fact that, given his content externalism, their minds have distinct intentional properties. His solution in *Psychosemantics* is to posit context-independent narrow contents, shared by the *Doppelgänger*; and his solution in *The Elm and the Expert* is to claim that such pairs are (by and large) nomically impossible or at best mere coincidences, and hence of no concern to cognitive theory, whose aim is to discover intentional laws.

Now it is fair, but nevertheless far from the last word, to reply that Fodor's externalism is insufficiently thoroughgoing. It is fair, because what Fodor is really committed to is the claim that intentionality – the thing that his denotational or externalistic theory is a theory of – is not really a mental feature. As he says:

> It is, to put the point starkly, the heart of externalism that *semantics isn't part of psychology*. The content of your thoughts ... does not supervene on your mental processes.[18]

Thus in *Psychosemantics*, broad contents are no more than our context-dependent way of indicating what is really in the mind – narrow content, the real stuff of psychology. And in *The Elm and the Expert*, broad contents are taken to be nomologically guaranteed to map one-to-one (by and large) onto aspects of the brain's computational operations, and are thus treated as (nomologically guaranteed but still) mere extrinsic signs of what is in the mind (namely, the computational processes). These views have some of the trappings of externalism, but do not go as far as "the mind ain't in the head," since they combine an *acceptance* of

(1) Content ain't in the head

with a *denial* of

(2) Content is in the mind.

Rather, according to Fodor, the mind is where computational processes are – in the head – while (broad) content is out in the world.[19]

But what Fodor starkly calls "the heart of externalism" – the denial of (2) – in fact renders externalism incapable of coping with intentionality, and hence the mind, since to deny (2) is to become impaled on the second horn of the Demonic Dilemma: to deny that content is in the mind is to deny that the mind is in itself directed at anything. That is presumably one reason why Fodor hankered so long for narrow content, since a resonance of the word "content" is that intentionality has been provided for.[20] Anyway, a much better way forward in the face of the Dilemma is to *accept* (2), in the manner of phenomenological externalism, so that the claim that semantics *is* part of psychology finds a place at the heart of externalism.[21]

Still, why do I say that this fair response to Fodor is nevertheless far from the last word? Here we need to consider the views of Colin McGinn. McGinn has argued for content externalism, and also claimed that the mind ain't in the head – "unlike mental models the mind itself is not located in the head, though it has its mechanical basis there."[22] Nevertheless, the overall shape of McGinn's account is indistinguishable from that of Fodor's, even though they disagree over some significant details. Both accept that intentionality is to be understood in terms of content externalism, and both accept that the *causal powers* of intentional states are to be narrowly individuated.[23] McGinn does not follow pre-*Elm and Expert* Fodor in speaking of narrow *contents* as what comport with this method of individuation, preferring to speak of narrow *aspects*,[24] since he (rightly) doesn't like the implication of the word "content" that something propositional is involved. But this is nonetheless hard to separate from Fodor's idea that narrow contents are radically inexpressible,[25] since presumably any proposition can be expressed in *some* possible language. In other words, such an inexpressible item isn't really propositional, or content, after all, and we thus move swiftly from Fodor to McGinn with barely a ripple. But if that is so, then the whole matter of whether the mind is in the head starts to look like a verbal dispute about what to *call* "mental" (or "mental, strictly speaking"). On both accounts, ascriptions of intentional states are normally answerable *both* to narrow, causally individuated internal structures (I), *and* to externalistically individuated content (E). For present purposes, the key disagreement is then whether the mental, strictly so-called, comprises I alone (Fodor) or I+E (McGinn). And how can this be an issue? Earlier I suggested that Fodor's externalism is insufficiently thoroughgoing, on account of its denial of (2). But now we see that McGinn appears to escape this by the simple expedient of so understanding the word "mind" that he can happily affirm (2), leaving everything else relevant unchanged!

The correct conclusion is not that, once content externalism has been conceded, the issue over "The mind ain't in the head" is merely verbal. It is, rather, that McGinn's externalism, like Fodor's, is insufficiently thoroughgoing.[26] Although their talk of content is intended to accommodate intentionality, and although they get as far as accepting externalistic morals about it, the fact remains that neither has a *rich enough conception* of content and its role in our mental life to do the intended job in the theory of intentionality. My argument for this comes in two parts. *First*, we need to give proper weight to the point, mentioned earlier, that content is a phenomenological notion, that the directedness of our thinking is, in the words of McDowell quoted earlier, "the most conspicuous phenomenological fact there is." *Second*, we need to give proper weight to the intensional facts of this conspicuous conscious life.

Content is a phenomenological notion precisely in the sense that our *conscious* mental life is as much imbued with content – directedness-at – as it is with items such as stabs of pain. It is thus "in" the mind in the same sense as sensations are: it is part of the configuration of subjectivity. Here is an excellent statement of the point by Galen Strawson, who speaks of "understanding-experience" or "meaning-experience":

> thinking a thought or suddenly remembering something or realizing that the interval between the perfect squares increases by 2 is as much of an experience as feeling pain. ... Episodes of conscious thought are experiential episodes. Experience is as much cognitive as sensory.[27]

Of course, one must embrace this without reverting to the hopeless empiricist approach where thinking is modeled on imaging or sensation. It is not that apprehending pains or images yields a model for grasping content: rather, on the contrary, our conception of the phenomenological must be sufficiently sophisticated for it to embrace episodes of conscious thinking as well as stabs of pain. Content appears *as itself* in consciousness: it is not that distinct contents have associated with them distinct identifying qualia or raw feels. They contribute *as themselves* to the phenomenology. And it is only thus that directedness-at or intentionality can figure in our conscious life.

Not only is it important not to construe these claims as meaning that content is to be modeled on sensation, but one must realize that the phenomenology of content is not merely a first-person matter.[28] Sometimes at least I can hear others' contents in their speech or see them in their gestures. Just as I can appear to myself as a thinker, as when I think consciously, so others too can appear to me as thinkers, as when I hear them saying or see them showing what they think. In this sense the phenomenological embraces some of the third-person, public aspects of thinking, speaking, and communicating: sometimes, at least, when we are communicating with others, the shared contents are as much a part of the scene of which we are conscious as are the colors of nearby objects.[29]

Elsewhere,[30] I have argued that the basic idea – that content is phenomenological yet in a way that embraces both the first- and third-person domains – can be illuminated using the idea of radical interpretation (not translation). It is possible to confront a form of life as a physical phenomenon yet have no understanding of it as a locus of thought, feeling, and other mental attributes. A form of life can be encountered as unintelligible, which means that its meanings are not manifest to the interpreter. In reflecting on the predicament of the radical interpreter we can then become clearer over what is involved in discovering how something, like a stretch of thinking or a piece of behavior, can be about something else: and this is part of the traditional problem of intentionality. Moreover, if the goal of the radical interpreter is to become able to understand the thinking of the members of the alien culture, then the radical interpreter has to get to the position of entertaining the thoughts that the aliens think themselves. To the extent that this can be accomplished, their meanings will be penetrated; to the extent that it cannot, they will not. The phenomenological dimension of content is then implicated as follows. In so far as the interpreter penetrates the meanings of the alien culture, the interpreter becomes capable of entertaining them for him- or herself in conscious thought (first-person aspect), and of perceiving them in the acts and utterances of the culture's members (third-person aspect). In making meanings manifest, the penetration process brings them into consciousness. Making meanings manifest *is the same thing as* embracing their phenomenology *is the same thing as* arriving at an adequate interpretation.

That is the first part of the argument against Fodor and McGinn. The second part involves care over the intensional facts of conscious life. Most agree that any account of thinking has somehow to accommodate the fact that referentially equivalent attributes such as

(3)   thinking that Cicero denounced Catiline

and

(4)   thinking that Tully denounced Catiline

need to be distinguished for certain purposes (e.g., sensitive interpretation). Few repudiate this *intensionality constraint*, although there is debate about whether it concerns the semantics of intentional states. More, there is almost universal assent to the (correct enough) idea that one needs to respect the intensionality constraint for reasons to do with the rationalization of behavior. Here, however, I want to insist on a further point, hardly ever mentioned. This is that the difference between (3) and (4) is not *merely* a reflection of rationalizing power, but is *also* a matter of phenomenology. In the first person, consciously thinking that Cicero denounced Catiline is not the same thing as consciously thinking that Tully denounced Catiline (imagine suddenly becoming aware of the identity). In the third person, hearing you say the one is not the same as hearing you say the other (imagine you affirm one and deny the other). Interpreting you as saying one is not the same as interpreting you as saying the other.

And what this all adds up to is that *broad content is intensional*. Given content externalism – just assumed here – content is broad. Given the two phenomenological points just adduced, not only is broad content *as content* a feature of conscious life; so is the intensional difference between referentially equivalent attributes such as (3) and (4). These points cannot be accommodated without a unitary conception of content, embracing both the mind's objects and *at the same time* the mind's take on these objects. At a stroke, the idea of potential harmony between the mind and its world is also introduced. It is not that, in the favorable cases, objects have an effect on my mind, which I somehow construe as a sign that I am indeed in contact with these objects. Rather, in the favorable cases, the objects present themselves to my mind, albeit (the intensionality constraint) under some mode or other:

> there are Fregean thought-constituents (singular senses) that are object-dependent, generating an object-dependence in the thoughts in which they figure. Two or more singular senses can present the same object; so Fregean singular thoughts can be both object-dependent and just as finely individuated as perspicuous psychological description requires.[31]

Returning now to Fodor and McGinn, their principal failing is that neither accommodates the foregoing phenomenological points, and the consequence that broad content is intensional. Indeed, although this consequence is a key message of McDowell's original paper on externalism,[32] it is usually not even noted as a possibility, much less considered, far less embraced, in the colossal externalism-related literature.[33]

Fodor is explicitly extensionalist about broad content, as shows in his treatment of what he calls "Frege cases," cases where "people who believe that Fa fail to believe Fb, even though a=b."[34] Of these cases he writes that they "make the relation between intentional laws and computational implementation problematic."[35] Fodor's problem is that, given content externalism as he understands it, believing that Fa comes out as having the same content as believing that Fb when a=b, even though "different computational mechanisms implement [these] ... broad beliefs."[36] But this alleged problem is generated solely by the assumption that broad contents are extensional: without this assumption, then even given content externalism and a=b, it does not follow that believing that Fa has the same content as believing that Fb.

McGinn is as explicitly extensionalist about broad content when he addresses this matter:

> The opacity of embedded "that"-clauses needs tectonic explication. How, for example, can a pair of contents both be about Venus – one expressed with "Hesperus", the other with "Phosphorus" – and yet it not be the case that both are attributable to any subject to whom either of them is?[37]

McGinn's "tectonic explication," just like Fodor's,[38] appeals to difference in implementation mechanism, the only disagreement here being over whether these mechanisms involve *sentences* (Fodor) or *models* (McGinn). On both accounts we are to distinguish the externalistically constrained referential or semantic aspect of an intentional state from what both authors call "mode of presentation," that which is supposed to introduce the dimension of intensionality. And in both cases "mode of presentation" is cashed out in terms of implementing mechanisms: in both cases E is extensional, I the bringer of intensionality. But in splitting intensionality from (broad) content in this way, neither Fodor nor McGinn is entitled to the metaphor of "presentation," and hence the necessary notion of fit or harmony that it conjures up.[39] They both just throw in the phrase as a borrowing from Frege without giving a thought to its implications or role in the theory of how the mind directs itself at objects, how objects present themselves to the mind. Put otherwise, while their approach to the intensionality constraint might seem to hold promise when attention is on the rationalization of behavior, they miss altogether the constraint's phenomenological implications, both in this third-person area and more generally.

Of course they are far from alone in this: and this is not all they are missing. For what it is worth, I think that McDowell's philosophy of mind, and in particular his seminal role in the reworking of Frege on the relations between *Sinn* and *Bedeutung*, figure among the most important contributions to analytical philosophy in the last century. But judging by the shape of the enormous literature on content, mine remains something of a minority view. One can only hope that things will be put right in the new millennium.[40]

Notes

1 J. McDowell, "Singular Thought and the Extent of Inner Space," in J. McDowell, *Meaning, Knowledge and Reality* (Cambridge, MA: Harvard University Press, 1998), pp.228–259, p.259.

2 As McDowell writes in "Singular Thought and the Extent of Inner Space," "The course of Cartesian epistemology gives a dramatic but ultimately inessential expression to Descartes's fundamental contribution to philosophy, namely his picture of the subjective realm" (ibid., p.242, note 27); and in the "Introduction" to *Mind and World*,

> It is true that modern philosophy is pervaded by apparent problems about knowledge in particular. But I think it is helpful to see those apparent problems as more or less inept expressions of a deeper anxiety – an inchoately felt threat that a way of thinking we find ourselves falling into leaves minds simply out of touch with the rest of reality, not just questionably capable of getting to know about it.
>
> (xiii)

(Subsequent page references to *Mind and World* are given in the text.)
3 "Singular Thought and the Extent of Inner Space," op. cit., p.243.
4 Ibid., p.249.
5 See J. Fodor, *Psychosemantics* (Cambridge, MA: MIT Press, 1987).
6 See J. Fodor, *The Elm and the Expert* (Cambridge, MA: MIT Press, 1994).
7 Ibid., p.38.
8 "Singular Thought and the Extent of Inner Space," op. cit., p.238.
9 See G. McCulloch, "Content Externalism and Cartesian Scepticism," in R. Sterne (ed.), *Transcendental Arguments* (Oxford: Clarendon Press, 1999), pp.251–270.
10 See C. Hookway, *Scepticism* (London: Routledge, 1990), chaps 1 and 2.
11 "Singular Thought and the Extent of Inner Space," op. cit., p.242.
12 Ibid., pp.241–242.
13 Ibid., p.258, note 57.
14 See G. McCulloch, *The Life of the Mind* (forthcoming), chap. 7.
15 Ibid., chap. 3.
16 See McDowell, "De Re Senses," in *Meaning, Knowledge and Reality*, pp.214–227, especially p.226, note 42.
17 Fodor, *The Elm and the Expert*, pp.1–2.
18 Ibid., p.38.
19 There is a quite striking parallel with Descartes at this point. In Fodor, Mother Nature ensures that our thinking *qua* processing in the head is directed at the "right" objects (something it cannot do for itself, as it were). In Descartes, the job is done by God's goodness. What neither author can do, however, is give any content to "right objects."
20 See McDowell, "Singular Thought and the Extent of Inner Space," op. cit., p.256, note 52.
21 This is the big idea in McDowell, "On the sense and reference of a proper name," in *Mind, Knowledge and Reality*, pp.171–198; and developed by Evans in *The Varieties of Reference*, J. McDowell (ed.) (Oxford: Clarendon Press, 1982).
22 C. McGinn, *Mental Content* (Oxford: Blackwell, 1989), p.210.
23 Compare here Fodor's *Psychosemantics* and McGinn's "Conceptual Causation: Some Elementary Considerations," *Mind* 100: 573–586 (1991).
24 McGinn, "Conceptual Causation: Some Elementary Considerations," p.583, note 13.
25 Fodor, *Psychosemantics*, p.50.
26 See McDowell, "De Re Senses," op. cit., p.226.
27 Galen Strawson, *Mental Reality* (Cambridge, MA: MIT Press, 1994), pp.6–7.
28 See G. McCulloch, *The Mind and its World* (London: Routledge, 1995), chap. 6.

29 As McDowell writes in "On the Sense and Reference of a Proper Name," "Comprehension of speech in a familiar language is a matter of unreflective perception, not bringing a theory to bear" (*Meaning, Knowledge and Reality*, p.179).

30 See G. McCulloch, "Intentionality and Interpretation," in A. O'Hear (ed.), *Current Issues in the Philosophy of Mind*, Philosophy Supplement no. 43 (Cambridge: Cambridge University Press, 1998), pp.253–271; and "Bipartism and the Phenomenology of Content," *Philosophical Quarterly* 49: 18–32 (1999).

31 McDowell, "Singular Thought and the Extent of Inner Space," op. cit., p.233.

32 That is, "On the Sense and Reference of a Proper Name."

33 For an exception, see F. Recanati, *Direct Reference* (Oxford: Blackwell, 1993).

34 Fodor, *The Elm and the Expert*, p.22.

35 Ibid.

36 Ibid.

37 McGinn, *Mental Content*, p.191.

38 See *The Elm and the Expert*, p.24.

39 "Singular Thought and the Extent of Inner Space," op. cit., p.160.

40 Many thanks for helpful comments to friends and colleagues – Rob Hopkins, Penelope Mackie, Harold Noonan, Tim Williamson, Elizabeth Wright – and to members of audiences in Oxford, St Andrews, and Sheffield. Above all thanks to John McDowell for his inspirational writings.

8

HUMAN NATURE?

Crispin Wright

McDowell's book consists of versions of the six John Locke lectures he delivered in Oxford in 1991, together with a four part "Afterword" elaborating on and defending various of their themes. It displays a level of philosophical ambition that, in both scale and general direction, is nothing short of Hegelian – indeed the author remarks[1] that he would like to view his text as a prolegomenon to a reading of the *Phenomenology of Spirit*. McDowell's agenda, like Hegel's, is shaped through and through by the challenge of overcoming the Kantian legacy of minds' alienation from an unknowable noumenal reality. But this is an essentially modern work. The approach is fashioned by a deeply respectful, if profoundly unsympathetic, reaction to certain fundamental epistemological themes in the writings of Donald Davidson and Gareth Evans. The Sellarsian and Strawsonian influences on McDowell's thinking are also very evident, and acknowledged. Quine and Rorty are extensively criticized. Wittgenstein and Gadamer are important allies.

In the broadest terms, the project of the book is as follows. McDowell believes that there is no hope of a satisfying vision of our place as rational, enquiring beings within the natural world if the latter is conceived in the currently dominant fashion. That conception elevates the sort of description of the world offered by modern physical science into a metaphysics of what the natural world essentially is: a "Realm of Law" – a domain of causal–nomological connection from which purpose and meaning are absent and whose complete description has no need of any of the vocabulary distinctive of minds and their activity. The modern "naturalism" in philosophy which attends this conception of Nature thus finds itself with a problem – that of finding space for the categories whereby we express our *Spontaneity*[2] – categories of meaning, intentionality, and normativity – in a world whose fundamentals are thought to be amenable to fully adequate description by modern natural science. One, eliminativist response is simply to repudiate the claim of those categories to represent anything real. A more conservative response – that of what McDowell styles *Bald Naturalism* – is to undertake a reductive or quasi-reductive[3] programme of the categories of Spontaneity: to disclose how the subject matter of Spontaneity reoccurs in another guise within, or somehow demands nothing beyond the Realm of Law. Set against both these tendencies would be a view which allows the adequacy of the modern conception of Nature but rejects the idea that Nature is all there is: an irreductive supernaturalism, as it were – McDowell coins the term *Rampant Platonism* – about our Spontaneity and the norms to which it responds. But it is the modern conception of Nature which sets up this unattractive, Homeric choice – between elimination or (quasi-)reduction of meaning, intentionality, and normativity, on the one hand, or an obscurantist metaphysical hypostatization of them, on the other – and it is this conception which McDowell aims to show us how to supersede. We should aim not to solve the difficulties of locating rational thought and intentional activity within the modern naturalist view, but to finesse them by accomplishing an improved – "relaxed" – conception of what should rank as *natural* – one which allows us to "take in stride," without any sense of eeriness or mystification, an acceptance that Spontaneity is *sui generis*, by emphasizing the thought that its distinctive concepts capture patterns in our natural way of living.[4] It is by this accomplishment that we can transcend the most fundamental of modern philosophy's characteristic dualisms: the dualism of mind on one side and a brutely external world on the other, and thereby go one better than Kant.

There are not many contemporary philosophers within the broader analytical tradition who would feel they had any clear idea how such a goal might be accomplished, let alone the confidence to try. The line of thought whereby McDowell hopes to succeed is unexpected and independently interesting. It begins with an epistemological dilemma: a problem about the relation between experience and our most basic empirical beliefs. The problem, to be reviewed in more detail below, is to attain a conception of the nature of experience which lets its relation to our empirical beliefs be a *rational* one and at the same time allows experience to emerge as a *real worldly constraint* on our thought. McDowell claims that when experience is conceived as by modern naturalism, there is an irreconcilable tension between these desiderata, and that only a radical refashioning of the concept of experience can provide for their simultaneous satisfaction – a refashioning whose availability has typically been quite overlooked by philosophers. It is in order for us to understand how the necessary refashioning *is* intelligible, and satisfactory, that a revised conception of what should count as natural is called for. What we need to make space for is precisely a conception of experience which opens the world up to us and thereby allows it to give us *reasons for* our beliefs.[5] But the world of modern science can exert only *causal* constraints; and experience, for modern naturalism, can only be an *effect* of our interaction with it. Modern science treats of Nature in a disenchanted form, as it were. So, according to McDowell, experience, as a natural process, is likewise disenchanted – divested of content – and thus disabled from playing the reason-giving role we need it to play. What it takes to put this right is the central preoccupation of his book.

The seesaw

The basic dilemma – what McDowell styles an "intolerable oscillation," or "seesaw" – has us in a bind between a pair of putatively hopeless views of the interaction between thought and the empirical world and of the justification of those of our beliefs most directly concerned with observable reality. The poles of the oscillation are a version of the Myth of the Given, on the one hand, and something along the lines of Davidsonian Coherentism on the other.

McDowell's thinking here is deeply conditioned by a spatial metaphor. Assume that the "Space of Reasons" – the realm of Spontaneity in which everything takes place that involves conceptual activity, intentionality, and rationality – is enclosed within a larger sphere: the realm of natural law which is the domain of brute nature, involves no conceptual activity, and is apt for description and explanation by natural science in its modern conception. Call this the Enclosure Model (this is not McDowell's term). Now there is, of course, a distinction between empirical beliefs which are rationally held and empirical beliefs held, for whatever cause – prejudice, wishful thinking, hypnotic suggestion, etc. – without reasons. In essentials what will be distinctive of the former is that they are *based on* experience. But there are no resources – this is McDowell's most fundamental contention – to recover a satisfactory conception of the needed idea of *basis* within the framework of the Enclosure Model.

The problem is generated by the principle that justification is essentially a rational relation. That seems to require that it can obtain only between *conceptually structured* items – things that carry or are somehow indexed by propositional content. But in that case the domain of justification must be restricted *within* the Space of Reasons – it cannot cross the boundary into the wider Realm of Law. So the wider world is left out in the cold, with no part to play in the justification of our most basic beliefs about it. Sure, it can play a *causal* role – it can impinge upon us in such a way as to induce particular beliefs. But for these beliefs, on the Enclosure Model, we will have, in McDowell's terminology, not reasons but only "exculpations."[6] We cannot be *blamed* for holding beliefs which the world sub-rationally prompts us to hold. But we cannot claim to hold such beliefs *for reasons* either.

That is one pole of the oscillation: the Coherentist pole, of which McDowell holds Davidson up as a representative. For the coherentist, the relation of justification does indeed call for conceptually structured terms and just for that reason "nothing can count as a reason for holding a belief except another belief."[7] Questions of justification have thus to be addressed by scrutiny of internal features of our system of belief; the nature of the relation between (items in) that system and anything brutely external to it cannot be a normative one.

I'll enquire a little further shortly into McDowell's grounds for thinking that this conception is intolerable. The alternative – so long as we stick to the

Enclosure Model – must be to try to hold that a genuinely normative relation of justification *can* somehow cross the boundary between the inner realm of Concepts and outer Nature. This is the dualism of Scheme and Content – of Concepts and non-conceptual input – which comprises McDowell's version of the Myth of the Given.[8] The idea would be, as he says, that the Space of Reasons can somehow extend beyond the conceptual sphere. But this McDowell flatly rejects: the relation of justification, he insists, demands terms which carry content – only such an item can entail, probabilify, be a reason for the judgment that P.

In sum, empirical thinking needs to be constrained by experience if it is to count as genuinely empirical. That encourages the Myth of the Given – the myth of items simply presented to us in experience and thereby constraining our thought about them. But the right kind of constraint cannot be merely causal, but must be rational. That requires that the items doing the constraining carry content. But the Given, as conceived, cannot carry content – by hypothesis, what is Given in experience are items from beyond the Enclosure. So it appears we cannot have empirical thought rationally constrained from outside. Which seems intolerable.

So up and down goes the seesaw. We want empirical thought to be subject to rational justification. We first try to live with the hopeless idea that contentless items can be justifiers. Then, failing with that, we try to live with the equally hopeless idea that there is no rational constraint from outside on our empirical beliefs but only causal influence. But neither position is stable.

The Bald Naturalist solution

Assuming that each pole in the Oscillation really is intolerable, what kind of solution might be possible? McDowell allows in Lecture IV that Bald Naturalism would – if sustainable – provide a way out in principle, and concedes it a certain attraction.[9] Now Bald Naturalism, in its clearest form prefigured earlier, will be a species of reductionism: the view that all states of affairs described using the vocabulary of Spontaneity are natural in the sense of allowing of re-descriptions that place them in the Realm of Law (so there will be at least a posteriori correct representations of such states of affairs in the language of natural science). In that case, I suppose the idea is, relations of justification – between experiences and basic empirical beliefs, say – may be re-describable in natural scientific language, so that the sharp boundary between the Space of Reasons and the Realm of Law erected by the Enclosure Model is broken down: there will be no deep difference in kind, according to Bald Naturalism, between the two domains – it is merely that we need and have yet to achieve a scientific understanding of the identity – the natural face, as it were – of the denizens of the Space of Reasons.

McDowell rejects this solution, I suppose, because he doubts that Bald Naturalism is a feasible program. Once one is clear, though, *what* he doubts to be feasible – what the Bald Naturalist is committed to – it may well seem quite obscure why Bald Naturalism may be supposed even to *promise* a solution to the problem as McDowell conceives it. Grant that only content-bearing items can be justifiers and justified. Suppose a certain occurrent experience justifies a certain belief. In such a case, what Bald Naturalism might conceivably supply is a naturalistic re-presentation of both ingredient terms and the relation between them. But the effect of such a re-presentation would surely have to be to *mask*, rather than explain, the normative relation between the two, since neither item will be re-presented as a something-that-P. Justifiers and justified may perhaps be identified with certain naturally occurring items within the Realm of Law, and brought under physical–scientific concepts accordingly. But that will not be to make sense – in a way that should alleviate any sense of strain between such talk and the assumptions of modern naturalism – of the discourse that deals with their normative relationship.

To illustrate the lacuna by a different example: it would, seemingly, be one thing to make a case that the beliefs and desires which rationalize a particular performance of an agent may be identified with certain neural items which are involved in the aetiology of the associated behaviour; quite another to maintain that the *rational* explanation they provide is thereby reduced to the associated *causal* explanation. Or again: it would be one thing somehow to find a natural property to serve as the referent of some evaluative concept; quite another to maintain that one thereby made sense of the associated evaluation. If the Bald Naturalist project is reductively to safeguard the place of the *categories* of Spontaneity within its austere world-view, then it will not suffice merely to execute a program of a posteriori identifications of reference; one needs in addition somehow to recover, within the naturalistic idiom, something of the characteristic *purposes and function* of those categories. (Indeed, unless that is accomplished, it is quite unclear with what right one could claim to have *identified* anything in the first place.)

Now, this is in effect an objection that McDowell himself brings against Davidson's anomalous monism about the mental.[10] Since he distinguishes Davidson's view from that of the Bald Naturalist, precisely because Davidson recognizes that

> the intellectual role of those spontaneity-related concepts cannot be duplicated in terms of concepts whose fundamental point is to place things in the realm of law[11]

we have to conclude that on McDowell's understanding, the Bald Naturalist is one who explicitly recognizes this obligation to attempt *more* than reference-identifying. So the general thesis is one of the replicability of the "intellectual" role of the concepts of ethics, logic, intentional psychology, etc., by concepts of natural science. It should already be clear independently of McDowell's strictures that that thesis is as desperately implausible as it is hazy.

144

McDowell's solution

McDowell's solution is to reject the contentlessness of experience. And this rejection takes a prima facie startling form: he writes

> We should understand [experience] not as a bare getting of an extra-conceptual Given, but as a kind of occurrence or state that already has conceptual content. In experience one takes in, for instance sees, *that things are thus and so*. That is the sort of thing one can also, for instance, judge.[12]

In the end, empirical judgments are justified not by other judgments but by experience. But an experience, as such a justifier, has to be thought of, McDowell is proposing, as itself a *passive* exercise of concepts – the very concepts which feature in the active judgment the subject may take it prima facie to justify. Note that this amounts not to a rejection of the Given as such, but a recasting of it. What is given in experience is essentially of the form: that P – that so-and-so is the case. "In experience one finds oneself saddled with content."[13] In rejecting the Myth of the Given, McDowell intends to reject a mythology about *what* is Given, and how, but not the very idea that anything is. In this respect, McDowell remains a foundationalist.

Re-enchanting the world

Taken just to this point, it might seem unclear how McDowell's solution involves a genuine alternative to the first pole of the Oscillation. Certainly he has reconfigured the concept of experience in a way at odds with the Myth of the Given as he characterizes it. But a reader might well wonder how anything essentially at odds with Coherentism has been proposed – since all that may seem to have been effected is an enlargement of the terms of the coherence relation. Before, we thought of coherence as essentially a relation on beliefs. Now, for basic empirical belief, we impose an additional requirement: coherence with *experience*, with the latter conceived as content-bearing after McDowell. But, for all that has been said, the relation between experience itself and the outer world need still not be conceived as a rational relation. It can still be a matter of brute causality, just as in the case – according to pure doxastic coherentism – of basic empirical beliefs.

What is really amiss with Coherentism in McDowell's view? Early in *Mind and World* it might seem that the basic objection is the spectre of "frictionless-ness" – the threat of what passes for rational empirical thought being unconstrained by experience and hence by the reality experienced ("Frictionless spinning in a void"). This image is not entirely happy, since a coherentist will want to reply that empirical thought, as the coherentist conceives it, *is* subject to tight rational constraints of intra-systematic coherence, with the basic input into the system no more optional, or "frictionless," than causality permits. The coherentist picture is that of a world impinging on us in experience, now thought of in brutely causal terms, and thereby sub-rationally inducing propensities in the experiencer to believe certain things which are then open to refinement in the light of rational coherentist constraints. Experience on this view is precisely not a justifier: it is the *source* but not the *arbiter* of our empirical beliefs. Justification, finally, can only have to do with how such beliefs bed down on the system of belief as a whole.

What is fundamentally wrong with that idea, in McDowell's view? One familiar worry concerns skepticism. Why should beliefs which are initially simply caused in us, and then go on to satisfy certain criteria of relationship to other beliefs which we are disposed to hold, enjoy any intrinsic likelihood of correct representation of the world which causes them? Once the initial causes of belief bear no rational relation to the beliefs caused, any merely intra-systematic constraints surely come too late – the causes of belief, consistently with the coherence of the overall system, could literally be anything at all. Yet justification, properly conceived, cannot bear a merely *extrinsic* relation to truth. We are wide open to radical skepticism otherwise. So we must find some other conception of justification than that afforded by coherentism.

This worry, if it were good, would remain even after experiences as well as beliefs are incorporated within the field of the coherence relation. Davidson, of course, is famous for an attempt to meet it head-on, arguing directly that the specter of massive error which it floats can be exorcized a priori by consideration of the constraints on content exerted by the mere fact of our interpretability.[14] But actually I doubt that a coherentist should take the worry seriously in the first place, since the robust correspondence conception of truth which it exploits – truth as fit with something brutely exterior – is or ought to be a casualty of coherentism itself. In any case, this is not McDowell's worry. He charges, rather, that Davidson's argument – of which he makes no internal criticism – "starts too late."[15] The real and prior concern, he suggests, is the availability of anything which could justly be regarded as *empirical content* once the impact of experience upon belief is conceived as merely causal.[16]

This point is crucial to the development of McDowell's argument, if I understand it at all, and it is therefore unsatisfactory that it is not more fully and adequately developed in the book. To be sure, the basic idea is not implausible. The thought will be, I take it, that the content of any judgment has to be fully determined in the rational – *internal* – relations it bears to other judgments and content-bearers at large. But causation is an *external* relation. That a belief is – merely – caused by certain experiences, or by the will of the Cartesian demon, or by the vat-controlling mad scientist, or whatever else, is nothing to determine its content. If there is to be such a thing as empirical content, then it requires an internal relation between judgment and experience; there is nothing in the mere fact that certain beliefs are characteristically *caused* in a certain way to determine their content at all. The root failing of the Davidsonian conception, in McDowell's view, is that it can find no room for genuine empirical content.

This suggestion, that empirical content requires more than causal connections between experience and beliefs, may seem both dogmatic and oversimplified. It is oversimplified, first, because nothing has yet been said about the content of our *theoretical* beliefs – *par excellence*, beliefs concerning unobservables whose states and processes do not directly impinge upon experience at all; and second, because it will certainly need qualification to accommodate even a modest degree of externalism about content (of which McDowell has of course been a strong supporter). It is dogmatic because it simply brushes aside the aspirations of those philosophers who have worked toward some form of "naturalised semantics."[17] But it had better be basically right if what seems to be the needed next step in McDowell's progression is to be well motivated. That step will be the thought that *the same point must hold for experience*, conceived as a content-bearer. What content an experience has will be essentially underdetermined by how it is externally induced. If an experience is to count as an experience that P, then it must sustain not merely causal but *rational* – internal – relations to potential items in reality.

So – if McDowell is right – not just experience, as a potential justifier of empirical beliefs, but the *real world* in turn, as that which is to be capable of impinging upon us in a way which induces experiences of determinate content, must be thought of as *conceptual*. We arrive at a conception of experience not merely as something which is intrinsically content-bearing, a passive exercise of concepts, but as also essentially an "openness to the layout of reality,"[18] where this openness is a matter of conceptual fit between the experience and the situation experienced. The world, as we must conceive of it, is indeed the Tractarian world: a totality of *facts*, where facts are essentially facts that P. Conceptual content, in McDowell's metaphysics, belongs to the very fabric of the world.

There is more to come. Someone could agree that this – as we might style it – sophisticated naive realism is demanded by a satisfactory orchestration of the notions of experience, justification, and truth and still worry about keeping company with McDowell when it comes to the full "re-enchantment" of the world that he attempts in the later lectures in the play with "Second Nature" and the generalization of Aristotelian moral psychology. It is a good question whether those later moves are not simply independent of the development just reviewed. But before coming to that, I will canvass some doubts about the initial basic move: the "conceptualization" of experience.

Experience as the passive exercise of conceptual capacities

It is a consequence of McDowell's proposal that, as he himself emphasizes, some radical refashioning is required of the way we think about the experience of infant humans and animals – in general, of the sensory lives of creatures who lack Spontaneity – who lack the conceptual vocabulary and powers involved in the critical formation of judgments. If my experience of the desk in front of me essentially draws – albeit passively – upon my conceptual repertoire, then that state is not one which can be entered into by a conceptless creature. Such a creature cannot have sense–experience, so conceived, nor can it occupy a state approximating a genuine experience in all respects save the exercise of concepts; for that would be another form of the Myth of the Given – such a state would be *raw material* for the conceptualization the creature cannot supply. As McDowell says, in his Kantian jargon: to the "co-operation between receptivity and spontaneity" involved in empirical judgment, the former is not to make an "even notionally separable contribution."[19]

So: it cannot be within a creature's consciousness in all respects as if it was seeing a tree except that it lacks concepts – though such a creature may of course show itself sensitive to its surroundings. And – here comes the rub – it also cannot be within a creature's consciousness in all respects as if it were experiencing pain – save that it lacks the concept pain. This does great violence. For our ordinary thinking finds no dependence of the capacity to experience pain on the possession of the concept; and it finds nothing for a pain to be if its essence is not to be found within consciousness.

McDowell, of course, has long been exceedingly well aware of this problem for his view. He regards it as something that calls, not for concern about the correctness of his position, but for "keeping one's head"[20] and much of the final lecture is devoted to a fresh attempt – wholly unpersuasive to this reader at least – to enlist Gadamer's help in an attempt to mitigate it. But ought it to have arisen at all? I shall consider two, mutually somewhat opposed doubts.

The immediate question is how soundly motivated is McDowell's conceptualization of experience? The key premise is that justificatory relations have to be contentual, and so can be sustained only by conceptually structured items. This is of course utterly ungainsayable when *inferential* justification is at issue – when justification consists in the adduction of supportive, independently attested claims whose acceptance is supposed to license the claim justified. But that is not the correct conception of perceptual justification – of the status of those of our beliefs which we form on the basis of what we take to be direct perception and consider to be justified thereby. McDowell proceeds as though in such a case experience has to take over something *akin* to the role played by belief in inferential cases: that non-inferential justification differs from inferential only in that the justifier is not a belief but some other content-bearing state. Call this the *quasi-inferential* conception of empirical justification. Generalized, the quasi-inferential conception would have it that each of our justified beliefs is justified by its relation to an antecedent *something-that-P*. What marks off the inferential cases, strictly so regarded, is that their justifiers are themselves beliefs. But what enforces the quasi-inferential conception? Might it be that in insisting, contrary to Davidson, that justifiers need not be beliefs, McDowell has unwittingly cut the ground from under the key premise that justifiers have to bear contentual relations to what is justified?

It might seem that, absent the quasi-inferential conception, we have nothing to stand in the way of the awkward, dubiously coherent thought that actually *nothing* justifies some of our justified – empirical – beliefs. But that is not so. McDowell's idea is that in experience, one has it appear to one that P. And this fact, the appearance that P, is then available to discharge something akin to the role that a prior belief plays in a case of inferential justification. But while it may not be clear what exactly to put in opposition to it, it is by no means obvious that this is the right picture in general of non-inferentially justified belief. Rather, if we take ourselves to have the capacity to arrive at knowledge, or justified belief of certain kinds without inference, that may undercut the thought that justification always requires a specific, content-sensitive justifier. It may be enough, for instance, that a belief is formed in circumstances when one (justifiably) takes the efficient operation of some appropriate faculty – perception, memory, mathematical intuition maybe – to be responsible for it. There would then be no need for the intermediary something-that-P – no need, indeed, for a justificatory Given at all, whether conceptual or not. Experiences would not be rightly conceived as the justifiers of perceptual beliefs. But nor would the justification of perceptual beliefs be a matter of their coherence within a larger system of belief. There is much more to say about this, but I cannot pursue it here. It is, though, surprising that McDowell – who is usually good at noticing unthinking analogies at work in our philosophizing – passes over the analogy he presupposes in the quasi-inferential conception.[21]

The second doubt about McDowell's conceptualization of experience contrasts with the foregoing by retaining the quasi-inferential conception, and granting McDowell that the justificatory potential of experience depends upon its being received as a carrier of content. However, it balks at the idea that sets up the difficulty with infants and animals – the idea that in order for experience to have this potential, the *very having of it* demands the exercise of conceptual capacities. McDowell sees no space between the ideas that experience is a brute Given – blind intuition with nothing to say – and his own preferred conception that it essentially draws on the passive exercise of conceptual capacities. But there is, of course, intermediate space. In order to avoid a non-justificatory Given, it is required that experience justifies by dint of conceptual content; in order to avoid the difficulty with animal- and infant-experience it is required that the mere occurrence of an experience does not require the exercise of conceptual capacities. These are not incompatible requirements. Both can be met quite simply if it is allowed that an experience of the outer world, while not itself ontologically dependent upon an actual exercise of conceptual capacities, is intrinsically such as to carry the information, for a suitably conceptually endowed creature, that P.

On this view, the very same event in my consciousness that constitutes experiencing the desk in front of me could take place even had I lacked any of the concepts by which I now give it shape. But what would then have taken place is nevertheless intrinsically such as to permit that particular conceptual shaping. So I, who do have those concepts, have no rational option, on receiving this particular experience, but to allow that it may – at least defeasibly – be so shaped. The justificatory use to which I put the experience thus does indeed depend upon the passive exercise of concepts, just as McDowell insists; and the experience is essentially such as to allow of that particular shaping. But its very existence does not depend upon its actually being so shaped.

This simple idea should not, I think, be identified with (anything akin to) Gareth Evans's conception of *non-conceptual* content (whatever the justice in McDowell's claim that Evans's idea is a version of the Myth of the Given). The claim, that is, is not that an experience can carry some form of content without being actively conceptualized – what I am suggesting is neutral on that – but rather that its role in justification demands only that it has the intrinsic potential to command a certain conceptual response from a suitably endowed thinker – not that such a response is constitutive of its very being. I can see nothing in the reasons which prompt McDowell to attempt to conceive of experience as essentially conceptually contentful which demands that it depend for its very existence on the *actual* exercise of concepts. Indeed, the resources for a more modest view are present in McDowell's own account. For *facts* too – the truth-makers to which, in experience, we are, as he holds, receptive – are likewise, on McDowell's view, essentially conceptually structured. But *their* conceptuality does not require that they exist only as *actually* conceived. McDowell is quite clear, as he had better be if the accusation of Idealism is to be as undeserved as he wishes,[22] that facts are conceptual only in so far as essentially conceiv*able*. So a fact is essentially such as, for an appropriate subject, to be conceived as the fact that P; but its existence – what makes for the truth of the proposition that P – need not depend upon anyone's actually exercising any of the concepts constituent in that proposition. What, then, is the obstacle to an absolutely parallel conception of experience? Of course it would be a version of the Given – but the Mythical component (of non-conceptual justification) is just what it aims to avoid.

This commonsensical suggestion is so salient that I find it hard to believe that McDowell does not somewhere intend to speak directly to it. But I have been unable to be sure where. Unless it is open to decisive objection, much of the dialectical progression of the first half of *Mind and World* is undercut. McDowell's proposal, that we should regard it as intrinsic to experience that it draws on the very conceptual resources involved in active, self-critical thought, will be supererogatory; we will be able to dismount from the seesaw without it, or the problem it gives with infant and animal experience.

Rampant Platonism, Second Nature, and *Bildung*

Still, the Oscillation, and its solution, was only to be a route into a more general insight. McDowell's diagnosis of why philosophers – even philosophers as skilled and perceptive as Evans and Davidson – altogether overlook the very possibility of his preferred conception of experience is independent of the obligatoriness of that conception.

The diagnosis runs like this. We share perceptual sensitivity with infants and non-conceptual animals. But such creatures are purely natural beings, and their sentience is an aspect of their animal, natural lives. So sentience should be an aspect of *our* natural, animal life too – but "it can seem impossible to reconcile the fact that sentience belongs to nature with the thought that Spontaneity might permeate our perceptual experience itself."[23] So the block, according to the diagnosis, is the combination of these three thoughts: (a) human sentience, like animal sentience, ought to be a purely natural phenomenon; (b) human sentience – on McDowell's conception – involves the exercise of concepts; (c) concept-exercise is *not*, in the relevant sense, a natural phenomenon – the Space of Reasons is not the Realm of Law.

The conception of nature that poses the problem – that nature is co-extensive with the province of the kind of intelligibility which is sought by natural science – can seem, McDowell concedes, "sheer common sense." The medieval mind did not clearly distinguish this kind of intelligibility from that which belongs to the Space of Reasons. But we – rightly – separate them sharply, and that is the source of our difficulty: it is, in McDowell's diagnosis, the root assumption that causes us to overlook the possibility of regarding experience as conceptual. For if our sensibility, our interaction with the world via experience, is through-and-through natural in this modern sense – if what goes on in experience has to be capable of being made complete sense of in terms of the categories of natural science – then it may seem that it cannot be anything *intrinsically* reason-giving or conceptual. So it looks as though McDowell's conception of experience must either involve a reversion to a pre-scientific superstition – "a crazily nostalgic attempt to re-enchant the natural world"[24] – or like a stubborn *supernaturalism*: either a nostalgic rejection of the modern conception of nature, a reversion to a cast of mind that looks for *meaning* in the "movement of the planets, or the fall of a sparrow,"[25] or an insistence that we place our participation in the Space of Reasons as a phenomenon which has nothing at all to do with what is (merely) natural.

If that is the diagnosis, how is the problem to be resolved? Suppose we accept, with McDowell, that, against Bald Naturalism, "the idea of knowing one's way about in the Space of Reasons, the idea of responsiveness to rational relationships, cannot be reconstructed out of materials which are naturalistic in the sense we are trying to supersede",[26] that is materials which belong to the Realm of Law. How in that case are we to avoid thinking of the Space of Reasons as an autonomous structure, independent of anything specifically human (since humans are *natural* beings, a species of animal), a structure to which, or so it may seem we have to think, we are somehow able to latch on by dint of some special – *supernatural* – capacity?

That is the key thought of Rampant Platonism. Yet McDowell does not think that we need have anything to do with that either. He is above all anxious to persuade us that it is possible to accept the autonomy of the Space of Reasons – that ordinary intentional psychology, ethics, logic, and mathematics do not need to be reconstructed or somehow made sense of in terms of the framework of modern Naturalism – without succumbing to the mythology which credits them with supernatural subject matters, to which only special, non-natural capacities enable us to respond.

This is potentially the most deep-reaching and important idea in the book. McDowell writes:

> To reassure ourselves that our responsiveness to reasons is not super-natural, we should dwell on the thought that it is our lives that are shaped by spontaneity, patterned in ways that come into view only with an enquiry framed by what Davidson calls "the constitutive ideal of rationality". Exercises of spontaneity belong to our mode of living. And our mode of living is a way of actualising ourselves as animals. So we can rephrase the thought by saying: exercises of spontaneity belong to our way of actualising ourselves as animals. This removes any need to try to see ourselves as peculiarly bifurcated, with a foothold in the animal kingdom and a mysterious separate involvement in an extra-natural world of rational connections.[27]

But I wonder how well it is possible to understand this suggestion. The key issue, evidently, is the precise contrast intended between Rampant Platonism, which involves supernaturalist mythology, and the "humanized" or "naturalized" Platonism which McDowell believes that we can take in stride, without reductive hankerings, once we have worked our way into a better conception of the natural. To help us achieve that conception McDowell advises that a prototype may be elicited from Aristotle's conception of ethical thought: a form of thought which is intrinsically human but which is nevertheless responsive to autonomous demands. He summarizes the Aristotelian conception like this:

> The ethical is a domain of rational requirements which are there in any case, whether or not we are responsive to them. We are alerted to these demands by acquiring appropriate conceptual capacities. When a decent upbringing initiates us into the relevant way of thinking, our eyes are open to the very existence of this tract of the Space of Reasons. Thereafter our appreciation of its detailed layout is indefinitely subject to refinement, in reflective scrutiny of our ethical thinking.[28]

So we should ask: why exactly is Aristotle's view, so characterized, not a form of Rampant (ethical) Platonism? Here is McDowell's answer:

The rational demands of ethics are not alien to the contingencies of our life as human beings. ... [An] ordinary upbringing can shape the actions and thoughts of human beings in a way that brings these demands into view. ... The rational demands of ethics are autonomous

– they do not need validation or interpretation from outside specifically ethical thinking –

but this autonomy does not distance the demands from anything specifically human ... they are essentially within reach of human beings (who have been) ... initiated into the structure of the space of reasons by ethical upbringing ... the resulting habits of thought and action are *second-nature*.[29]

The key features of Aristotle's conception which, as McDowell would seem to intend, serve to distinguish it from anything "rampant," thus appear to be these:

(i)   that the correctness of ethical judgment is constrained by "contingencies of our life";
(ii) that it needs only an ordinary, unmysterious ethical education to initiate people into "the rational demands of ethics";
(iii) that correct ethical judgment is "essentially within reach" of our ethical thinking.

But how exactly do these considerations sustain the crucial distinction that McDowell is trying to draw? The first, the idea that correct ethical judgment is sensitive to contingencies of human life, may seem like a mere banality. It is merely banal for instance that, had we possessed different needs and concerns, then our assessment of the ethical value of specific practices and institutions might well have been different; and there is no reason why any ethical platonist, of however extreme or "rampant" a stripe, need deny it. Compare: had our beliefs been different, then we would have regarded our logical commitments as different – hardly the same thing as saying that logic is constitutively sensitive to contingencies in human belief. To be sure, that suggests a less banal interpretation: perhaps McDowell intends that, had certain contingencies of human life been different, then different *principles of ethical evaluation* which are not at present cogent would have become so – that *general moral norms* are hostage to contingencies of human nature. That idea would indeed be at odds with the notion that ethical truth is constituted in some supernatural sphere. But it wants argument, in detail. And if that were the suggestion McDowell intends to be making, it would anyway seem to have no defensible analogue for logic – or any domain of necessary truth. Yet logic, no less than ethics, is a sphere for which McDowell wishes to commend the humanized platonism of second nature which reflection on Aristotelian ethics is supposed to help us understand.

The import of the second and third considerations seems to be equally ambiguous and undeveloped. Why should Rampant Platonists find any difficulty in the idea that it takes only an ordinary training to trigger the exercise of the special non-natural epistemic capacities in which they believe? What exactly is the problem in that combination? And what does it mean to say that ethical truth is "essentially within reach" of human beings who have had the appropriate upbringing? Presumably the point is not meant to be hostage to the occurrence of otherwise rational but morally ineducable psychopaths. Is it the suggestion that moral truths are necessarily recognizable by ordinary moral thought? That may seem attractive. But the analogous thesis for logic and mathematics is of course contestable, and highly contested. And besides, if a philosopher thought that ordinary moral thinking involved the exercise of non-natural capacities, why would it cause a problem for this view to allow – if it is so – that moral truths are essentially decidable in principle? There is no evident tension.

McDowell thinks we can attain the distinction between Rampant Platonism and his recommended "naturalized" platonism by a judicious invocation of the notion of Second Nature and by taking on something of the concept that features in German philosophy as *Bildung*.[30] I am skeptical whether it would be possible for even the most willing and open-minded reader to glean any sufficiently clear understanding of the matter from the account in Lecture IV. The root idea seems merely to be that we can free ourselves of the temptations both of (bald) naturalistic reconstruction of the subject matters and epistemology of normative discourses and of a contrasting platonistic mythologizing of them if only we remind ourselves often enough, with the appropriate Aristotelian and German texts open, that these express forms of thought into which it comes naturally to us to be educable. But it is simply not explained how that is supposed to help. It is perplexing to find so vital a distinction for its author's purposes confined to so unfinished and merely suggestive a formulation. We need more.

The discussion in Lecture IV is not, indeed, McDowell's last word on the matter. The contrast is invoked again in §3 of Lecture V to underpin a proposal about the interpretation of Wittgenstein on rule-following and is further emphasized in various passages of summary in the final lecture.[31] But matters do not get significantly clearer. Thus apropos of his preferred reading of Wittgenstein, McDowell writes:

> The idea is that the dictates of reason are there anyway, whether or not one's eyes are opened to them ... [by] ... a proper upbringing.

And there is no obligation on us to try to understand how they can be objects for

> an enlightened awareness, except from within the way of thinking such an upbringing initiates one into.

This is, McDowell asserts,

> quite distinct from rampant platonism [in which] ... the rational struc-
> ture within which meaning comes into view is independent of
> anything merely human so that [our capacity] to resonate [sic] to it
> looks occult or magical.

For naturalized platonism,

> the structure of the space of reasons has a sort of autonomy; it is not
> derivative from, or reflective of, truths about human beings that are
> capturable independently of having that structure in view. [But] ... the
> structure of the space of reasons is not constituted in splendid isolation
> from anything merely human. The demands of reason are essentially
> such that a human upbringing can open a human being's eyes to
> them.[32]

This offers nothing new. It is of course open to McDowell to *define* a rampant
platonist view as one according to which the "demands of reason" are *not*
essentially such as to be accessible to a normal human upbringing. (I pass over
the fact that, naturally read, McDowell's words bear interpretation as implying
a problematical insistence that logical truth must be decidable.) But it
becomes no clearer in these passages than it was made in Lecture IV why it
might be supposed to follow – if indeed it does follow – from our natural
educability into responsiveness to the "demands of reason" that both the epistemology and the ontology of discourses which feature the categories of
Spontaneity can with clear conscience be regarded as fully "natural" – that is,
that no non-natural capacities are involved in responsiveness to the "demands
of reason," and that there should be no temptation toward naturalistic reductive construal of normative discourses like ethics and intentional psychology.
Someone so tempted will doubtless be in the grip of a certain restrictive
conception of what there is: probably precisely the idea that reality is
exhausted by the Realm of Law. McDowell's aim is to show how it need not be
a kind of supernaturalism to repudiate that restriction. But if someone is
puzzled about how in the natural world, as he or she conceives it, there can be
such things as "demands of reason" – how there can be a real subject matter
for various forms of normative discourse – some massive unstated assumption
would seem to be at work in McDowell's suggestion that we can teach him or
her otherwise simply by a reminder, however eloquently elaborated in terms of
the concepts of *Bildung* and the acquisition of a Second Nature, that our initiation into such discourses is a matter of the perfectly ordinary human
upbringing which our nature equips us to receive.

Now, one can see what kind of assumption *would* serve the purpose. What
McDowell needs is a way of channeling the philosophical pressure that modern

naturalism generates away from a direct obsession with the subject matter of normative discourses and onto their learning and practice instead. I believe an illuminating prototype of the needed readjustment is provided by the Fregean treatment of certain kinds of abstract object which I and others have elaborated and recommended.[33] The goal, in the most general terms, is to achieve a perspective from which the good-standing of a discourse is somehow provided for first, without attempting any prior direct engagement – on questionably motivated assumptions – with the metaphysics and epistemology of its proper objects and concepts. Thus we do not ask directly what sort of things numbers, say, could be and how one might know about them. Instead, we ask how arithmetic, and the ordinary statements whereby it is applied, get their meaning and how that meaning might be grasped. Once those questions have been given the right kind of answer, the mere integrity of the language-game carries the ontological and epistemological issues in its wake and there is no space for a residual concern about the place of the subject matter of arithmetic in the natural world or the knowability of its objects by human beings. I take this general form of inversion – "language-games first; ontology second" – to be a way of assimilating one of the deeper readjustments of the philosophy of language of the *Tractatus* that Wittgenstein made in his later work. Although Wittgenstein is not the most explicitly prominent of the cast of characters in *Mind and World*, I believe McDowell would freely acknowledge Wittgenstein's influence on his discussion in this general respect. However, the crux is, of course, how one sets about motivating the inversion, and what kind of work is conceived as going into the disclosure of "good-standing" for a discourse which, for whatever reason, causes concern. Disclosing such good-standing must involve showing that the statements of the discourse in question may quite legitimately be regarded as true or false – and that the distinctive objects and properties with which they deal may consequently be viewed as genuine, without further reductive obligation – in the light of nothing beyond the standards which we actually normally apply within the discourse. One approach in this connection which I myself have followed is via the development of so-called *minimalist* conceptions of truth and truth-aptitude.[34] A different though not incompatible line is taken by Huw Price's functionalist treatment of the concepts of truth and fact.[35] But McDowell seems to recognize no definite theoretical obligation in this direction. (Naturally not: philosophers are not supposed to *construct* anything.) This makes his treatment, to this reader at least, almost wholly unsatisfying. It is not of course *irrelevant* that a competence in normative discourses is one product of a normal human education. But the point, however fancy the packaging, hardly measures up to the fixation of the entrenched dilemma between Rampant Platonism and reductionism, and it is, disappointingly, unclear what more to the purpose *Mind and World* ultimately has to offer. I fear that not many of those who have so far failed to see the point of this kind of inversion, or to get a sense of its liberating power, will be moved to a different view by McDowell's treatment here.

* * *

I do not think, then, for the reasons I have explained, that either of the main contentions of Mind and World – that experience must be conceived as conceptual, and that one should look to a conception of Second Nature for a reconciliation of the normative with the natural – is developed with convincing clarity; but they are original suggestions on profound, central problems, and either may yet prove to be a lasting contribution. In any case it would be quite unjust to close without emphasizing that this is, on any reasonable count, a very impressive book. There is no doubting the importance to contemporary Western philosophy of the direction of its main endeavor, and the philosophical power and charisma of its author leap out from almost every page. It contains discussions in detail of many issues – privacy, non-conceptual content, action and bodily movement, the Cartesian self, epistemological skepticism, and, in the Afterword, additional detailed consideration of ideas of Davidson, Quine, Rorty, and Wittgenstein – that I have not touched upon in this notice and which will get and repay careful study. In a certain sense, it is also a work of Kantian exegesis, and will be read with profit by interpreters of that philosopher. Throughout, the text is extremely carefully crafted and displays such a flowing, confident, forcefully idiosyncratic style that philosophically impressionable readers are likely to be overwhelmed by the example which it presents.

That is the main trouble. If analytical philosophy demands self-consciousness about unexplained or only partially explained terms of art, formality, and explicitness in the setting out of argument, and the clearest possible sign-posting and formulation of assumptions, targets, and goals, etc., then this is not a work of analytical philosophy. Any professional who sets him- or herself to work through it will rapidly conclude that, before one can assess, let alone appropriate its achievement, there will be a need for *constructive exegesis* – for a reworking of the characteristic idiom of the book and the exploration of interpretative hypotheses – to a degree which one normally associates only with the study of writers from the past, before the academic professionalization of the subject. At its worst, indeed, McDowell's prose puts barriers of jargon, convolution, and metaphor before the reader hardly less formidable than those characteristically erected by his German luminaries. Why is this? It cannot be that he thinks that the care and rigor which we try to instill into our students is merely a fetish, unjustified by anything in their projects or the philosophical subject matter. Is it that he views the kind of deconstruction of existing research programs in analytical philosophy to which his work is directed as something which cannot be accomplished save by writing of quite a different – rhetorical or "therapeutic" – genre?[36]

I don't know the answer to that question, but the stylistic extravagance of McDowell's book – more extreme than in any of his other writings to date – will unquestionably color the influence it will exert. If that influence is largely toward renewed efforts on the agenda – to new work on the hard epistemological questions about the interface between thought and experience, and to a re-examination of the assumptions that generate the dualism of norm and

157

nature that we have anyway somehow to overcome; if so, then, to that extent, its influence will be all to the good. But the fear must be that the book will encourage too many of the susceptible to swim out of their depth in seas of rhetorical metaphysics. Wittgenstein complained that "The seed I am most likely to sow is a certain jargon." One feels that, if so, he had only himself to blame. McDowell is a strong swimmer, but his stroke is not to be imitated.

Notes

1 Preface, p.ix. All page references are to *Mind and World* unless otherwise stated.
2 McDowell's writing is scaffolded by a characteristic jargon of Kantian (and Sellarsian) contrasts: Spontaneity vs. Receptivity; Sensibility vs. Understanding; Concepts vs. Intuitions, the Space of Reasons vs. the Realm of (Natural) Law, and so on.
3 McDowell allows (p.73) that Bald Naturalism need not involve actual reductive identifications of denizens of the Space of Reasons with items recognized in the Realm of Law: "What matters is just that ideas whose primary home is the space of reasons are depicted as, after all, serving to place things in nature in the relevant sense." It is not terribly clear what sort of latitude he means to leave but – one possibility – a number of philosophers have supposed, for instance, that the mere *supervenience* of ethical discourse on descriptions of natural fact is somehow already sufficient to show that ethics makes no distinctive ontological demands. However, the matter is certainly not straightforward. Since McDowell advises that we should "set our faces" against Bald Naturalism, it would have been better if he had been more explicit about the options he considers open to it besides the strictly reductive – which is indeed widely regarded as Quixotic.
4 p.78.
5 p.42.
6 p.8.
7 At p.310 of Donald Davidson's "A Coherence Theory of Truth and Knowledge," in Ernest LePore (ed.), *Truth and Interpretation: Perspectives on the Philosophy of Donald Davidson* (Oxford: Blackwell, 1987), pp.307–319.
8 This version of the Myth wants distinguishing from a "Myth" which Quine and Sellars are famous for rejecting. McDowell's Mythical Given is non-conceptual input, conceived as presented in sentience anyway, whether brought under concepts or not. By contrast, the Myth rejected by Quine is the (two-way independent) empiricist Myth of a base class of empirical judgments whose acceptability is settled just by the occurrence of episodes of sentience, independently of whatever collateral beliefs a subject may hold – a Myth of one–one mandating relations, as it were, between experience and a basic range of *synthetic* statements (in the sense of "Two Dogmas").
9 p.76.
10 pp.74–76.
11 p.74.
12 p.9.
13 p.10.
14 In "A Coherence Theory of Truth and Knowledge."
15 p.17.
16 Lecture I, §6, *passim*.
17 Which may be exactly what they deserve. For a useful catalog of the problems, see Barry Loewer's "A Guide to Naturalising Semantics" in Bob Hale and Crispin Wright (eds), *A Companion to the Philosophy of Language* (Oxford: Blackwell, 1997).

18 p.26.
19 p.9.
20 From p.300 of his "One Strand in the Private Language Argument" in *Grazer Philosophische Studien* 33/4: 287–303 (1989).
21 We may expect that he would express disquiet about the foregoing proposal along similar lines to his fundamental concern about coherentism: that to reject the quasi-inferential conception is to have no story to tell about the determination of empirical content.
22 McDowell's rebuttal of the charge occurs at pp.26–27 and following, and pp.39–40.
23 p.70.
24 p.72.
25 Ibid.
26 p.77.
27 p.78.
28 p.82.
29 Selected from pp.83–84.
30 p.84.
31 For example, at pp.109–110, and at p.123.
32 pp.91–92.
33 See, for example, Bob Hale's *Abstract Objects* (Oxford: Blackwell, 1987), and my *Frege's Conception of Numbers as Objects* (Aberdeen: Aberdeen University Press, 1983).
34 See my *Truth and Objectivity* (Cambridge, MA: Harvard University Press, 1992).
35 Huw Price, *Facts and the Function of Truth* (Oxford: Blackwell, 1988).
36 He does write at one point (pp.94–95) as if we ought to welcome a supersession of "ordinary modern philosophy," but he does not seem in that passage to have in mind more than the supersession of the kind of project of constructive rehabilitation which modern naturalism encourages.

POSTSCRIPT TO CHAPTER 8

Crispin Wright

The discussion in the first part of "Human Nature?" of the *Mind and World* "seesaw" or "oscillation" substantially overlapped with my comments in a *Philosophy and Phenomenological Research* Book Symposium, where McDowell contributed an expectably unbending response.[1] Responses to responses are subject to a law of diminishing returns; but there is more to say and I am grateful to Nicholas Smith for giving me an opportunity to reply. Whether returns have indeed diminished is for readers of this volume to judge.

To recap a little: the problem that preoccupies McDowell in the first half of *Mind and World* is how best to conceive of experience if it is to exert a genuinely *rational* influence on – provide reasons for, not merely causes of – basic empirical beliefs. The poles of McDowell's "oscillation" both think of experience in the same way, as "occurrences in consciousness that are independent of conceptual capacities"[2] – a kind of brute impingement on awareness. One – Coherentism – accordingly concedes that experience is indeed not a rational influence (justifier) but merely a causal source of beliefs, whose justification, properly so regarded, is then confined to their relations to other beliefs. The other – the "Myth of the Given" – tries to maintain that experience, even conceived as a brute impact, can somehow justify basic empirical beliefs nevertheless. But that, supposedly, is hopeless. So: the seesaw is powered by two incompatible thoughts about experience conceived as brute: it had better be a justifier – but that is a Myth – so it cannot justify, and the best we can do is Coherentism – but that is radically unsatisfactory – so it had better be a justifier – but that is a Myth – so it cannot justify, and so on.

Obviously it is crucial to McDowell's treatment of the issue that we cannot comfortably settle for either station. I think the respective cases for thinking so offered in *Mind and World* remain undeveloped (in the case of Coherentism) and simply unconvincing (in the case of the Myth). The principal weakness in the latter, to which I shall return, derives from McDowell's failure to characterize the targeted error sufficiently sharply. Let me observe again that he does not dismiss the idea that something *is* "given" in experience: he believes in a *conceptual* given – what he regards as mythical is, rather, the notion of a given which is both justificatory *and* "independent of conceptual capacities." He does not argue for this incompatibility but just asserts it, and I do not know how he would rebut an awkward customer who just counter-asserted that "occurrences in consciousness that are independent of conceptual capacities" can justify. But I believe one could agree with McDowell about that – and grant him that Coherentism is radically unsatisfactory – yet still be unpersuaded that his refashioning of experience is called for. The key issue turns on the interpretation of the dangerously imprecise "independent of conceptual capacities." The weakness in the rebuttal of Coherentism, by contrast, remains its dependence on a thesis about the necessary conditions for empirical content – or "objective purport" (p.365) – which, correct or not, McDowell leaves inchoate.

I shall confine my observations to three headings: McDowell's reaction to my comments on his treatment of Coherentism; his attempt to enlist Wittgenstein's support in defense of his conception of experience; and his reactions to two suggestions I made about ways we might "dismount the seesaw" without conceptualizing experience.

Coherentism and content

McDowell embraces not just essentially conceptualized experience but a view of the world as conceptual too: a world of Tractarian *facts* – of conceptually structured states of affairs. It seemed to me useful, in trying to understand this, to consider a kind of half-way house position: an Extended Coherentism which allowed experience to carry conceptual content (without worrying too much about how it gets it) and regarded justification as a matter of coherence over a larger domain including both beliefs and experiences, but which viewed experience itself as standing in merely causal relations to the world. The point of considering this position was to focus on the question: what is McDowell's most fundamental dissatisfaction with Coherentism? If it were just the consideration which impels one side of the seesaw – the uncomfortable thought that Coherentism denies experience any properly justificatory role – then this adjustment would successfully still the movement without any need for the additional "re-enchantment" of the world involved in thinking of it as a totality of facts that P. So it seemed reasonable to conclude that the real dissatisfaction lay elsewhere: precisely in the point about which McDowell finds me "gratifyingly clear," that there is an issue about how Coherentism, even of this extended variety, could make a place for anything amounting to genuine empirical content. It would follow, if that is a good concern, that it is a precondition of the objective purport of the beliefs based upon it that experience stands not (merely) in causal relationships to the world but sustains *internal* relations to it, relations which would accordingly demand the conceptually structured nature of the latter. In brief: the "re-enchantment" of the world would emerge as a precondition of the objective purport of the beliefs which experience is apt to justify.

Given that it led me to "gratifying clarity" about a central point, it seems mean-spirited of McDowell to dismiss this train of thought as "a very uncooperative attempt at spelling out my drift" (p.426). He complains that he wanted experience to be conceived as "sensory consciousness of objective reality" from the start and that his thought never moved through a half-way house with experience *first* conceived as carrying conceptual content, and *then* construed as direct receptivity. But these complaints reveal a misunderstanding. I did not intend to ascribe to McDowell any "interim conclusion." My point was *meant* to be cooperative – but it was not to speculate about McDowell's actual ratiocinative sequence, still less to try to *spell out* the "crucial transcendental thought" about the problem Coherentism is supposed to have with objective purport. Rather it was to eliminate a compromise position which might seem, to a Coherentist, to be responsive to the need to have experience as a justifier, and to bring out that and why McDowell had better have a further concern about Coherentism which would not be met by this compromise. That further concern is, again, the "crucial transcendental thought": that, as I should express it, merely causal – hence external – relations to a subject matter cannot sustain beliefs – or experiences – being *about* that subject matter. But my attempt was not to spell this out – that is, make a case for its cogency, which I do not know how to do – but to show how McDowell's position must be understood as demanding it, both to stop Extended Coherentism from stilling the oscillation and to enforce the first stage of "re-enchantment."

McDowell continues to misread me when he writes that "Wright charges the interim conclusion ... with [an] oversimplification: it says nothing about theoretical beliefs" (p.427). The charge is not of oversimplification but, again, of omission, and it bears not on any "interim conclusion" but on McDowell's master thought about the failings of Coherentism, that it cannot accommodate the "objective purport" of basic empirical beliefs. Theoretical beliefs, for present purposes, are precisely those which do not concern aspects of reality which are open to direct awareness. One way of understanding the master thought about basic empirical beliefs would be this: that in order for such a belief to be just that – to have a content concerning some aspect of the objective empirical world – it has to be possible for the very facts in virtue of which it is true, or false, to exert a rational control over its acceptance. That *seems* to be McDowell's (nowhere elaborated) idea. Suppose it is right. Well, presumably *that* constraint cannot be met by any theoretical beliefs, since – *qua* theoretical – their truth-makers are not items of our awareness and connect only causally with things which are. A weaker version of the master thought would make it a necessary condition of a belief's having objective empirical purport that experience, conceived as direct awareness of states of affairs, exerts, perhaps indirectly, a rational constraint on it. And theoretical beliefs can meet *this* constraint, it would seem, since what controls their acceptability is how well they are able to participate (coherently!) in a system in which basic empirical beliefs also participate. But the question has to be faced: what bestows the content on such beliefs in virtue of which they do or do not so participate? The stronger master thought addresses that question for basic empirical beliefs. But it would be merely dogmatic (or ostrich-like) to assert without further ado that their satisfaction of the weaker constraint is enough to do the job for theoretical beliefs. After all, that need demand no more than a network of *formal* liaisons with basic empirical beliefs.

In brief: McDowell wants to say that Coherentism gives rise to, and cannot address, a legitimate concern about empirical content. I want to say that, in so far as I have a sense of what this concern consists in, McDowell's own response would seem to leave it no better addressed for empirical beliefs about non-observable subject matters. He responds that "all I need is a version of the picture Sellars gives in §VIII of 'Empiricism and the Philosophy of Mind.'" But Sellars in that particular section of his famous paper is concerned with repudiation of a *distinct* Myth of the Given – the Myth of the Synthetic Statement, if I may so put it (see note 8 to "Human Nature?"). Perhaps McDowell thinks that to see that and why there are no pure synthetic statements is to see how satisfaction of something like the constraint embodied in the weaker of the two master thoughts allows "objective purport" to suffuse across the totality of our empirical beliefs. If so, then to appropriate his riposte to another of his commentators (p.408), that seems like magic to me.

But I confess to shadow-boxing, absent any clear statement of what exactly the "transcendental discomfort" about Coherentism and empirical content comes to, and any clear case that it is a discomfort that ought rationally to be felt. That omission remains *my* principal discomfort with McDowell's treatment of Coherentism. McDowell himself seems not to feel any deficiency here; just as Davidson and his followers seem not to feel McDowell's "transcendental discomfort" with their management of the notion of empirical thought.

Animals, infants, and Wittgenstein

To conceptualize experience is to regard any episode of experience, properly so viewed, as involving a *having it seem to one that P*. Someone might observe[3] that in a hallucination, or dream, one can also have it seem to one that P and hence that there is a tension between McDowell's conceptualism and his well-known rejection of the conception of genuine sense-experience and, say, dreaming, as sharing a "highest common factor," a type of event or state essentially ingredient in both. But I do not think he has a difficulty in *this* respect. One can quite comfortably hold that there are a variety of ways in which it can seem to one that P which have no factor in common in the sense McDowell is concerned to deny: that they are not, in particular, to be conceived as events of the same species differing only in their causes but rather, despite their subjective similarities, as occurrences of essentially differing (onto)logical structure. To have it seem to one that P in the course of genuine sense-experience is to stand in a relation of direct awareness to items in the objective world; to have it seem to one that P in the course of a dream, or hallucination, is quite another thing. Sure, one can *mistake* one state for the other; so there is undeniably a subjective similarity captured by the shared description, "having it seem to one that P." But that no more enforces the idea that the items in question have a type of essential ingredient in common than a parallel conclusion is enforced by the mistakability (in suitable circumstances) of a mirror image for the object from which it originates.

The real difficulty is the one I urged in "Human Nature?": that such a conception of experience – experience as essentially a having it seem to one that P – must restrict the capacity for experience – both of the outer and of an "inner" world – to conceptually endowed subjects. Only a thinker capable of grasping the thought that P can have it seem to him or her that P. McDowell continues to try to give the impression that this is a bearable, perfectly intuitive consequence, to be taken in stride. He writes:

> Wright depicts the conception of experience I recommend as some-thing everyone has reason to resist, because of its implications about non-possessors of conceptual capacities. He formulates an implication of my conception like this: "It cannot be within a creature's conscious-ness in all respects as if it were experiencing pain – save that it lacks the concept pain." And he says "This does great violence." But violence to what? A creature can be *feeling pain* though it lacks the concept of pain.
>
> (p.429)

But this bluff attempt at a distinction – in effect, we are invited to suppose that there are two ways of suffering: *feeling* pain and *experiencing* it – should seem merely sophistical, provided that we follow McDowell's own advice and keep a firm grip on the thought that, in the cooperation between "recep-tivity" and "spontaneity," the former "does not make an even notionally separable contribution."[4] That stops us thinking – and is precisely intended so to do – of something which a conceptless creature merely feels – its pain – as *of a kind with* something which goes on within our awareness when we experi-ence pain in McDowell's fuller sense of "experience." *That* would be a "notionally separated" contribution by "receptivity" if anything was. So McDowell's position requires him to regard the surface grammar of "feeling pain" and "experiencing pain" as misleading in its implication of a common component. Contrary to the impression suggested by the common occurrence of "pain," the two conditions literally *have nothing in common*. An animal in pain does not stand in one kind of relation to (an instance of) a certain type of state to which a human in pain stands in another – a different modality of awareness, as it were. To think that way is exactly to make the prohibited notional separation.

What goes missing on the resultant view is any role for empathy or projec-tion in the range of broadly evaluative responses – sympathy, outrage, sadistic satisfaction, delight, etc. – which we have toward the suffering or pleasures of the conceptually innocent. Events and states whose occurrence makes no conceptual demands on their "owner" cannot be understood on the model of events and states which essentially draw upon a conceptual repertoire, events and states which essentially go with *thought*. So it seems that such broadly evaluative responses become groundless, or even unintelligible: where do we look for a satisfactory conception of what is bad about the suffering of an animal or infant *per se* if its state cannot be conceived by analogy with the awful thing that we sometimes *experience*, and if what is awful about the latter depends essentially on its being experienced *as* awful, as falling under that concept? McDowell confidently reaffirms that no damage of this kind is done by his view. But mere confident reaffirmation will not make it true.

Part of what drives his confidence is the belief that the opposed conception is committed to something Wittgenstein exposed as hopeless: sensations as private. McDowell agrees that it is true

> if you like (the wording is not mine), that, according to me, for such a [conceptless] creature to feel pain cannot be for things to be a certain way within its consciousness – the way they are within our consciousness when we feel pain. This does violence to an inclination to suppose that that is what feeling pain, as such, is. But that is not, as Wright suggests, a bit of philosophically uncontaminated common sense. On the contrary, the idea that for a creature to feel pain is for some state of affairs to obtain within its consciousness, from which it may or may not go on to an actualisation of a conceptual capacity, is just the supposed conception of the private object, which is conclusively exposed as hopeless by Wittgenstein ... it is simply a way of taking Wittgenstein's point to say that the idea of states of affairs within consciousness is applicable only where we are already thinking in terms of actualisations of conceptual capacities. This leaves the fact that non-possessors of conceptual capacities can feel pain completely unthreatened.
>
> (p.429)

McDowell's idea would seem to amount to this: that a conception of sensation as something which essentially draws on conceptual capacities represents the only escape from the dilemma between a Cartesian dualism of private objects and outward appearances on the one hand and, on the other, some form of reductive naturalism. This is too large an issue to hope to explore adequately within a short compass, but I think neither that those three proposals – Cartesianism, (bald) naturalism, "McDowellism" – exhaust the options nor that Wittgenstein's discussion either tends or was intended to establish that they do. Philosophizing about sensation simply misses its intended subject matter if it leaves no place for those features of the concept from which the dualistic impulse springs – features which ground a perfectly *innocent* conception of privacy. Here are some examples:

it is often, just in the ordinary run of things, very difficult, even impossible to know what others are feeling;

a subject can in principle be as good as you like at concealing her sensations;

it is the merest platitude that my pains do not hurt anyone else, whereas my hand is a potential object of experience for anyone;

any of us, not just animals and infants, may on occasion be unable adequately to express our feelings; and may quite properly and intelligibly report that we cannot say how we feel;

sometimes it is necessary to experience a sensation for yourself if you are to know what it is like;

it is reasonable to suppose but not absolutely certain that a baby's finger, trapped in a door, feels much the way yours would; and that a biting horse-fly on a cow's skin feels much the way it would on yours.

The conception illustrated by these remarks is constitutive of our ordinary notion of sensation precisely in the sense that a range of putative states of a subject for which analogues of them were inappropriate would just on that account not properly be regarded as *sensations* at all. To be sure, such talk can encourage – can seduce us into acquiescing in – a folk-explanation, or perhaps better, a *model* which does indeed view sensations, and feelings generally, as objects, or states of affairs, whose nature is Cartesian: a model which represents sensations as events within an inner theater to which, necessarily, only a single subject can bear witness. On that model, only the subject can view her own sensations and directly know what they are like, with the familiar consequence that there can be in the end no reason to suppose that any two subjects share the conceptual repertoires under which they respectively taxonomize their inner lives. But I take it to have been a principal point of Wittgenstein's treatment of the issues that we should separate what properly belongs to the "language-game" from the troublesome features of the model whereby we try to represent the way its moves have meaning.

Whatever might be his view of the others, McDowell seems to suppose that the sixth remark above not merely permits the Cartesian model but *demands* it – that to think of an animal's feelings in certain circumstances and those of an articulate human in similar circumstances as being of the same general kind cannot but be interpreted as a commitment to Cartesian privacy. But the sixth remark, as it seems to me, belongs with the others as, indeed, a "piece of philosophically uncontaminated common sense." What is under attack in the famous sections of the *Investigations* is not the conception of sensations as private – in effect, the conception of sensations as *sensations* – which is innocently at work in those various commonplace ways of talking, but the philosophical model of privacy to which we succumb when we accede to the Cartesian picture. It is on the implications of that model for the idea that we have genuine concepts under which we acknowledge and report our sensations that Wittgenstein's attack focuses: in brief, if it is successful, the result is that there is nothing for competence with such a concept to consist in if the subject matter it may purportedly be used to characterize exists in Cartesian privacy. So the *model* – not the ways of talking to which it is applied – is undercut. The upshot of the attack, if it is sustained, is not that it is simply wrong to think of sensations as private but that the Cartesian model of privacy – the inner theater of observation from which all but a single witness are excluded – merely induces misunderstanding of the kinds of ways of talking, illustrated above, which variously express their privacy. Sensations are indeed private, if to say so is merely to advert to the kinds of ways of talking about them illustrated; but they are not private in any sense which would require that it becomes a mere metaphysical hypothesis whether we respectively bring them under a common conceptual vocabulary.[5]

On this reading, McDowell's idea of inner experience as conceptual is exactly *not* "a way of taking Wittgenstein's point"; for it is wholly anti-Wittgensteinian in spirit to see the effect of his work on this issue as being to correct ordinary linguistic practice, as reflected for example in the sixth remark, rather than to adjust a philosophical misunderstanding of that practice. It seems to me that it is simply no implication of that adjustment that conceptless creatures are barred from experiencing any of the sensations which we are accustomed to ascribe to other adult humans and ourselves. When we ascribe pain to an animal, we mean to ascribe to it a state which, *qua* pain, we think we fully understand and to whose assimilation to what we ourselves can experience there is no conceptual barrier. On McDowell's reading, taking Wittgenstein's thought on board would involve that this way of thinking is forfeit: that our mutual intelligibility can be safeguarded at the cost only of deep disanalogy between our inner lives and those – if it still makes any sense to think of them as having inner lives – of the conceptually inarticulate. That conclusion seems to me to be neither desirable nor required – either as a reading of Wittgenstein or as a self-standing proposal about what it takes to escape from Cartesianism.

Dismounting the seesaw (I)

If the foregoing is accepted, then we now face a bind: how *are* basic empirical beliefs to be conceived as justified if not by intra-systematic relations of coherence – supposing the correctness of McDowell's "crucial transcendental thought" – nor by experience conceived as a brute impingement on consciousness, nor by experience conceived as by McDowell? In "Human Nature?" I suggested two possibilities.

The first turns on discarding what I called the *quasi-inferential* conception of how non-inferentially justified beliefs are justified. The quasi-inferential conception (i) calls for something content-bearing to do the justifying (e.g., having it seem to one *that P*) and (ii) requires the content of the justifier to stand in certain kinds of relation to that of the justified (in the best case: identity). On this type of view, non-inferential justification is just like inferential except that it is not other *beliefs* that serve in, so to speak, the premise position, but the non-doxastic content-carrying input states of certain presumed cognitive faculties – perception, on McDowell's view, but a similar story could be extended to memory, logical intuition, and our faculty for self-knowledge.

I suggested that McDowell's thinking about his problem was controlled by this quasi-inferential conception, and that it is not mandatory. For a view is at least structurally possible which dispenses with the content-specific justifiers in which, in their different ways, both a strictly inferentialist Coherentism and the quasi-inferential conception of McDowell believe. On McDowell's view, justification for those basic empirical beliefs to which one moves directly, without any element of inference, is provided by the relation between their content and that of the experiences which move one to them. For Coherentism, their justification is a matter of the relations between their content and that of the beliefs already participant in one's presumed coherent system of belief. But for the view now canvassed, what justifies a belief to which one is just directly moved is one's concurrent entitlement to the presupposition that it is the product of the operation of some appropriate and effectively functioning cognitive faculty. This type of justification is content non-specific in the sense that the specific content of the targeted belief plays no role in determining that it is justified (save perhaps in the very general way that only a belief with a certain *type* of content could sensibly be deemed to be the product of a germane type of cognitive faculty).

McDowell rejects the claim that his thinking is controlled by the quasi-inferential conception – but it manifestly is. Look at what he actually says by way of riposte:

> Unsurprisingly, I do not think this diagnosis fits. ... If it were not for distortions inflicted on our thinking by philosophy, I think it would be obvious that the idea of observational judgement, in particular, involves "a specific, content-sensitive justifier" – namely, the fact observed. The point of the idea of experience is that it is in experience that facts themselves come to be among the justifiers available to subjects; that does not represent experience as a quasi-inferential intermediary between facts and judgements, as in Wright's two-step reading of my thought. It strikes me as obvious enough that observational judgements have specific content-sensitive justifiers – apart, as I say, from philosophically generated distortions – for the thought to stand

on its own feet. It does not need to be defended as a conclusion from something more general, such as a quasi-inferential conception of justification.

(p.430)

Part of this protest is spurred by the misreading I mentioned earlier: McDowell's reception of my play with Extended Coherentism as an attempt to depict the movement of his own thought. This seems to have encouraged him to equate a quasi-inferential conception of the justificatory role of experience with the idea that experience serves as an "intermediary," in a fashion inconsistent with his direct realism. But the quasi-inferential conception is simply the general idea that, in order for any belief to be justified, something must justify it which stands in an internal relation to its specific content. This idea is quasi-inferential precisely because it inherits from inferential justification its insistence on the kind of relation between justifier and justified which obtains when the justifiers are a set of antecedent beliefs whose content precisely sustains an inference to that of the belief to be justified. And this conception is unmistakably in control of McDowell's thinking about the issue: when he talks of *facts* as doing the justifying for empirical beliefs, he precisely invokes what are, in his view, a range of justifiers which owe their justificatory relations to being individuated by their content – they are facts *that P* – and to the content of the beliefs they purportedly justify. This is exactly an instance of the kind of thinking which, according to the view presently entertained, is not mandatory.

It is worth pursuing McDowell's riposte a little. We sometimes speak of proofs as justifying mathematical beliefs, but of course this is inept unless elliptical: nobody is justified in a mathematical belief by a proof of which he or she is *unaware*, even if it exists. Speaking of "the fact observed" as a justifier is inept in the same way, since if facts really could carry the weight of the first term of the justification relation, there would be no need to experience them in order to be justified in one's empirical beliefs. McDowell should therefore stick to saying that it is indeed *experience* which justifies, with reminders when necessary that experience is being conceived as direct awareness of external fact. But now it is worth asking *how* exactly experience, so conceived, is supposed to *justify*: why should a having-it-seem-to-one-that-P which is as a matter of fact an "episode of openness to the layout of reality" be taken to warrant the belief that P? The answer, for one who conceives of such seemings as, in the best case, instances of "openness to the layout of reality," must be that one is normally entitled to take them as precisely that. For if one was for some reason agnostic about their status – if, say, one somehow had good reason to suppose (falsely) that now and for the next few hours, it would be a strong possibility (as likely as not) that one would be suffering very extensive hallucinations while actually lying in a hospital bed – then one's (as a matter of fact) continuing experience of reality would lose its justificatory force. Even McDowellian experience, then, is not an *unconditional* justifier: a suitably conducive background of collateral general belief is required in any case, however experience is conceived. There is therefore a question why/whether McDowell's account differs in any important respect from the present proposal, at least so far as its potential to save the justificatory character of experience is concerned.

The present proposal, developed no further, says nothing about the nature of experience. It could be augmented by a view of experience as the carrier of conceptual content, or non-conceptual content, or no content at all – a "brute impingement" on awareness. It does not matter what experience is: on this view, it can justify the beliefs it (causally) encourages if (but only if) placed in the correct collateral doxastic setting – one which, one way or another, entitles a thinker to take the content of the beliefs to which her experience inclines her as a likely reflection of the nature of the world. Whether or not content, of whatever sort, is assigned to experience as well is – once it is recognized that a conducive collateral doxastic setting is required in any case – a question with no bearing on its capacity to justify.

At this point, of course, it should begin to seem that this proposal is actually a bit of an impostor: we are presented not so much with an alternative idea about the justification of basic empirical beliefs, contrasting both with McDowell's and with those in play in the two "seesaw" positions, as with a more developed, counter-attacking version of Coherentism – a version which, rather than conceding that experience is not a justifier at all, argues that, precisely because justification is always holistic, any *conscious phenomenon whatever* can be a justifier and need stand in no internal relation to the content of what is justified. Here again, therefore, is where it would be important for McDowell to be able to make good the claim, essential to his rejection of the Myth of the Given, that it is a kind of solecism to think of experience, when conceived as non-conceptual, as capable of justifying anything. The Coherentist counter-attack, again, consists in the thought that even if conceptual, experience will not justify in the wrong doxastic setting; and if the doxastic setting is right, letting experience carry conceptual content in common with a candidate empirical belief adds nothing to its justificatory power. The template in any case is that justification accrues in virtue of (one's being aware of) something's happening which one is entitled to take as an indicator of the truth of the candidate belief, and it is all the same whether that something is a McDowellian experience that P or, say, a loud noise. My first proposal, then, pursued a little, merely takes us back into and extends McDowell's debate with Coherentism. And as before, his master card will have to be the "crucial transcendental thought" that conceptual experience, conceived as direct awareness of a conceptually structured reality, cannot be dispensed with in any account which can save the possibility of objective empirical purport. It is that issue, and not the question which drives the seesaw – the question of making out how experience can play a role in the rationalization of belief – which is fundamental.

Dismounting the seesaw (II)

I return, finally, to what I continue to find most unconvincing about McDowell's main argument in the first part of his book. Suppose that he is right that experience can only justify if conceived as carrying conceptual content. And grant the point that so conceiving of experience gains no advantage over Coherentism unless it is also thought of as directly responsive to the world: that is, as not just caused by it but *disclosing* it. These two points call, as we have noted, for a Tractarian ontology: the world of our experience must be a totality of *things that are the case*, facts that P. In *Mind and World* McDowell devoted some effort to repudiating the idea that this metaphysics is idealist in any pejorative sense. But it would be just that if we supposed that facts – like experience, on McDowell's view – owe their being to *actual* conceptual activity, so that any particular fact would not so much as exist unless actually conceived by some thinker. If the position is not to be idealist, then facts, as self-standing states of affairs, have to be mere conceiv*ables*. They are individuated by conceptual content, but do not depend for their existence on anyone's actually thinking – or even being actually capable of thinking – their content.

It seems to me just obvious to ask now: why cannot this conception of a fact, which McDowell enthusiastically embraces and to which he is anyway committed, be applied to episodes of brute awareness? Why should not a man's sensory awareness of certain items in his environment – his experience of the cat sitting on the mat, say – be conceived as just such a (relational) fact: a fact consisting in his standing in a certain mental relation to a chunk of material reality. It would only be in bringing concepts to bear on this relational fact that it would be registered as an experience that P, and hence become able to contribute toward justifying the belief that P. But it could obtain unconceptualized in just the same way as the fact that P itself. So on this view, there is simply no good need so to refashion the concept of experience that it is barred to animals and infants.

When McDowell argues that, if we are to dismount the seesaw, we must cease to think of experience as consisting in "occurrences in consciousness that are independent of conceptual capacities," he would appear to conflate a weaker and a strong version of the claim. The strong version is just what he goes on to recommend: experience is an activity of conceptually endowed subjects that draws on their actual conceptual capacities. The weaker claim is: the justificatory *potential* of experience depends on its being, as it were, *readable*; it does not actually have to be read, however, in order to exist (any more than a newspaper). So the question is: even granting, against the more developed Coherentism latterly outlined, that experience has to be conceptual if it is to justify, why do we need more than the weaker understanding of this in order to dismount the seesaw? To be sure, if we had *already* discarded the very idea of brute experience, there would only be the stronger option. But McDowell's reason for discarding it was precisely to safeguard the justificatory potential of experience. And to have justificatory potential, merely, it is enough for experience to be a relational fact, available for but not owing its existence to the operation of concepts.

McDowell responds:

> I am baffled by Wright's second suggested line of resistance. I cannot see the "absolute parallel" he claims, between the idea of a fact as a thinkable that does not depend on anyone's thinking it, on the one hand, and, on the other, the idea of an occurrence in consciousness that is not an actualisation of conceptual powers but nevertheless such as to "sustain" or "command" [my words in "Human Nature?"] a particular conceptual articulation. If an item ontologically independent of anyone's thinking it is in view as a *thinkable*, there can be no problem about the idea that someone *might* think it. But there is a problem about "sustaining" or "commanding" conceptual articulations, the supposedly parallel optional extras in Wright's alleged counterpart. Can Wright separate the language of "sustaining" and "commanding" from the idea that one rather than another conceptual articulation is correct in the light of the supposed occurrence in consciousness? If not, then the proposal is simply, and obviously, a version of the Myth of the Given.
>
> (pp.430–431)

Well, I am perfectly content not to "separate the language of 'sustaining' and 'commanding' from the idea that one rather than another conceptual articulation is correct in the light of the supposed occurrence in consciousness." McDowell's idea was that in experience, I bring a fact to conceptual awareness: it appears to me *that* P. So the fact that P "sustains" and "commands" that particular conceptual articulation – that is just a fancy way of saying that I recognize it for what it is. And, someone running the line that so baffles McDowell will say, my awareness of that fact is, in just the same way, recognized for what it is by the conceptual articulation: *it appears to me* that P.

McDowell charges that this is just the Myth of the Given all over again. But either it is not or else it really is not at all clear what the supposed Myth is, and what, according to *Mind and World*, is wrong with it. What McDowell officially *said* was mythical was: the notion that justification can accrue to a belief from something which merely causes it and stands in no conceptual (internal) relationship to it. But the weaker claim does not controvert that; it allows that an experience is justificatory only as and when actually conceptualized – "read" – questioning only whether this justificatory potential has to be actualized – via an actual "reading" – in order for experience to exist at all.

Of course, the conception now in play of experience as material for recognition is just Scheme/Content dualism of the kind which Davidson famously rejects. McDowell too, for his own reasons, sets himself the task of "overcoming" that dualism. The intentions of its author notwithstanding, the question which *Mind and World* leaves open is: why should we want to overcome it? Not, anyway, in order to explain how experience can justify. The overcoming of dualisms is a good thing only when the duality is bogus; otherwise, it is just the missing of distinctions.

Notes

1   *Philosophy and Phenomenological Research* 58: 2 (1998). My contribution is at pp.395–402. McDowell's Reply to his Commentators – Brandom, Collins, Peacocke, Rorty, and myself – is at pp.403–31, with the discussion of my contribution at pp.425–31. There is a précis of *Mind and World* by McDowell at pp.365–368.
2   Ibid., p.425. All subsequent references to McDowell's *Philosophy and Phenomenological Research* Reply are included in the body of the text.
3   As William Wringe did to me, in discussion. This would not go for all choices of 'P' though – a dream, for instance, could not involve a genuinely *demonstrative* content (on plausible views of demonstrative content).
4   *Mind and World*, p.9.
5   "So in *what* sense are they private, then?" The question may seem almost irresistible. But it asks, in effect, for a better model: *another* way of underwriting the habits of thought and talk illustrated above. Let me remind you of Wittgenstein's response. This is from *Investigations*, 109:

> We must do away with all *explanation*, and description alone must take its place. And this description gets its light, that's to say its purpose, from the philosophical problems. These are, of course, not empirical problems; they are solved, rather, by looking into the workings of our language, and that in such a way as to make us recognise those workings: in *despite of* an urge to misunderstand them ... philosophy is a battle against the bewitchment of our intelligence by means of language.

Recall also *Investigations*, §§654–655:

> Our mistake is to look for an explanation where we ought to look at what happens as a "proto-phenomenon". That is, where we ought to have said: *This language game is played*.

> The question is not one of explaining a language game by means of our experiences, but of noting a language game.

That we should settle for this kind of deflationary position seems to me to be one of the hardest things to accept in Wittgenstein's later philosophy. But that it should be accepted is, it seems unmistakable, his view. The Cartesian conception of privacy is exactly something to which we succumb when we misunderstand the workings of our language, and specifically, the kinds of locution illustrated by the six examples. And his recommended moral is, not that we abandon any of those ways of talking, but that we resist the temptation of trying to underwrite them; that is, to construct a general picture of the nature of their subject matter and our relations to it which would explain why it is all right to talk in such ways.

I have explored this general idea further in "Self-knowledge: the Wittgensteinian legacy," in C. Wright, B. Smith, and C. Macdonald (eds), *Knowing Our Own Minds* (Oxford: Clarendon Press, 1998), pp.15–45.

McDOWELL'S MIND AND McDOWELL'S WORLD

Hilary Putnam

John McDowell's *Mind and World* has already evoked a number of reactions from prominent philosophers, including some enthusiastic ones, some violently negative ones, and various forms of "not getting it." I am on the enthusiastic side myself, but, nevertheless, I find *Mind and World* an enormously difficult book – as difficult as it is important – and my primary aim will be to evaluate its contribution, as I see that contribution, and only secondarily to voice a few criticisms.

Quine has spoken of bringing our beliefs about the world before "the tribunal of experience." In *Mind and World* McDowell agrees that this is what we must do, but he argues forcefully that Quine's conception of experience as nothing more than a neuronal cause of verbal responses loses the whole idea that experiences can *justify* (and not merely cause) beliefs. McDowell's overarching aim is to determine conditions experience must satisfy if it is to be genuinely a *tribunal*.

McDowell also wishes to understand a certain dialectical movement in philosophy after the rise of modern science, a dialectical movement which he sees as having been up to now primarily an oscillation between unworkable positions. Showing that the opposing unworkable positions do not exhaust the available alternatives will, McDowell believes, enable us finally to give philosophy peace with respect to one important set of issues.

In McDowell's narrative, as in most contemporary accounts of the emergence of the modern period in philosophy, an initiating role was played by the appearance of a new conception of nature, one that we might call the Galilean (or Newtonian) conception. This conception McDowell refers to as the conception of nature as lying "in the realm of law." Laws, in this post-Galilean sense, no longer involve Aristotelian final causes; they simply describe – with a precision previously unimagined, one might add – nomological relations between events.

One of the positions that McDowell attacks – Coherentism – was only formulated as an explicit theory in the late nineteenth century, but McDowell sees the problem that gives rise to that position as having been present long before the position itself assumed a fully explicit form. According to Coherentism, if nature is the realm of law in this new (teleology-free) sense, it cannot *simultaneously* be a realm of reason: nothing purely "natural" can also *rationally warrant*. The Coherentist concedes (what it would be crazy to deny) that the deliverances of our senses are *natural* occurrences. The problem for Coherentism is that if this is so, and if nothing that is purely natural can also rationally warrant anything, then it follows that those deliverances do not justify our beliefs about the world.

The threat faced by any position that accepts this result goes beyond mere skepticism about warrant, however. (The sort of skepticism one might meet by saying "the chain of reasons has to end somewhere.") McDowell points out that if our beliefs lack rational connections to experiences – if experiences are *only* causes of those beliefs, and not also *justifiers* – then it is impossible to see how our beliefs have *empirical content* at all; we lose our grip on how we are believers at all.

The position that McDowell opposes to Coherentism, "the Myth of the Given," posits that justification begins with some sort of brute confrontation with something "outside the space of reasons," an unconceptualized experience (Gareth Evans and Christopher Peacocke are contemporary representatives), while Coherentism (represented by Donald Davidson) says that nothing can justify a belief except another belief, and simply accepts that experiences do not justify beliefs, although beliefs about experiences do. But, McDowell argues, neither position is workable. Both are disasters.

McDowell points out that there is an alternative that has been overlooked throughout the long history of this problem. What Coherentism and the Myth of the Given share is the assumption that if the deliverances of the senses are purely natural, then they cannot also be conceptually structured. It is the picture of sensory experience as non-conceptual that drives the Coherentist to deny that they can justify anything and the believer in the Myth of the Given to postulate that there is a form of justification that is non-conceptual, and hence not subject to rational criticism.

The key to seeing that experiences can simultaneously be purely natural occurrences and conceptually structured is to recognize with Kant that even if perceptual experience ("receptivity") is *passive*, that does not mean it is *non-conceptual*. Although my experience of, say, the blue patch on the wall has causes and effects, like any other natural event, it does not follow that it must lack conceptual content. The claim which McDowell repeats most often and most insistently is that our experience, say, of the blue color, or of the patch on the wall, or of the blue patch (if the viewer does not know what a wall is), involves our conceptual powers, what Kant called our "spontaneity." McDowell does not say that the experience is an *exercise* of those powers – because that would invite disastrously idealist readings – but he does say that our conceptual powers are involved, or in play, albeit *passively*.

Our first task will be to understand what this means.

Well, what it means to say that my experience is of a blue patch on the wall is that I perceive *that* there is a blue patch there. The content of an experience is at the same time a fact about the world. The picture is that experience involves "openness to how things anyway are," *and* it justifies beliefs. This fits nicely with the direct realism about perception that McDowell argued for in previous writings,[1] but the argument of *Mind and World* does not, according to McDowell, presuppose the arguments given in those writings.[2] The dialectic he was concerned with in those writings is a dialectic which leads to a seesawing back and forth between direct realism and various "interface" theories of perception;[3] the dialectic McDowell is concerned with here leads to a seesawing between the Myth of the Given and Coherentism. One of my problems with McDowell's strategy has to do with precisely this separation that McDowell sees between the two sets of issues.

But first a word more on what McDowell is claiming when he says that our conceptual powers are in play in perceptual experience. To set aside a possible misunderstanding at once, McDowell is not claiming that all experience involves *verbalized* thought. Of course we do not think "that is blue" every time we see something blue, or "that is a pencil" every time we see a pencil, and so forth. Obviously not all conceptual activity involves words. Nevertheless, when we perceive the color of the patch on the wall we have the *potential* to think such thoughts. Even if we do not have a name for the color, or for the particular shade, we have the potential to think of it as "that particular color" or "that particular shade," for example. This much might, of course, be granted by a philosopher of mind like Christopher Peacocke, who believes that the "content" of the experience is, in itself, *non-conceptual*. Where McDowell differs from Peacocke is in holding that the experience is not to be thought of as merely the efficient cause, or trigger, of the verbalized thought. According to McDowell, the experience is a *taking in* of the fact that a blue patch is presented. Like the verbalized thought, the experience has a propositional content (and presupposes that we have the requisite concepts) and like the verbalized thought it can justify, or probabilify, beliefs. Indeed, it normally justifies the proposition that states its content. Under normal conditions, seeing a blue patch on a wall *justifies* the belief "I see a blue patch on the wall" and does not merely *cause* it.[4]

Thus, what McDowell means by saying that our conceptual powers are "drawn on" in experience, albeit "passively," is not anything mysterious, nor is this to be construed as psychological speculation of some kind; it is articulated by the work that this idea has to do: to show *how* experience involves "openness to how things anyway are." If we put aside temporarily McDowell's difficult (and fascinating) discussion of experiences with "inner accusatives" (e.g., experiences of pain, or of after-images) and confine our attention to experiences of how it is "out there," what McDowell is saying is that such experiences, when they are experiences in what McDowell calls "the demanding sense" (when they function in the justification of belief), are intrinsically about the outer world, and the possibility of having them depends on the possession of the relevant world-involving concepts. They are not inner signs with a magical

176

connection to the outer world, but takings in of how it is (in the best case), or how it seems to be (in more problematic cases), with the outer world.

The issue of direct realism

When I encountered *Mind and World* I naturally read it in the light of the direct realism that McDowell defended in such papers as his 1982 British Academy Lecture, "Criteria, Defeasibility, and Knowledge." When I read an ancestor of the present essay to the Central Division of the American Philosophical Association, to my surprise I discovered that McDowell regarded the issues as entirely independent.[5] What I want now is to turn away from *Mind and World* for a while, and examine the direct realism issue as McDowell saw it in that earlier paper (and, I believe, as he still sees it). One of my standing questions, as I have indicated, is whether the two issues – the issue of the involvement of our conceptual powers in perception, and the issue of direct realism – can really be kept apart. I myself believe they cannot be, and that McDowell's book would have been far more persuasive if he had linked them explicitly.

To see the issue McDowell discussed in his 1982 lecture, let us recall that in "modern" (i.e., post seventeenth-century) philosophy, experience has almost universally been conceived of as something "inside" us, something in a private mental theater (identified by materialists with the brain, of course). A famous argument for this view[6] might be called "the highest common factor argument" (the term "highest common factor" is McDowell's). The argument goes like this: if someone is under the illusion that they see a blue patch on a wall, or dreams that they do, etc., the experience (it is claimed) is, or anyway could be, "qualitatively identical" with a "veridical" experience of seeing a blue patch. So *there is something in common*, a type-identical *etwas*, that is "presented" whether the experience is veridical or not. The *etwas* is certainly not "out there" in the external world, since it can be presented when there is no real blue patch. So it is "inner," or "private," or "mental," etc. (proponents of the traditional view differ about which adjective to use here). And thus, in one stroke, we arrive at the standard conception of experience, or of what G. E. Moore would have called the "object" of experience, or of the "content" of experience, as an interface between us and the "external world," where the requisite notion of "externality" gets its sense entirely from the conception of the interface. With one stroke the whole modern problematic, with all its epistemological and ontological involvements, is in place.

What the 1982 McDowell wanted us to do (following, in this respect, the lead of John Austin and of the later Wittgenstein) was to scrap the whole idea of a "highest common factor," and with it the idea of "sensations" (or "non-conceptual contents" etc.) as an interface between us and the familiar objects that we see, touch, hear, smell. With the traditional idea of "sensations" gone, gone too is the idea that colors and other so-called "secondary" qualities are "dispositions to produce certain sensations in us," and hence not properties of the objects themselves. The way is clear to what I have elsewhere called a "second naiveté."[7]

But what of those "non-veridical experiences"? Of course they occur, and although, as Austin points out, this is a much rarer occurrence than the epistemology books would lead one to suppose, they can be *indistinguishable* from "veridical experiences." But no one should suppose that if one cannot "qualitatively distinguish" experience A from experience B, it follows that some "quality" of the two experiences is *numerically identical*. In fact, when the highest common factor argument is explicitly stated, instead of being smuggled in via the use of some such expression as "qualitatively identical," it collapses on the obvious fact that while experiences can, indeed, be indistinguishable, *indistinguishability is not a transitive relation*, and numerical identity is. As both Austin and McDowell (in "Criteria, Defeasibility, and Knowledge") argue, when I only seem to myself to be seeing an X and when I am really seeing an X the experiences may be similar, even "qualitatively indistinguishable," but it does not follow that they have a numerically identical "object," nor is it necessarily the case that the "non-veridical" experience has an "object" at all. When I seem to myself to be seeing a blue patch on a wall but I am not, I *may* be seeing something else, for example a mirror image or a hologram, or may not be seeing – or "perceiving" – anything. Hypostatizing "experiences" (or their "objects," or their "contents") does not *explain* anything; on the contrary, it generates many of the insoluble "problems" of traditional philosophy.

"Non-conceptual content": further remarks

At least one philosopher – Russell in *The Analysis of Mind*[8] – held a belief in non-conceptual content *in conjunction with* a certain sort of direct realism. This is a rare position, and I should like to digress for a moment to say why it is so rare.

Russell's turn to direct realism (about 1919) was inspired, as he tells us, by American "New Realism," and particularly by William James's "Radical Empiricism." James believed that, in practice at least, we cannot succeed in factoring experience into a non-conceptual part and conceptual "add ons."[9] Russell, however, proposed to think of a blue patch on a wall as something that can be experienced *directly* and nevertheless to think of the experiencing, or being presented with, the blue patch as non-conceptual (or, in his terminology, non-"mnemic"). The only way Russell suggested this might be the case is that the same entity, the blue patch, might be both a physical thing and a part of someone's mind. This suggestion only makes sense given a "neutral monist" metaphysics, which Russell adapted, with significant alterations, from James's *Essays in Radical Empiricism*.[10] McDowell, in contrast, thinks of our minds as simply a subset of our abilities, goings on, etc., and certainly did not intend (and does not now intend) to propose a new ontology, "neutral monist" or otherwise.

I have gone into this to illustrate the point that if one thinks of the "contents" of experience as "non-conceptual" then it will be virtually impossible also to think of them as "out there." The very extremity of Russell's metaphysical speculations (and of James's, and at times G. E. Moore's) brings out the difficulty. The direct realist idea of experience, as a taking in of how it is in the world, virtually requires one to see experience as conceptually structured, since it is only in that way that we can identify the content of experience, the content which is to be identified with part of the content of the world, with something formal rather than material – to use Aristotelian terminology. The opposite move, the move Russell made, of identifying the content of experience with something material, is what led him, in the context of his post-1919 direct realism, to a neutral monist metaphysics.

But does McDowell avoid the problem?

To some, however, it may seem that McDowell's talk in *Mind and World* of the contents of the mind and the contents of the world as being "identical" lands him in exactly the sort of metaphysical extravagance that James and Russell landed themselves in. Suppose, to stick to our example, I see a blue patch. On McDowell's view, the fact that the patch is blue (or, if I notice the particular shade without already having available a predicate for it, the fact that the patch is *that* color) is part of the content of the world, and, after I perceive it, it (the numerically identical "it") is part of the content of my mind. Is this not "neutral monism" all over again? Indeed, is not quantification over "facts" already an example of metaphysical extravagance?

There are a number of issues here which it is important to disentangle. According to Quine's doctrine of ontological commitment – a doctrine popular with many philosophers – to quantify over Xs, where Xs may be, in the present context, "facts," is *ipso facto* to "commit oneself to the existence" of Xs, where committing oneself to the existence of Xs is to think of them as *objects*. For example, quantifying over numbers is to claim that certain imperceptible objects exist: "The words 'five' and 'twelve'," Quine writes, "name two intangible objects, numbers, which are *sizes* of sets of apples and the like."[11] Appearances to the contrary notwithstanding, I have not forgotten that my present topic is McDowell's philosophy, and not Quine's. My point is simply that one need not agree with Quine that every time we use an expression which we are prepared to symbolize with a backwards capital E we thereby claim that an *object* exists; and if the quantification is "abstract," that an *intangible* object exists. In short – and I hope that McDowell agrees with me here – worries about "ontological commitment to abstract entities" are, as a rule, bunk.

Quantification over "facts" notoriously runs foul of another famous Quinean (and Davidsonian) doctrine: "no entity without identity." The only proposed criterion for the identity of "facts," it is said, is the synonymy of the expressions used to describe them. The fact that *p* is identical with the fact that *q* just in case the sentences "*p*" and "*q*" are synonymous.[12] And Quine supposedly showed that synonymy and analyticity are hopelessly unclear notions. Hence, even if we were willing to "bloat our ontology" – by countenancing facts as further "entities" (i.e., objects) along with numbers – we should not do so because of the lack of an "identity criterion." But (1) *even in the case of things that really are objects*, objects that we quantify over every day, *their* identity conditions are undefined in at least some conceivable cases, as Wittgenstein long ago noted.[13] Quine himself admits[14] that there are no specified precise boundaries for *mountains*, for example; and that means that there are objects (e.g., pieces of terra firma with precisely defined boundaries including Mt. Everest) such that it is *undefined* whether they are or not identical with Mt. Everest. But even Quine does not conclude that *mountains do not exist*. (2) The Quinean arguments against synonymy/analyticity all depend on the assumption that the defender of synonymy believes that judgments of synonymy are available in some way which makes them *unrevisable*. Quine's arguments are powerful and important against such notions of conceptual truth; but the right moral to draw is that we should reject those notions, not conclude, absurdly, that judgments of synonymy are somehow without content or importance.[15] It is perfectly possible to hold that there is a difference between conceptual and empirical knowledge while also holding that both kinds of knowledge are *revisable*.[16] For all of the above reasons, quantification over facts, I am arguing, need not involve hypostatization. And, in the absence of an objectionable reification of facts, it is not sinful.

On the other hand, if we do reify facts, or if we suppose that is what McDowell is doing – as we must, if we suppose that mere quantification over facts is tantamount to reification – then it may well seem to us that his story must amount to what Brian Skyrms once called "Tractarian Nominalism."[17] As Skyrms described the position, the Tractarian Nominalist holds that the world consists of *facts* not things. To say that my cat exists is to say that there are such facts as the fact that my cat likes fish food best and does not drink milk.[18] Now, if we take McDowell (1) to be reifying facts, and to be saying (2) that "the world" is just the totality (or the conjunction) of all the facts (as in Tractarian Nominalism), and (3) that my mind is the totality of its contents, among which are the facts that it perceives or conceives to be true, then we have indeed a variant of the neutral monist picture. As in neutral monism there is a single kind of object of which the world consists – only now it is not James's "pure experience," but *facts* – and my mind consists of the same kind of object, and some parts of my mind are also parts of the "external" world. Even if McDowell is not a Tractarian Nominalist – even if he supposes that the world consists of both facts and objects which are not facts (so that there are tables and chairs and also facts about the tables and chairs) – still the picture of a certain kind of object being both "out there" and "in here" has the same problematic features as Aristotle's talk of a certain kind of object, the "form" of what is perceived, as being both out there (with its matter) and in here (in my psyche, but minus its matter).[19]

But in both cases – McDowell's case and Aristotle's – what is written is objectionable *only* if one supposes that reification is involved. And in McDowell's case, at least, I do not think that reification is involved. As I understand it, what McDowell is saying is simply that what is involved in cases of successful perception is nothing other than the taking in of the fact that things are thus and so. On *this* conception, the same proposition – for example, "that is a blue patch on the wall" – is fit to describe how it is in the world and fit to describe the content of an experience. As Pamela Kribbe put it,[20] McDowell's position is a "postmodern Aristotelianism": with respect to at least part of their content, mind and world are "formally identical."

It is at this point that I am puzzled by McDowell's vigorously expressed belief that *Mind and World* does not presuppose direct realism.[21] If we combine McDowell's own direct realism of "Criteria, Defeasibility, and Knowledge" with the doctrine of *Mind and World*, we get the following account: when I perceive that the patch is blue, I take in the fact that the patch is blue, and I do not do this by forming a mental intermediary, a sense datum, which merely *causes* me to form the belief (thought of, very often nowadays, as a "formula in mentalese") that the patch is blue. That the patch is blue is at one and the same time a fact about the world and an exact description of something I experience. This aspect of the world and this aspect of my experience are "formally identical" (to borrow Pamela Kribbe's term), but that does not mean that some *object* is both a piece of the wall, or wherever the patch may be, and a piece of my mind.

On the other hand, if we suppose that there *is* a mental intermediary, and *merely* argue that that intermediary is not "blind" (in Kant's sense), but conceptually informed, what happens? We may have avoided the Myth of the Given, but at the cost of postulating an inner realm of Kantian "representations," entities which are simultaneously "in us," but mysteriously refer (intrinsically) to what is "out there." This is a view which McDowell himself denounced as incoherent as recently as 1992, when he denounced

> a way of thinking in which we try to combine conceiving the mind as an organ of thought, so that what an episode of thinking is in itself is a mental manipulation of a representation, with supposing that an episode of thinking has its determinate referential bearing on the world intrinsically. Putnam's cogent point is that this combination pushes us into a magic picture of the reference of the supposed mental symbols, and hence into a magical picture of the powers of the mind.[22]

Surely, conceiving of experiences as inner objects which intrinsically have "referential bearing on the world" would be a "magical picture"; and to add that the inner objects are not "symbols" because they have no description *except* in terms of their contents would not make it any the less magical (instead of a magical picture of the reference of ordinary symbols, we would have a picture of magical symbols).

"Non-conceptual content" revisited

That *in some sense of "conceptual"* successful *perception* has a conceptual aspect seems undeniable. What is more questionable is whether one can maintain, as McDowell attempts to do, that all *experience* involves our conceptual powers in the strong sense that McDowell requires.[23] Indeed it seems, reading *Mind and World*, that McDowell has no room for the notion of an experience that is not *perceptual at all.* And it seems to me that in McDowell's discussions of his disagreements with various other writers, including Peacocke and Gareth Evans, this issue is not disentangled from the issue as to whether perception has non-conceptual content in the sense in which the sense datum, as it is in itself prior to interpretation, might be thought of as the non-conceptual content of the perceptual experience by someone who holds a sense datum theory (or a materialist counterpart of such a theory).

McDowell's argument against non-conceptual content is, let us remember, that such content cannot intelligibly *justify* any belief; not even a belief about *it.* At most it can be an efficient cause of such a belief, and an efficient cause is not a justification. But if I have experiences which fall short of being perceptions – if, say, I see a patch of color without attending to its particular shade or its particular shape – the very question of justification does not arise. This possibility is ruled out by Kant, on the ground that an experience (a "representation," in Kant's terminology) to which I could not prefix "I think" would be "nothing" to me, or to my knowledge. Perhaps McDowell would endorse this argument. But it seems a bad argument to me, because it ignores the fact that one may be aware that one has an experience falling under a determination without being aware of the exact determination: I may be aware of the blue of a patch without being aware, in the sense of *having knowledge*, or even belief, of the exact shade of blue involved. Yet it seems natural to say that I sensibly experience a shade, and not just "some blue or other."

Another traditional argument against this possibility comes from the empiricist dictum, taken over by some British idealist thinkers, that *esse est percipi*. At least in the case of experiences, this has often seemed self-evident. Yet the consequences are quite paradoxical. Bradley, for example, who invented the "speckled hen" example, reasoned as follows. Suppose I look at a speckled hen. My experience is of speckles – say of red speckles against a white ground – if the hen is white with red speckles. But for no N is my experience of N speckles (since I don't perceive the speckles as having a determinate number). Hence, he thought, the appearance has the property "having a finite number of speckles" but for each N it *lacks* the property "having N speckles." Visual appearances are, on Bradley's view, Ω-inconsistent! (Of course he did not use this term.)

I shall simply say, for the record, that in my view when I see a hen with, as it might be, 50 red speckles on it, I think that part of the "richness" of my experience lies in my awareness that what I am *experiencing* outruns what I am *perceiving.* I do not perceive 50 red speckles, but it does not follow that I do not in some sense *experience* them. Neither the Kantian nor the empiricist reason for maintaining the contrary view seems to me at all compelling.

There is another problem with assimilating all experiences to perceptions or seeming-perceptions (which is connected with, if I do not misunderstand it, McDowell's way of accounting for what I just called the "richness" of experience: he simply postulates a vast number of perceptual experiences[24]. There is (as I would put it) no sharp line between experiences which are perceptual and ones which are not. On any view much of what I perceive/experience is not *judged* at the moment. If right now as I am writing this essay, I shut my eyes and rely on short-term memory, I am aware that a moment ago the coffee urn was within my visual field, yet I formed no such judgment at the time. My ability to form such a judgment, even if I did not actually form it, shows that I "perceived" the coffee urn; this is, as I understand it, McDowell's view, and it seems (so far) quite reasonable. But counterfactuals are tricky, and it is quite unclear – perhaps intrinsically unclear – just which counterfactuals of this sort are true, or even have a truth-value. Could I have formed the judgment that the box of Passover Matzah on my right (which was, in some sense, in my visual field as well) was there a moment ago? I have no idea; I am not even sure what the question means. This is no problem for a view like the one I am urging, according to which there need not be a definite line between "perceptions" and "experiences," but a view which wants to maintain (1) that all experiences are perceptual *and* (2) that for each perceptual experience there is either an occurrent judgment whose content is identical with the content of the experience[25] or else a true counterfactual to the effect that the subject could have formed such a judgment *and* (3) to do justice to the "richness" of experience is, it seems to me, in trouble.

The alternative I propose does not, however, involve a return to the idea that some experiences do not involve our conceptual powers *at all*. Rather, it seems to me, the proper view to take is that some experiences are *preconceptual* in a sense exactly analogous to the sense in which some experiences are *preconscious* (and the fact that it makes no sense to suppose there is a sharp boundary in the one case is closely connected with the fact that it makes no sense to suppose there is a sharp boundary in the other).

Efficient causation

Earlier I reported McDowell's argument against non-conceptual content, namely that such content cannot *justify* any belief, not even a belief about *it*. At most it can be an efficient cause of such a belief, and an efficient cause is not a justification. To McDowell, the second premise of this argument seems self-evident. But is it?

We can, perhaps, see why the premise seems obvious if we recall McDowell's discussion of Davidson's views about perception in *Mind and World*.[26] Davidson holds that perceptual experiences (which, on his "anomalous monist" view, are

Davidson

token-identical with neural events) *cause* but do not *justify* beliefs about what is perceived. The denial of a justificatory connection between perceptual experiences and beliefs about what is perceived is disastrous on McDowell's view, and it indeed seems profoundly counterintuitive. I shall explore this issue further in a moment. But the idea that efficient causation is not justification is a point of agreement between Davidson and McDowell. And indeed, given the *sort* of efficient causation that Davidson has in mind, the idea is perfectly reasonable.

On Davidson's view, although perceptual experiences, like mental events in general, cause other mental events (e.g., beliefs), this causal connection is not a type–type connection. There are no causal laws of the form: events of mentalistically characterized type A cause events of mentalistically characterized type B. Rather individual "token events" cause other "token events" by virtue of their *physical* properties, according to the strong (exceptionless) laws of fundamental physics, and the relevant physical properties vary from member to member of a mentalistically characterized type. It does seem obvious that if my "visual experience" of seeing a lot of people in this room is identical with a brain event, and the connection between that brain event and my belief is that it physically causes another event which is "token identical" with the event of my believing that there are a lot of people in this room – causes it, that is, by virtue of some physical connection which has no nomic relation at all to the fact that the brain event *is* an experience of a lot of people in a room, *and* there is no other sort of "mental causation" to provide an additional link between the first event, characterized as a visual appearance of a lot of people in a room, and the second event, characterized as a belief with a certain content – then the experience is not *justificatory*. A mere physical impact (which is all the visual experience is, on Davidson's view) cannot justify a belief, in the sense of providing a warrant for it which can be rationally discussed or evaluated. And if accepting the idea that our beliefs have no warrant outside of the system of beliefs itself is the epistemic disaster that McDowell argues it is (and I think he is clearly right on this point), then we have no choice but to reject this whole picture of experience.[27] The fact that Davidson is McDowell's clear target explains, I believe, much of the structure of his argumentation.[28]

However, Davidson's position is probably a minority position, to put it mildly, among philosophers of mind. Today, many more – perhaps most – philosophers of mind subscribe to some form of functionalism, and one misses so much as a reference to this position in *Mind and World*. Functionalists have a complex attitude to Davidson's denial of the possibility of "type–type" identities between mental properties and physical properties. As a rule, they reject Davidson's *arguments* completely, even if they also, for different reasons, deny that mental properties can be directly identified with properties definable in the vocabulary of physics. In addition, they reject Davidson's view that causality requires exceptionless laws of the sort found only in fundamental physics. Instead of Davidson's "anomalous monism," they subscribe to the view that mental properties can be identified with *computationally described* properties of organisms, that is with properties of our "software," such as running such and such programs, or having such and such a computational architecture. Such properties are supposed to be "realized" by physical properties in individual brains and nervous systems, but not necessarily by the same physical properties in *all* brains and nervous systems (which is why direct identification of mental properties with physical properties is impossible). And they are supposed to have causal relations with one another, causal relations by virtue of their functional characterizations, and not just by virtue of some "token identity" they bear to physical events with physical connections which are "anomalous" with respect to those *functional* characterizations. In short, the functionalist position is that mental events, including experiences and beliefs, have causal connections of a very special sort. A functionalist would simply not see why an experience, conceived of as a functionally characterized brain event, could not be both a cause and a justification of a belief, characterized as another functionally characterized brain event.

The bearing of functionalism on the issue about "non-conceptual content" is, however, less clear. If "non-conceptual contents" are just what used to be called "qualia," as I suspect, then functionalists divide into those who think that qualia are also functional states, and those who (like Ned Block, and, in a different way, like myself when I was a functionalist[29]) think that some other story will have to be told about qualia, because the writ of functionalism does not run so far. Functionalists of the first kind, *total functionalists, as we might call them,* believe that any brain event complex enough to be identified with a visual appearance must have an extremely complex structure, and extremely complex functional relations to any event complex enough to be called a belief. Such functionalists might well feel happy with McDowell's insistence that if appearances are to justify beliefs, then they must have conceptual structure; indeed, one functionalist, Steve Leeds,[30] has proposed that qualia are sentence-like objects, and that is certainly being structured like beliefs. Believers in the irreducibility of qualia to functional states and events, on the other hand, are likely to identify them with the "non-conceptual content of experience" that Peacocke speaks of and that McDowell attacks. Of course, from a direct realist point of view, what people call "qualia" (e.g., the colors we sensuously experience in perception) are publicly accessible properties of surfaces and not mysterious private objects at all. The possibility of keeping or returning to common-sense realism about colors and the other so-called "secondary qualities" is, it seems to me, one of the most attractive features of the direct realist position that McDowell has played such a central role in reviving.

Naturalism and "bald" naturalism

The fact that certain views of Davidson's are such an important target for McDowell no doubt accounts for the somewhat idiosyncratic way in which he sees the naturalist camp in present-day analytic philosophy. Naturalism is, to be sure, an extremely fuzzy label, covering a wide variety of metaphysical and epistemological positions.[31] Today, a central issue for naturalists – making it such was one of Quine's central achievements, whether one accepts or rejects his views – is the status of intentional notions, such as reference, truth, and meaning. With respect to these notions, naturalists of the more "tough minded" variety – McDowell calls them "bald naturalists" – can be divided into *reductionists* and *eliminativists*. The reductionists – for example, Fodor, Dretske, Stalnaker – seek to reduce intentional notions to causal and/or information-theoretic notions, while the eliminativists – for example, Paul and Patricia Churchland – hold that the intentional notions have no more right to be taken seriously than does the notion phlogiston or the notion witch. To complicate the picture, there are also deflationists who hold that some version of the "disquotational" account of reference and truth solves all the problems, and that the whole issue is a pseudo-issue.[32]

In McDowell's description, however, what unites all "bald naturalists" is the belief that the complete description of the world can be given in the language of natural science. The world as described in that language is subject to laws, and perhaps Steven Weinberg's phrase for the kind of theory he hopes we are fast approaching, "a theory of everything," exactly captures the spirit of this "bald" sort of naturalism. A milder version of this position is represented by Quine, and by Bernard Williams in *Ethics and the Limits of Philosophy*.[33] According to this milder version, this scientific description of the world – Williams calls it the "absolute" description – is the one we must use when our interest is in describing reality as it is in itself, but other concepts, in particular the intentional ones – in *Ontological Relativity and Other Essays* Quine speaks of these as constituting our "second grade conceptual system"[34]– are necessary and legitimate in everyday life, for pragmatic reasons.

But Quine and Williams and the eliminativists are actually rather atypical naturalists. Today, or so it seems to me, the great majority of naturalistic philosophers of mind and language are still inclined to hope that some version of the functionalist program in the philosophy of mind and some version of a causal theory (or, perhaps, an information-theoretic theory) of reference will succeed. Now, I myself have come to think that these programs are hopeless. The versions of these programs, including the version I put forward in my youth, when they are precise enough to evaluate, are open to disastrous counterexamples, and the remaining versions are so vague as to amount to the hope that the intentional will be reduced to the non-intentional "we know not how." As I have recently argued, functionalism today is not cognitive science but science fiction.[35] In *Mind and World*, however, these positions are not so much as mentioned, and this seems to me either a serious oversight or, if the omission is intentional, a tactical error.[36]

Perhaps another source for McDowell's oversight/tactical error (in addition to the preoccupation with Davidson) is McDowell's commitment to Sellarsian terminology. Sellars himself divided our concepts into those which belong to the realm of law, or the space of law, which he thought of as modeled on physics, and the realm of reasons, or space of reasons, which he thought of as comprising our normative notions (both in ethics and in epistemology).[37] McDowell sees the issue facing naturalism as a choice between bald naturalism as he understands it, that is a reductionism which seeks to reduce our normative notions to notions in the realm of law, or, alternatively, to do without them, and his own liberal version of naturalism, which "re-enchants nature" by allowing us to use normative notions without reduction and without apology. But, once again, this misses the fact that the great majority of present-day naturalists would opt for a third option, the one McDowell does not discuss, namely to try to reduce the notions of the realm of reasons to notions in what Fodor calls "the special sciences," that is to notions which do not qualify for full citizenship in the realm of law[38] as Sellars understood it (whether they qualify under McDowell's construal is not clear), but which are not part of Sellars's "space of reasons" either, because they are not normative. (Geological concepts are frequently used as an example of concepts which a naturalist may use with good conscience without worrying about reducing them to concepts of physics.)

To his credit, however, McDowell does take pains to make clear that he is not attacking experimental work and model building in cognitive science, when that work is distinguished from reductionist claims. Making that distinction clear is obviously a delicate issue, but I agree with McDowell that it is of the highest importance.

"Re-enchanting nature"

It was Max Weber who talked of the "disenchantment of nature," meaning by that not the idea that intentional notions, or even normative notions used in connection with natural science (e.g., simplicity, coherence, or warranted assertibility), should be eliminated or viewed as merely subjective – that thought, as far as I know, never crossed Max Weber's mind – but referring rather to the "discovery," which he claimed we are forced to accept if we are committed to scientific honesty, that objective values are an illusion. When McDowell speaks of the need for a naturalism which "re-enchants nature," he is deliberately coupling the issues of accepting the intentional notions and the normative notions used in connection with natural science (the epistemic norms, as it were) without reduction and without apology with the issue of accepting our ethical notions – not only the more abstract ones, but also the so-called "thick" ethical notions, such as cruelty or compassion – without reduction and without apology. Although he devotes only a few pages to this issue, they are exceptionally deep and luminous, especially when they are read (as I think they need to be) in the light of McDowell's well-known papers defending a species of common sense realism in ethics. I agree with McDowell that the issues are, in a sense, the same with respect to both these sorts of notions, and further agree that realism in ethics need not commit one to any sort of dogmatism. But McDowell's position is often assimilated to what he himself dismisses as "rampant Platonism," and we badly need – and I would like to use this opportunity to enter a plea for – a book-length treatment by John McDowell of the issues surrounding the "realism" controversy in ethics.

Notes

1 See, for example, "Criteria, Defeasibility, and Knowledge," in John McDowell, *Meaning, Knowledge and Reality* (Cambridge, MA: Harvard University Press, 1998), pp.369–394.

2 The reason that it does not presuppose those arguments is that the thesis that experience is conceptual in the sense indicated above, on the one hand, does not, by itself, rule out *all* possible sense-datum theories (it only rules out ones on which sense data are, as it were, "mute"), while, on the other hand, it does rule out certain forms of direct realism (those forms according to which our direct perception of the "external" world is itself a confrontation with something unconceptualized – McDowell interprets Evans's view, for example, as presupposing such a form of direct realism).

3 This is the dialectic I discussed in "The Dewey Lectures 1994: Sense, Nonsense and the Senses; An Inquiry into the Powers of the Human Mind," *Journal of Philosophy* 91(9) (September 1994).

4 The Kantian provenance of this claim is obvious, and is stressed by McDowell.

5 In his reply to my APA paper, McDowell accused me of crediting him "with aims I don't have, and not crediting me with aims I do have." And he went on to complain that

> Putnam evidently thinks my primary aim is to insist on "direct realism" about perception, to reject a picture in which perceptual experience makes contact with the world only at an interface. He talks as if this interface conception is simply *there* as a problem for us, because of how modern philosophy has unfolded. To defend "direct realism" in this sort of spirit, one would need to undermine all the rationalizations philosophers have concocted for the interface conception. That is why it bothers Putnam that I don't go into the Argument from Illusion and all that. He thinks I make my book unnecessarily difficult by presupposing earlier work on such topics.

6 For a devastating criticism of this argument, see John Austin's *Sense and Sensibilia* (New York: Oxford University Press, 1962), chap. V.

7 See my "The Dewey Lectures, 1994."

8 See Bertrand Russell, *The Analysis of Mind* (London: Macmillan, 1921).

9 "Does a man walk with his left leg or with his right leg more essentially? Just as impossible it may be to separate the real from the human factors in the growth of our cognitive experience" (*Pragmatism* (Cambridge, MA: Harvard University Press, 1975), p.120).

10 See William James, *Essays in Radical Empiricism* (New York: Longman, 1912).

11 "Success and Limits of Mathematization," collected in Quine's *Theories and Things* (Oxford: Blackwell, 1953), p.149. There are, however, deep tensions in Quine's thinking: for example, between thinking of "exist" as univocal, and admitting that it admits of both "objectual" and "non-objectual" interpretations. Moreover, even when Quine clearly thinks of "exist" as univocal, he equivocates (or, perhaps, he is torn) between thinking of the univocality of "exist" as something trivial (what better standard of univocality do we have, he asks in effect, than how something looks

when properly "regimented"?) and thinking of it as involving a substantive claim, the claim that being committed to the existence of abstract entities (when quantification over them cannot be explained away as "non-objectual") is doing something he calls "positing" intangible objects, objects whose existence has to be inferred from the contribution that positing their existence makes to the success of prediction, particularly in physics.

12 Use-mention purists should replace the quotation marks with Quinean "corners" in this last sentence. Professional mathematicians would, of course, write this sentence without quotes *or* corners, and damn the use-mention worry. As Martin Davis long ago remarked to me, "what a formula in corners means is just what a mathematician would mean if he wrote the formula without the corners."

13 See, for example, *Philosophical Investigations*, §80.

14 In "What Price Bivalence?", *Journal of Philosophy* 78: 90–95 (1981).

15 See my "Pragmatism," *Proceedings of the Aristotelian Society* 95 (part 3): 291–306 (1995).

16 Fallibilist conceptions of conceptual truth were, indeed, common at one time – for example, in the writings of Josiah Royce.

17 See Brian Skyrms, "Tractarian Nominalism," *Philosophical Studies* 40: 199–206 (September 1981).

18 Since, according to Tractarian Nominalism, only facts "really exist," in the metaphysical realist sense, and the model-theoretic argument of my *Reason, Truth and History* (Cambridge: Cambridge University Press, 1981) did not involve changing the truth-conditions of whole sentences, but only involved permuting the individuals (which do not have real existence), the upshot was that at least one kind of metaphysical realist – the Tractarian Nominalist – need not be bothered by the model-theoretic argument. My purpose in bringing Tractarian Nominalism up in the present context does not have to do with the model-theoretic argument against metaphysical realism, of course.

19 See "Aristotle After Wittgenstein," in my *Words and Life* (Cambridge, MA: Harvard University Press, 1994), pp.62–84.

20 In her Nijmegen doctoral dissertation.

21 See note 5 above. Of course, McDowell's reason for saying that *Mind and World* does not presuppose the "direct realism" of "Criteria, Defeasibility, and Knowledge" *is not* that he has *given up* that view.

22 "Putnam on Mind and Meaning," *Philosophical Topics* 20(1): 45 (Spring 1992).

23 Here I have in mind the experience of mature, conceptually competent human beings. The issue of the experience of small children and animals is much more difficult.

24 *Mind and World*, pp.56ff.

25 For simplicity, I ignore "non-veridical" perceptions in this formulation.

26 *Mind and World*, p.137ff.

27 Of course, this is something we should do anyway if we reject the conception of our experiences as a sort of internal interface between ourselves and the objects we perceive.

28 Richard Rorty is another target, but Rorty repeatedly cites Davidson as his authority on these points.

29 My view at that time was that "qualia" are *physically* – not functionally – characterized brain events. See *Reason, Truth and History*, chap. 4.

30 Stephen Leeds has proposed this in "Qualia, Awareness, Sellars," *Noûs* 27: 303–330 (1993).

31 For a good account of the vagueness of the notion as it figures in contemporary debate, see Steven J. Wagner, "Why Realism can't be Naturalized," in Steven J.

Wagner and Richard Warner (eds), *Naturalism* (Notre Dame, IN: University of Notre Dame Press, 1993), pp.211–254.

32 Rorty hovers somewhere between this camp and Davidson's.

33 See Bernard Williams, *Ethics and the Limits of Philosophy* (Cambridge, MA: Harvard University Press, 1985).

34 See Quine, *Ontological Relativity and Other Essays* (New York: Columbia University Press, 1969), p.24.

35 See my essay (listed as "Putnam, Hilary") in Samuel Guttenplan (ed.), *A Companion to the Philosophy of Mind* (Oxford: Blackwell, 1994).

36 In his introduction to the 1996 edition of *Mind and World* McDowell disclaims the very need to rule out bald naturalism – it is enough, he now says, to show the sort of reduction bald naturalists seek is not necessary. In my view this is quite mistaken.

37 With respect to the intentional, Sellars, like Carnap in "Truth and Confirmation," in *Readings in Philosophical Analysis*, H. Feigl and W. Sellars (eds), (New York: Appleton Century-Crofts, 1949), was a thoroughgoing disquotationalist.

38 The concepts of the "special sciences" do not qualify because their concepts are not reduced to those of physics, and their "laws" contain *ceteris paribus* clauses, and thus are not laws at all, in Sellars's sense.

Part IV

TOWARD ETHICS

10

ATTENDING TO REASONS

Charles Larmore

Introduction

Nothing separates me so much from John McDowell as my conception of the prospects of philosophy. Before I turn to his magnificent book, *Mind and World*,[1] and examine in particular his account of the mind's responsiveness to reasons, I want to lay out the point of view that, despite a large measure of agreement, fosters the sense of dissatisfaction I shall be expressing.

Philosophical reflection, I believe, has no natural end. The solution we propose to a philosophical problem generally brings in its wake new difficulties we did not face before. We may find it necessary to rethink our other commitments. Or we may run up against further questions whose existence we did not previously suspect. Philosophy is subject to a law we might call "the conservation of trouble." To a certain extent, the situation is no different in the various sciences and other organized forms of knowledge, or in life itself. It is a general truth that the more we learn, the more we see that we have yet to figure out. In philosophy, however, the conservation of trouble takes on a more complex and daunting form, because of the nature of the problems at issue. Philosophical problems are typically fundamental in character, their implications ramifying through different areas of our experience, and as a result many disparate considerations turn out to be relevant to their solution. At the same time, they also show a remarkable cohesiveness. Their various elements tend to be so interconnected that our judgment about how well any particular aspect has been handled hinges on our conception of the problem as a whole. These two features conspire to give the problems of philosophy a peculiar intractability. Only a comprehensive solution will do, yet none seems able to tie together in a convincing way the many diverse factors involved. The theory that recommends itself when certain elements are regarded as crucial looks doubtful or even wrong-headed when the problem is approached from another angle, where different considerations weigh more heavily.

In consequence, piecemeal resolutions of the sort employed in the sciences seldom work in this domain. Philosophical problems resist being broken down into manageable puzzles solvable to everyone's satisfaction and deeper questions which we can leave for a later time. Notoriously, philosophy achieves few settled results. Everything stands open to question from some, not implausible, point of view. Reflection seems fated therefore never to be at rest. No argument or vision succeeds in one regard without falling short in another.

Most philosophers would agree of course that philosophy up to them has been locked in controversy. Yet few have felt at home in this state of affairs, and many have imagined that they, single-handedly or as part of a movement, had managed to get beyond it. Some, of course, have persuaded themselves that they have arrived at definitive answers. Others have supposed that they possessed a method by which philosophical problems would eventually yield to a step-by-step resolution after all. Neither sort of stance wins many converts or keeps them for very long. A third reaction, increasingly common over the past century, has been to seek a more radical way out. The problems of philosophy have proven so intractable, it is said, because they rest upon assumptions which, though naturally seductive, betray confusion. Progress is to be achieved, not by the solution, but by the dissolution of problems, not by the construction of theories, but by the diagnosis of the misconceptions that give rise to the apparent need for theory. Philosophy at its best consists in curing us of the philosophical impulse.

No one championed this conception more ardently than Ludwig Wittgenstein, of course. "The real discovery," he exclaimed in the *Philosophical Investigations*, "is the one that makes me capable of stopping doing philosophy when I want to. – The one that gives philosophy peace, so that it is no longer tormented by questions which bring *itself* in question."[2] Wittgenstein's quietism has been enormously influential, despite the inescapable paradox that manifestly lies at its heart. For how, we must ask, can showing up the mistaken assumptions underlying some philosophical problem amount to anything other than putting better views in their place? And must not these views be of a similar scope and thus provide the makings of a positive theory of the phenomena in question?

Many readers of Wittgenstein, dismissing his quietism, have undertaken to expound the actual positions implicit in his writings. Not surprisingly, these ideas exhibit the traits of all good philosophical theory: they accord well with certain things, but they have to strain to accommodate others. In philosophy, there is no true escape from difficulty. The only way that philosophy can be at peace with itself is to accept that tranquillity of mind must forever elude it. The unendingness of philosophical reflection is the true expression of the human condition, and Montaigne provides a better model than Wittgenstein. "There is no end to our inquiries," Montaigne wrote, "our end is in the other world. It is a sign of narrowness of mind when the mind is content, or of weariness."[3] Or as Thomas Nagel has formulated this outlook,

> It may be that some philosophical problems have no solutions. I suspect this is true of the deepest and oldest of them. They show us the limits of our understanding. In that case such insight as we can achieve

depends on maintaining a strong grasp of the problem instead of abandoning it. ... Unsolvable problems are not for that reason unreal.[4]

The purpose of these meta-philosophical remarks has been to define the spirit in which I shall discuss the central theme of McDowell's *Mind and World*. Modern philosophy, he observes, has found insuperable the problem of understanding how thought can be both shaped by experience and responsive to reasons. Experience is regarded as the way the world impresses itself upon us in accord with causal laws, yet experience can serve as a tribunal for our thinking only if it provides us with reasons for belief, and reasons involve a normative relation to the world. McDowell's claim is that this problem proves so difficult only because of the dominance of the modern, "disenchanted" image of the world, which divests nature of everything normative. We need to adopt a broader naturalism that does not reduce nature to the domain of law-governed processes described by modern science. If we recognize that the way we are caught up in the natural world through our sense-experience already involves the exercise of conceptual capacities, which training and tradition have made our "second nature," we will be able to see ourselves as at once part of nature (broadly conceived) and guided by reasons. We will have bridged the deep-seated dualism of mind and world and made out how norms, reason, and thus freedom too – understood not as the absence of constraint, but as the heeding of reasons – fit into the natural order.

No book undertaking to establish so much could fail to represent a bold project, and in my opinion the philosophical ambition of *Mind and World* is matched by the power of its results. Nonetheless, I also regard McDowell's book as importantly flawed by his own understanding of what he has achieved. McDowell is determined to deny that he is engaged in laying out a substantive philosophical theory. A "naturalized platonism" is the name he gives his point of view, the idea being that though reasons are to be understood as being "there anyway," whether we recognize them or not, this platonistic thought is tamed by the insistence that our responsiveness to reasons betokens nothing supernatural, only that second nature which stems from appropriate upbringing. Hence this naturalized platonism, so he claims, "is not a label for a bit of constructive philosophy" (p.95). It amounts to no more than shorthand for a set of "reminders" that dispel the assumptions responsible for the chief problem of modern empiricism. It is the sort of discovery, McDowell declares in echo of Wittgenstein, that "gives philosophy peace" (p.86). He too aims at curing the philosophical impulse, even if the affliction is bound to recur (p.177).

McDowell, however, is in no position to promise peace. In reality, he has embarked upon the construction of a comprehensive theory of mind and world, and his failure to see that enterprise for what it is keeps him from realizing how his overcoming of one problem leaves him, in fact, faced with another, no less difficult. The notion of "second nature" identifies the means by which the mind is responsive to reasons. But it does not tell us what reasons themselves are, if reasons are supposed to be, as he himself avers, "there anyway," forming a possible object of knowledge. What precisely is a reason, and how can there exist, independently of our beliefs about them, normative entities of this sort? What must the world be like, if it is to be understood as containing reasons? McDowell believes that such questions will evaporate, if only we take to heart the import of the idea of second nature. "The response we should aim at being entitled to, if someone raises a question like 'What constitutes the structure of the space of reasons?', is something like a shrug of the shoulders" (p.178). Shrug his shoulders he certainly does. Yet the problem remains all the same. The very things McDowell says to explain how experience can function as the tribunal of belief make it necessary to wrestle with understanding how reasons can form part of reality.

Experience and reality

To see why the nature of reasons cannot be dismissed as an idle question, let us look more closely at McDowell's analysis of the travails of modern empiricism. The enduring difficulty, he remarks, has been that the idea of "experience" is expected to contain two distinct features, which can seem to resist combination. Experience is a causal notion, denoting the way the world impinges upon us, but it is also a normative notion, signifying a source of reasons for belief: the world having been found to be thus and so is supposed to give us reason to believe this or that. In the classic terminology of Wilfrid Sellars favored by McDowell, experience belongs to the "logical space of reasons," defined by relations of warrant and implication, at the same time as it apparently falls within that space of causal processes which forms the object of modern scientific inquiry and has no place for normative relations. Thus, the perplexity.

One common solution has been to hold that relations of justification find their terminus in experiences of the world where certain contents of thought, often called "sense data," directly impose themselves upon the mind. Experience can appear to be a notion at once causal and normative, if it grounds our beliefs about the world in the way that the world, at the outermost bounds of our conceptualization of it, acts causally upon us. The ultimate basis of belief will then be the (sensible) Given. But the well-known trouble with this "foundationalist" approach is that the Given cannot serve as a justification for belief, if it lacks conceptual articulation; yet to the extent that it is shaped by an understanding of the world we already possess, it cannot count as simply "given."[5] The alternative to the Myth of the Given, notes McDowell, has usually been some species of coherentism, which rejects the idea that the world itself provides any rational constraint upon our beliefs. Part of the causal order though they obviously are, beliefs find their warrant only in how they cohere with our other beliefs. "Nothing can count as a reason for holding a belief," writes Donald Davidson, McDowell's paradigm of the coherentist position, "except another belief."[6] Experience itself, understood as the tribunal at which belief is held accountable to the world, no longer has a role to play. The trouble with this position is also familiar. Coherence theories of knowledge turn the very possibility of knowledge of the world into a mystery. They threaten to make our web of beliefs appear "a frictionless spinning in a void" (p.50), whereas knowledge involves thought's answerability to the way things are; that is, to the world itself. The dilemma, however, is that in pursuing this latter intuition, we seem destined to end up again at the idea of the Given.

To cut the Gordian knot, McDowell argues, we must jettison the assumption that underlies both these positions and that creates the problem in the first place. The mistake is to assume that the points at which the world acts causally upon us cannot consist in the exercise of our conceptual capacities. Foundationalists suppose that such points somehow initiate conceptual thinking, and coherentists that they are, by their nature, unsuited to instruct our thought. But in fact the conceptual is unbounded, extending all the way into our causal dependence on the world. We need to hold on to the idea that the world is given to us in experience, yet also recognize that it is given as already possessed of conceptual structure, already bound up in relations of warrant and implication. In McDowell's view, the obstacle to acknowledging this truth, the preconception responsible for perpetuating the seesaw debate between foundationalists and coherentists, is, as I have said, a modern, impoverished idea of nature, one that strips nature of everything normative and immures it within the space of law-governed processes. The receptivity of experience, properly construed, shows up the deficiency of that idea. For at such moments the mind is at once part of nature, in being shaped by it, and also participant in the "space of reasons."[7]

"In experience," so McDowell puts his position, "one takes in, for instance sees, that things are thus and so" (p.9). Clearly, the content of such experience – "that things are thus and so" – is not a preconceptual Given, to which we could only point, speechlessly as it were. Yet for such experience itself to embody a receptivity to the world, that content also cannot be a judgment we make *about* what is given to us, for then the given element in experience would have been located, once again, beyond the bounds of the conceptual. Instead, that very content must be what is given in experience, and it thus must be, in the absence of error, part of the world itself. Anything short of this conclusion reintroduces the Myth of the Given, and the only other alternative is to reject altogether the receptivity of experience, denying the existence of an independent reality, as an idealist might, or refusing it any epistemological significance, as the coherentist does. Our thought cannot therefore be understood as forever operating at one remove from the world, as though what it conceives were always some picture or "representation" of things and not the things themselves. Through experience, the mind latches directly onto reality and follows the conceptual articulations of the world itself.

McDowell is in no doubt about this implication of his views. "*That things are thus and so,*" he argues, is the conceptual content of an experience, but if the subject of the experience is not misled, that very same thing, *that things are thus and so*, is also a perceptible fact, an aspect of the perceptible world. ... Thinking does not stop short of facts. The world is embraceable in thought.

(pp.26, 33)[8]

Yet it is also significant, I believe, that he sometimes slips in laying out his conception. Later on in *Mind and World*, he remarks that he does not want to "disallow the question what the conceptual contents that are passively received in experience bear on, or are about," and his answer is that "they are about the world, as it appears or makes itself manifest to the experiencing subject" (p.39). Disallowing such a question, however, is precisely what McDowell should have done. The content of experience ought not to be regarded as being *about* the world, since then thought could not be understood as reaching up to reality itself; it would have to stop short at some representation of it. Experience may count as being *of* the world, but the content of experience, or what we experience, had better be seen as the world itself in so far as it makes itself manifest to us. For the only reason not to identify the content of experience with the very fact that things are thus and so is the notion that what is strictly speaking given in experience must be something – a preconceptual something – out of which the thought that things are thus and so is constructed. Then, conceptual content will have been restricted to the judgments we make about experience, to our "spontaneity" (following the Kantian terminology McDowell is fond of), instead of figuring in our "receptivity" as well. And such, of course, is the misstep to be avoided.

I point out this lapse, not simply to make clear McDowell's actual position, but also to underscore how unconvincing and indeed obfuscating is his denial that he is proposing a piece of "constructive philosophy." True, McDowell has rejected an assumption – the idea that experience cannot be at once given, that is, causally dependent on the world, and conceptually structured – which has been a large part of the problem in seeing how experience can act as a tribunal of belief. And I am convinced that he is right to do so. But what he puts in its place goes well beyond a mere reminder or "a truism dressed up in high-flown language" (p.27). His arguments contain the makings of a full-scale theory of the mind's relation to the world that is no less ambitious than the sort of representationalism which, as I have indicated, forms the ultimate object of his attack. The fact that his conception hews more closely to what our self-understanding would be, if freed from that assumption, does not make it any less a theoretical construct; that is, any less a set of theses requiring systematic elaboration and giving rise to further questions.

For consider: McDowell is committed to regarding the world itself, not just our understanding of it, as conceptually structured. "We have to suppose," as he declares elsewhere, "that the world has an intelligible structure, matching the structure in the space of *logos* possessed by accurate representations of it."[9] This proposition is scarcely an innocent truism. It is a claim of considerable moment and brings into play an age-old spur to metaphysical speculation. How can we avoid wondering why there should be such a natural sympathy or pre-established harmony between mind and world? For just this reason, philosophers resolved to be "post-metaphysical" want nothing to do with McDowell's idea of the mind's intimacy with the world.[10] I share his conviction that in experience the world impresses itself upon us as the knowable world it is.[11] But nothing is gained by pretending that such a view does not stake out a substantive philosophical position.

Experience as a tribunal

McDowell's approach removes one obstacle to conceiving how experience can serve as a tribunal of our thinking, yet other obstacles remain, and they embody questions which cannot be exorcised, but have to be tackled. Let us grant that it is the world itself in articulate form, the fact that things are thus and so, which is given to us in experience. Certainly, the thesis is not without its points of obscurity. If, for example, receptivity involves the exercise of conceptual capacities, then the way we experience things to be must be capable of error, and not just errors that reflect the limits of the capacities deployed (as when our perception leads us astray in cases of optical illusion), but also errors that consist in failing to exercise these capacities correctly – as when in normal cases we simply mistake the color of the table before us. How, one might wonder, can such mistakes be understood, if not (as McDowell would have to deny) as judgments wrongly made about what was given to us in sense? I mention this difficulty as a minor illustration of the "law of the conservation of trouble." But again, I want to grant the thesis (indeed, I believe it to be true), since my aim is to focus on a larger problem still remaining, namely, the fact that the thesis falls crucially short of explaining how experience can have the function of a tribunal.

In order for experience to be something to which we are accountable, it has to be such as to provide us with reasons for believing this or doubting that. We may be given in experience the world itself, or the fact that things are thus and so, but unless that fact gives us in turn reasons for belief, experience cannot instruct us in what to think. To be a tribunal, experience must present us, not merely with facts, but with facts seen to have a bearing on the course of our thinking; otherwise, experience cannot be said to stand in judgment over our attempts to understand the world. McDowell may thus be right that in experience the mind can grasp directly the way things are. But that truth does not suffice to establish the sort of empiricism he intends to redeem. For the fact that things are thus and so cannot be equated with the reason we thereby think we possess to believe this or that (nor does McDowell show any inclination to make such an identification).[12] After all, one might agree about the fact, yet dispute the existence of the reason. There is, to be sure, a relation between the two: without the fact, the reason would not obtain. But the fact that things are thus and so is not the same as the reason to believe this or that; it "gives" us that reason or "constitutes" that reason, or, as we may more impressively put it, the reason is "supervenient" on that fact.

We will not therefore have vindicated experience as a tribunal, until we have made sense of how it can yield reasons for belief. One account would be that the ways things are made manifest to us in experience serve as reasons only to the extent that we take them as such or give them that role. Reasons are not something we discover, so it might be said. They consist only in a status we confer upon the things in the world which we do discover, a status expressing our decision about the evidential force which those things will be held to possess. Deep philosophical pressures push in the direction of this perspective, and I will come back to them later on. For the moment, however, I want to point out that our self-understanding usually runs along different lines. Reasons, we suppose, are in general something which we discover. They are not created by us; they are there waiting to be discerned, and we may miss them, if we have not learned enough or focussed our minds enough to make them out. From this point of view, experience can serve as a tribunal for our thinking precisely because the reasons for belief we draw from it are reasons we suppose it discloses by way of the facts it makes known to us. Were we ourselves to make up what weight, if any, those facts have for our thinking about the world, experience would be a tribunal only in some etiolated sense.[13]

Now McDowell's various statements show that he shares a robust conception of experience and of the reasons it provides. He observes, to be sure, that even if "how one's experience represents things to be is not under one's control ... it is up to one whether one accepts the appearance or rejects it" (p.11). Yet the judgment one then makes, though an exercise of spontaneity or freedom, is regarded by McDowell as being *responsive* to reasons (pp.xxiii, 79, 84), reasons that are "there anyway" (pp.82, 91), "whether we know it or not" (p.79). A reason, so conceived, cannot consist in our own taking one thing to count in favor of another; it has to be a relation of warranting that really obtains and that it is our business to acknowledge. The mind's responsiveness to reasons is a theme that unmistakably pervades McDowell's book and sustains his attempt to rehabilitate the basic truth of empiricism. All the more dismaying, therefore, that he shrugs off the need to explain the nature of reasons themselves. Without such an account, he has not made clear how experience can be, not just an "openness to the world" (p.111), but also (by way of that) a tribunal for belief. He has only asserted that it is so.

Why this reluctance to face the question squarely? I have already noted McDowell's professed hostility to "constructive philosophy," belied though it is by his actual practice. Not by accident, I suspect, this aversion to positive theory becomes particularly inflexible, when the character of reasons as such would seem to call for analysis.

To see why this may be so, let us pause for a moment to consider what we have to be willing to say about the space of reasons, if we regard it as constituting an order that is "there anyway," awaiting our response. Suppose that some fact of physical nature gives us a reason for accepting a belief about the world. The reason, as I have observed before, cannot be identified with that fact itself, if only because people can agree upon the fact, yet deny or be unsure that it provides any warrant for the belief. The reason is the bearing that fact has upon what we are to believe: it consists in that fact being such as to count in favor of the belief in question. A reason is thus not something physical, but neither can it be equated with anything psychological – at least if our point of departure is that reasons are an object of knowledge and not merely an expression of our own commitments, a status we bestow upon the facts we meet with. The belief that we have a reason cannot be the same as the reason itself, since that belief turns on our assuming that we would have the reason, even had we not discovered it.

Some philosophers hold that the only reasons any person has are "internal" reasons, ones which individuals can grasp by deliberating on the basis of their existing beliefs and desires (their given "motivational set").[14] Whatever the truth of this thesis, internal reasons themselves cannot be reduced to elements of our psychology. A man who concludes that his present convictions give him a reason for belief or action, does not suppose he has this reason because he believes he has it; he believes he has it because he supposes it is his in point of fact, deliberation making no sense if not aimed at figuring out what reasons one really has. Though the internal reasons such a person has depend on his perspective being as it is, they are not therefore any item in his mind. Such a reason obtains given where he stands, yet he may fail to recognize its existence, and if he succeeds, his grasp is a grasp, not of his thought at the time or in its future tendency, but of a demand (conditional, to be sure, yet no less prescriptive) about how he ought to think.

In general, reasons are essentially normative entities, and they resist identification with anything physical or psychological precisely to the extent that their normativity is regarded as irreducible. Now McDowell endorses the *sui generis* character of the space of reasons. Reasons, he holds, are not to be reduced to physical phenomena belonging to the domain of the natural sciences, as the proponents of what he calls "bald naturalism" suppose to be possible. Nor can they be in his view simply an expression of our own commitments, for then one could hardly say of reasons, as he does, that they represent "requirements of reason that are there whether we know it or not" (p.79). These convictions would appear to entail a fundamental rethinking of the reigning conception of what there is. The world, that is the totality of what exists, would have to encompass, not only the two dimensions of physical nature and minds, but also a third, normative order of reasons.[15] No wonder that, with his quietism, McDowell is determined to skirt the challenge, declaring that "there is no need for constructive philosophy, directed at the very idea of norms of reason" (p.95).

In the end, however, this indifference only cripples his own enterprise. Without some account of what reasons are and of how they fit into the architecture of the world, we can have no real comprehension of what is meant by our responding to them. To that extent, we will have failed therefore to show how experience can be a tribunal.

Platonisms

This conclusion will impress itself on us all the more if we look at the way that McDowell, using moral thinking as a paradigm, proposes to talk about responsiveness to reasons without worrying about what reasons may be themselves. It is in virtue of our "second nature," he declares, drawing on Aristotle's discussion of ethical character, that we are keyed in to the space of reasons. "The ethical is a domain of rational requirements, which are there in any case, whether or not we are responsive to them" (p.82), but we are able to grasp them only because of the upbringing and cultivation of sensibility that endow us with the conceptual capacities necessary to discern them. They are not visible in the absence of character. The demands of ethics will not come into view, if one looks at ethical life "sideways-on" (p.83), taking up a standpoint outside it and checking its forms of thinking against the way the world appears from that detached perspective. The study of ethics, as Aristotle remarked,[16] is of little profit to young people lacking moral experience.

In just this way, McDowell argues, reasons in general – not only moral reasons, but the full gamut of reasons for belief and action – will disappear from sight, if we seek them in the world as it must look if dissevered from our conception of it as placing demands on our thinking. Then the world will appear as merely the disenchanted realm of law-governed processes, the object of modern natural science. Our eyes are open to the reasons there are, only so long as we deploy those forms of understanding that training has made our second nature and that show us a world to which our thought is answerable (p.84).

There is much to be applauded in McDowell's theory of second nature. One of its merits is the insight that, in regard to the question of objectivity, moral judgment stands on a par with other species of normative judgment, including those at work in the sciences. Far too often the debate about whether morality is a form of knowledge proceeds as though morality were a special case, to be taken up once the rest of one's world-view is already in place. If moral judgments can properly be said to be true or false, what sort of things, it is asked, can they be considered to be true of? That the world should contain, along with mind and matter, such things as moral values then strikes many (like J. L. Mackie) as too "queer" to be believed, and thus it becomes easy to regard moral judgments, not as descriptive, but as only expressing our own preferences. Expressivism, however, looks far less hospitable, once we recognize that moral judgments are essentially judgments about the moral reasons we have and that they thus form one kind of judgment, amongst others, about the reasons there are. For then expressivism's rejection of the idea of moral knowledge entails that there can also be no knowledge of how in general we ought to think, even about the realm of physical nature. The perennial debate about whether there can be moral knowledge really concerns the possibility of normative knowledge as such.[17]

McDowell was not always so clear about this point. In the early 1980s, he sought to rescue the notion of moral knowledge by way of a parallel between values and secondary qualities, though even then he put his finger on the key disanalogy: the object of a moral judgment is taken to "merit" our response whereas a dispositional property such as a color can merely cause it.[18] McDowell's move to a more satisfactory view was signaled in his Lindley Lecture of 1987, where he observed that a proper epistemology of moral judgment should center on "the notion of susceptibility to reasons."[19]

A second strength of McDowell's theory of second nature is its overcoming of the common opposition between reason and tradition. We learn from experience only to the extent that our thinking is shaped by forms of sensibility and understanding that are ours primarily because we have been brought up in them. Such traditions of thought are not immune of course to scrutiny and correction, but critical reflection, as McDowell likes to say, is best compared to Otto Neurath's famous image of the sailor who repairs his ship at sea. Only within our existing web of belief can we find the resources essential to determining which elements have become problematic and what solutions would count as appropriate, so that revision is always piecemeal, though sometimes radical all the same (p.81).

The exercise of reason does not then consist, as a certain modern individualism supposes (p.98), in peeling away the force of tradition so that we may stand face to face with the real. History itself, by the *Bildung* it gives us, is our mode of access to reality.[20] Stripped of all the standards and habits of mind it has inherited and forced to begin again from scratch, our moral thinking must lose its bearings, and the same is true for our ability to grasp every sort of reason for belief or action. Even scientific thinking, as it aims to display the world as simply a system of law-governed processes, normatively mute, proceeds by adapting its inheritance from the past. Internal reflection of this kind is not a second-best mode of inquiry, whose results need to be relativized in the light of a more direct confrontation with the world as it is. It is the very nature of reasoning. Nothing, McDowell points out,[21] could therefore be more wrongheaded than to argue (as "bald naturalists" are wont to do) that the disenchanted world of modern natural science alone is real, because the idea of there being reasons we must acknowledge arises only within a certain way of conceiving the world. On such grounds, any articulate thought would have to count as but a "projection."

Yet for all its virtues, this conception of second nature is not a point at which philosophy can come to rest, much as McDowell would like to believe so. Once "the bare idea of *Bildung* is in place," so he maintains, "no genuine questions about norms" remain (p.95). But this is simply not true. We have been told the conditions under which we are able to apprehend reasons, but not what reasons are themselves. How can any account of our responsiveness to reasons be complete, if it skimps on a systematic explanation of the object of our response and of its place in the overall scheme of things? McDowell's refusal to take on this topic amounts to a failure to show that experience – and experience as he wants to understand it, as an openness to the world – is truly a tribunal for belief.

Of course, laying bare the nature of reasons, when one credits them with being irreducible to anything else and with being there independently of our knowledge of them, can hardly prove an innocent business. As I have indicated, it runs in the face of the prevailing view of the world as but mind and matter. It can only be the kind of constructive or substantive theorizing which McDowell aims to shun. He himself mentions only one sort of speculation about the ontology of reasons, the position he calls "rampant platonism," and this undoubted piece of philosophical extravagance serves as his excuse for refusing to get into the subject. Rampant platonism views reasons as "constituted independently of" (p.77) or "in splendid isolation from anything merely human" (p.92), and as a result it turns our ability to respond to them into something "occult or magical": it fails to see "the demands of reason [as] essentially such that a human upbringing can open a human being's eyes to them" (p.92). The position does not seem very attractive. But is this really the shape our thinking must take if we do not believe that the idea of second nature tells us everything we would like to know about reasons as such?

Describing the order of reasons as a third ontological dimension of the world (a way of talking McDowell is sure to deplore), I observed at the same time how reasons, though irreducible, depend on the physical and psychological facts being as they are. Nothing in the willingness to take seriously the reality of reasons and the questions it raises obliges us to suppose that they inhabit some remote Platonic heaven. To deny an essential connection between the reasons there are and the way things otherwise happen to be would seem in fact to betray an ignorance of the very notion of what a reason is. Nor are we driven to reject training and tradition as the means by which we tune in to the demands of reason, just because we think that the irreducibility and objectivity of reasons, to which McDowell himself is committed, call for a deeper account and one which can be nothing less than metaphysical. After all, second nature is our mode of access, not what we thereby get hold of. If a "naturalized" platonism limits itself (as McDowell defines it as doing) to an appreciation of second nature's importance, then venturing beyond its confines does not plunge us into the only other sort of platonism he seems willing to envision. Forsaking quietism does not entail losing touch with the human condition.

The conservation of trouble

My aim, however, is not to paint an irenic picture of where speculation about these matters will lead. On the contrary, trouble waits just around the corner.

McDowell's assumption is that second nature is clearly immune to any charge of being "occult or magical." Upbringing and the transmission of tradition are incontestably part of what makes us human, and they draw upon capacities belonging to us as the kind of natural organisms we are (p.84). Responsiveness to reasons cannot appear mysterious, he supposes, when it is seen to be rooted in second nature.

Yet here again attention has been focussed solely on the means of access, and not on the object thereby disclosed. Once we recall that it is reasons which our second nature is supposed to make known to us, the situation clouds over. Reasons, I have noted, cannot be physical or psychological in character, if they are taken to be irreducible and objective in the way McDowell himself favors. How then can reasons operate as causes, as they certainly must do, if their existence is to explain our coming to grasp them? Our usual understanding of causes involves locating them in space and time. Yet how can a reason occupy a spatial or temporal position? Perhaps reasons can be placed in time, as when we say that a certain reason obtains at one time and not at another. But assigning reasons a spatial location, as though one could talk about the distance between them, is manifestly ridiculous. As a rule, we suppose that cause and effect are spatially contiguous, or that the one leads to the other along some path in space, or (as in so-called mental causation) that they are successive states of some spatially situated entity. Have we any real idea of how the denizens of the "space of reasons" can act in the world, if they have no locus in physical space? The physical and psychological features of the world that give us reasons for belief and action are certainly in space, and no mystery surrounds how they can act on us. But reasons themselves, it will be recalled, cannot (given McDowell's point of departure) be identified with these features, however much they may depend on them. The snag, then, is conceiving how reasons as such are able to move us.

Loath to delve into the question of what reasons themselves are, McDowell never addresses this difficulty, of course. But he does make a point of observing that, for his vindication of experience as a tribunal to succeed, reasons must be able to act as causes (p.71, note 2).[22] After all, the idea of a responsiveness to reasons makes no sense if reasons are denied a causal influence. Where there is no action, there can be no response. That is why McDowell quite rightly insists that the proper contrast to the space of reasons – the organizing principle, in other words, of the modern scientific image of nature – is not the space of causal relations, but the space of law-governed processes. And thus, the predicament I have just sketched is his, whether he chooses to acknowledge it or not.

The problem of how reasons can be causes, when irreducible to physical or psychological phenomena, provides one of the strongest motivations for maintaining that the truth must lie instead with that view of the world which McDowell dubs "bald naturalism." There is only confusion, it can seem, if we imagine that the space of reasons consists in anything other than law-governed processes of the natural world, explicable in the terms of modern science. To many reasons look "spooky" (pp.94, 95), despite McDowell's assurances, if they are assumed to be both *sui generis* and causally active in the world. The sensible approach, one easily concludes, is to regard reasons for belief and action as simply the expression of our own commitments, and not as anything "there anyway," awaiting our discovery: the reasons there are are simply the reasons we take there to be. For our commitments themselves are psychological phenomena, and their place in the causal order of the world should pose no problem of intelligibility.

Far be it from me to want to argue that this sort of naturalism represents in the end the position to embrace. Formidable obstacles lie in that direction as well. Not the least of them is indeed the expressivist analysis of reasons which it typically begets,[23] since that analysis implies that strictly speaking there can be no such thing as normative knowledge, no truths to be discovered of how we ought to think. My own conviction is like McDowell's that the mind is answerable to the world and to the reasons it gives us. But I also believe that he has not truly shown how experience can thus be a tribunal and that standing in his way is most of all a conception of philosophy which serves him ill. Denying the constructive vision that animates his work only blinds him to the problems he has yet to face. They are not problems which melt away, once we break loose enough from a disenchanted view of the world to see in our second nature an attunement to the demands of reason. They are problems his own platonism, tame though it be, is obliged to reckon with, and their difficulty accounts in large part for the enduring attraction of the modern naturalism he opposes.

On these fundamental matters, there can be then no peace in philosophy. Here, as elsewhere too, philosophy is always in trouble, and to seek a cure that will give it rest is to mistake for an affliction the very vitality of thinking. Philosophy itself heeds the demands of reason when it lets reflection follow where it is pulled, instead of hankering to bring it to a close.

Notes

1   John McDowell, *Mind and World* paperback edition (Cambridge, MA: Harvard University Press, 1996). All subsequent references to this book will be in the text.

2   Wittgenstein, *Philosophische Untersuchungen*, §133: "Die eigentliche Entdeckung ist die, die mich fähig macht, das Philosophieren abzubrechen, wann ich will. – Die die Philosophie zur Ruhe bringt, sodaß sie nicht mehr von Fragen gepeitscht wird, die *sie selbst* in Fragen stellen."

3   Montaigne, *Essais* III.13 ("De l'expérience"): "Il n'y a point de fin de nos inquisitions, notre fin est en l'autre monde. C'est signe de raccourcissement d'esprit quand il se contente, ou de lasseté."

4   Thomas Nagel, *Mortal Questions* (Cambridge: Cambridge University Press, 1979), p.xii.

5   The difficulty finds perfect expression in C. I. Lewis, *Mind and the World Order* (New York: Scribner's, 1929). Without the Given, he writes, "there would be nothing which [knowledge] must be true to" (p.39), yet "in a sense," he goes on to acknowledge, "the given is ineffable, always" (p.53).

6 Donald Davidson, "A Coherence Theory of Truth and Knowledge" (1983), quoted by McDowell on p.14 of his book.

7 It is therefore wrong, McDowell argues (p.71, note 2), to suppose that the proper contrast with "the space of reasons" is "the space of causal relations." Nature as the disenchanted object of modern science really forms the space of "law-governed processes," since reasons themselves can be causes. There is an important problem here for McDowell's approach which I take up in the final section.

8 See also his essay, "Knowledge and the Internal," pp.395–413 in McDowell, *Meaning, Knowledge, and Reality* (Cambridge, MA: Harvard University Press, 1998).

9 McDowell, "Two Sorts of Naturalism" (1995), p.178 as reprinted in McDowell, *Mind, Value, and Reality* (Cambridge, MA: Harvard University Press, 1998).

10 Such is the reaction, in their different ways, of Richard Rorty ("The Very Idea of Human Answerability to the World: John McDowell's Version of Empiricism," pp.138–152, in his *Truth and Progress. Philosophical Papers*, vol. 3 (Cambridge: Cambridge University Press, 1998)) and Jürgen Habermas (*Wahrheit und Rechtfertigung* (Frankfurt: Suhrkamp, 1999), p. 43).

11 Some may object to McDowell taking the world to be "everything that is the case" (p.27), the totality of facts, in other words, and not the totality of objects about which facts can be asserted. The supposed distinction, however, seems to amount to little more than alternative ways of speaking. The objects which make up the world are not bare "things-in-themselves," but objects having such and such features, their having them being what is meant by the facts being thus and so.

12 He writes, for example, that appearances – the way we experience the world as being – "constitute" (not: "are") reasons for judging the world to be that way (p.62).

13 This is precisely the perspective which Rorty, in his critique of McDowell, urges that we should adopt.

14 Such is the view in Bernard Williams's famous essay, "Internal and External Reasons," in *Moral Luck* (Cambridge: Cambridge University Press, 1981), pp.101–113. McDowell himself has argued against the view in "Might There Be External Reasons?" (1995), pp.95–111 in his *Mind, Value, and Reality*. Important though it is, this debate leaves untouched the question of the metaphysical nature of reasons.

15 In developing this line of thought in *The Morals of Modernity* (Cambridge: Cambridge University Press, 1996), chapters 4 and 5, I wrote therefore of the need to move beyond the naturalistic world-view. While also rejecting the sort of *Weltbild* I had in mind, McDowell terms his own standpoint a "relaxed naturalism" (p.89). I suspect the sense of relaxation comes from not pursuing the consequences of his position.

16 Aristotle, *Nicomachean Ethics* 1095a2–4, 1095b4–6, 1142a11–16. See McDowell, *Mind and World*, p.80 (note 13), and also his essay "Two Sorts of Naturalism" in *Mind, Value, and Reality*, pp.167–197.

17 I pursue this theme in *The Morals of Modernity*, chapters 4 and 5.

18 See McDowell, "Values and Secondary Qualities" (1985), p. 143 in *Mind, Value, and Reality*.

19 McDowell, "Projection and Truth in Ethics," p.162 in *Mind, Value, and Reality*.

20 Cf. also "Some Issues in Aristotle's Moral Psychology," p.37 in *Mind, Value, and Reality*. On this point too, I feel particularly close to McDowell. See my *Morals of Modernity*, chap. 2.

21 See in particular McDowell, "Two Sorts of Naturalism," p.187 in *Mind, Value, and Reality*.

22 The point is an essential part of his critique of Davidson's coherentism. See in particular his essay "Scheme-Content Dualism and Empiricism," pp.87–104 in Lewis Hahn (ed.), *The Philosophy of Donald Davidson* (Chicago and La Salle: Open Court,

1999). Oddly, he writes in "Two Sorts of Naturalism" (pp.186–187 in *Mind, Value, and Reality*) that while science is led to its conclusions "because of the causal influence of the fact that things are thus and so, ... there is no analogue to that in ethics." So great a difference there cannot be, if ethical thinking, like scientific thinking, hinges on a responsiveness to reasons.

23 A good example of this alliance of (bald) naturalism with an expressivist theory of norms is Allan Gibbard, *Wise Choices, Apt Feelings* (Cambridge, MA: Harvard University Press, 1990).

11

BILDUNG AND SECOND NATURE*

Rüdiger Bubner

I

McDowell's powerful and complexly argued book starts from Kant's central dictum "thoughts without content are empty, intuitions without concepts are blind."[1] McDowell is driving at the Kantian discovery of *spontaneity*, that specific achievement of subjectivity whose beginning and ground lies not outside but within itself. Of course, this is something the idealist successors of Kant had already focussed on: from Fichte to Hegel, they were convinced that the deepest secret of transcendental philosophy lay in spontaneity, if only the idea were worked out properly.

The idealists tried in their various ways to penetrate that mystery, and in doing so changed the meaning of spontaneity into a principle of *system-exposition*. McDowell proceeds by the very different means of modern philosophy of language. He does not have a system in mind. In philosophy there are no absolute proofs, everything depends on the degree of plausibility with which the respective reasons are brought in, elaborated, and joined together. My impression is that McDowell is generally more interested in freely pursuing intricate lines of thought than clarifying a method or strategy. Certainly for me, those philosophical texts that provoke the reader's intellectual activity are preferable to those written with a dry, suffocating clarity.

In the following I will devote myself to a particular thesis from the *middle section* of McDowell's book. The point developed there is that spontaneity must be independent yet stand in genuine union with *nature*. At the same time, however, the excesses of the idealist systems – which draw a new concept of nature from the principle of subjectivity, one that does not succumb to the bare opposition between mind and "disenchanted" nature – must be avoided. There is no striving for a conclusive "reconciliation" of subject and object. Nevertheless, it is necessary to move beyond the evacuated concept of nature which modern scientism bequeaths to us. Spontaneity is not some synthesizing or ordering power that stands opposed to an anonymous sphere of sense data, contingently impinging on us from the outside and thereby providing the basis for all empirical knowledge.

A concept of nature which would again be a bearer of sense must include the practice of our spontaneity. It is *our* nature that is actualized through the practice of our spontaneity and we do not stand helpless in the face of a "bald naturalism." At this point, defenders of the Kantian view who do not want to pay the price of Kantian dualism or to take on the "monistic" consequences of idealism have recourse to Aristotelian ethics (pp.78ff.). That, by the way, is a line which *hermeneutics* from the early Heidegger to Gadamer has also pursued as an alternative to the modern ideal of knowledge.[2] The intention was to show that standards of rationality should not be formulated only in terms of the methodical confrontation with nature understood as the totality of what is empirically given. To show this is also to bring out the reductionism of the philosophical paradigm of modernity.

For there is a rationality arising from our nature as human beings, passed on through a process of cultural evolution, which orients us in our practical lives. As humans we are dependent on ethics. But ethics is not limited merely to questions of individual preference, or of which norm to act on. Ethics does not result from the interaction between autonomous subjects. On the other hand, of course, we cannot simply rely on mother nature, as if there were something definitively given to us by nature. In truth we are dealing here with a "second nature," which we first must shape: "our nature is largely second nature" (p.91).[3]

However, the ethical claims that provide our nature reveal themselves only to the right point of view:

> When a decent upbringing initiates us into the relevant way of thinking, our eyes are opened to the existence of this tract of the space of reasons. ... We can so much as understand, let alone seek to justify, the thought that reason makes this demand on us only at a standpoint within a system of concepts and conceptions that enables us to think about such demands, that is, only at a standpoint from which demands of this kind seem to be in view.
>
> (p.82)

Once awoken to the right point of view, the field of relevant intuition extends to the formation of conceptual capacities owing to which we are able to make claims:

> If we generalize the way Aristotle conceives the moulding of ethical character, we arrive at the notion of having one's eyes opened to reasons at large by acquiring a second nature. I cannot think of a good short English expression for this, but it is what figures in German philosophy as *Bildung*.
>
> (p.84)

II

Indeed the concept of *Bildung* played a decisive role in classical German philosophy from Herder to Wilhelm von Humboldt. The original meaning of the world *Bildung* was something like "formed according to an inner picture (exemplar or original model)." From then on the concept signified a program of cultural formation and development that reckoned with the variability of the individual and the unforeseeability of the individual's defining context. *Bildung* takes place in the upbringing and civilizing of the subject, who must emerge from a state of being driven by instinct with intelligible and recognizable forms of social behavior. In relation to the subject, *Bildung* means the discovery of possibilities and capacities whereby character is shaped, not only in the direction of a socially fixed and pre-given ideal of virtue, but in the acquisition of a personality. Everyone has the means of realizing this end, but it takes a lot of effort to bring it into concrete existence.

With the stabilization of desirable modes of behavior in the individual subject, which take shape from the flow of life within and from the outer pressure of changing circumstances, the *culturalist* concept of *Bildung* extended to the whole of humankind. The philosopher of history Herder thought that humanity might have a historical *telos* which remains to be fully realized. The changing circumstances of history, in which no iron laws prevail, must be continually used and transformed into so many occasions and opportunities to refine and heighten the human value of society. History as the continuing history of the *Bildung* of humankind has the complex logic of a "Phenomenology of Spirit" – the central theme of Hegel's teleological reconstruction of the history of our species. In the English-speaking world Charles Taylor has contributed much toward the rediscovery of these insights.[4]

After these short remarks on the historical career of the concept of *Bildung*[5] let me return to McDowell and his project. It must be made clear that *Bildung* as a modern concept assumes much more of the subject's power of spontaneity than what Aristotle had in mind with his talk of a second nature. Second nature, in which we are introduced to the practical challenge of ethical relations, reveals a static anthropology set against the background of the Greek *polis*. Not the individual, but the citizen, definitely counts most. That is why generalizable forms of durable processes of character-formation are reckoned with and not the productive unrest of the critical intellectual. With "second nature" we consciously step back behind the level of reflection of a modern *Bildung*.

Of course Aristotle had in mind those institutions which we as human beings, who are properly called "political animals," are naturally inclined to establish. We are dealing here with those structures made available by way of tradition so that each new generation can find its way about with them. At least in Aristotle's view, without the *polis* to belong to, man is not human, but either a beast or a God.[6]

It is important that to borrow thus from the German tradition, which McDowell expressly refers to when invoking the term *Bildung*, in no way opens up a special realm of autonomy split off from our animal nature. In the realization of second nature we are not freed from natural conditions. We just fulfill a task given to us, like a dowry, from birth. Rationality, even in its most refined achievements, never distances us from nature. It rather completes a limited conception of ourselves: we are nothing but a piece of nature, even if we make nature into an object of our knowledge. In the sense of second nature, nature and rationality pervade each other, they do not need to be bridged. "Meaning is not a mysterious gift from outside nature" (p.88).

III

Here McDowell takes up Wittgenstein's much discussed "logical behaviorism." When I raise my arm, so Wittgenstein had claimed, nothing proceeds parallel to it that I can record as some kind of mental event. Arm raising and the intention to do it go together. In other cases there may be merely mechanical, unintended arm movements, as experienced sometimes by people in shock or by the unfortunate sufferers of Parkinson's disease. And there are likewise intentions not carried out, mere wishes or fantasies that never get acted upon. Again, the formula modified from Kant is correct: "Intentions without overt activity are idle, and movements of limbs without concepts are mere happenings, not expressions of agency" (p.89).

Once this point is taken seriously, some of the literature that surrounds Wittgenstein on the topic of embodied movement vanishes into thin air. For the repeated insistence that there is no independent sequence of inner events running parallel to the bodily movements of the agent merely drives away a myth, the myth characterized by Gilbert Ryle as "the ghost in the machine." Logical behaviorism, which dryly assures us that beyond observed bodily movements there is nothing of significance, plays down the role of culture in agency. It belongs to second nature in the aforementioned sense that actions are expressed in bodies which are with us from birth. But as agents we relate to what this body does in an essentially different way from the way we relate to happenings "out there," which may have nothing to do with us.

Whether the wind slams the window, or whether we shut it to keep ourselves warm or cool, it looks all the same from the remote stance of the disengaged observer. Aristotle says that kithara-players in particular can judge the practice of kithara-playing; in other words, that such a practice underlies assessments of "correct" and "incorrect," without having to touch on moral or aesthetic norms. The point is not that kithara-playing is a cultural activity conforming to criteria of aesthetic taste. The pleasure of the listener is not the main issue. It is rather that the playing is a praxis which one can prosecute skillfully, ably, elegantly, and so forth, rather than awkwardly, clumsily, or coarsely. The judgment concerns the meaning of the act itself.

As an expression of agency, every act has its own meaning. An act is not a happening that could take place without agency, either by accident or as an effect of causal laws. Nor is it accompanied by inner stirrings according to the misleading dualism of the inner and the outer. Agency, at least in the normal case, does not involve influencing an observer or making an impression on the public. It is not a piece of theater of the everyday. Action realizes a possibility which the agent possesses, thanks to his or her natural faculties. It is rooted in a person's spontaneity, but it can be trained and perfected culturally. The agent has moved beyond the primitive state of the "Given" once he or she has been provided with a *Bildung* and has developed his or her second nature.

This is the space of our *social* encounter. In connection with Herder, Charles Taylor has spoken of "expressivism." In brief, we tend to shape our action not just by following egoistical goals, pursuing useful work or manipulating our environment. Through acting we typically allow ourselves to be understood by others, where we belong, where we stand, and what as a whole we would like to achieve with others. Such communication takes place originally on the occasion of our intelligible action. We require no mediating intentions external to what we do. Social embodiment incorporates our ability to act and is not built upon it as if at some metalevel. "Agency" does not call for an autonomous theory of communication.

However, *social philosophy*, in an explicit sense, is not McDowell's interest in *Mind and World*. He is concerned with epistemology in the widest sense, without of course excluding its practical aspects. But our world-relation is not explained, as it is in the varieties of pragmatism from Dewey to Davidson, by the practical exigencies of the subject–object relation and the difficulties of successful problem solving. If spontaneity provides us with the first keys to the world, then we are already intellectually active and so in conformity with our nature before we engage practically in this or that environment. We are endowed with a world and do not prepare what is pre-given to us for socially useful ends. The origin of the relationship between mind and world lies in a deep-seated potential of the subject and does not arise from a Darwinian, evolutionary struggle with the environment in which we find ourselves driven by the instinct of self-preservation.

IV

Spontaneity arises from our essence and is developed in the production of a relation to the last horizon of our thought, action, and understanding. In this respect McDowell follows Gadamer's hermeneutic conception and turns his back on the standard conviction of the analytic school, that is, of the basic explanatory power of language. Spontaneity is not simply another word for the mastery of language as rule following. Against Dummett's classical claim, for example, that thought can only be found in the space of language, McDowell defends – from the point of view of "*Bildung*" – the claim that with the learning of language we acquire an initiation into the space of reasons. We do not just learn unproblematic language use. Through language acquisition we open ourselves to the world and so raise ourselves above stimulus-determined animal behavior.

Openness to the world means a general orientation of the understanding, and with that something new comes into play. One must recognize here the role of tradition. Human spontaneity never begins at zero point, and therefore it brings us essentially to the course of *history*. In the end this hermeneutic turn taken by McDowell is not developed further. It does show, however, that *Mind and World* takes up a perspective that converges between linguistic analysis and hermeneutic understanding.

It is best to begin our consideration of the problems raised but not explored by McDowell with the innocent sounding concept of a "form of life." The philosophy of the later Wittgenstein together with its followers in social philosophy, as well as the general hermeneutic movement in continental philosophy, all refer to the *pre-givenness of forms of life*. It seems at first to be an abstract web of loosely connected forms of specifically contextualized rule-governed behavior. Over and above that, however, one must take into account the origins of the forms of life, their career in the ups and downs of social customs and manners, the hierarchies they fall into within a general cultural point of view. Then forms of life take on the complexion of traditions.

For forms of life are essentially more than the conditions of functioning language games. Seen from within the ordinary course of linguistic interaction, and so in the light of a pragmatic theory of language, forms of life certainly appear as marginal phenomena. Compared with the analysis of the relevant rules of use, forms of life are not the main consideration. With the concept of "second nature," however, we can consider the structure of forms of life as such; that is the remarkable event of the achievement of the establishing of a culture. Each subject who enters into the course of a *Bildung* represents a concrete case of socialization. The institutions of social interaction, together with their normative character, must already be pre-given. That means that we grow into these institutions in the course of our biography, their validity tested by time and made self-evident through countless earlier processes of "*Bildung*."

That which is self-evident in an existing society corresponds to the sum of those things which are not, from the outset, radical and permanently struggled over or contested. However, the self-evident is also not fixed for all time, as it is in the fictitious social contract of the classical doctrine of natural rights. For such a decision to contract must logically overcome the superior power of natural contingency. In contrast to that, the self-evident outlines show the always already articulated understanding of a society with regard to the world in which each individual – who is opened to this understanding through the "*Bildung*" process – is to live.

Consequently we arrive at a certain dialectic of *Bildung* and second nature. Processes of *Bildung* are not simply ways of organizing information about the validity of norms. And the realm within which norms are valid is not a fact which can be studied as a bee colony is studied by a natural scientist. We are dealing with our own second nature, something we must endeavor to realize through our very concern with *Bildung*. And vice versa, second nature loses its fundamental ability to endure through time, as well as its stability in the face of conflicts, when and in so far as we do not all affirm it together time and again in daily action.

If one takes this consideration seriously, then the category of the form of life points in a further direction, over and above the characteristics of the self-evident. And this direction seems to be decisive. It becomes apparent when one considers how the Aristotelian conception of ethics, which is rooted in politics, is defined in a quite general sense by the role of the citizen. Even where a post-modern "anything goes" holds sway, affiliation to cultural spheres proves to be identification with the particular form of second nature which is pre-given to us in our specific situation. Such bonds connect those involved with the social and political order, since their practical relation to the world is pre-structured through them. In a decisive way human beings gain recognition as citizens. Their second nature goes over and above anthropological determination in being *political*.

Aristotle, and with him the ancient conception of politics, is not at all concerned with the historical dimension, and could not get muddled up with it. But it is a matter with which we must wrestle today. There is, so to speak, never second nature at first glance. Its naturalness is essentially transformed through change. That is basic to the historicality of the always-already structure of understanding which marks for us available forms of life. Long before the individual finds and cultivates his or her social roles, cultural structures have already been put in place. The institutions we are generally able to affiliate ourselves to precede us by whole epochs. The beginning of *Bildung* and the bindingness of norms never coincide.

V

Let me conclude with a brief comment placing the problem just sketched in the history of philosophy. If McDowell consistently proceeds from the Kantian discovery of spontaneity, he signs up much less to the systematic consequences Kant himself drew from it. Without explicitly discussing the difference between Kant's epistemology and moral philosophy, it is obvious that McDowell is not inclined to follow Kant in the division he sets up in the first and second Critiques. If Kant bases our knowing relation to the world on spontaneity, in a countermove he makes our practical commitment to the categorical imperative of pure reason free of all preceding world-relations. We ought to act in each situation as if we were the original legislator for the whole of humankind. No second nature, no ethical customs, no conventionally acquired roles of citizenship can support us in that.

The absolutist moral philosophy of the pure, unspoiled, non-empirical reason systematically requires a dualism of practical autonomy and the theoretical world-relation. This extremely bold construction was explicitly directed against the predominant Aristotelianism of Kant's day. It was Kant's intention to provide us at last with an ethic which would be consistent with the necessity and strictness of the natural laws formulated by science. Without exception, philosophy after Kant has given up on this project. Hegel, for example, from his early writings to his mature philosophy of right, worked toward an alternative. This alternative took a direction which invites comparison with McDowell's intentions, although the contemporary author of *Mind and World* holds to no philosophy of right in the strict Hegelian sense (pp.44, 186).

The world in which we live is, for Hegel, universally shaped by spirit, in the meanings that surround us and in the cultural models we obey. The general determination by spirit of our world-relations overcomes Kant's dualism. It may be the real ground of the historicism which Hegel made popular and which finds a clear echo in contemporary hermeneutics.

Notes

* Translated from the German by Nicholas H. Smith.
1 Kant, *Critique of Pure Reason*, A51. Page references in the text are to *Mind and World*.
2 See H.-G. Gadamer, *Truth and Method*, tr. Joel Weinsheimer and Donald G. Marshall (New York: Crossroad, 1992), II, 2,2 b.
3 Compare Aristotle, *Nicomachean Ethics*, II, 1.
4 See Charles Taylor, *Hegel* (Cambridge: Cambridge University Press, 1975), and more recently, Terry Pinkard, *Hegel's Phenomenology: The Sociality of Reason* (Cambridge: Cambridge University Press, 1994).
5 The concept also plays an important role in Humboldt's reforms of the university in the nineteenth century, but I shall leave that aside.
6 *Politics*, 1253 a 4.

12

RE-ENCHANTING NATURE*

J.M. Bernstein

Disenchantment and re-enchantment

There is an overarching correspondence between the program of John McDowell's *Mind and World* and the writings of T. W. Adorno.[1] At the last, both contend that the very possibility of there being rational knowing and meaning depends upon displacing the disenchanted conception of nature (and so society) that is a product of the domination of natural science over the modern world-view.

Briefly, McDowell's epistemological argument is this: assume, however indeterminately, that rational belief building must be answerable to the deliverances of the senses if it is not to spin in a frictionless void, where the notion of the rational includes some notion of reason being self-determining (autonomous), and where sensibility is conceived of as a natural capacity mediating rational mind with extra-mental nature. Now if one interprets this natural capacity in the light of the conception of law-like nature bequeathed to us by natural science, then one will face an interminable oscillation between a "bald naturalism" (p.xviii) that upholds the empiricism requirement by forsaking the autonomy of reason, reducing the space of reasons to the space of law; and a coherentism that aims to resolve the difficulty by surrendering the role of sensibility and experience, thus making nature at most only causally but not rationally relevant to epistemic claiming. Coherentism's dismissal of a fundamental role for experience easily leads back to the worry about emptiness, with bald naturalism the most plausible alternative. The villain of this piece, what underpins the "transcendental anxiety"[2] expressed by the interminable oscillation, is the conception of the natural provided by natural science, since it is this conception which makes the sensible separate, one is tempted to say "transcendentally" separate, from the conceptual. The transcendental separation of nature from the space of reasons, the natural from the normative, is the disenchantment of nature, nature becoming thus a thing wholly apart from human activity and meaningfulness; significant activity and meaning, including knowing, cannot survive the separation, which is precisely what the transcendental anxiety appropriately feels and expresses. Assume that the transcendental anxiety is not narrowly epistemological but also expresses the

217

pervasive modern anxiety about the possibility of meaningfulness in general, about whether a wholly secular form of life can be rationally coherent and affectively satisfying; then Adorno's position converges with McDowell's.[3]

Relief will come, McDowell avers, if we can loosen the grip of the scientistic conception of the natural, since only so doing will allow an overcoming or dissolution of the separation of the conceptual from the natural. If another conception of nature were permitted, a nature of second nature, then it in turn would allow a notion of experience as the actualization of conceptual capacities in sensory consciousness. Hence the sensible would be both natural and normative, belonging to nature and the space of reasons: nature would be re-enchanted. McDowell and Adorno both consider the solution to the transcendental anxiety as thus involving a demonstration of how there can be knowledge that is not further translatable into science, where the route to uncovering this form of knowledge is through an interpretative appropriation of Kant's epistemology, above all his dictum that concepts (thoughts) without intuitions are empty and intuitions without concepts are blind. Instead of epistemically blind causal episodes, empirical experience is of conceptualized intuitions, hence of items always already mediated by and within the space of reasons. And for both McDowell and Adorno what is meant to save this solution from collapsing into idealism, the flat *imposition* of human meaning onto a meaningless natural world, is that the space of reasons, while *sui generis* and thus not reducible to or derivable from law-governed nature, is itself natural, the way that humans as "living animals" (p.104) negotiate and shape their environment. While our nature is largely a "second nature" (p.87), our access to it is through ordinary processes of maturation and education, the *Bildung* of the human infant into the socialized adult self. Because second nature is still nature, then its identification amounts to a partial re-enchantment of the natural world (p.88); because what our second nature enables us to be sensitive to is the conceptual content already inherent in the world, then re-enchantment is of both subject and object.

Only the slimmest nuance separates McDowell and Adorno at this juncture: what McDowell conceives of as a transcendental dissolution of the anxiety Adorno would portray as utopia. While McDowell believes his critical diagnosis of the transcendental anxiety directly provides a re-enchantment of nature, Adorno construes the reconciliation of norm and nature as something that could transpire only as the consequence of radically transformed social practices (the likelihood of which he was notoriously less than sanguine about). In certain moods, this difference may be as nothing, certainly in comparison with what is shared, the only difference between the two a matter of having different dialectical purposes situated in adjacent but different philosophical settings. But this cannot be quite right. If McDowell allows Adorno his setting in which the disenchantment of nature and the sway of scientific (logical/mathematical) reason are socially and historically actual (and not merely projections from mistaken philosophizing), then his transcendental point cannot be satisfying, cannot bring relief from the anxiety since the very thing he requires for his purposes, another (conception of) nature, will remain actually unavailable and thereby necessarily in dispute: can there be a nature that is neither the nature of mathematical physics nor anthropomorphic, the mere projection of human meaningfulness on to nature? If the transcendental anxiety of contemporary epistemology is not just philosophers ignoring the obvious resolution, the one McDowell and Adorno aspire to, must not there be a pressure on contemporary philosophy that makes the options of coherentism (in cultural terms: the autonomy of the sign) and bald naturalism all but irresistible and the alternative, re-enchanted nature, all but unintelligible?

The view that the transcendental anxiety is the philosophical inflection of a social actuality requires a more differentiated conception of the space of reasons than McDowell acknowledges. Not all forms of reasoning conduce to significant meaningfulness or a re-enchanted natural world because not all forms of reasoning possess the conceptual resources to acknowledge or account for the *normative dependence* of experiences on the objects they are about. It is surprising that McDowell is not alert to this possibility since it is utterly central to Weber's idea of the disenchantment of nature and society – if you disenchant nature you necessarily disenchant society since as animals we are also parts of nature – that there occurs with it a disenchantment or *rationalization of reason*.[4] The rationalization of reason includes both a practice of reasoning and a conception of what is involved in that practice that in the course of the last couple of hundred years has become practically and theoretically dominant; it is not only the mathematical reasoning of the natural sciences, but its practical analogues: the bureaucratization of social institutions, the mechanisms of a capitalist economy, the pervasiveness of instrumental reasoning in practical affairs. Rationalized reason, reasoning finally in its most austerely procedural and/or formal or formalizable posture, what Adorno calls "identity thinking" wherein each new item is made to fit within a pre-existing and ideally unchanging conceptual scheme, is the fundamental medium through which nature and social experience have become disenchanted. Making rationalized reason itself rather than its attendant epistemology central is necessary if we are to understand how nature could have been disenchanted or how that disenchantment could continue to matter to social life or why it exerts so powerful an influence over philosophical thought.

Bald naturalism and versions of coherentism are critical targets of Adorno's endeavors, but they are simply the latest and most recent avatar of identitarian thought,[5] which includes most formatively and importantly Kant's own handling of the relation between concept and intuition.[6] For Adorno critical idealism and bald naturalism are different versions of the same, fundamentally idealist conception of reason, a reason which in its a priori foundations and scientific utopian telos is so abstract, reified, and independent of its objects that it bears no trace of them, no trace of its worldliness, in its basic modes of operation. This entails that the re-enchantment of nature can only occur through a

219

critique of formal reason rather than epistemological dualism. By focusing on the epistemological upshot rather than the cause of disenchantment, McDowell distorts his most central ideas; by relying on the problem posed by the dualism between coherentism or conceptual scheme (norm) and the Myth of the Given (p.88), he skews his position toward the very idealism he means to resist.[7]

Finally, it is logically inconsistent for McDowell not to reflectively historicize his position since the crux of his naturalizing of Kant, his Hegelianism, involves dropping Kant's dualism between concept and intuition, form and content, that is caused by Kant's regarding space and time as a priori forms of intuition.[8] For McDowell, if we concede the possibility of a second nature and thus the idea that experience involves the actualization of conceptual capacities in sensory consciousness, then we have not closed the gap between mind and world, rather we have discovered that it is already closed, there was no gap to overcome. It is this which allows McDowell to conceive of his project as diagnosis and therapy rather than theory building. But it is equally what must make the objects of his reflection not a priori forms but socio-historical formations of reason. Logically, then, McDowell's endeavors internally presuppose a genealogical account, an explicating of the coming-to-be of the duality between coherentism and bald naturalism as philosophical reflections of wider social processes. This, of course, is just what Critical Theory's notion of a dialectic of enlightenment has meant to provide. McDowell cannot deny Adorno his dialectical purposes.

Despite all this, might it not still be the case that McDowell's view, unknown to itself, does project the very utopian conception of knowing and nature Adorno aims at, and hence that the two projects do complement one another, converging in their finale? Perhaps, more or less, within bounds. But it would be odd if McDowell's bypassing of the sources of transcendental anxiety and his belief that re-enchantment is currently available did not somehow infect the contours of his position. Eventually I shall want to say that the mark of avoidance occurs in his conception of experience: the one he offers cannot explicate the possibility of real re-enchantment, or rather, what he offers as experience is the disenchanted view of it: experience as *Erlebnis* rather than *Erfahrung*. But before getting there I want to put a little more pressure on the conception of nature that would be neither the nature of mathematical physics nor a mere projection. The notion of second nature seems to me to underestimate what is needed for re-enchantment; something more in the way of a living and animate nature is required. Whether my offerings on this topic are friendly refinements or corrections I leave undecided. To see how such Adornoian thoughts about nature are directly relevant to McDowell's epistemological reflections, I will begin by considering two potentially lethal objections to him.

Two criticisms of McDowell

Both the criticisms I want to canvass appear in Crispin Wright's critical notice of *Mind and World*. The linchpin of McDowell's solution to the problem of how

the perceptual experience of empirical items can justify ordinary empirical judgments is to contend that what is perceived is not a mere thing but a fact (that
P). Hence, the appearance that P plays the role in perceptual experience that
prior beliefs play in inferential justification. Wright worries at this thesis from
two angles. On the one hand, he is concerned about the very nature of
McDowell's analogical strategy: why should non-inferentially held beliefs be
conceived of as being justified in just the same way that inferentially held
beliefs are? It may be enough, Wright suggests, that "a belief is formed in
circumstances when one (justifiably) takes the efficient operation of some
appropriate faculty – perception, memory, mathematical intuition maybe – to
be responsible for it."[9] This is a poor objection since it begs the very issue with
which McDowell is concerned: unless there is some content-sensitive justifier
to appeal to, then any other appeal – say, that I was directly facing the object,
my eyes were open, the lighting standard, etc. – while relevant, will nonetheless
spin in a vacuum.[10] If this way of stating his worry is not convincing, Wright
nonetheless has a reasonable concern, namely, that as well as analogy we should
expect there to be more of a disanalogy between those beliefs that are inferentially held and rationalized in discursive thought, and those beliefs
non-inferentially held because based on direct perception. Too quickly assimilating non-inferentially held beliefs to those inferentially justified threatens to
disqualify the specificity of sensory experience in relation to discursive thinking,
yet without the analogy the demand for rational justification rather than exculpation in this area collapses.

Wright's second pass at this problem fares better, and it is incompatible with
the original statement since it grants that the justificatory potential of experience depends upon its carrying cognitive content. His worry relates to the
extreme all-or-nothing way McDowell deals with the cognitive content of experience: either experience is conceived of as a brute Given or it is construed as
essentially drawing on the passive exercise of conceptual capacities. It is the
sharp character of this either/or that is the source of McDowell's problems with
infants and animals: since for him having an experience does involve the actualization of conceptual capacities in sensory consciousness, then our experience
of pain, for example, may be analogous to what infants and animals suffer when
they are in pain, but it cannot, by definition, be the same experience (because
their "experience" is had without drawing on conceptual capacities). As Wright
pointedly comments, this does "great violence"; our ordinary thinking "finds no
dependence of the capacity to experience pain on the possession of the
concept; and it finds nothing for a pain to be if its essence is not to be found
within consciousness."[11] It is a singular feature of extreme experiences of pain
that they involve the weakening to the point of collapse of our capacity for
intending the world and speaking it; pain dissolves language, reducing the
human to its animal substratum. In extreme instances of pain we become all but
worldless. But even with our capacity for intentional comportment broken, the
pain remains.[12] How now might we distinguish ourselves from our animal

221

brethren? This does make the extremity of McDowell's either/or disconcerting. Wright suggests in opposition that there is room for an intermediate space, one in which an experience of the outer world "while not itself ontologically dependent upon an actual exercise of conceptual capacities, is intrinsically such as to carry the information, for a suitably conceptually endowed creature, that P."[13] One might think that there must be room for such a conception of experience if it is going to be intelligible how we can *learn* from experience, have new experiences, learn new concepts.[14] Must not there be the possibility of our experiencing something, it having a significant shape and character to it, and yet it being as yet nothing we can discursively articulate? Does not McDowell's all-or-nothing make learning, so *Bildung*, itself a magical process where we leap from meaningless chaos into the demands of reason without intermediaries? If there is no intermediary space, then are we not, in fact, again facing a dualism of non-conceptual givenness versus conceptual articulation?

Wright's second objection, although more difficult to state clearly, is also best conceived as a worry about missing intermediaries in McDowell's story. Again, for McDowell, to be inducted into the human form of life is to become able to appreciate the rational demands things and persons make on us. He exemplifies this way of thinking in his characterization of Aristotelian ethical thought.

> The ethical is a domain of rational requirements, which are there in any case, whether or not we are responsive to them. We are alerted to these demands by acquiring the appropriate conceptual capacities. When a decent upbringing initiates us into the relevant way of thinking, our eyes are opened to the very existence of this tract of the space of reasons. Thereafter our appreciation of its detailed layout is indefinitely subject to refinement, in reflective scrutiny of our ethical thinking.
>
> (p.82)

The question now arises as to why exactly this view is not a form of rampant (ethical) platonism. We know that McDowell's answer to this question is that

> exercises of spontaneity belong to our way of actualising ourselves as animals. This removes any need to try to see ourselves as peculiarly bifurcated, with a foothold in the animal kingdom and a mysterious separate involvement in an extra-natural world of rational connections.
>
> (p.78)

If I have understood Wright correctly, his doubt is that the reasonable claim that exercises of spontaneity are a way of living out and actualizing ourselves as animals by itself does anything toward vindicating the claim that we are not bifurcated creatures, animals who *also* possess the power of reason. Even for a rampant platonist it will be the case that we require education and training, *Bildung*, in order to achieve insight into the space of reasons. If the space of reasons is as *sui generis* and autonomous as McDowell presents it, is calling it "second nature" any help in understanding it as *natural*? How are the facts of our animality meant to be present in our habitation of the space of reasons? If all the emphasis is placed on how exercises of *spontaneity* are our way of actualizing ourselves as animals, where spontaneity is just another name for the *sui generis* space of reasons, how can our animality, and hence what we share with other sentient creatures, be intrinsic to rationality?[15]

Anthropomorphism and living nature

Spontaneity is, indeed, our way of actualizing our animal life, but if this is going to be a form of naturalism then *what* is so actualized must have as great a speaking role as the manner, the *how*, of its actualization.[16] What is actualized through spontaneity is, initially and always in part, our animal life. What enables us to identify those aspects of our cultural life that have their origin in our animality is, precisely, their comparability with the behavior of the higher mammals: seeking out food, hunting, protecting our young, mating, bonding, clustering into families, interacting ("socializing" and acting in concert) with non-familial others, forms of aggression and territoriality, sensitivity to pain and protecting ourselves from hurt, learning mature forms of behavior through play, displays of strength or desirability, etc. To agree that human forms of nurturing the young, for example, are not reducible to the behavioral patterns through which our nearest animal relations nurture their young is not, for all that, to accede to the claim that our nurturing is *sui generis*, wholly formed by the demands of reason. Are not the fundamental aspects of nurturing–protecting, attending to and doting on, providing with security, concernfully training for adult life – features that need to be seen in the light of what we share with the other higher mammals (of not being born fully equipped for the world and thus in need of an "extended" process of maturation) if they are to be understood aright? And hence is not "animal-nurturance" *what* is realized in our conceptual practices of nurturing? Animal forms of behavior, if I can so put it, are meaningful or proto-meaningful, certainly purposive, without as yet being conceptual; conceptuality exploits and elaborates a potentiality for explicitly conceptual meaning that is already there.[17]

The issue is not whether McDowell acknowledges that animals are not mere things, possessing an environment if not a world (p.115), and even a proto-subjectivity, it is rather that he always conceives of reason and language as dirempting us from our own animality, rationalizing it.[18] Hence, despite himself, in construing the space of reasons as *sui generis* and that of essentially free beings, McDowell operates with a dualistic scheme of a first nature subject to law (or that is appropriately "hard-wired") and a second nature subject to the demands of (free) reason, hence with an antithesis of history (reason) and nature. About this antithesis Adorno comments:

> The traditional antithesis of nature and history is both true and false; true, in so far as it expresses what the moment of nature underwent; false, in so far as it apologetically recapitulates, by conceptual reconstruction, history's concealment of its own natural outgrowth [*Naturwüchsigkeit*].[19]

If this remark is to be intelligible, then the moment of nature that underwent petrification by being turned into a law-governed totality, what Kant calls "empirical reality," cannot be equivalent to the nature that is revealed through mathematical physics since that nature just is a law-governed totality. Rather, the nature that has been discounted by rationalized reason is the nature whose operations are not strictly reducible to the natural-scientific paradigm, the nature intrinsic in and the counterpart of our embodiment (and the embodiment of creatures biologically like us). For such animals, like ourselves, objects appear relative to embodied needs and desires: things to be eaten, places for hiding or making a home, objects to be attacked and defended against, things to be protected and nurtured. Because the way in which objects appear in this scenario is relativized to our embodiment, and the embodiment of creatures like us, and hence is proto-meaningful, it does not follow that this relativization or qualification in their appearing is a work of *projecting* (proto-)meaning on to them. On the contrary, much of the point of claiming that we are *parts* of a wider natural world (shared with the higher mammals), and that our forms of activity are a natural outgrowth from more primitive forms of animal behavior, is to deny that meaningful behavior is *sui generis* or an unconditioned imposition of meaning onto an otherwise meaningless flux. We could not ethically (conceptually) care about preventing unnecessary suffering unless suffering pain was "already" something which beings constituted like ourselves naturally sought to avoid.[20]

Let us call the nature that is implied by our embodiment "circumambient nature." Now the core of Adorno's account of the rationalization of reason turns on his contention that it was formed through the enlightenment project of demythologization. Enlightenment is always the critique of myth; what defines a content as mythic from the perspective of enlightenment is that it originates from an illegitimate anthropomorphism, the projection on to nature of what is merely human. In the first instance, identifying anthropomorphic projections was easy: gods, demons, spirits, in short all supernatural phenomena. These surely are projections, things not there otherwise than through our placing them there. However, enlightened thought never possessed a clear criterion for what counted as a mere projection – what is there because we have actively put it there versus what is there "anyway" – other than that it was *relative* to us. But once that idea is adopted, once anything relative to our embodied standpoint on the world is counted as a (mere) projection, then all of what I have identified as circumambient nature becomes suspect. Only what can be understood as belonging to an independent and fixed order of things can count as being fully objective, as there anyway. Bald naturalism, the absolute conception of knowledge, the idea of a view from nowhere, or according privilege to items capable of having the widest possible cosmological role are all different expressions of the thesis that true objectivity is only available to wholly de-relativized objects, to Kantian empirical reality.[21] Since, arguably, all the parts of living or circumambient nature are relativized to, at least, other parts of living nature if not the totality of it, then circumambient nature, which I am contending provides the conditions for the intelligibility of human practices, comes to be counted as merely subjective, as anthropomorphic.

In his critical notice of McDowell, Wright contends that the potentially "most deep-reaching and important idea" in *Mind and World* is the attempt to reassure ourselves that our responsiveness to reasons is not supernatural but our way of actualizing ourselves as animals. I agree. However, in the previous section I also endorsed Wright's complaint that McDowell's way of fleshing out his thought was unconvincing as it stood because it was too idealist, or, as I interpreted Wright, lacking in intermediaries. I have now made a quick if hesitant step toward locating those intermediaries; they are, in the first instance, objects as they appear to or are relativized with respect to our embodied, animal selves as those selves are elicited through comparison with the higher mammals, and hence, by extension, the interdependent system of living nature in which objects depend on other objects through mechanisms other than that of mechanical causality.[22] Animal activity, antecedently to conceptual practices, maps out *lives* with shapes and distinct physiognomies. The kind of passive synthesis that McDowell analyzes in terms of the passive exercise of concepts is thus better first comprehended as forms of response to stimuli and patterns of activity that animal embodiment affords.[23] Animal bodies with their complex patterns of purposive behavior, and not disembodied consciousnesses, are the original synthetic faculties.[24] Unless the space of reasons is considered as evolving from animal routines, as supervening on those routines, elaborating, re-determining, and extending them, spontaneity cannot be our way of actualizing ourselves as *animals*.

A combination of piety, wanting to distinguish us from those animals most like us, and the remarkable success of Newtonian physics contrived to support a bad analogy between illusory items that were projections of the human onto given nature and those items that are the counterparts to embodied animal activity. That analogy generated the stark contrast between items physically there anyway and items whose sense or meaningfulness is necessarily relativized to a standpoint or perspective. Once that contrast becomes decisive, then all forms of situated responsiveness become perspectival takings (projective views of) what is in itself (causally) there anyway. Hence, it is the denial of the relative autonomy of circumambient nature from mechanical nature that yields the epistemological dilemma of what is merely subjective (perspectival and projective) versus what is truly objective.

But the bad analogy and the contrast between the relativized and unconditioned it generated could not have continued to weigh socially and historically unless something within our conception of reason itself correlated with them. When the space of reasons is conceived of as antecedent to and independent of its objects, free and self-determining in itself, and ideally fixed and unchanging, when what it is for an item to be significant is for it to be brought within the compass of the space of reasons so conceived, then, *a fortiori*, circumambient nature is rationally discounted and the space of reasons becomes *sui generis*.

Priority of the object

The considerations of the previous section can be regarded as anticipatory components of a genealogical critique of bald naturalism and scientific rationalism. How now can we connect the genealogical naturalism of circumambient nature with McDowell's and Adorno's more purely epistemological concerns? Both Adorno, emphatically, and McDowell, more quixotically, share a basic thesis of modern reductive naturalism. Adorno states the thesis this way:

> Not even as an idea can we conceive a subject that is not an object; but we can conceive of an object that is not a subject. To be an object is also part of the meaning of subjectivity; but it is not equally part of the meaning of objectivity to be a subject.
>
> Rather, by priority of the object is meant that the subject, for its part an object in a qualitatively different sense, in a sense more radical than the object, which is not known otherwise than through consciousness, is as an object also a subject.[25]

Adorno attempts to state the thesis of the priority of object in austere terms: while we can conceive of objects that are not themselves subjects, we cannot but conceive of the subject as also an object, as one object among or within a world of objects. He thinks this thesis follows from the simple reflection that every thinking is a thinking about something, whether that something is a physical object, artifact, or abstract object. The important items here for our and Adorno's purposes are medium-sized material objects; these objects, Adorno avers, must be not reducible to the thoughts about them, otherwise thought would idle, remaining locked within its own discursive movements. The object of thought must be conceived as capable of resisting and so determining what is thought about it. This fails to occur when empirical knowledge is de-contextualized, where the paradigm case of the de-contexualization of empirical knowledge is treating an empirical object or event as rationally intelligible only if it is a deductive consequence of a natural law which is itself a member of a deductive system of law. The more pure, logical, formal, procedural, or mathematical a consideration of an object or event is, the more it abstracts from the qualitative specificity, the sensuous particularity of the object or event to the ideal point at which the object or event becomes nothing but the shadow of the thought about it. Hence, the more objects are considered in the light of what can be known about them a priori, or the extent to which a priori norms of thought determine empirical knowledge (where the a priori is *the* expression of the spontaneity and so self-determining normativity of reason), the more subjective that knowledge is. For Adorno, de-contextualized knowings are subjective because they are determined by what belongs to pure reason (mathematics, logic, a priori categories) alone and, thereby, comprehend what is from the point of view of reason alone rather than from its placement within the context of at least circumambient nature. It is for this reason that Adorno regards a program like that of bald naturalism, which at first sight appears to be a hyper-objectivism, to be unduly *subjective*. Conversely, "if one wants to reach the object … its subjective attributes or qualities are not to be eliminated, for precisely that would run counter to the priority of the object."[26] Adornoian naturalism requires that those attributes of objects traditionally regarded as the quintessence of subjective qualities projected on to them be, in truth, the fundament of their objectivity, that through which they are provided with their independence from the cognitive subject.

Appearances to the contrary notwithstanding, these reflections cannot be epistemologically self-moving; behind them lies a debate about two competing conceptions of nature: the nature of bald naturalism versus circumambient nature. For both it would be true to say that the subject is also object while not all objects are subjects; hence, for both the object possesses priority. For both forms of naturalism, bald and circumambient, the object, nature, is temporally and ontologically prior to subject: nature temporally precedes the appearance of the human, and the human is a part of the natural world. Because both forms of naturalism claim ontological and temporal priority for their conception of nature the issue between them requires sorting differently, say, epistemologically.[27] From an epistemological perspective it thus matters terribly that we perceive in the abstractions from ordinary experience purveyed by bald naturalism an undue subjectivism.

The short route to making good this claim turns on the contention that the epistemological subject must be a living animal (p.104), where the argument for that conclusion is approached through reflexive epistemological considerations.[28] A knowing agent's awareness of itself must be conceived as, at least, an *experiential* path through a world existing independently of the agent; that is, I am cognitively self-aware only if I can distinguish my experiences of the world from the world they are experiences of, and I am cognitively self-aware only in virtue of that ability.[29] The epistemologically primary way in which the inner is dependent on the outer is through the way in which my awareness of myself emerges as a correlation between my changing experiences of the world (as uniquely mine) and the relatively stable world those experiences are of. Crucially, what those experiences are of are the appearances of sensuous particulars. If this feature of Kant's transcendental program is granted, it follows that the epistemological agent must be conceived as possessing powers of sensibility, passive powers, and powers of spontaneity that are, at least, intimately related to one another. That is, for knowing to get started sensible experiences of the world are ineliminable because *qua* agent of knowledge that sensible stratum of experience alone provides the conditions of self-awareness. Because sensible experience of an objective world alone provides the conditions of identity and self-awareness of the epistemological agent, then the appearing world of sensuous particulars must represent the permanent condition of cognitive subjectivity, the permanent arena in which such subjectivity emerges and has its cognitive life. Sensible nature is epistemically primary in relation to all other possible objects of knowledge because it is the permanent arena of cognitive activity. Hence, what occurs as circumambient nature from the perspective of philosophical ethology occurs epistemologically as the relatively stable order of the appearances of sensuous particulars; and what epistemology adds to philosophical ethology is the role of sensuous particulars in providing the necessary conditions of self-consciousness.

In Lecture V, McDowell argues against Kant that a "free-standing idea of formal subjective continuity" (p.103), the correlate of the "I think" that must accompany all my representations that Kant offers in the Paralogisms, while well-taken in opposition to the Cartesian ego, is not itself adequate; the knower of sensible nature cannot itself be essentially non-sensible.

> [T]he idea of a subjectively continuous series of states or occurrences in which conceptual capacities are implicated in sensibility – or, more generally, the idea of a subjectively continuous series of exercises of conceptual capacities of any kind, that is, the idea of a subjectively continuous series of "representations", as Kant would say – is just the idea of a singled out tract of a life. The idea of a subjectively continuous series of "representations" could no more stand alone, independent of the idea of a living thing in whose life these events occur, than could the idea of a series of digestive events with its appropriate kind of continuity.
>
> (p.103)

While this is unquestionably too quick, its point seems right: if representations are those of sensible nature, then their vehicle, sensibility itself, cannot be passed over. But sensibility is not a power of the disembodied mind, but of the living body. The medium of perceptual consciousness is the whole living body of the subject. Hence, the sense in which we cannot but conceive of the subject as an object is the sense in which it is a living body whose proximate objects are those sensuous particulars belonging to circumambient nature. So saying might well lead us to think that if philosophical ethology requires epistemology, the converse is equally true. This should be unsurprising; after all, what exactly is it that pressures McDowell in wanting some form of naturalism if not the independent claim of the naturalism of circumambient nature? Is not McDowell implicitly relying on that naturalism in employing the idea of a "living thing in whose life these events occur" against Kant's abstraction? And hence, can the necessity at stake here be purely epistemic, or must it not nod in the direction of the necessities of circumambient nature?

What McDowell fails to see in his critique of Kant is that what pressures Kant to treat the "I think" as abstract is not solely either his concern to protect the a priori from material contamination or his worries about the Cartesian ego; what equally forces Kant to abstract the self from its embodiment, making it a sheer point of view on the world, is that the "empirical world" was for him nothing but a law-governed totality, hence the kind of world that would leave no room for exercises of spontaneity. It is this fact, above all, which makes the space of reasons in Kant *sui generis*; and it is precisely the *sui generis* character of Kant's account of the space of reasons, its a priori origin, that, conversely, makes the understanding insensitive to circumambient nature.[30] There is, then, only the slimmest line separating Kant's transcendental subjectivism and bald naturalism – indeed nothing other than the evanescent and insubstantial "I think" itself; and if one is aggressively Kantian, one will say that the bald naturalist is but a Kantian rationalist who has forgotten the contribution of reason itself to the idea of there being a rational order of nature. Kant's transcendentally grounded and a priori constitution of *the* view from somewhere, the "I think" that must accompany all my representations, and the attempt to provide a view from nowhere are both determined by and expressions of the abstraction of agent and object from circumambient nature. At least here it is well to remind ourselves that Kant himself did not regard the inclusion of material nature in the space of reasons, the doctrine of transcendental idealism, as re-enchanting nature; the establishment of normativity all the way down, the space of reasons as having no outside, is not equivalent to the establishment of human meaningfulness as a component of a wholly natural world. Kant thought that project doomed (by natural science); only freedom beyond or outside or adjacent to rational nature would secure the worth of human pursuits. Implicitly, McDowell's naturalizing of Kant must presuppose a train of thought of this kind.

What supports the correlation between Adorno and Horkheimer's statements that, on the one hand, "Abstraction, the tool of enlightenment, treats its objects as did fate, the notion of which it rejects: it liquidates them," and, on the other hand, "the disenchantment of the world is the extirpation of animism," or even, "enlightenment ... compounds the animate with the inanimate"[31] *is the equivalence of the epistemological notion of appearances of sensuous particulars with the genealogically presupposed order of circumambient nature.* The epistemological wrongness of abstraction as the mechanism for concept formation (pp.7, 18–23) cannot be fully stated in formal terms because what is abstracted from, in the final instance, is circumambient nature with its interdependent system of proto-meanings. The object liquidated is the living thing and its (practical) life; and it is liquidated by abstracting from its proto- and actual forms of meaningfulness, and re-determining them as tokens of natural law. What enlightenment in the form of Kant's empirical realism, or bald naturalism, or, practically, bureaucratization or the domination of exchange value over use value, abstracts from and/or supervenes on is circumambient nature and its cultural elaborations.

Without reference to circumambient nature the role and status of appearing sensuous particulars remains theoretically indeterminate. Consider Adorno's argument that the apparent subjective attributes of objects are in fact borrowed from the object. It must assume that the appearing sensible features of sensible objects are irreducible because they, in fact, make the object what it is. But this assumption must presuppose that something essential is lost, liquidated, in taking up a reductionist stance; unless that something is the *life* and proto-meanings of circumambient nature, the force of the claim remains indeterminate. Here is Adorno's statement:

> If one wants to [cognitively] reach the object ... its subjective attributes or qualities are not to be eliminated: precisely that would run counter to the primacy of the object. ... If the subject does have an objective core, the object's subjective qualities are so much more an element of objectivity. For the object becomes something at all only through being determinate. In the determinations that seem to be attached to it by the subject, the subject's own objectivity comes to the fore: all of them are borrowed from the objectivity of the *intentio recta*. ... [T]he supposedly pure object, lacking any admixture of thought or intuition, is the very reflection of abstract subjectivity: only it makes the Other like itself through abstraction. Unlike the indeterminate substrate of reductionism, the object of undiminished experience is more objective than that substrate. The qualities which the traditional critique of knowledge eliminates from the object and credits to the subject are due, in subjective experience, to the object's primacy; that is what we were deceived about by the ruling *intentio obliqua*.[32]

I take the turning point in this argument to be the claim that if subjects have an objective core, if the subject thus is something other than a geometrical location in space, then this will be due to just those qualities which it shares with objects that traditionally have been designated as merely subjective. Hence, what makes those qualities *more* objective than, say, the microscopic or abstract primary qualities of things is that they alone make the object determinate, and thereby constitute the subject as *object*; that is, epistemically insert the subject into the object world. And while secondary qualities, narrowly understood, are part of this story, the thicker protocols and proto-meanings of circumambient nature, animal life in all its differentiation and practical complexity, is necessary in order to make the argument hold. We are epistemically inserted in the world via the sensible features we share with perceptual objects because that – always reflexive – insertion is not purely epistemic; reflective self-insertion recapitulates the contextualization of animal life in its living environment.

Epistemologically establishing the priority of the object succeeds, finally, only if it presumes that the order of appearances of sensuous particulars overlaps with, in part, the order of circumambient nature. Hence, if the partial re-enchantment of nature requires the rehabilitation of circumambient nature, the question arises as to how we can conceive of perceptual takings of sensuous particularity in its qualitative density as significantly objective, as something upon which the subject *depends*, and hence as sustaining the priority of the object, without losing the normativity of the space of reasons. How can the space of reasons be a repository of proto-meanings it does not originate? How is the very idea of a space of reasons, rational demands, compatible with naturalism and the priority of the object?

Shades and samples: dependence all the way up

In order to ensure that *what* is actualized through exercises of spontaneity is our animal life I have insisted that there must be intermediaries. To insist upon intermediaries is to argue against McDowell's (and Kant's) contention that "receptivity does not make an even notionally separable contribution to the co-operation" (p.9) between receptivity and spontaneity. Adorno entitles this richer notion of receptivity "undiminished experience [*Erfahrung*]";[33] hence, he thinks that the deepest consequence of the rationalization of reason is the reduction and epistemic disenfranchisement of experience, and that a future, utopian philosophy would be "nothing but full, unreduced experience in the medium of conceptual reflection."[34] Experience, then, is for Adorno the crucial epistemic intermediary, that item which, in Wright's terms, will have the "intrinsic potential to command a certain conceptual response from a suitably endowed thinker" without that conceptual response constituting its "very being."[35] It has this intrinsic potential because it is already mediated by "intelligent" (but non-conceptual) animal embodiment and behavior.

McDowell, of course, is correct to deny that receptivity, as our power of sensibility, should be understood as submerged in the realm of law; receptivity is also a power of synthesis, hence a form of passive synthesis. But passive synthesis should be, in the first instance, associated with accomplishments of animal embodiment rather than the passive exercise of conceptual capacities. Even in its most primitive forms, human experience, however immediate it appears, is mediated by our animal life. Because it is *our* animal life which is at issue, then there is reason to believe that our passive powers are not identical with the passive powers of the higher mammals; further, there will be complex ranges of experience that we would not possess unless we led the conceptually structured lives we do. Hence, experience must be strongly enough tied to our animal life so as to permit the thought that some of it, at least, is all but the "same" as that possessed by the higher mammals, while being synthetically complex enough to command a conceptual response of a certain kind, and must be subject to elaboration such that even richly articulated cultural phenomena can be "experienced" as well as thought.[36]

While I am unsure what would demonstrate that all these criteria were satisfied, the minimum necessary for sustaining the relative autonomy and independence of sensible experience would be to show the priority of the object over the subject *in the concept*: concepts must be dependent on the objects they are about. McDowell, in his anxiety to avoid the Myth of the Given, focuses all his energy on demonstrating that there is normativity all the way out (or down); by introducing a richer concept of circumambient nature, which McDowell requires anyway, I have attempted to mitigate some of that anxiety by simply denying that we ever directly face that kind of givenness.[37] Nonetheless, if the idea of normativity all the way out is not to collapse into idealism, then there must be as well *dependence all the way in (and up)* so that the concept is marked by and beholden to our encounter with its object. Only a conceptual order in which concepts *remained* dependent on experience could be an order of an enchanted nature. This provides us with a formal distinction between the conceptual orders of disenchanted and enchanted nature: in the conceptual order of disenchanted nature the meaning of a concept is determined *solely* by its inferential role in a system of concepts, while for enchanted nature the meaning of a concept must *also* make essential reference to the experience to which the object of the concept gives rise. Only this latter can bind conceptual meaning to an appropriate empirical context, namely, one involving the appearances of sensuous particulars. In order to begin fleshing out how this is possible, two ideas of McDowell's are helpful.

If we are to consider experiences of objects as normatively beholden to them, hence, at one level, as fully *responses* to the layout of the world, then we are going to need to say that an experience of P requires that we are sensorily directly exposed to P, that our experience of P is, in part, brought about by or *caused* by P.[38] For this thought to run we must not conceive of the opposite of the space of reasons as our being in only causal relations to objects. As McDowell (p.71, note) and Adorno[39] both insist, the right contrast with the space of reasons is the realm of law. But the realm of law is, at least for Adorno, the primary expression of identity thinking which associates conceptuality with generality (p.104), and hence with the priority of the universal over the particular. Once this occurs, then nothing particular can be cognitive in its own right, and we will easily suppose that the ordinary empirical concepts employed in everyday judgments are suppressed or implicit causal laws. As Adorno comments:

> The process of demythologization has had a twofold effect upon causality, the legatee of the spirits held to be at work in things: it has both confined it [to the model of causal chains] and reinforced it in the name of law.[40]

Freeing causality from the spell of the universal should enable it to contribute to the space of reasons.

The second idea of McDowell's that can be of help here turns up in his treatment of the problem that experience, of color, say, is too fine-grained to be called conceptual throughout. In this instance I want to split the difference between his claims and those who, for these cases, want to say "that the content of experience is *partly* non-conceptual" (p.56). McDowell's correct critical point here is to suggest that with the help of demonstratives like "that shade" we can give expression to a concept of a shade no matter how fine-grained. "Why not say," McDowell asks,

> that one is thereby equipped to embrace shades of colour within one's conceptual thinking with the very same determinateness with which they are presented in one's visual experience, so that one's concepts can capture colours no less sharply than one's experience presents them?

> (p.56)

All that is required in order to assure ourselves that what we have in view here is a genuine conceptual capacity is that the capacity employed to embrace a color in mind, one activated in the presence of the original sample as designated by "... is coloured *thus*",[41] is able to persist beyond the duration of the experience itself. But this does not show, quite, what McDowell claims: even if conceptual understanding *can*, in principle, be as fine-grained as experience, that does not entail that experience is conceptual all the way out or that experience is not weakly concept transcendent for two reasons. First, even if *any* portion of my current experiential field can be conceptualized, not *all* of it can be. Actual experience is always more fine-grained, complex, richer, and hence more dense than any conceptual grasping of it. Phenomenologically, part of what distinguishes the experiential from its conceptual uptake is that the former is indefinitely fine-grained and dense. It is because experiential fields are dense that we are minded to regard conceptualizations as but thin determinations of them, where determinations are further contextualizations of open-ended contextual arenas. And one inference that can be drawn from that claim is that experiential fields are potentialities for conceptual determination that in themselves must therefore be indeterminate. Second, the possibilities for not just me but those of my community determining an experiential field will necessarily track interest. Our experiential fields relating to snow or coconuts will be very different from those had by the indigenous inhabitants of Norway or Brazil. But this too entails that experiential fields are intrinsically indeterminate. Hence, both individually and communally experience is, because indeterminate, weakly concept transcendent.

To think otherwise is to imagine that for each *possible* shape of experience there a priori corresponds a unique demonstrative. So imagine for each shape of experience that there must be possible a unique photograph, and that for any particular object or state of affairs there will be (ahistorically? atemporally?) some definite number of photographs that would exhaust the possible experiences of the object or state of affairs. (Ignore for a moment the fact that any photograph that is standing in for a "… is coloured *thus*" might itself be found complex – in value, intensity, hue, shading.) Is not this notion of exhaustion or the wish for it (the fantasy of experience like nature cut at the joints) what seems odd and unnecessary here? Take Edward Steichen's project of taking a thousand photographs of the same cup and saucer.[42] Imagine each does indeed manage a distinct physiognomy. There seems no end to it; and yet, for all that, it is the same cup and saucer. In saying that they (cup and saucer) and, by analogy, experience, exceed their photographic capture[43] (and each photographic capture exceeds or shapes what we thought our experience of the object was – otherwise photographs would never teach us anything), neither arbitrariness nor nominalism are invited; if they were photography would be pointless. But if neither arbitrariness nor nominalism are lying in wait, and certainly no sub-perceptual scientific story is either (it is not any such which the photographic analogy brings to the fore), then where is the force of McDowell's insistence that there be actualizations of conceptual capacities that are not exercises of them? Why not say that each determination of an experiential field is just a further or other determination of it without claiming either that the field is *essentially* indeterminate (as if wholly unjointed as in the Nietzschean fantasy of a random flux as the background to our interested predications) or essentially determinate, fixed. If this is a conceptually consistent position, then McDowell's insistence exceeds its support and, if my denials are correct, it is unnecessary for the success of McDowell's transcendental project.

Conversely, there are two very good reasons for thinking experience must be indeterminate without being essentially indeterminate: (i) it explains how human possibilities (of action and perception) can be lost (and not just go into hiding), which is what Weberian disenchantment exposes (certain possibilities of determination are lost when certain possibilities of action are lost); and (ii) it enables the possibility of novelty or creation or innovation. But (i) and (ii) are just the flip sides of the fact that humans are historical beings rather than merely having a history. McDowell, in assuming the propriety of Gadamer's second-nature thesis, assumes we are historical in this way, but he does not show how that claim fits his conception of experiential determinacy.

McDowell wants to claim that an aspect of experiential content need not be conceptualized to be conceptual; if this requires that experience be essentially determinate all the way down it is implausible in itself and incompatible with a truly historical second nature. But without the claim for determinacy all the way down (as what conceptuality all the way down entails), then the force of the thesis that there are aspects of experiential content that are conceptual without being conceptualized is not really distinguishable from the "partly conceptual" thesis, where the latter means, roughly, "determinable and thus suitable for conceptualization without containing any feature antipathetic to that suitability." But why should McDowell require more than this?

Life: the natural basis of the normative

That concepts can be, contextually, as fine-grained as experience provides the right kind of intimacy between experience and conceptualization; that experience, in fact, is *always* richer than its current conceptualization gives experience the immediacy and independence from conceptuality we normally suppose it to have while providing it with the right kind of material and causal credentials. Yet, if we are to consider conceptualization as fundamentally a *further* determination of experience rather than, as in identity thinking, the subsumption of already determinate particulars under universals, then we will need to consider general concepts (like "red" or "sad") as particular elaborations and extensions of cases like that in which the concept in question is grasped like "... is coloured *thus*" is grasped. General concepts enable the discrimination and recognition of experientially dense phenomena. But this does not quite accurately state what is needed. One reason for thinking that the paradigm of conceptually grasping something is a case where that grasping is expressed through demonstrative reference is that in those cases the experiential content of the concept is a component of it. If this were not so, then the empirical content of a perceptual experience would be *exhausted* by all the true inferences that could be drawn from it, in which case perceptual experience itself would reduce to "blind" input.[44] And this, of course, brings us back to the issue of the specificity of perceptual experience which, in McDowell's handling, so troubled Wright.

Adorno's way of attempting to capture what is at issue here is to say that all empirical concepts are organized along two different axes: sign and image, communication and naming, function and substance, rationality and mimesis, etc. Each of these is intended as a re-description of the relation between concept and intuition which gives back to intuition some level of independence from conceptuality narrowly understood. Generalizing from the case of " ... is coloured *thus*," the argument for some measure of independence can now be stated as the thesis that *ideally all (empirical) predicative identification incorporates a moment of non-predicative identification.* And while acts of non-predicative identification are expressed with the aid of demonstratives, non-predicative, perceptual judgments themselves are not *fully* discursive, where full discursivity is fleshed out in the thought that the empirical content of a judgment is equivalent to the totality of the true inferences it licenses.[45] As McDowell rightly comments in a slightly different context:

a perceptual demonstrative thought surely homes in on its object not by containing a general specification, with the object figuring in the thought as what fits the specification, but by virtue of the way this sort of thinking exploits the perceptible presence of the object itself.

(105)

I take it that what McDowell has in mind here by exploiting the perceptible presence of the object is something like from my perceiving you in pain I immediately seek to remove the object causing it. In such a case, my reaction would be suitably object dependent.[46] But while that begins to show that conceptual exploitation need not be equivalent to discursive articulation, it bypasses the precise way in which the original perception in question is fully cognitive but not discursive; but it is cognition without (full) discursivity that is the crux of non-predicative identification, and by extension, the specificity of perceptual judgment.

To state the same hesitation from a different angle, nothing in my exploitation of McDowell's account of "... is coloured *thus*" demonstrates why we might be *required* to make essential reference to experience in the employment of standard empirical predicates. Standardly, concepts are learned in more chaotic ways than through direct experience, and nothing within the account of experience thus far offered explains why it would be emphatically *wrong* to rationalize our conceptual scheme so that objects became nothing but shadows of it. McDowell helps us see how experience can enter into conceptual understanding, but not how it must so enter.[47] Is it not now the case that empirical color perception is not emphatically experiential, that for us color awareness generally does involve the seamless incorporation of intuitions in concepts? Is not that fact the chagrin with which every Matisse canvas, for example, resounds? Color perception has been rationalized, and because rationalized is not any longer emphatically experiential. Arguably our color experience is now disenchanted – Erlebnis rather than Erfahrung.

Part of the reason why color perception cannot be pivotal for demonstrating the experiential contours of conceptuality is because for it the equivalence between the appearing of sensuous particularity and the order of circumambient nature has been severed. Or, more directly, Kant never meant the subordination of intuition to concept to block the scientific rationalization of perceptual experience and hence never meant to establish the rational autonomy of perceptual experience. What on its own will establish the normativity of perceptual experience does nothing toward establishing the worth of the objects of experience, their significance. If empiricism in McDowell's sense is the doctrine of the relative autonomy of sensory experience, its irreducibility, then empiricism is not a narrowly epistemological thesis.

If this is correct, then it entails that there is no direct epistemological route that can demonstrate why an empirical concept *must* make essential reference to the experience to which the object of the concept gives rise. The normativity of conceptuality is not epistemologically free-standing; the idea of a space of reasons that is self-moving or rooted in the spontaneity of the intellect will not do the job. On the contrary. There is normativity in the conceptual sphere only because the conceptual is already practical and ethical. In order to uncover the normative requirement that concepts be dependent on experience we need to re-inscribe the equivalence between the appearing of sensuous particulars and circumambient nature. The wrong of rationalization is cognitively or rationally wrong because it is an ethical wrong; it is the destruction of the living.

In order to give this idea a moment of hope, I need a case in which an ordinary predicative concept must be thought on the basis of its non-predicative sense if its empirical content is to be grasped at all, where not so doing carries consequences beyond the cognitive. I do not know of anywhere in Adorno where such a demonstration can be found. However, in the midst of Wittgenstein's private language argument I think there is an argument connecting object dependency with ethical normativity *überhaupt*.

> And can one say of the stone that it has a soul and *that* is what has the pain? What has a soul, or pain, to do with a stone?
>
> Only of what behaves like a human being can one say that it *has* pains … .
>
> 284. Look at a stone and imagine it having sensations.—One says to oneself: How could one so much as get the idea of ascribing a *sensation* to a *thing*? One might as well ascribe it to a number!—And now look at a wriggling fly and at once these difficulties vanish and pain seems able to get a foothold here, where before everything was, so to speak, too smooth for it.
>
> And so, too, a corpse seems to us quite inaccessible to pain.—Our attitude to what is alive and to what is dead, is not the same. All our reactions are different.[48]

As I read him, Wittgenstein is here attempting to question the Cartesian (and Kantian) picture of interiority by contending that it is not souls or minds that feel pain but bodies. But in order for this to have the force he wants, Wittgenstein attempts to show, *from the outside*, that bodies cannot be the dead or lifeless or unfeeling or mechanical *things* that the picture that drives one into Cartesian interiority makes them appear to be.

Wittgenstein is here contending that there is something basic, categorial in our apprehensions of mere things, dead things, and living ones, and that in making these discriminations we are not blindly subsuming these different kinds of objects under different (categorial) concepts, but that our apprehensions are somehow *responses* to the objects, guided and governed by their forms of appearing – too smooth, wriggling, inaccessible to pain.[49] In these cases the smoothness or motionlessness of the stone, the wriggling of the fly, and the inaccessibility to further hurt or pain in the corpse are not external properties of these objects, not mere empirical predicates picking out properties capturable in a normal predicative judgment or assertion ("the fly is wriggling"), but, at least here, features of those objects *experienced* as marking them off from one another, and hence as providing us with utterly different and incommensurable orientations toward them – "All our reactions are different" in the different cases. Hence, my judgment of the fly as living *orients* my relation to it in the sense of regulating the appropriateness or inappropriateness of other conceptual responses. In judging the fly as living, "is living" is not a simple determining or classifying of the experiential manifold, but a judgment that attunes us to that manifold generally; it is presupposed in all our reactions to things like that, it orients the kinds of meaningfulness our application of predicates to that kind of object can have. As Wittgenstein says in rebutting the interlocutor who thinks that the stones and flies are just things that, as it so happens, behave differently, "I want to intimate to him that this is a case of the transition 'from quantity to quality'." To let a little enchantment in: wriggling is something like the form of the fly, it is a bit of nature's cipher that we decode or determine into the categorial predicate "is living." In this instance "is living" is a *material* a priori predicate. What makes the predicate a priori is its controlling of "all" our reactions. What makes it material is that its a priori power is not detachable from the exemplary instances through which it is announced. It is an a priori distinction that imposes itself on us.[50]

Or, as we might now be tempted to say: it is *the* a priori distinction that is here imposed on us, for in controlling the direction of "all our reactions" it is equally announcing or introducing into our reactions the very idea of normative appropriateness, of our taking a normative attitude.[51] If normativity is more than the thin notion of having a reason for a belief this is because there are kinds of objects in the world, the living ones, that demand to be responded to differently than other things, the mere ones and the dead ones; if all our reactions are not different, then we will treat the animate as if inanimate, doing it incalculable harm thereby. But the introduction of normativity is "intuitive" just as the distinction between left and right is a matter of intuition – what can be pointed to but inevitably misrepresented when construed as merely discursive. That there can and must be such material a priori predicates is thus what demonstrates that the concept's empirical meaning outruns its discursive employment.

While Wittgenstein's big game here is to contend that the distinction between the psychological and the merely physical lies in the division between the living and non-living, and not between inner and outer,[52] and hence the key to establishing the intimacy of the relationship between inner and outer is to reanimate (and so re-enchant) the body, he is simultaneously concerned to show how this reanimation requires non-predicative forms of identification. It is thus no accident that he states just a few lines later, "one can imitate a man's face without seeing one's own in a mirror;" a remark that I interpret, in the context of the above, as claiming that mimetic behavior is a form of (intransitive) understanding that has its source in the structures of meaningfulness that animate objects possess.[53] To think of perceptual judgment on the model of mimetic behavior is prescient since in the latter case we can make no sense of the idea that one could grasp the meaning of a thing in that way without the presence of the object governing one's response utterly. The presence of a mirror, that is mediation through internal reflection, would make mimetic understanding non-mimetic, so removing the object from its controlling role and replacing it by an internal self-relation. If the model of mimetic response is how Wittgenstein intends us to interpret our understanding of the fly's wriggling, our non-predicative identification of it, is there any reason not to suppose that more mundane empirical concepts ought to have their empirical meaning in just the same way?[54]

If the fly's wriggling is what orients us in relation to it, and this possibility of orientation affects all responses to it and what is like it, then there is a deep entwining of the normative and the natural. But the reason that the natural here is within the space of the normative is because the natural is already in itself normatively constituted. Reason lives off that if it lives at all; hence, the disenchantment of nature is brought about by the subsumption of circumambient, living nature by the system of law-like nature, and that work of subsumption (or supervenience) can generate a transcendental anxiety because it, in fact, destroys a necessary condition for normativity.

Conclusion

The best defense of McDowell's "quietism" is that a passage from Wittgenstein like the one just commented upon can still be found disconcerting and illuminating, something that can enable an aspect of our practices to dawn on the reader; I take the moment of dawning and orientation to be the having of an experience, *Erfahrung*. If the case has the range I am claiming for it, the dawning of that aspect is equivalent to coming to see nature as, however partially, enchanted. The best criticism of McDowell's quietism is that the material a prioris that Wittgenstein brings to our notice have only the slightest grip on the actual details of the practices, institutional and non-institutional, that they should be orienting. But this goes back to the first wedge I inserted between his and Adorno's thought: the actual characterization of the space of reasons we inhabit. McDowell seems to believe that this space is just there for appreciating and refining once we have been inducted into it. But this ignores the way in which practices shape contents. To use an analogy, it is not just that our tastes in fashion change, requiring ever new shifts in perception to be aware of them; they change with actual changes in the clothes that are on the rack;[55] that was the point of my indeterminacy thesis. And if the clothes on the rack all presume to dress the human body in suits of armor and corsets of steel, then nothing much of the animal body is going to be detectable to resist those fashions other than the mystifying hurt they cause. Rationalized reason – Weber's "iron cage" – generates practices that do dress the body in suits of armor and corsets of steel. No dawning of an aspect or shift in perception, say our coming to find the clothes on the rack intolerable, will by itself provide alternative garments, or indeed reveal the lineaments of the noble animal body these uniforms have so deformed. Wittgenstein's reminder does not re-enchant the world for us, but rather, as a piece of negative dialectics, reveals all we have lost.

Notes

* This essay is an expanded and revised version of my article "Re-enchanting Nature," *Journal of the British Society for Phenomenology* 31(3): 277–299 (October 2000).

1 All bracketed page references in the body of this essay are to the paperback edition of *Mind and World* (Cambridge, MA: Harvard University Press, 1996).

2 John McDowell, "Précis of *Mind and World*," *Philosophy and Phenomenological Research* 58(2): 366 (June 1998).

3 I am assuming that the interminable oscillation between coherentism and bald naturalism can be widened so that the former stands for any view which would wholly extract human meaningfulness from its natural setting, from Kantian rationalism to Nietzschean self-making, and the latter any program of reductive naturalizing.

4 While the issue of the disenchantment of the world has been palpably absent from analytic epistemology over the past fifty years, it has been the driving thought of three important works of moral philosophy: Alasdair MacIntyre, *After Virtue* (London: Duckworth, 1981); Bernard Williams, *Ethics and the Limits of Philosophy* (London: Fontana Press, 1985); Charles Taylor, *Sources of the Self: The Making of Modern Identity* (Cambridge, MA: Harvard University Press, 1989).

5 "Subject and Object" (hereafter: SO), in A. Arato and E. Gebhardt (eds), *The Essential Frankfurt School Reader* (New York: Urizen Books, 1978), p.505.

6 In this I agree with Michael Friedman's complaint that McDowell makes too little of the fact that Kant's account of the relation between concept and intuition was fundamentally designed to close "the Platonic gap between mathematical reason and sensible nature" ("Exorcising the Philosophical Tradition," *Philosophical Review* 105(4): 438 (October 1996), p.32 of this volume), although Friedman is heading in exactly that wrong Kantian direction. The rationalization of reason or identity thinking is a shorthand way of speaking about, first, the displacement of reason (*Vernunft*) by the understanding (*Verstand*), and, second, the modeling of the activities of reason on those of the understanding. I take these two shifts together to be what, ultimately, disenchants nature.

7 Which is another complaint raised by Michael Friedman, "Exorcising the Philosophical Tradition," op. cit., pp.463–464 (pp.46–47 of this volume).

8 For a defense of this line of thought in McDowell see Sally Sedgwick, "Hegel, McDowell, and Recent Defenses of Kant," *Journal of the British Society for Phenomenology* 31(3): 229–247 (October 2000).

9 Crispin Wright, "Human Nature?," *European Journal of Philosophy* 4(2): 244 (1996) (p.149 of this volume).

10 In contending that there is "no need ... for a justificatory Given at all, whether conceptual or not" (ibid.) Wright does appear here to be settling for exculpation: beliefs are simply what happen when we are in the appropriate circumstances and using the appropriate faculties correctly (causal regularity, or "normalcy," thus displacing actual normativity). This, then, is a version of the idea of empirical beliefs simply "whelming up" out of non-cognitive states about which McDowell is rightly suspicious.

11 Ibid., p.243 (p.148 of this volume).

12 See, above all, Elaine Scarry, *The Body in Pain: The Making and Unmaking of the World* (New York: Oxford University Press, 1985). This way of making the point places the emphasis on our identity with other animals rather than the denial of their feeling the "same" pain as us. McDowell of course believes that animals feel pain, perceive, etc. And he adopts Gadamer's notion that animals have an environment if not a world. That moves in the right direction, but would still leave my point untouched since my suggestion here is that in extreme pain an environment is all *we* have. What finally I am concerned with is a systematic notion of nature that, again, is neither the nature of mathematical physics nor subject to the charge of anthropomorphism like the idea of a second nature is.

13 "Human Nature?," op. cit., p.244 (p.149 of this volume).

14 Although I shall not be able to elaborate on it here, I take the space defined by the intersection of concept acquisition, concept extension, and the production of new concepts to be the one in which we require some notion of experience that is not already concept saturated. In order to make this space a theoretical pivot I would need to show that, broadly speaking, concept learning, conceptual change, rather than concept possession should be at the center of our understanding of cognitive experience and rationality. My account of experience at the end of this essay is meant to point in this direction.

15 Officially, it is only in relation to the realm of law that the space of reasons is *sui generis*; this leaves space for the mediations I am proposing to be necessary for the very possibility of second nature even on McDowell's own account. This and his adoption of the Gadamerian notion of environment leave open the possibility that my line of thought at this juncture is a friendly addition rather than criticism.

16 For the analogous thought stated in epistemological terms see SO, p.502.

17 It is well to remember that with the higher mammals, at least, purposive activities are "learned" and hence "taught"; the young are "trained," their behavior, when appropriate, "punished" and "corrected." Hence, the young of the higher mammals do things "correctly" and "incorrectly." Not all purposiveness is like this – the purposive activities of frogs and spiders is not – but some is. So one way of pushing the thesis I want to achieve would be to ask: can we make sense of rational activity apart from purposive activity? And can we make sense of purposive activity (what is subject to learning and correction) apart from purposive routines (unlearned behavior)? And can we make sense of purposive routines apart from (their emergence from) purposive systems?

18 John McDowell, "Reply to Commentators," *Philosophy and Phenomenological Research* 58(2): 412 (June 1998).

19 *Negative Dialectics* (hereafter: ND), tr. E. B. Ashton (London: Routledge, 1973), p.358.

20 For an elegant defense of the thought that pain is intrinsically normative for the higher mammals see Christine M. Korsgaard, *The Sources of Normativity* (Cambridge: Cambridge University Press, 1996), pp.144–160.

21 For the absolute conception of knowledge see Bernard Williams, *Descartes: The Project of Pure Enquiry* (Harmondsworth, Middlesex: Penguin Books, 1978), pp.244–249; for "the view from nowhere" see Thomas Nagel, *The View from Nowhere* (New York: Oxford University Press, 1985), chap. 6; and for the explanatory privilege of items with a "wide cosmological role" see Crispin Wright, *Truth and Objectivity* (London: Harvard University Press, 1992), pp.196–201. I detail the argument of this paragraph in my *Adorno: Disenchantment and Ethics* (Cambridge: Cambridge University Press, 2001), chap. 2. Most of the present essay draws on material from chap. 6 of that work. This presentation of it is extremely abbreviated.

22 I here must simply assume that the attempt to reduce biology to physics is misbegotten. For an excellent first go at an anti-reductionist account of biology see John

Dupré, *The Disorder of Things: Metaphysical Foundations of the Disunity of Science* (Cambridge, MA: Harvard University Press, 1993). And for a recent thinking about animality related to the one here see Alasdair MacIntyre, *Dependent Rational Animals: Why Human Beings Need the Virtues* (Chicago: Open Court, 1999).

23 Within the tradition of European philosophy the idea of locating the "pre-history" of reason in living nature goes back to Schelling, and achieved some semblance of formal statement in Maurice Merleau-Ponty's *Phenomenology of Perception*, tr. Colin Smith (London: Routledge, 1962), and *The Visible and the Invisible*, tr. Alphonso Lingis (Evanston, IL: Northwestern University Press, 1968).

24 If animal bodies are indeed intermediaries, somehow between the merely causal and the fully rational, then nothing is gained by trying to determine whether their responses are cognitive or causal. On the contrary, the implication of the line I am taking is that it has been the desire to determine an answer to that question that has produced the epistemological distortions McDowell is seeking to dissolve. *In seeking a domain of intermediaries, my intention is to make the notions of meaning, conceptuality, reasons less precious and unique than they standardly have been.* Hence I am denying that there is a place where responding stops and rational response begins. Once one begins to concede proto-subjectivity or proto-meaning or proto-language to the brutes, then the metaphysical motivation for seeking out differences becomes suspect. As part of this suspicion, I would have to include the Austin, Strawson, Williams denial that there is a large metaphysical/philosophical issue around freedom and determinism – which is to insist on and not to deny all the practical and political issues in that area.

25 The first passage is from ND, p.183, the second from SO, p.502.

26 SO, p.502.

27 Any question of explanatory priority at this juncture would necessarily beg the epistemological issue.

28 The long route would be the core argument of Adorno and Horkheimer's *Dialectic of Enlightenment* that modern rationalism as exemplified by Kant and scientism are, despite themselves, forms of instrumental knowing, hence forms of knowing that emerge from, are natural outgrowths of, the drive for self-preservation.

29 This is a necessary but not sufficient condition. I can only count myself fully self-conscious when I conceive of my responses as normatively governed and situated; and that only occurs through interaction with other self-conscious agents. But since on my account those other agents must also be animal selves, then for me the crucial element will be how I perceptually distinguish bodies that actualize their animal lives through spontaneity and those whose plasticity of response marks them out as less in self-possession of themselves than that.

30 The issues here, which come to a head in Kant's treatment of purposiveness in the third *Critique*, are immensely complex. For a first go at sorting out these issues see my "Judging Life: From Beauty to Experience, From Kant to Chaim Soutine," *Constellations* 10(7): 157–177 (June 2000).

31 *Dialectic of Enlightenment*, tr. John Cumming (New York: Seabury Press, 1972), pp.13, 5, 16.

32 SO, pp.502–503.

33 Ibid.

34 ND, p.13.

35 "Human Nature?," op. cit., p.245 (p.150 of this volume).

36 Because I am urging a *continuum* from the really hard-wired way in which some animals actualize their lives through the more plastic routines of the higher mammals to our spontaneous mode of actualization, then I am bound to split the difference between the simplistic "factoring" model (p.64) adopted by Evans, and McDowell's overly strong two ways of living out an animal life. McDowell's model is

more nearly right than Evans's, but it needs to be made radically plural: gorillas live out their experience of pain differently than cats, and cats differently than mice, and mice differently than spiders. The samenesses and differences are analogical but objective all the way down.

37 If the Given is equivalent to the description of what is as belonging to the realm of law, then the correct way to account for it is as the result of some highly elaborate conceptual work of de-contextualizing the objects of circumambient nature, and re-contextualizing them in the space of law. Despite its different overall conceptual orientation from that being pursued here, the best account of the logic of de-contextualizing and re-contextualizing remains Martin Heidegger's *Being and Time*, tr. John Macquarrie and Edward Robinson (New York: Harper and Row, 1962).

38 This is beautifully pitched in McDowell's "Having the World in View: Sellars, Kant, and Intentionality," *Journal of Philosophy* 95(9) (September 1998), where, following Sellars's idea that in perceptual experience claims are "evoked or wrung" from the perceiver, the specificity of the perceptual is thought in terms of its involuntariness: "But they are actualized with an involuntariness of a specific kind; in a visual experience an ostensibly seen object ostensibly impresses itself visually on the subject" (p.441). Nothing in the critique of Sellars – the fine demonstration that the role of sensation in thought is transcendental and hence that it is the object known and not sensation that does the basic epistemic work of "guiding" – changes those aspects of *Mind and World* that I find unsatisfactory.

39 ND, pp.265–270. Adorno is here attempting to show how Kant's concepts of freedom and causality are both bound to a particular historical conjuncture.

40 ND, p.267.

41 This phrasing is adopted by McDowell in his "Reply to Commentators," op. cit., p.417, in order to block an objection by Christopher Peacocke. The point is to let the demonstrative correspond to a real fineness of discrimination. Because this fineness is necessarily contextually constituted, as I shall suggest momentarily, the refinement does not remove the *question* of indeterminacy, which is one way, mine, of construing Peacocke's complaint.

42 I am here drawing on Stanley Cavell, *The World Viewed: Reflections on the Ontology of Film*, enlarged edition (Cambridge, MA: Harvard University Press, 1979), pp.120, 185–186. In insisting on the indeterminacy of experience, I am insisting upon an unavoidable vagueness in designation. For a powerful defense of the thought that endorsing ineliminable vagueness is the crux to Wittgenstein's philosophy of language, see Mark Sacks, "Through a Glass Darkly: Vagueness in the Metaphysics of the Analytic Tradition," in David Bell and Neil Cooper (eds), *The Analytic Tradition: Meaning, Thought and Knowledge* (Oxford: Basil Blackwell, 1990), pp.173–196.

43 Or not. I am not denying, and I suppose Steichen was secretly hoping, that at some point variations (of shaping, angle, distance, focus, etc.) might themselves come to seem arbitrary, pointless, variation for its own sake. Would this show the determinacy McDowell desires? No, only that indeterminacy can be boring, empty, pointless – humanly and so epistemologically. Gerhard Richter's photographs of his paintings (after photographs) reveal those paintings to contain possibilities of art that are invisible from the perspective of the painting as ordinarily perceived. I take these photographs – each of which is of just one exact portion of the painting, but each taken from a different perspective (aerial, side-ways on, etc.) so that they do not "add up" to the painting – to perfectly realize how an unnoticed portion of experience can become a "… shaded-and-textured *thus*" without it seeming as if just that possibility was emphatically there prior to all the conditions through which it was realized. But this is to say there could be no totality of conditions that could be specified that would constitute the actualization of a conceptual capacity that was not its

exercise short of its exercise for all cases (and probably any). This is because the exercise itself is multiple and complex – which is the point of my photographic analogy.

44 My point in putting the matter this way is to drive a wedge between McDowell's version of normativity – which, like Adorno's, follows Kant (against Hegel) in attempting to preserve a privilege and specificity for first-person experience – and that found in Robert Brandom's *Making it Explicit: Reasoning, Representing, and Discursive Commitment* (London: Harvard University Press, 1994). A wholly inter-subjectively constituted account of normativity will make first-person experience *mere* entry and exit points (transitions) with respect to the discursive realm, and the discursive realm identical with conceptuality and normativity. The idea of entry and exit points is the fate of animal embodiment in discursive idealism. So my thesis here is that McDowell requires the generalization of the "… is colored *thus*" thesis in order to hold the line against Brandom. My further contention is that he cannot sustain the exemplary character of the "…is colored *thus*" analysis unless he concedes to my revisions concerning experience and, more radically, the attaching of the order of experience to the possibilities made available by circumambient nature.

45 In *Adorno: Disenchantment and Ethics* (New York: Cambridge University Press, 2001), I attempt to explicate the possibility being asserted here in terms of an extension of Kant's theory of reflective judgment in relation to determinative judgment. All the arguments of this essay are snapshots of lines of thought pursued in the book. The italicized portion of the previous sentence might be considered a re-determination of the thesis of empiricism.

46 This is insufficiently nuanced. More accurately, McDowell's thought is that what constitutes my grasping of this as a case of pain, where say it is a kind of pain I have not seen before, is its setting within a conceptual context wider than it. For this, see "Intentionality and Interiority in Wittgenstein," in his *Mind, Value, and Reality* (Cambridge, MA: Harvard University Press, 1998), esp. pp.214–217.

47 His strategy works differently: he presupposes the transcendental weight of the thesis of empiricism, and then shows how only the actualization of conceptual capacities in sensory consciousness enables that weight to be appropriately recognized; it is recognized and suppressed in the transcendental anxiety expressed in the oscillation between coherentism and bald naturalism.

48 *Philosophical Investigations*, tr. G. E. M. Anscombe (Oxford: Basil Blackwell, 1953), §§283–284.

49 For simplicity, I am taking Wittgenstein's metaphorical "too smooth" as descriptive of the stone; even if the stone were rough, however, nothing would change in the basic story, it would be just harder to lay out quickly.

50 Which is why, of course, it is so fragile; because it is so experience-dependent it possesses no powers of resistance to a rationalized reason that demands objects fit patterns of rational articulation that emerge solely from reason itself (on the presumption that there are such).

51 This would be the beginning of a critique of Brandom's contention that normativity is instituted through the taking up of a normative attitude, and that nothing lies behind this attitude (hence it is a form of "normative phenomenalism") other than the attitude and the practices consequent upon having it. See *Making It Explicit*, pp.32–37, 47–50, 626–627.

52 I am here following the conclusion drawn by Marie McGinn, *Wittgenstein and the Philosophical Investigations* (London: Routledge, 1997), p.153. I am grateful to my former colleague Stephen Mulhall for bringing this portion of Wittgenstein's thought to my attention.

53 Those already aware of Adorno's thought will recognize that all my remarks in this section have been oriented by his claim that the disenchantment of the concept has dominantly involved eliminating from it its mimetic moment.

54 Of course, this generalization is here rhetorical and gestural; in this context, however, I would hope that the gesture is not thought of as groundless. I have previously used this account of the Wittgenstein passage in my "Judging Life: From Beauty to Experience, From Kant to Chaim Soutine," op. cit., p.162.

55 I am grateful to Elijah Millgram for suggesting this analogy to me.

13

BETWEEN HERMENEUTICS AND HEGELIANISM

John McDowell and the challenge of moral realism*

Axel Honneth

In the past two decades John McDowell has, with admirable consistency, sought to establish a position in moral philosophy programmatically entitled "moral realism." Although this expression had previously been used for theories that treated moral values as objective components of the world – that is to say, as strictly independent of our perceptions, beliefs, and practices[1] – McDowell's moral realism has a quite different character. According to McDowell, moral reality is disclosed to us in its full objectivity only in connection with rule-governed behavior, which can be conceived as a "second nature" of human beings owing to the fact that it arises from the socialization and education (*Bildung*) of our first nature.[2] The idea of such a "second nature" – suggested in ways that are hard to disentangle by Aristotle, Hegel, Wittgenstein, and Gadamer – is supported by a subtle moral phenomenology that is meant to show how far we are able to perceive moral facts in the same direct way as we perceive colors, odors, and other secondary qualities. The phenomenology seeks to determine whether the moral characteristics of persons or the moral qualities of an action concern phenomena that are not extraneous additions to a reality but are rather experienced directly within the framework of our everyday practices.[3] Thanks to our second nature, it is empirical experience – our sensory receptivity, as McDowell puts it – that enables us to take in the qualitative constitution of the world. Hence this version of moral realism amounts to the idea that our moral beliefs and judgments reflect not the intersubjective efforts of human beings but rather the demands of reality itself.

Now such a conception need not of itself be quite as eccentric as it may seem at first glance. For the claim might simply be that in the development of their forms of life and everyday practices, and thus in the formation (*Bildung*) of their "second nature," human beings had to take into account the constraints imposed by their first nature. To put it pointedly, the normative rules of our practices would then express a world existing independently of us in the sense that there are given human needs, vulnerabilities, and dispositions which we unavoidably have to consider in our intersubjective action. The particular diffi-

246

culties of McDowell's position only appear, however, when it is compared with another approach in contemporary moral philosophy that likewise takes its departure from the idea of a "weak naturalism." In recent years Jürgen Habermas has sought to give his discourse ethics a stronger realist turn by attempting, in a non-scientistic manner, to conceive our moral demands as part of a learning process through which we continue the natural evolutionary process at the cultural level. Here too the idea of a "second nature" of human beings is combined with the "realist" notion that in the normal execution of our learned everyday practices, which represent the results of a collective learning process, we are in a position to perceive moral facts.[4] If we also bear in mind that Habermas speaks of the need for a "hermeneutic of natural history" in his presentation of "weak naturalism," we can see that the theoretical foundations of both approaches are probably much closer than their authors may currently be aware. But in stark contrast to McDowell, for Habermas the situations in which our moral certainties are disrupted are characterized by a compulsion toward a justificatory practice that can no longer be backed by perceptual judgments centered in the lifeworld. Rather, the practice of justification puts these judgments into brackets, as it were, in order to test the universalizability of intersubjectively raised validity claims. Hence, at the reflexive level of such practical discourses, the normative idea of impartiality, understood as an "equal consideration of all the relevant interests," takes the place of a commonly accepted, evaluatively disclosed world.[5]

Conversely, the idea of a problem-oriented suspension of our everyday certainties now raises the question of how McDowell's moral realism tries to accommodate the possibility of a critical examination of moral norms. It is true that McDowell's approach emphasizes the need for a rational analysis of the experienceable world of moral facts, but in the first instance it is not entirely clear how we are supposed to conceive the interplay of moral perception and justification. In what follows I would like to pursue the conjecture that there is an unresolved tension in McDowell's theory, which has the hermeneutic idea of the happening of tradition standing right next to the Hegelian idea of a directed formation (Bildung) of the human spirit. On the one hand, McDowell depicts the formation of our perceptual capacity according to the model of an anonymous happening of tradition which leaves no room for the perceptual testing of normative claims; on the other hand, however, he also plays with the thought of a rationally mediated learning process, which cannot be understood in a consistent manner without at least the temporary interruption of our everyday certainties. I shall proceed first of all by clarifying the epistemological presuppositions that provide the home for McDowell's idea of a "second nature" of human beings. This background should ensure that we keep in view from the outset the close connection between the ideas McDowell developed in Mind and World and his moral realism (I). Only in the second step shall we focus more precisely on how McDowell justifies the idea that in normative contexts we act in an "always already" perceptually disclosed world of moral facts. Here our concern is to reconstruct as exactly as possible the considerations that speak in favor of the idea of a faculty of moral perception (II). In the third section I turn finally to McDowell's attempt at accommodating the process of rational justification. We shall see here that the procedure for coping with moral disagreement brings into relief the unfortunate consequences that arise from the unresolved tension in McDowell's conception (III).

I

In his book *Mind and World*,[6] which also lays down an epistemological foundation for his meta-ethical position, McDowell undertook to rehabilitate empiricism under non-scientistic presuppositions. Seen as a whole, the argument is that owing to their perceptual capacity, human beings have retained a kind of receptiveness to demands issued to them from the world itself.[7] McDowell's complex train of thought takes its departure from a diagnosis of the difficulty we have in coming to terms with Sellars's famous attack on "the Myth of the Given" – a central theme in analytic philosophy.[8] As soon as we see clearly that the world is not given to us directly in our experiences, but that experiences for their part are always already theoretically impregnated, we draw the "coherentist" conclusion that the truth of our statements is determined only by their internal relations of fit. But according to McDowell, the coherentist position – which in the book is represented by the work of Donald Davidson – is fundamentally unstable, and even Kant, owing to his reverence for the scientism of his time, only half-heartedly held on to it: on the one hand there is the "world," thought of as a space governed by natural laws and causal dependencies; and on the other there is the "mind," in which we act only according to rational standards, unimpinged upon by reality. Contemporary philosophy generally, no less than Kant's two-world doctrine, is far from making sense of the pragmatic certainties of everyday understanding because it lets the human practice of justification be carried out independently of the rational demands of the world itself. Even if we grant that reality exerts causal influence on our mental activity, we do not have a view of the mind as receptive to the world through sensory mediation.

McDowell wants to cure us of this split between "mind" and "world," between the rational standpoint of procedural reason and reality conceived as the realm of natural laws, by outlining an alternative epistemology. And as for so many philosophers of the first half of the twentieth century, it seems to him that the royal road to such an overcoming of the modern two-world idea lies in a new interpretation of human experience.[9] In contrast to the other, older attempts, McDowell takes his departure from moral rather than cognitive experience: at the point in his book where an alternative conception is first sketched, Aristotle's ethics appears as the paradigmatic example of a successful synthesis of reason and nature (p.78ff.). McDowell must carry out two steps, which at first sight look hardly connected, before he can present this ethical approach as the basis for a solution to his epistemological problem. The first step involves tracing back the unfortunate dualism of mind and world to the modern tendency to conceive reality as a logical realm in which law-like natural dependencies hold sway. This tendency results in what Max Weber called the "disenchantment" of nature: a "bald," blunt naturalism which no longer permits the idea that reality may be charged with meaning (a) (Lecture IV, §6). The second step, however, consists in showing how "practical wisdom" is understood within Aristotle's ethics as a kind of habitualized responsiveness to moral reasons. Above all, the importance of this is that moral knowledge possesses a circular structure in so far as the ethical significance of a situation can only be grasped if we already have some comprehension of the weight of ethical demands (b) (Lecture IV, §7). The decisive point of McDowell's argumentation follows from his attempt to relate these steps to each other so that Aristotelian ethics appears as an exemplary alternative to the scientistically evacuated concept of nature: since Aristotle considers moral knowledge to be the habitualized result of an education (*Bildung*) of human nature, he can describe the "second" nature of human beings as the horizon within which we possess a faculty of experiencing the demands of reality itself (c).

(a) With the first step in his argument McDowell sets a theoretical course that is of prime importance for the development of his alternative model. On account of it, the initial epistemological problem is traced back to the ontological relation between reason and nature. McDowell forges links to questions of ontology with the thesis that "mental blocks" reaching far back into the early history of modern thought are responsible for the "uncomfortable situation" in contemporary epistemology. To see why "coherentism" can seem the only option facing the refutation of a conceptually unmediated given, we need to unearth the intellectual source of a particular image of human sensibility, which with Kant was already bound up with a scientistic concept of nature. According to this tradition we can understand the receptive capacity of human beings, their ability to experience, only as part of a law-governed conception of nature, while conversely human conceptual spontaneity must be ascribed to a realm of reason, where only rational grounds have force. But once the world is divided up into these two ontological spheres, our rational activity can no longer permeate "all the way out to the impressions of sensibility themselves" (p.69) because only causal effects hold sway there. That to which human beings have a sensory or receptive relation must from now on remain outside the practice of justification, so that knowledge finally shrinks into an operational exercise in the "logical space of reasons." In the end, it is this ontological tradition, the subsumption of human sensibility under the laws of a scientistically understood nature, which McDowell holds responsible even for the coherentism of a Donald Davidson. If the empirical given is always already conceptually structured, but otherwise has only causal effects on the human senses, our cognitive activity takes place in an enclosed "space of reasons" in no kind of "contact" with the world. There is no longer a mental continuum stretching between "nature" and "reason" that would allow us to show how we arrive at empirically contentful knowledge by following a single chain of reasons that begins with sensory experiences.

The kind of mental blocks that McDowell holds responsible for the regrettable situation of contemporary epistemology also provides him with the therapeutic means for remedying that situation. McDowell's strategy is to reach back, by rehabilitating a pre-scientistic concept of nature, to an intellectual location where human conceptual capacities are not yet separated from their natural endowment. If within traditional epistemology the possibility of a "friction" with reality is kept from view – because empirical experience itself cannot be granted any rational content – so in the counter-move an idea of conceptual "spontaneity" must be won back that also characterizes "states and occurrences of sensibility as such" (p.76). But such a synthesis of concept and experience is only restored under the condition that nature is not reduced to a sphere of lawlike connections. Nature must itself be understood as a space of potential intellectuality. To that extent we require, as McDowell says, an expanded naturalism that re-enchants "nature," not by charging it with meaning, but by bringing about a kind of continuity between nature and human "reason." For only if we are able to presume that human rationality is continuous with natural processes can we understand our sensory capacity at once as a natural endowment and as an ability rationally to comprehend reality.[10]

The brief hints regarding the essential features of such an expanded naturalism found in *Mind and World* can at first sight easily arouse the impression that McDowell is readopting motifs from Schelling. In addition, one can hardly help making certain associations with the tradition of philosophical anthropology established in the first third of the twentieth century by Scheler, Gehlen, and Plessner.[11] The relevant point of departure at this juncture is McDowell's thesis that we share with dumb animals a "perceptual sensitivity to features of the environment" (p.69). However, in contrast to other highly evolved primates, whose sensory receptivity is on the whole bound to instinct (p.115), human beings possess a sensibility which on account of its distance from the environment is already shot through with "spontaneity." Hence we can say that the human senses are conceptually structured in so far as they allow us to perceive the world rationally. McDowell now sums up the position suggested by these remarks in the one proposition that human beings realize themselves through a way of life characterized by "exercises of spontaneity" (p.78). In order to make explicit the Aristotelian provenance of this formulation, he turns in the second step of his argumentation to a brief account of Aristotle's ethics.

(b) However, McDowell has to make a detour if he is to clarify the extent to which Aristotle's ethics represents a paradigm for the idea of an expanded naturalism. According to the dominant interpretation of Aristotle – adverted to in the book only through a brief reference to Bernard Williams and Alasdair MacIntyre – Aristotle wanted to extract the principles of his ethics from the facts of an independently given nature. Even though teleological assumptions are also supposed to play a strong role here, from McDowell's point of view that would just amount to an early form of scientistic naturalism. Against this interpretation, McDowell must be able to show that Aristotle's derivation of the concept of moral virtue from objective facts about human nature had a wholly different meaning.[12] He has to show that Aristotle's intention was to comprehend ethical knowledge as an exercise of natural powers that are an extension of the processes of nature. McDowell's alternative interpretation thus rests on the concept of "second nature." Of course it is not just his interpretation of Aristotle that depends on this notion, but the idea of an expanded naturalism as a whole.

McDowell's concept of "ethical character," like Aristotle's, occupies a middle position between mere habit and rational deliberation. Virtue is distinct from mere habit because it is supposed to contain a particular insight or "wisdom"; on the other hand it is distinct from rational reflection because it represents a molded, habitualized condition of human character. The difficulty here arises from the need to comprehend something as an almost bodily, spontaneously performed routine which is at the same time an intellectual operation of the mind. And it looks as if the problem can only be resolved if we understand virtue to be the result of a socialization process through which the practical intellect of human beings – their moral consciousness – receives the lasting shape of a character that is "at home with" moral requirements. Over and above this, McDowell tries to show that for Aristotle virtue so conceived forms, as it were, the hermeneutic horizon within which we must always already be situated when dealing with moral problems. The mere fact of grasping a particular situation as involving a moral conflict, which we want to deal with rationally, tells us nothing but that we let ourselves be guided by an ethical pre-understanding in reaching, albeit in a circular fashion, the cognitively correct solution. What McDowell refers to as the rational "self-scrutiny of an ethical outlook" (p.81) takes place according to the same model of a hermeneutic circle. Even in the case where we have to submit the standards of our moral habits to critical revision, the connecting thread can only be that "practical wisdom" which already makes up the core of our moral character. As moral subjects we always already act against a horizon of moral knowledge, which we can never step out of even when it has become highly questionable. Rather, completely in accordance with Gadamer's idea, such revision and critique is carried out only in the form of the innovative application of an encompassing traditional knowledge.

Of course the links to McDowell's opening question are forged only with the proposal that this hermeneutic conception of "ethical character" be imposed on the concept of second nature. And by that nothing more is meant than that the virtues form intellectual habits and to that extent represent quasi-natural behavioral tendencies that are the result of cultural socialization processes. But if the term "second nature" were to be so minimally restricted, it would not really be clear whether it amounted to more than a reformulation of what we commonly call culture. In order to make the connection with "first" nature, which features in the idea of an expanded naturalism, McDowell must give the expression a stronger meaning.[13] Here the thought emphasized earlier comes into play, namely that humans realize themselves as living, organic beings in the form of an orientation to reasons. Often McDowell uses this formulation as an allusion to the continuity that exists between first nature and human forms of life. The fact that we speak of virtues acquired through socialization as a second "nature" must mean, then, that we understand them as an extension of potentialities that are laid down in the "normal human organism" (p.84). More simply, we could say that the first nature of human beings, their bodily qualities, makes possible the development of moral habits that are mediated by reasons. And from here we can follow Wittgenstein in the speculation that under normal circumstances we cannot avoid noticing in the human voice, even in human facial expressions generally, a capacity for linguistically organized rationality.[14]

It is not hard to recognize why this form of naturalism sets up an alternative to the scientistic understanding of nature. For to understand ethical character as a realization of organically determined potentialities means that nature is certainly not reduced to a realm of causally effective dependencies; rather, it is to interpret nature as a process involving the gradual facilitation of specific forms of life. But because the classification of such organic potentialities can only be carried out from the viewpoint of our own form of life, we have to do it, in the end, through the idea of a hermeneutic of natural history. With the properties we deem to be characteristically human as our guiding theme, we reconstruct natural history as a layered order of the living that terminates in our cultural form of life. But even this form of naturalism does not solve the problem that provides the real point of McDowell's treatment of Aristotle's ethics. For that requires a further, third step, in which it is shown how far the assumption of a second nature of human beings goes along with the claim that our senses have a rational content.

(c) Within the framework of a hermeneutic of natural history such as has just been sketched, we do not conceive nature as a blind, law-governed sphere given independently of us. Rather we understand ourselves as included in the processes of nature in so far as we interpret them as ascending stages of organic productivity, at the end of which stands our own rational form of life. McDowell now draws the further conclusion that under the premises of such an expanded naturalism, the scientistic spell cast over human sensory capacities from the outset of modernity disappears. Human receptivity, our perceptual capacity, need no longer be interpreted as a component of a realm of natural law; rather we can conceive it as an organic element of the form of life through which we realize ourselves as natural beings. According to McDowell, this train of thought leads to a conclusion that provides the key theoretical yield of his conception of second nature: namely, that with the proper education and socialization, our senses are in a position to perceive the demands of reality itself (p.82).

The significance of this conclusion depends much more than it seems at first sight on how we understand "reality." As he first makes clear again in connection with Aristotle's ethics, for McDowell "reality" cannot be collapsed into what we are now describing as the realm of law. The idea of an expanded naturalism has exactly the opposite aim of widening our idea of nature so as to accommodate intellect and rationality within itself. As soon as the conceptual activities through which we reproduce ourselves in specific ways as animal beings are ascribed to nature, the idea of "reality," through which we determine our relation to the world, must also be changed. The "facts" we refer to must then be understood as furnished with the reasons by which we rationally orientate our action. With Heidegger, to whom McDowell does not refer in his book, this thought can be formulated so that the world of human beings is always already disclosed according to their activities. Reality is also supposed to have a rational structure in so far as it is always already enriched with those meanings that belong to the normal course of human existence. McDowell makes it clear that this relation cannot be understood as one of projection or construction. As he puts it in connection with Gadamer's formulation of the same idea:

> For a perceiver with capacities of spontaneity, the environment is more than a succession of problems and opportunities; it is the bit of objective reality that is within her perceptual and practical reach. It is that for her because she can conceive it in ways that display it as that.
>
> (p.116)

The way in which McDowell refers to Marx's *Economic and Philosophical Manuscripts* also speaks in favor of an interpretation of his position as similar to the one developed by Heidegger in *Being and Time*. McDowell cites with approval Marx's expression that nature without alienation would be the "inorganic life of man," and commenting on this, he remarks that the essential thought here consists in the idea that the "rest of nature," or that which does not belong to the organic body of human beings, is to be conceived as "in a different way, my body also" (p.118, note 9). Therefore the world, how it moves human beings on account of their conceptual capacities, is not the ontological counter-sphere to the logical realm of reasons. Rather, because it has already been disclosed, worked upon, or transformed for the most part through our rational activities, the world extends into that realm in such a way that it confronts us with "rational" demands. Hence McDowell can interpret human socialization, and thus the introduction of children into "second nature," as a process through which we acquire the conceptual capacities that make access to the objective world of reasons possible. Again in connection with Aristotle, this means that the moral formation (*Bildung*) of human beings involves the mediation of rational competencies with whose help we are able to work out the meaning of the domain of rational demands:

> The ethical is a domain of rational requirements, which are there in any case, whether or not we are responsive to them. We are alerted to

these demands by acquiring appropriate conceptual capacities. When a decent upbringing initiates us into the relevant way of thinking, our eyes are opened to the very existence of this tract of the space of reasons.

(p.82)

This talk of "eyes," which we find in the last sentence, of course has more than a merely metaphorical character. With this formulation McDowell would like to make clear that we must really conceive of our moral knowledge as a perception of ethical states of affairs. If the human world for its part has a rational structure and therefore projects into the logical space of reasons, then empirical experience has validity as a sensory apprehension of those demands that issue from the reality itself. Concept and intuition merge with each other not because human beings have some extraordinary capacity at their disposal, but because the rational content of the world is disclosed to them only to the degree that they have learnt, in the process of their self-formation (*Bildungsprozesse*), to adjust their perception conceptually to the corresponding requirements. It is this socialization model of perception that provides the core of McDowell's moral realism.

II

Up to this point it remains unclear whether the realist position McDowell draws out of his Aristotelian conception of second nature in *Mind and World* should be interpreted in a pragmatic or in a representationalist sense.[15] The pragmatic reading is favored not just by the reference to Marxian instrumentalism, but also by the underlying affinity with early Heidegger, who sought to understand the world in terms of our practical "involvement" with it. According to this conception, we need to understand the rational control which reality exerts over our thought as epitomized by the resistances we encounter in the pursuit of our practical aims in the world. Assuming that we experience reality as a sphere of "rational" requirements, it makes sense to speak here of a rational content to our perception: within the framework of our practices, we observe the world as an ordered multiplicity of states of affairs, which must be understood as "rational" in the sense that they furnish us with reasons for the orientation of our actions. Of course, in the pragmatic conception such experiences lose their justifying function the moment practices hit against problems that make their continuation impossible. For then we are forced to put our perceptions into brackets, so to speak, by isolating their propositional content in such a way that it can play the role of a hypothesis in a renewed intersubjective practice of justification. The same change in attitude, which pragmatism deems necessary in situations of cognitive disruption, also allows us to suppose that qualitative cognitive experiences take on the propositional content of a claim: from the perception of something *as* something, we as it were distill the content of the experience so as to yield hypothetical statements *that* something is the case. Such purified claims can then function at the reflexive level of justification as potential reasons for accepting a belief.[16]

The representationalist paradigm is distinguished from this pragmatic model above all by the fact that it tries to clarify our access to the rational content of the world in terms of a mere passive reception. The rational demands of reality are not disclosed to us in the framework of our goal-directed activities, but are represented in the mind more or less correctly with the aid of our senses. We could say that according to the pragmatic model, the rationality of the world lies in our "practical reach" (p.116),[17] whereas according to the representationalist paradigm, it lies within our "theoretical reach." Our understanding of the relation between cognitive experience and justification, between perception and critique, will depend on which of these possible interpretations we prefer. It is a particularly crucial feature of the argumentation of *Mind and World* that it seems to hover between these two alternatives. The points at which primacy is given to practise are at least as numerous as those that express the representationalist view of minimal empiricism. It is no different for moral theory, as sketched by McDowell in several supplementary essays to *Mind and World*. Here the ambivalence between praxis and representation is repeated in the form of an unresolved tension between two interpretations of what a "moral education" (*moralische Bildung*) can mean.

In his meta-ethical writings McDowell has developed in detail just the principles of the basic normative idea laid out in his remarks on Aristotelian ethics in *Mind and World*. However, these essays enable us to recognize much better that the point of the idea of second nature in the field of moral theory consists in its providing, with the help of value realism, a cognitivist framework for virtue ethics. The point of departure is again a specific concept of "virtue," interpreted with reference to Aristotle within a naturalistic version of Gadamer's hermeneutics. The "virtues," or a "virtuous character," thus refer to a holistically integrated web of behavior whose moral quality is recognized only from within the perspective of a "tradition," which itself must be conceived as the result of an intellectual transformation from the "first" to the "second" nature of human beings.[18] Once a subject has been successfully socialized into such a moral culture, that which is ethically required is disclosed to the subject only through the circular application of traditional knowledge to each new situation. "New" here can only ever have a relative meaning, for behavior that has become our "second nature" has provided us with a pre-understanding in the light of which facts are always already morally significant. In this respect moral knowledge is not conceived according to the model of a deduction from supreme, universal moral principles, as Kant thought, because that would miss out the fact of prior familiarization with a life-praxis. Rather we can hold on to Wittgenstein's idea, according to which we are only able to recognize moral rules by familiarizing ourselves with a corresponding practice.[19]

Now this very general point only explains why, according to the hermeneutic model, we should base ethics on a specific concept of "phronesis."[20] But it still does not help McDowell realize his aim of defining hermeneutic pre-understanding as a knowledge of moral facts, and thereby of establishing the analogy with propositional truth. In order to be able to give virtue ethics such a cognitivist direction, McDowell must carry out three theoretical steps which, while closely bound together, are better taken separately. He must first bestow upon what Gadamer calls "pre-understanding" the perceptual significance of a sensory grasp of moral facts (a); second, within the context of this theory of perception, he has to explain what we understand by "morality" when we refer to the rational demands of a perceivable world (b); and third, he must make intelligible how, under the given premises, we are able to conceive the interplay of perception and reflection, of factual assertion and moral justification (c).

(a) The defense of virtue ethics in the strong sense of a cognitivist moral theory first of all requires that McDowell interpret the hermeneutic idea of "pre-understanding" as a knowledge of facts. He performs this cognitivist transformation by elaborating the thesis that values, like secondary qualities of human perception, are accessible when they satisfy the normalcy condition of being shaped through a corresponding "pre-understanding."[21] McDowell's train of thought can be summed up as follows. The formation of a "second nature" of human beings, and thus their socialization into a moral culture, also results in a modeling of their inclinations and evaluative ways of seeing. This means that from now on, human perception is conceptually structured in that the world presents itself to us as a horizon of morally loaded states of affairs. Hence we now observe the relevant features of persons, actions, or situations as morally commendable or contemptible in the same way as we perceive the lion as an animal which merits the response of "fear." Of course our perception is only furnished with a sensitivity to moral facts under the normalcy condition of moral socialization. But since this sensory capacity is internally tied to the corresponding motivations – due to the character of "second nature" – we do not need to assume, in Humean fashion, the existence of a subjective desire to locate an effective "reason" for acting on the perceived state of affairs. Rather the perception of a moral fact suffices to move us rationally to the appropriate action.[22]

(b) Conspicuously, up to this point McDowell has not made any progress in his attempt at defining the phenomena to be covered under the term "morality." The reason for this must be the hermeneutic conviction that whatever counts as morally "true" or "false" is only disclosed from the internal perspective of a particular tradition. However, such relativistic caution would not allow us to distinguish "moral" facts from other states of affairs in the world. In this respect it is necessary, despite all the emphasis on hermeneutic pre-understanding, to determine at least in general terms the unity of all the facts we designate as "moral." McDowell does not solve this problem in a pragmatic way – say through an account of the goals or purposes we seek to secure with the help of morality. Rather his solution consists in the surprising proposal that by giving the Kantian idea of the categorical imperative a moral realist turn, we can understand it as pointing to the special status of moral facts.[23] In our perception, those states of affairs which we experience as morally meaningful accordingly possess the extraordinary quality of being able to "silence" all the different points of view on our practical actions. Under the normalcy conditions of a successfully completed socialization, the morally perceived facts have a categorical effect on us, in so far as we feel compelled to act in accordance with the imperatives that provide the rational content of our perception. The advantage of such a strategy, of course, is that it allows McDowell, within the framework of his hermeneutic naturalism, to retain for morality the strong sense of unconditionally valid norms. While Aristotelian considerations in general tend to align moral judgments with evaluative reflections on the constitutive goals of life, here they are consistent with the Kantian idea that in the conflict of perspectives morality has priority because it involves categorical duties. However, the advantage of this strategy comes at a price, namely that it can only provide a circular definition of morality. We know what is "moral" only in view of the effect moral facts have in rationally silencing all conflicting points of view, without that providing an external criterion for what it is that makes a fact "moral." Since no further, independent determination of "morality" is thinkable under McDowell's premises, we are forced to the conclusion that every object perceived with the validity of an imperative is a "moral" fact. It is irrelevant whether this fact satisfies the further criterion of the requirement to take other persons equally into consideration; the point is just that we encounter something with categorical normative validity only internally to a lifeworld.

(c) Now such a picture of morality soon raises the question of how reflection and rational argumentation acquire their significance within the horizon of habitual, perceptually supported moral certainties. With McDowell we must distinguish two aspects of this question, since entry into a moral view of the world, and rationally reaching an understanding within a particular way of seeing, involve different kinds of cognitive process. In the first case, there is an issue about whether, and if so how, we are able to be moved into developing a sensitivity to moral facts; in the second case, there is the problem of how we have to understand the influence of rational considerations within an already disclosed world of moral facts. The first issue concerns an implication of the idea of "second nature," namely that we are able to understand the adoption of a moral view of the world not simply as the outcome of a rational conviction or influence. Someone who has not been socialized in the appropriate ways will be moved through rational arguments into developing a moral sensibility just as little as someone closed to modern music will be persuaded into enjoying twelve-tone music. Rather, in both cases a kind of conversion process is required, because the feel for moral points of view, like the ear for music, is the result of a shaping of character that affects the motivational structure of a person as a whole.[24] The ability to use practical reason is therefore an adjustment of character, and we must be able to think of moral reasons as always already furnished with a motivational power – a power which, according to the competing view, must come from the outside if those reasons are to become effective for action. Conversely, it follows that such reasons for their part cannot motivate or move a person to adopt a moral view of the world.

However, once a person has become successfully socialized into a moral view of the world and therefore possesses a sensitivity to moral facts, the quite different question of the relation between habitualized certainty and rational reflection arises. For now there exists a motivational readiness to be convinced by practical reasons, and beliefs are henceforth exposed to the argumentative pressure of justification. McDowell repeatedly emphasizes that the second nature of human beings should not be understood as a rigidly fixed pattern of behavior; on the contrary we must regard it as the rational capacity to be oriented by moral reasons through the habitualized virtues.[25] But this position naturally gives rise to the problem of how the sensitivity to reasons for action acquired through socialization interacts with the simultaneously developed sensitivity to moral facts. It is hard to make the proposal of rehabilitating moral realism by way of hermeneutics consistent with all the emphasis on the importance of critical reflection. For how can the world of moral facts be understood as so porous, fragile, and open that the power to call facts rationally into question can be developed at any time? Or to formulate the question differently, in the case of moral beliefs how must we conceive the connection, which according to McDowell somehow must exist, between factual assertions and the practice of justification?

The answer McDowell provides for this question is captured in the image of "Neurath's boat."[26] We find here a metaphor for the hermeneutic premise that the standards in light of which we are able to question rationally a given content of our tradition can be obtained only by an immanent appeal to the particular tradition itself. Transferred to the case of the moral view of the world that McDowell has in mind, this picture implies our use of practical reason is limited in so far as it must remain within the horizon of traditional standards and criteria. It is not decontextualized, universal principles of morality, but rather the leading ideas of our cultural heritage which we are able to enlist for questioning established moral ideas and subjecting them to revision. But the proposal so outlined, no less than Gadamer's talk of the epistemic authority of tradition, does not actually answer the question it is meant to answer: namely, how we conceive the rational mobilization of traditional moral principles in face of a world given to us in our perception as always already morally contentful. In order to clarify this point, it will help to take a closer examination of McDowell's notion of "moral education" (*moralische Bildung*).

III

There are probably two types of situation that are paradigmatic for showing how breakdowns in our everyday moral certainties take place in a manner that must initiate a process of critical reflection. Let us suppose with McDowell that the world is normally given to us according to our second nature as a sphere of moral facts. These cognitive certainties break down time and again in at least two ways: on the one hand, when in the course of our actions new challenges arise for which our perceptual faculty is not prepared; and on the other hand, when those involved face a discrepancy in the observation of a moral fact that cannot be rectified simply by reference to a perceptual error. Regarding the first case, just think of the technological innovations that make possible social practices or operations with no historical precedent, and thus for which no schemata of moral evaluation are available. Concerning the second case, for the sake of simplicity think of situations in which two subjects describe one and the same state of affairs with evaluative vocabularies so different that mutual correction at the level of perception is impossible. Both types of situation are of course chosen to put in question a premise that McDowell seems to take for granted in his concept of "second nature": namely, that morally shaped lifeworlds, thus lifeworlds in which evaluative distinctions are used as the means for describing reality, are always sufficiently flexible and self-contained so as not to bring about situations of perceptual uncertainty or observational discrepancy. Even if we grant the unlikely possibility that there may once have been such homogeneous, change-resistant cultures, every historically mobilized, differentiated society excludes them. Here moral uncertainties arise as new facts are judged and intersubjective differences regarding the evaluative description of states of affairs become a regular feature of the social lifeworld. In such a context, which today is normal, we can ask how the widening or correction of familiar moral certainties is appropriately described.[27]

If places can be found at all in McDowell which bring into view the possibility of intracultural differences, and thus of a fragmented and plural "second nature," they end up confronting his own idea with an absurd sounding alternative. For as soon as we no longer assume the effectiveness of a common practice of evaluative judgment, we seem, on McDowell's suggestion, to be confronted with the idea that the solution to moral conflicts should take place according to the model of a deduction from context-free principles of moral reason. But such an idea would not do justice to the circularity of moral judgment-formation grounded in the fact of ethical pre-understanding. All in all, then, the assumption is to be characterized as erroneous. That is why we have no option, so he concludes, but to assume a common horizon to evaluative practices even in the case of moral conflicts, which we must fall back on a bit more deeply as required. As we could say, going beyond McDowell, in cases of discrepancies we reach agreement only to the extent to which we succeed in advancing that level of our ethical tradition at which evaluative agreements still exist. Thus, in view of conflict cases, the "critical demand of reason" of which McDowell speaks consists in the attempt to comprehend that circular movement of the understanding through which the particulars of an individual case are disclosed in the light of a shared traditional knowledge. But this hermeneutic proposal, the one that seems plausible for McDowell to hold, actually leaves the interesting question unanswered: namely, how the recourse to, and also the advancement of, such uncovered common ground is supposed to take place, so that a rectification of the differences in moral evaluation becomes possible on the same basis as the cooperative undertaking of the "pursuit of truth." Above all, however, it is unclear from this process of reflection what role should be played by those moral facts which, according to McDowell, only represent the ontological complement to the second nature of a shared moral life praxis.

It is not difficult to see that such a cooperative enterprise must begin with the general attempt at putting into brackets perceptual judgments centered in the lifeworld. It is indeed correct that in the early stages of the arbitration of moral disagreements an effort may be made to bring one's conversation partner to change his or her perspective so that he or she is in a position to have a "more appropriate" view of the disputed matter. But in general, such perceptually focussed attempts at correcting a view quickly founder on just those "normalcy conditions" of moral perception which for their part make up a core of the original dispute. Of course if McDowell's analogy with secondary qualities is convincing, then the appropriate perception of the moral facts is subject to certain normalcy conditions in the same way as the "correct" perception of a color is bound to the adoption of the suitable standpoint. The opponents in a moral disagreement will therefore realize straightaway that at the center of their debate stands the question of which starting point is "normal" or appropriate because it allows for the correct perception of the disputed matter. To that extent the moral facts, disagreement about which sparks the controversy, have already lost their justifying power by the first stage of the dispute. The participants must abstract from that which they see "there" qualitatively before themselves: they must describe the situation with different evaluative concepts and collectively adopt a reflexive standpoint from which they are reciprocally able to judge the appropriateness of their abandoned points of view.

Now it is clear that judgments about the normalcy conditions to which moral perception is subject do not refer to "objective" standards in the same way as these might be given in the case of color perception. While here references to the time of day, the incidence of light, and one's particular perceptual capacity can be relevant, the reflexive solution to a discrepancy in moral perceptions does not come without reference to normative criteria. The validity of a particular standpoint for perceiving a state of affairs or events as morally appropriate can only be determined intersubjectively; only in this way can the moral rightness of the hermeneutic point of departure be assessed. In cases of moral disagreement there is no norm-free equivalent of those places and times which can serve as guiding principles for deciding discrepancies in color perception. To that extent, the adversaries in a moral dispute cannot avoid scrutinizing their traditional knowledge with a view to whether it contains normative principles or points of view which in general can be abstracted, and so be suitable as overriding reasons for the justification of the particular standpoint. And "overriding" here has only the restricted meaning of an inclusion of the perspective of those who ought to be convinced of the inappropriateness of their previous standpoint. However, this need for decentering, which is inherent in moral discourses as soon as the level of qualitative perceptions is left behind, possesses the quality of a certain "interminability." For in order to able to justify a particular standpoint, each of the two parties will, by way of countermoves, extend the circle of those before whom the internal, traditionally mobilized reasons must prove convincing. This process of mutually enforced generalization provisionally hits upon limits only when, with reference to the "moral community," a maximal circle is reached with respect to those for whom the offered reasons are justifiable, since each is granted a say in the balanced judgment of the appropriateness of a standpoint. It follows from the logic of universalization just sketched that, in cases of moral disagreement, the normalcy conditions of perception can only be assessed mutually, by including each person as a respected, legitimate addressee of the justification. What validly counts as "normal" when we argue over the appropriateness of our moral perceptions can only be elucidated systematically in terms of the agreement of all those potentially involved. Of course by now there is a far more difficult question: how an agreement can be achieved between the opposed parties about where the limits of the "moral community," whose members must be regarded as entitled to a judgment, ought to lie. Here the category of "Bildung" can be brought into play with a meaning different from the one it usually has in McDowell's writings. While McDowell follows Gadamer in using the term "Bildung" to refer above all to an anonymous process of historically effective mediation of tradition, we can also conceive Bildung as Hegel did: that is, as a process of unavoidable learning, and thus of "ongoing formation" (Fortbildung).

Now at first sight it is not at all easy to determine how the speech situation as hitherto described enables us to make reference to some kind of "progress." The question is: does the possibility of appealing to a learning process which allows certain reasons to appear as superior, better, or more valid play a decisive role in the intersubjective judgment of the appropriateness of a standpoint? This brings to light a difficulty that is connected with the fact that, in McDowell's account, moral facts possess not just a justifying force but a defining one. For the participants are supposed to know what makes up morality only from the special weight accorded to moral facts in virtue of them "silencing" all the other points of view. This means that the participants in a moral dispute, in which such facts have immediately been put on hold, find themselves in the apparently paradoxical situation of not properly knowing why they seek to generalize, and thereby to justify, the particular perspective of the commonly shared tradition. If McDowell's observation is correct, they lack, as it were, a sense of the goal for the sake of which they attempt to bring about an intersubjective determination of the correct, "normal" perceptual perspective. However, this situation would appear differently if we were to suppose that the participants conceive of their cooperative undertaking itself as a systematic expression of what morality consists in; that is, as an attempt at reaching an agreement on those consensual norms that enable us to manage our interpersonal relations in view of all legitimate claims. But with such a premise we introduce the theoretical presumption that moral socialization amounts to something more than the transmission of a holistically connected web of virtuous behavior. Rather, in the process of becoming practised in second nature, subjects would also learn that their acquired behavioral dispositions express moral norms that have significance as consensually generated rules for interpersonal relations. Such a description of moral socialization departs from McDowell's concept with the thesis that the acquisition of virtuous dispositions simultaneously awakens a sense for the principles according to which their underlying norms are constructed. We not only become practised in moral ways of perceiving and the corresponding types of response, but in the same way also learn to understand these web-like behavioral dispositions as the limited embodiment of principles which ought to regulate our interactions and relationships legitimately through the consideration of justified claims.

Under such an alternative description, which does not relinquish the idea of "second nature" but lends it a stronger, principle-oriented character,[28] the continuation of the discourse schematically outlined above would also of course appear differently. We could assume of the participants that their appeal to a common tradition, which has become necessary in order to resolve their perceptual discrepancies, would have to be guided by the unifying principle that was merely embodied differently in their behavioral dispositions. It is this comprehensive principle, which is nothing other than an intersubjectively shared understanding of the meaning of morality, that not only ensures that the participants in discourse know what it is to repair "Neurath's boat" but also gives their reflexive endeavors a certain picture of the way ahead. The appropriate standpoint, which the participants attempt to ascertain with a view to rectifying their perceptual discrepancies by looking for the generalizable reasons in their collectively shared tradition, must also always be proportionate to what are appropriately considered as the legitimate claims of all those potentially involved. And here, at this point, our sketch of a moral discourse makes apparent that it is possible to use a criterion of progress. For our interpersonal relations can be justified more or less, be better or worse, corresponding to the dimensions of inclusion and extension of the claims of those involved. Accordingly, however inclusive and complex the concepts of the person used by us are, a disputed perspective must prove itself superior to the others in the fact that it does more justice to the articulated claims of other persons and therefore be more likely to gain the potential agreement of all those involved.

For the issue that interests us here, it is of secondary significance whether this idea of moral discourse is further explicated in terms of the "transcendental" force of argumentation itself or a deep-rooted common understanding of morality. For the decisive point about the suggested alternative is that it presents the conflict-conditioned transition from the moral certainties of "second nature" to the reflexive management of disagreement in a different way than McDowell's view. We must first of all grant that, as a rule, a moral life-world does not just consist in a web of habitualized behavior. Over and above that, it contains an intersubjectively shared understanding of the principles of construction of the corresponding schemata of response. For without the reflexive surplus of such shared moral principles it would not be possible to understand the hermeneutic achievement of repair appropriately. The subjects must repair their broken lifeworld without the help of moral facts as soon as they come across situations of conflict in their modes of moral perception. But if we acknowledge the mediating role of such shared meaning for morality, we must also grant the possibility that the intersubjective process of managing disagreement through argument brings to bear a certain pressure toward learning. Since subjects refer to one and the same set of moral principles in the restoration of their moral common ground, they must try to expand their common tradition so that both standpoints can be expressed in the newly secured agreement, with a resulting increase in the claims that are taken into consideration. In this respect the sense of morality, which goes beyond actually existing perceptual faculties, acts like an authority that compels entry into argumentation, allowing the mediation of tradition to take the direction of an expansion of the moral community. Where we have disagreement, second nature, conceived as a fragile network of socialized value convictions, is not simply reproduced as effective history; it is also morally expanded under the reflexive efforts of the participants.

It is clear that with this alternative interpretation, the meaning of what McDowell calls the "weak naturalism" of his theory also changes. If the moral form of life of human beings always contains a reflexive surplus, which consists in the common understanding of the underlying principles of morality, then nature continues not merely in the form of a recognition of virtuous behavior. Rather, this happening of a "second nature" assumes the form of a learning process which shows itself to advantage whenever crises and disagreements in the lifeworld compel reflexive problem solving. It follows that "*Bildung*" does not have the form, suggested by Gadamer, of an anonymous happening of tradition; rather it has the form characterized by Hegel as a successive realization of practical reason. However, even a process of formation (*Bildung*) of this kind remains within the boundaries imposed upon it by the structure of the moral form of life of human beings. That is why its results can always be translated back into shared perceptions that disclose a unified world of moral facts.

Notes

*   Translated from the German by Nicholas H. Smith.
1   Compare Peter Schaber, *Moralischer Realismus* (Freiburg, 1997); Jean-Claude Wolf, "Moralischer Realismus. Neuerscheinungen zur angelsächsischen Ethikdiskussion," *Allgemeine Zeitschrift für Philosophie* 1: 63–71 (1990).
2   See McDowell, "Two Sorts of Naturalism," in *Mind, Value and Reality* (Cambridge, MA: Harvard University Press, 1998), pp. 3–22.

3 See McDowell, "Values and Secondary Qualities," in *Mind, Value and Reality*, pp.131–150.

4 See Jürgen Habermas, "Einleitung: Realismus nach der sprachpragmatischen Wende," in Habermas, *Wahrheit und Rechtfertigung* (Frankfurt/Main: Suhrkamp, 1999), pp.7–64; and "Richtigkeit versus Wahrheit. Zum Sinn der Sollgeltung moralischer Werte und Normen," op. cit., pp.271–318.

5 Jürgen Habermas, "Richtigkeit versus Wahrheit," p.305.

6 *Mind and World* (Cambridge, MA: Harvard University Press, 1994). Page references in the text are to this work.

7 The title of Richard Rorty's essay on McDowell picks out this point: "The Very Idea of Human Answerability to the World: John McDowell's Version of Empiricism," in Richard Rorty, *Truth and Progress. Philosophical Papers*, vol. 3 (Cambridge: Cambridge University Press, 1988), pp.138–152.

8 See Wilfrid Sellars, *Empiricism and the Philosophy of Mind* (Cambridge, MA: Harvard University Press, 1997).

9 Compare the overview in J. Freudiger, A. Graeser, and K. Petrus (eds), *Der Begriff der Erfahrung in der Philosophie des 20. Jahrhunderts* (Munich: Beck, 1996).

10 On this claim see Michael Williams's illuminating analysis in his "Exorcism and Disenchantment," *Philosophical Quarterly* 46: 99–109 (1996).

11 Andrew Bowie attempts to bring out the proximity to Schelling in his "John McDowell's *Mind and World* and Early Romantic Epistemology," *Revue Internationale de Philosophie*, no. 197: 515–554 (1996). The classical formulation of a "hermeneutic of natural history" within the tradition of philosophical anthropology can be found in Helmuth Plessner, *Die Stufen des Organischen und der Mensch* (Berlin/New York: de Gruyter, 1975).

12 Julia Annas follows the same lines in her interpretation of ancient naturalism; see Julia Annas, *The Morality of Happiness* (Oxford: Oxford University Press, 1993), especially chap. 3.

13 Michael Williams stresses this point in "Exorcism and Disenchantment," p.104.

14 Compare Virgil C. Aldrich, "On What it is Like to be a Man," *Inquiry* 16: 355–366 (1973).

15 On the possibility of both kinds of reading, see Andrei Denejkine, "Sind wir vor der Welt verantwortlich?" *Deutsche Zeitschrift für Philosophie* 6: 939–952 (2000).

16 The need for a transition from perceiving "as" to the proposition "that" is brought out very clearly in Carleton B. Christensen, "Wie man Gedanken und Anschauungen zusammenführt," *Deutsche Zeitschrift für Philosophie* 6: 891–914 (2000).

17 Though McDowell uses this expression rather differently.

18 See McDowell, "The Role of Eudaimonia in Aristotle's Ethics" and "Two Sorts of Naturalism" in *Mind, Value and Reality*.

19 See McDowell, "Wittgenstein on Following a Rule," ibid., pp.221–262.

20 For the now classical formulation, see Hans-Georg Gadamer, "Über die Möglichkeit einer philosophischen Ethik," in Gadamer, *Gesammelte Werke*, Bd. 4 (Tübingen: Mohr, 1987), pp.175–188; in English "On the Possibility of a Philosophical Ethics," in Gadamer, *Hermeneutics, Religion and Ethics*, tr. Joel Weinsheimer (New Haven, CT: Yale University Press, 1999).

21 See McDowell, "Values and Secondary Qualities."

22 See McDowell, "Might there be External Reasons?" in *Mind, Value and Reality*, pp.95–111.

23 See McDowell, "Are Moral Requirements Hypothetical Imperatives?" ibid., pp.77–94.

24 See McDowell, "Might there be External Reasons?", esp. p.101.

25 See McDowell, "Two Sorts of Naturalism," esp. p.188ff.

26 See McDowell, "Some Issues in Aristotle's Moral Psychology," *Mind, Value and Reality*, pp.23–49, esp. p.36ff.; "Two Sorts of Naturalism," p.189ff.

27 It is at this point that Jan Bransen raises his objections in Bransen, "On the Incompleteness of McDowell's Moral Realism," unpublished manuscript (1999).

28 Of course Lawrence Kohlberg's investigations of moral socialization point in this direction. See, for example, Kohlberg, "Stage and Sequence," in D. Goslin (ed.), *Handbook of Socialization Theory and Research* (Chicago, 1969). (In German, "Stufe und Sequenz: Sozialisation unter dem Aspect der kognitiven Entwicklung," in *Zur kognitiven Entwicklung des Kelinkindes* (Frankfurt/Main: Suhrkamp, 1974), pp.7–255.) Even if we do not share the details of Kohlberg's model of stages, the idea of a gradually increasing abstraction from moral conventions enforced by socialization and a corresponding growth in orientation to principles can still be defended.

Part V

RESPONSES

14

RESPONSES

John McDowell

Let me begin by expressing my thanks to Nicholas Smith for conceiving this project and overseeing its execution, and to the contributors for taking trouble over my work.

Part I Philosophy after Kant

Richard J. Bernstein

Bernstein's generous essay amplifies and makes more definite my vague suggestion that some of my thinking is Hegelian, at least in spirit. It may seem ungrateful to pick on his objections, which are few and muted. But some comments may be helpful.

Bernstein thinks I aim to reconcile "nature as the realm of law and nature as encompassing spontaneity." He says this would require rethinking the disenchanted conception of nature, and he complains that I do not say how that is to be done. I think this objection misses the mark. In my view there is a disenchanted conception of *something*, which needs no rethinking (though there is room for improvement in my way of describing it). What it is a conception of is reality in so far as it can be made intelligible by the methods of the natural sciences – not the natural as such, as we can be confused into supposing. The idea of the realm of law (or, preferably, some improvement on it) persists into the outlook I recommend, without needing to be rethought. My talk of the realm of law is a gesture toward describing the conceptual organization characteristic of the natural sciences. But I resist counting this as a conception of nature. I do not have nature as the realm of law still in my picture, needing to be rethought so that it can be reconciled with nature as encompassing spontaneity. The point is that the realm of law must not be allowed to usurp the position of the natural. If we prevent it from doing so, we remove the supposed difficulty about how spontaneity can be *sui generis* even while its operations are natural.

Bernstein says "we need to know how to answer those who claim that ultimately a science based on the disenchanted concept of nature will (or may) prove sufficient to fully account for what McDowell wants to single out as spontaneity." I doubt that there is any way to win over people who are convinced of that. And in any case, my purposes do not require it. I do not need a knockdown argument that spontaneity is *sui generis*. All I need is to show how taking spontaneity to be *sui generis* does not pose the philosophical threats it can seem to pose. That removes a motivation – the only one relevant to my concerns – for making the claim Bernstein says we need to know how to answer, and it leaves us safe, at least in respect of the philosophical dangers I consider, in disbelieving it. There need be no question of establishing that disbelief is the right stance.

Bernstein thinks I "struggle nobly" with a problem about the mentality of non-human animals and prelinguistic human beings. I think the supposed problem is an illusion. I shall discuss this in my response to Crispin Wright.

Bernstein says "we need a deep analysis of causality, and where it fits in relation to a disenchanted concept of nature and the spontaneity of reason." I am inclined to say the main obstacle in the path of seeing an unproblematic fit between causality and spontaneity is just this idea that causality calls for a deep analysis – and, more specifically, that the analysis is supplied, or at least begun, by connecting causality with law. That is what makes it hard to see how the operations of a *sui generis* spontaneity can hang together causally, among themselves and with other things. Donald Davidson has a justly celebrated answer to what is in effect that question, made pressing in that way: operations of spontaneity must be redescribable in other terms, which enable them to be subsumed under law.[1] But does this give due weight to the thought that operations of spontaneity can show, for instance, causal efficacy on their faces as the operations of spontaneity they are, even while we know nothing about the postulated redescriptions? And anyway, why should we connect causality with law? More generally, why should we think anything needs to be said, at that depth, about the very idea of cause?[2]

Michael Friedman

The first of the historico-philosophical "oddities" Friedman finds in my account relates to "the Platonic gap between mathematical reason and sensible nature" – a conception according to which sensible nature is beyond the reach of mathematical intelligibility. Friedman's point is that it is strange to suggest the modern scientific revolution blinds us to the power of a Kantian strategy for ensuring that such a gap does not open, when the very point of the scientific revolution was to extend mathematical intelligibility beyond the superlunary realm to the whole of nature. He is clearly right that such a suggestion would be strange. But why does he think the point impinges on me? This shows that he has not engaged with what I try to do in my book. And this failure to make contact ramifies through what he says. It would take at least as much space as his essay occupies to explain this in detail. I shall confine myself to some remarks about the first and last of the "oddities," and, at the end, some remarks about Friedman's fundamental failure of sympathy toward post-Kantian idealism and my attempt to align myself with it.[3]

The point of the Kantian strategy I consider is to ensure, not that sensible nature is within the scope of mathematical intelligibility, but that thinking is intelligibly of objects at all. If we find it mysterious that thinking is of objects, it can be helpful to see a role for conceptual capacities in an account of the direct presence of objects to thinking subjects in perceptual experience. That is secured by envisaging states or episodes of sensibility that are themselves actualizations of conceptual capacities. But this is hard to sustain, I suggest, because conceiving these occurrences or states as operations of sensibility would have to be placing them in nature, and conceiving them as actualizations of conceptual capacities would have to be placing them as Sellars says we do when we conceive something as a case of knowledge – placing them in the space of reasons. And a scientistic conception of nature makes it look as if these cannot be combined, unless we take it – against Sellars and surely against Kant – that the layout of the space of reasons can be naturalized in the appropriate sense. So what a scientistic conception of nature obscures, according to me, is a Kantian strategy for ensuring that a gap does not open up between conceptual thinking of any kind – not just applied mathematical thinking – and its subject matter. Nature figures here, not as something that threatens to be beyond the reach of mathematical understanding, but as what threatens to disqualify sensibility from being shaped by conceptual capacities in ordinary perceptual awareness of reality.

In the Sellarsian image, placing something in the space of reasons is seeing it as an exercise of rationality, a case of responsiveness to reasons as such. As Friedman uses the image in setting out his first "oddity," placing something in the space of reasons would be making it intelligible in the way a mathematical physicist makes things intelligible. But that is the sort of thing Sellars *contrasts* with placing in the space of reasons. My Sellarsian use of the image goes missing here.

I exploit Kantian thinking to consider the question how it is possible for empirical thought to be of objects at all. Friedman centers his reading of Kant on the question how the exact sciences – pure and applied mathematics – are possible. Of course it is indisputable that that is a Kantian concern. As Friedman notes, it structures the *Prolegomena*. But does this concern provide the best approach to Kant for us? Looking at Kant from this angle, we have to give a central position, as Friedman does, to Kant's conception of the a priori structure of our sensibility, which figures directly in his answer to the question "How is pure mathematics possible?" and indirectly in his answer to the question "How is pure natural science possible?" And from this point of view Kant's success stands or falls with the acceptability of his philosophy of pure mathematics – which seems to imply that it falls. I abstract from this framework a conception of how sensibility and understanding are interwoven in experience that is clearly Kantian in spirit, and potentially helpful in making sense of the objective purport of empirical thinking, in a way that is detachable from the credentials of Kant's philosophy of mathematics. Here the understanding figures as the faculty of concepts in general, not just pure concepts, and Sellars's image fits because conceptual activity in general is essentially responsive to reasons: not just the logical and mathematical reasons that Friedman concentrates on, but – as Sellars frequently insists – material reasons also (as when visible smoke leads someone to believe there is fire in the vicinity). And I do not need to say anything about Kant's idea that our sensibility has its own a priori form.

Of course Friedman could object to this putatively charitable exploitation of Kantian thinking, which certainly ignores much that mattered to Kant. But the first "oddity" indicates that he does not even get it into view.

Friedman's last "oddity" reflects the same failure to address the potential problem about placing in the space of reasons that concerns me. I talk of a threatened extrusion of meaning from nature. Friedman thinks I take this to be the basis for a threatened extrusion of rational relations from nature. As before, he takes this in the sense of a threat to the idea that nature is intelligible by the methods of the exact sciences. A threat with this structure and basis does arise, he says, but only after Quine. The Marburg neo-Kantians flirted with a platon-istic exclusion of rational relations from nature, by abandoning Kant's appeal to the pure forms of our sensibility, which was essential to how Kant ensured that the Platonic gap did not open. This threat of a reopening of the Platonic gap was temporarily averted, in logical positivism, by "the linguistic doctrine of logico-mathematical truth," according to which "the logical structure constituting the space of reasons does not subsist in an autonomous ontological realm but rather in the meaning relations of our language." Quine undermines this reassurance by arguing that there are no facts of the matter about meanings, which would imply, by the linguistic doctrine, that there is no such thing as "the logical struc-ture constituting the space of reasons." And Quine does this by applying a conception of the factual that is naturalistic in the sense of the outlook I trace to the modern scientific revolution. Only now, according to Friedman, can such a naturalism "make rational normative structures as such look 'spooky'."

This too makes no contact with my thinking. In the frame of mind that concerns me, it is not that an extrusion of meaning from nature threatens to lead to platonism about logico-mathematical reasons. Logico-mathematical reasons in particular are not especially at issue, and the connection between rationality and meaning goes the other way round. A scientistic conception of the natural generates a potential difficulty about responsiveness to reasons as such (of any kind, including material reasons) – a difficulty that can perfectly intelligibly have begun to make itself felt before hostility to psychologism, which Friedman depicts as the fruit of the "pure logic" tradition, came to explicit expression. This potential difficulty about responsiveness to reasons opens into a potential difficulty about meaning, because we can make sense of meaning only in a context in which we can make sense of responsiveness to reasons. These connected difficulties can intelligibly have taken shape as a felt spookiness long before anyone had occasion to propound a linguistic doctrine of logico-mathematical truth. Perhaps a "problematic of an opposition between reason and nature" that fits Friedman's bill – a threatened reopening of the Platonic gap on the basis of an extrusion of meaning from nature – makes sense only with the wreckage of the linguistic doctrine, but that is irrelevant to the problematic I concern myself with.

Friedman locates Davidson only as succeeding Quine in this historical progression. This makes for a peculiarity in his reading of Davidson. Davidson's thinking about the difference between thought and talk about the mental, on the one hand, and thought and talk about the physical world, on the other, chimes with the tradition, much older than Quine, in which *verstehen* is distinguished from *erklären* and the *Geisteswissenschaften* from the *Naturwissenschaften*. This feature of Davidson's thinking lies close to the problematic I am concerned with. Arguing as he does that "McDowell's problematic" makes sense only after Quine, Friedman must either deny this feature of Davidson's thinking or claim that it has nothing to do with "McDowell's problematic."

Friedman credits me with the idea

> that passively received impressions become experiences of an objective world ... only by being *taken as such* by the active faculty of the understanding; by being subject, that is, to the perpetually revisable procedure through which the understanding integrates such impressions into an evolving world-conception.

This enables him to argue, against my aim of vindicating a common sense realism, that "the crucial notion of *independence* is, in the end, given a purely coherence-theoretic reading." But this does not fit the conception of experience I recommend. In my picture, actualizations of conceptual capacities in receptivity are already, in conforming to that specification, at least apparently revelatory of an objective world, and, when all goes well, actually so. They do not need to be turned into experiences with objective purport by being so taken. The point of invoking the perpetual obligation to rethink a world-view is to help make it intelligible that these "passively received impressions" already have objective purport – not to indicate a way in which intellectual activity can somehow make experiences of an objective world out of items that are in themselves less than that.

Friedman's reading here belongs with his lack of sympathy for anything that smacks of post-Kantian idealism. Kant's successors definitively abandon the idea that our sensibility has its own autonomous a priori form, and the sharp boundary Kant places between understanding, constrained by sensibility, and unconstrained reason.[4] In Friedman's view, the effect is "a tendency to distance rational thought from sensible experience and to minimize the empiricist elements in Kant's own conception." He finds it absurd to suppose such an outlook might vindicate common sense realism.

Friedman acknowledges that in Hegel's ethical thinking a descendant of Kantian reason is "historicized." This marks a departure from Kant, who exempts reason from any essential situatedness in human life. Now a Hegelian conception of reason's autonomy in theoretical thought reflects just such a non-Kantian conception of reason as essentially situated. That reason is unconstrained in theoretical thought does not mean that we invent the world. What figures in a different conception as constraint from outside by sensible experience is incorporated within what is now conceived as the free unfolding of rational activity. The empiricist elements in Kant's own conception are not minimized, but reconceived.

Of course motivating and explaining the reconceiving would take a great deal of work. But Friedman proceeds as if he thinks he knows in advance that any such project would be hopeless. I surmise that this impatience with Kant's successors, with whom I express an affinity, is partly responsible for his uncharacteristically hasty reading of my book.

Robert B. Pippin

Usually people who criticize my Hegelian echoes think, like Friedman, that I go too far with the idealistic theme of subjectivity as source. Pippin thinks I do not go far enough. So I attract objections from opposite sides – I must be doing something right.

Pippin's criticisms are partly based on mischaracterizing my appeal to nature. He has it carrying a transcendental load that (as he knows) I do not mean it to carry. He cannot see how I can avoid putting more weight on it than I purport to.

My proposal is that, even though conceptual activity as such is spontaneous, its objective purport becomes unmysterious if we can see how the very conceptual capacities that are freely exercised in making up our minds can also be operative in states or episodes in which objective reality is directly present to us. That is secured by the idea of actualizations of conceptual capacities in sensibility. This idea can seem incoherent, on the ground that sensibility is part of our natural endowment, whereas actualizations of conceptual capacities as such are not within the scope of natural-scientific understanding. It is in this connection that I offer my "reminder" that, philosophical prejudices notwithstanding, it is easy to take the notion of second nature in stride. The sole point of the reminder is to display that seeming incoherence as illusory.

The transcendental work – the work of making objective purport unmysterious – is done here by the idea that conceptual capacities figure not only in free intellectual activity but also in operations of receptivity outside our control. Nature is relevant only in connection with a possible threat to that idea.[5]

I do not suppose that either of these roles for conceptual capacities is intelligible except in combination with the other. So if we need to talk about answerability to each other, when we make sense of the normative setting in which free intellectual activity takes place, answerability to each other must be an essential element in the conception of objective purport I envisage. I am not reluctant to acknowledge that a social framework matters to the very idea of the conceptual. Indeed I insist on it. Pippin, in contrast, writes as if in my picture an individualistically conceived taking in of reality somehow serves *instead* of "Hegelian talk of social bases of normativity," as the foundation of an account of the very idea of objective purport.[6] That is why he thinks my appeal to second nature would need to be more substantial than the mere reminder he knows I want it to be. He cannot see how I could pretend to supply the substitute basis for understanding objective purport that he thinks I envisage, without giving nature a more foundational role than I acknowledge attributing to it.

This comes to a head when Pippin says (in a note about my exchanges with Robert Brandom):

> McDowell's claim is that there would be nothing for a "context of justification" [the sort of thing that "Hegelian talk of social bases of normativity" aims to capture] to be *about* if we could not account for [the objective purport of experiences] independently of it.

Here "independently of it" is exactly wrong. What I urge against Brandom is that we cannot make sense of discourse-governing social norms prior to and independently of objective purport. Answerability to each other in discourse is not a self-standing foundation on which we could construct a derivative account of how talk and thought are directed at reality. That is not to propose, as Pippin says I do, that we should simply reverse the order. In my picture answerability to the world and answerability to each other have to be understood together. That is very like something Pippin says, wrongly taking it to correct me.

In the ethical context too Pippin represents me as needing the notion of second nature to do more than I want. I agree with him that we should not "buy into [Aristotle's] or any other account of species-specific and determinate forms of *natural* actualization" – as if an appeal to nature could somehow substitute for reflection, under a constant obligation to find, or try to make, common ground with our fellows, in getting straight what we have reason to do. I am skeptical whether such a conception of a role for appeals to nature is Aristotle's either.[7] The point of my appeal to second nature here is simply to help bring out that there is nothing "queer" (as J. L. Mackie claimed)[8] about the idea of a capacity to know what there is reason for one to do, if the capacity is understood as the result of being initiated into an ethical community. Talk of proper upbringing makes sense only within a formed ethical outlook, which would be needed to give determinate content to that use of "proper." The point is not to reach through to some independently accessible truths about nature that could supposedly validate the content of such an outlook.

Pippin makes heavy weather of the idea that capacities that belong to spontaneity are in play in states or episodes of receptivity. I see no promise of explaining the idea, as he suggests, by appealing to judgments of perception as conceived in the *Prolegomena*. Kant says judgments of perception, unlike judgments of experience, have only subjective validity, and I take it this implies, or perhaps even means, that they do not have objective purport – they do not reach out to the layout of the objective world.[9] But experiences, as I conceive them, already have objective purport themselves. At their best, they are cases of having objective reality directly available to one. They do not need further acts of judgment before objective purport can be on the scene. That would be a version of Friedman's misreading of me, according to which we confer objective purport on experiences by taking them a certain way.

In this context Pippin cites several passages from Kant, but not the one place where I believe Kant gets the idea he is groping toward into helpful shape. This is A79/B104–5 of the first *Critique*, where Kant says: "The same function which gives unity to the various representations *in a judgment* also gives unity to the mere synthesis of various representations *in an intuition*." I exploit this remark in my Woodbridge Lectures, which Pippin mentions so approvingly that it is puzzling why he thinks the question in what sense capacities that belong to spontaneity are in play in actualizations of receptivity is so pressing for me. I think the answer must lie in his conviction that I need the idea of nature to do heavy transcendental lifting. This makes him unable to see how close the presence of objects in experience is, in my putatively Kantian conception, to the objective purport of judgments. In different terminology, that remark of Kant's says that the logical form of an intuition is none other than the logical form of a possible judgment of experience. The difference between intuitions and judgments is only in what this shared form informs: free intellectual activity in one case, operations of receptivity in the other. What goes missing, in my view, if we try to do everything with the idea of free intellectual activity is not nature, as Pippin supposes, but receptivity.

Pippin is surely right that the central image in the German idealist tradition is one of legislating for ourselves. But the idea of subjectivity as source needs delicate handling if it is not to put at risk the fact that, as Pippin puts it, "we cannot legislate arbitrarily." The point of the image is that subjection to norms should not be an infringement on freedom; we are authentically subject only to norms whose authority we acknowledge. Thus the norms that bind us are our own dictates to ourselves, not alien impositions. But any intelligible case of agency, legislative or any other, whether on the part of an individual or a group, must be responsive to reasons. It makes no sense to picture an act that brings norms into existence out of a normative void.[10] So the insistence on freedom must cohere with the fact that we always find ourselves already subject to norms. Our freedom, which figures in the image as our legislative power, must include a moment of receptivity. This fits at various levels, one of which is the responsiveness to experientially available facts – which can be conceived as norms for belief

– that I consider. One way of putting the point is to say subjectivity deserves either three cheers, if its autonomy is understood properly, so as to include the moment of receptivity, or none, if it is not – not two, as Pippin suggests.

Pippin is also surely right that Hegel's thought tends toward ultimately leaving nature behind. It is only his overestimate of the role nature needs to play for me that makes him think this marks a contrast with me. Once my reminder of second nature has done its work, nature can drop out of my picture too, leaving the moment of receptivity to dissolve pseudo-problems stemming from the appearance that radical autonomy would make objective purport impossible.

Hegel shows no interest in engaging sympathetically, as I try to, with the way a restrictive conception of the natural motivates supposing that – in my terms – spontaneity cannot be *sui generis*, on pain of being spooky. To put it mildly, Hegel is not good at making his way of thinking inviting to people who find it alien in that sort of way. Piecemeal exorcisms, such as the one I offer, can in principle surely help, by showing outsiders ways of entering into Hegel's work.

Part II Epistemology

Barry Stroud

Stroud thinks some of what I say about impressions suggests that I do not think they can be, at their best, simply cases of perceiving, for instance seeing, that things are objectively thus and so – or, if I do think so, that I do not think that fact about them is enough to explain how they ground empirical beliefs. In fact I think the idea of perceiving that things are thus and so – or perhaps I should say *an* idea of perceiving that things are thus and so – goes well with my conception of experience as, in the best cases, taking in part of the world – a conception whose original point is precisely to make it clear how experiences can ground beliefs. But the idea of perceiving that things are thus and so that fits my bill does not have implications Stroud insists on.

Stroud says: "A person who sees that it is raining judges or believes or otherwise puts it forward as true that it is raining." I think that is simply wrong about a perfectly intelligible notion of seeing that something is the case. And this other notion is the right one for my purposes.

Certainly one will not *say* one sees that p unless one accepts that p. But one can see that p without being willing to say one does. Consider a person who thinks her visual experience does not put her in a position to say how things are in some respect. But she later realizes she was wrong about that, and says something on these lines:

> I thought I was looking at the tie under one of those lights that make it impossible to tell what color things are, so I thought it merely looked green to me, but I now realize that I was seeing it to be green.

According to this quite intelligible remark, it was true at the relevant past time that she was seeing the tie to be green, but at that time she did not in any way put it forward as true that the tie was green. She does now, but that is irrelevant to Stroud's claim that the seeing itself must have involved endorsement or acceptance. She withheld her assent from the appearance that the tie was green that her experience presented her with – an appearance that was actually the fact that the tie was green making itself visually available to her. Stroud thinks withholding one's assent from an appearance is incompatible with seeing that things are that way. But this person, as she now realizes, did see that the tie was green, though she withheld her assent from the appearance.

Her having her visual impression *was* her seeing that the tie was green, and it was not itself a matter of accepting, in any way, that the tie was green. In the case I have described, the subject considered the question of the tie's color, and accepted the less committal proposition that the tie looked green. But the content of the impression was that the tie was green, not this less committal proposition that she accepted. Stroud's question – "Do we always have an impression of something less than that things are thus and so every time we see that things are thus and so?" – does not arise.

Our subject accepted the less committal proposition, but having an impression is not to be identified with accepting such propositions, any more than it is to be identified with accepting the more committal proposition that constitutes the impression's content. An impression is something like an invitation – a petition, as Robert Brandom puts it in his contribution to this volume – to accept a proposition about the objective world. Our subject refused the invitation, but responded to it to the extent of accepting a proposition about how things looked to her. But one need not respond, even to that extent, to the invitation to belief that an impression is. Whether one does depends on the direction of one's attention, a topic I do not think we need to consider when we give a basic picture of perceptual experience. (I do not consider it in *Mind and World*.) On the basis of the claim that "experience involves awareness," Stroud says "it cannot be that in receiving an impression that is an appearance there is no acceptance or judgment at all." His idea is that there must be acceptance at least of a proposition about how things, say, look. But I think receiving an impression, having things appear to one a certain way, does not itself imply accepting anything, not even that things appear to one that way. The awareness that experience involves is a matter of its being *possible* for "I think" to accompany representations, to echo Kant – not of its actually accompanying them.[11]

Davidson refuses to credit perceptual experience with reason-giving capacity, and Stroud puzzles over my dissatisfaction with this. He makes it look as if I merely trade on some unfortunate wording on Davidson's part. As far as Stroud can see, there is nothing in Davidson's thinking to prevent him from acknowledging the reason-giving capacity of, say, seeing that something is the case. But the closest Davidson gets to the idea of seeing that something is the case is the idea of acquiring the belief that something is the case as a result of sensory occurrences. That is how Stroud too thinks seeing that something is the case would have to be understood, and that is the basis of his puzzlement. Stroud writes: "'Believe' is perhaps not the best word to capture the attitude of acceptance or endorsement involved in perception, especially if it suggests actively making up one's mind." But my problem with the suggestion is not met by insisting, correctly enough, that belief-acquisition can be involuntary. My problem is that I think we need an idea of perception as something in which there is no attitude of acceptance or endorsement at all, but only, as I put it, an invitation to adopt such an attitude, which, in the best cases, consists in a fact's making itself manifest to one.

That is what I find missing from the legendary chicken sexers whom Stroud mentions.[12] They acquire beliefs, in fact knowledge, to the effect that, say, a chick is male, as a result of the operations of their senses, but they do not accept that male and female chicks look (or smell) any different to them. I think there is no ordinary sense in which they see (or perhaps smell) that a chick is male, though in the Stroud–Davidson sense they do. The point is not that they are unable to say what features they rely on in applying the concept *male*. As Stroud says, there must be concepts that can be recognized to apply directly, not on the basis of features of their compliants other than that they are compliants. The point is, rather, that the purchase of the chicken sexers on the propositions that their skill enables them to know is quite unlike our purchase on what we, for instance, see to be the case. They cannot find in their perceptual experience impressions whose content is that a chick is male, or that it is female. They find themselves with beliefs to that effect, and, knowing their skill, they have good grounds for an unspecific belief about the etiology of such beliefs – that if they find themselves believing, in the relevant circumstances, that a chick is male, or that it is female, that traces back somehow to the fact that it is male, or that it is female. But finding oneself believing something, even if one has, in that way, good grounds for supposing one's belief is true, does not amount to having something's being the case perceptually manifest to one. And that is what perceiving something to be the case is.

Robert Brandom

In my view Brandom is wrong to suppose Sellars has no room for the non-judgmental justifiers that experiences are in my conception. It is true that what Sellars calls "sense impressions" are not suited to stand in justificatory relations to judgments. But much of the point of "Empiricism and the Philosophy of Mind" is to explain a conception of *experiences* – not what Sellars calls "sense impressions" – according to which they "contain claims." I think this conception is very like the one I propose in *Mind and World*. There I thought I had to defend the conception against Sellars, misreading him (under Brandom's influence) much as Brandom does, but I try to set things straight in my Woodbridge Lectures.

Brandom thinks I would agree that the legendary chicken sexers have observational knowledge that, say, a chick is male. But when I first responded to his invitation to consider the chicken sexers as exemplifying non-inferential knowledge on his minimal conception (the broader of the two notions between which he places my conception of experience), I said that, although their sayings of "It's male" or "It's female" clearly express knowledge, "it seems plain to me that … these sayings are *not* intelligible as *reports of observation*."[13] Observational knowledge is knowledge acquired by perceiving something to be the case, and in my view the chicken sexers do not perceive chicks to be male or female.

As Brandom notes, the chicken sexers are in the same position, with regard to the justification of the relevant beliefs, as third-person observers might be. I think he underplays how different this is from the position that, according to me, characterizes people who perceive how things are. The chicken sexers find themselves with inclinations to say things, which they can supply with justification only by adducing considerations external to what is available to them in their present angle on reality – considerations about the skill that they know they have acquired. These inclinations to say things would not even intelligibly amount to beliefs were it not for that external context. If the chicken sexers were to restrict themselves to what is available to them in their present angle on reality, the inclinations would be no more than yens to make certain utterances, rationally and causally unaccountable to them. The inclinations are unlike mere presentiments only in that something unspecific is known about their etiology, though only by going outside themselves. When one sees how things are, in contrast, a warrant and cause for one's belief that things are that way is visibly *there* for one in the bit of reality that is within one's view. I think it would be absurd to be frightened out of the "intuition" that this difference matters by an insinuation that it may be "residually Cartesian."

Brandom asks whether his imagined physicist has impressions of the presence of mu mesons. I agree that this is an interesting question. Perhaps we should say the physicist's ability to tell whether mu mesons are present owes its status as knowledge-yielding to the physicist's having available, in the relevant cases, a cogent inferential basis for knowledgeable claims, even though the physicist does not make the claims on that basis. That is not true in the case of the ability to look and see what color something is, or what shape.[14] Perhaps this is an alternative to supposing the physicist has impressions of the presence of mu mesons. I do not know what to say about this. But I do not see why this should make it urgent to wonder whether the distinction I insist on in clearer cases – separating, say, an ordinary ability to see that something is cubic from the chicken sexers' ability to tell whether a chick is male – is Cartesian in some disreputable sense. Perhaps, indeed, the boot should be on the other foot. Is there anything to be said for the idea that Brandom's broader notion is the only notion we need – rather than just a way of accommodating odd cases like the chicken sexers – except that so restricting ourselves indulges a phobia of the very idea of states or episodes of consciousness? That is surely an over-reaction to the unsatisfactoriness of classical Cartesian thinking.

The other of the two positions between which Brandom locates me is that perception is immediate awareness of secondary qualities. He formulates the conception of secondary qualities I derive from Gareth Evans like this: "To take φ to express a [visual] secondary quality concept, is to take it that one cannot count as having mastered the use of 'φ' talk unless one has also mastered the use of 'looks-φ' talk." But as far as I can see, a formulation on these lines fits sophisticated mastery of any observationally applicable concept, primary or secondary. Sophisticated mastery of an observational concept must include awareness of fallibility, awareness that appearance and reality can diverge. Evans's point about secondary quality concepts is rather that their very content cannot be specified without invoking what it is for them to figure in appearance. What it is for something to be red is for it to be such as to look red (to certain perceivers in certain circumstances), whereas what it is for something to be cubic can be spelled out in terms of how cubic things take up space, without need for invoking how cubic things look or feel.

Brandom asks whether there could be perceptual experience without experience of secondary qualities. I think there is an interesting question hereabouts, but I am not sure that secondary qualities are the right focus for it. The older concept of proper sensibles might be a better focus. Perhaps the proper sensibles of vision are the same as the visual secondary qualities, but the concepts of proper sensibles and secondary qualities are not the same. I find it plausible that the different senses have their proper sensibles, and that there is no visual experience, say, without experience of the proper sensibles of vision. But I have no settled view on the question. Here too, I think it would be absurd to suggest – as Brandom does in connection with his final question, about whether there are impressions, in my sense, of normative states of affairs – that the very intelligibility of my conception of experience turns on having an answer to the question.

Charles Taylor

In Taylor's "Inside/Outside" picture, the Outside (the world) is a realm of law. The epistemological problem this picture poses is that knowledge requires a boundary at which the spontaneity of the understanding somehow makes contact with "a world under adamantine, post-Galilean 'laws of nature'." Events at this boundary would have to partake both of the Galilean character supposedly possessed by knowable reality, and of the allegiance to reason that governs the zone in which knowing occurs. And this combination seems to be impossible.

This is not the picture I aim to dislodge. In the way of thinking that concerns me, the realm of Galilean law does not figure as what we would like to have knowledge of but have problems seeing how we could get into the right kind of contact with. The epistemological difficulty is not about the possibility of knowledge of the world of natural science in particular, but about the possibility of empirical knowledge, and more generally empirical thought, *überhaupt*.

Making up one's mind is an exercise of freedom. If empirical thinking is to have objective purport, that freedom must be rationally constrained by receptivity. And the Galilean conception of nature poses an apparent problem about how spontaneity could be rationally constrained by receptivity. The operations of receptivity would have to be goings-on in nature. According to the Galilean conception, that would mean that the idea of such occurrences belongs in the framework of the realm of law. But many people have found it plausible that the logical framework constituted by the realm of law cannot be aligned with the logical framework we are moving in when we say one thing rationally constrains another. And this separation of logical frameworks yields an argument that experience cannot both be receptivity in operation and stand in rational relations to belief.

This double character for experiences is not the double character of Taylor's boundary events. The double character of Taylor's boundary events – that under one conceptualization they would have to be displayed as both Galilean and spontaneous – reveals them as impossible. But I show how the double character of experience that poses my apparent problem – that experiences are both states or episodes in which "things 'impress' themselves on the senses" and, as such, epistemologically significant – is innocent.

The first of Taylor's two "continentally" inspired moves is to suggest that "the foundationalist project" is another source of the idea of a brute input to the knowing mind. I do not see why Taylor thinks foundationalism is extra to anything I consider. He depicts the foundationalist impulse as a felt need to "peel back all the layers of inference and interpretation, and get back to something genuinely prior to them all, a brute Given." That is just the temptation I consider. Where Taylor's foundationalist says "It can't be interpretation all the way down," the proponent of the Given I discuss says "It can't be actualizations of capacities belonging to spontaneity all the way out." The imagery is different, but the thought is surely the same.

Taylor focuses, as I do not, on the methodological context for the idea of foundations in its Cartesian form. But why should it have come to seem that proper method requires building from a basis of brute inputs, inputs independent of our capacities for reflective thought? Why should it not have seemed, rather, that proper method requires a careful check for coherence? The way I handle the idea of the Given points to an answer to this question. Thought's hold on the world can easily seem to be in question if we play up the idea that making up one's mind is an exercise of spontaneity, while we see spontaneity as operating in a logical space alien to the one that comes into focus in the Galilean conception of nature. It is intelligible that it might seem to help with this felt difficulty if we could see receptivity as yielding brute inputs for cognitive activity. So the temptation to foundationalism can be understood from the standpoint of my book. Taylor thinks foundationalism is extra to my story, and my story centers on the Galilean conception of nature. So Taylor must see foundationalism as separate from the ascendancy of that conception of nature. By contrast, the picture I have sketched points toward an explanation of why the foundationalist temptation should have become gripping, in a new way, precisely when the Galilean conception was coming into its ascendancy.

Taylor's second "continental" move is a reaction to my taking issue with Gareth Evans, who claims that the content of experience is non-conceptual. Taylor's worry is that in doing so I deny myself insights from Heidegger and Merleau-Ponty, according to which conceptual capacities are embedded in a pre-intellectual mode of living in the world.

But Evans portrays empirical judgments, not as *embedded in* a holistic background of pre-conceptual coping, but as *based on* non-conceptually received content. In Evans's picture, the relevant non-conceptual content is no less "particulate" than the content of the judgments that are based on it. Evans conceives empirical judgment as converting already particulate non-conceptual content into conceptual form. This is not the view of conceptual content that Taylor applauds, in which particulateness emerges out of an "undelimitable background" of pre-understanding. When I object to Evans, it is not with a view to setting my face against the idea of a background.

It is true that I do not exploit the idea of a background of pre-understanding. I am not sure how much of a divergence this reflects from Taylor's "continental" thought. Part of the seeming divergence may come from the fact that Taylor works with a notion of conceptual capacities according to which they are in play only when things come into focus. I do not see why we should accept this connection between conceptuality and determinacy.

Taylor does not emphasize my insistence that actualizations of conceptual capacities must be seen as manifestations of life, as opposed to operations of a pure intellect. Perhaps if he had, I would have seemed less distant from the idea of a background that he wants to urge.

Anyway, how much would it have helped me if I had made much of a background of pre-understanding? I agree with Taylor that there is something between spontaneity in what he calls "the strong Kantian sense, turning crucially on conceptual, reflective thought," on the one hand, and conformity to Galilean law, on the other. We need this middle ground for thinking about non-human animals, and it is what is supposed to be occupied by pre-understanding even in our case. But the difficulty that concerns me arises because making up our minds about the world is an exercise of spontaneity in precisely the Kantian sense. The problem is how spontaneity in that sense could be rationally constrained by receptivity. This difficulty would not be addressed by appealing to spontaneity in the weaker sense that Taylor thinks my argument must involve. What my project requires is that we see how spontaneity in the strong Kantian sense, although it is indeed "freedom" in the sense of something "full-blown, reflective, self-possessing, radical," is exactly not an "emancipation from nature," as Taylor suggests Kantian spontaneity would be.

Two quick remarks about Taylor's last section. First, it is not obvious to me that Davidson's principle of charity diverges in the way Taylor suggests from one that is ontologically based, so as to be irrelevant to questions about intercultural understanding. Davidson's principle, properly understood, surely requires looking for common ground – if necessary engaging in conceptual innovation for the purpose – with candidates for understanding whom we initially find unintelligible. Second, it is surely not Davidson's fault if people base objectionably ethnocentric social science on misreadings of him.

Part III Philosophy of mind

Gregory McCulloch

Most of McCulloch's essay is of course congenial to me. But I have reservations about his "small reservations."

McCulloch says, about the connection he questions between intentionality and justification, that according to me the views I set it against, traditional empiricism and Davidsonian coherentism, "share the root defect of conceiving the impact of world on mind in at best merely causal terms, leaving no room for the normative idea of justification." That is not right. Traditional empiricists want experience to serve as the rational basis of knowledge. The trouble about an empiricism that falls into the Myth of the Given is that it conceives experience in a way that will not cohere with that desideratum. The desideratum is there, and that is why arguing that the Given cannot meet it is so distressing to traditional empiricists.

In *Mind and World* I look for a way to conceive experience so as to conform to the desideratum. In traditional empiricism the point of giving experience its foundational status is epistemological, but, as McCulloch notes, I think the epistemological questions empiricism addresses give expression to an underlying worry about thought's contact with the world, knowledgeable or not. This worry reflects the thought that if we cannot see how experience could stand in relations of warrant to empirical belief, we put at risk our entitlement to the very idea of empirical objective content. I aim to characterize a non-traditional empiricism that, by definitely avoiding the Myth of the Given, rescues that inchoately transcendental thought from the wreckage of traditional empiricism.

My aim is not to recommend externalism about content apart from any context. As McCulloch in effect suggests, that could be done in a way that might be less vulnerable to objection, say by deploying Twin-Earth arguments. My aim is to defend a non-traditional empiricism that retains the thought, inchoately present in traditional empiricism according to me, that the possibility of empirical objective content depends on a rational connection between experience and empirical belief. Giving up that thought would be giving up the very project of *Mind and World*. Perhaps I should do that, but to suggest I should is not to express a small reservation.

This point impinges on the *ad hominem* way McCulloch puts his skepticism about whether a justificatory context is necessary to intentionality. I say the idea of the Given is a response to a threat that external constraint goes missing, and McCulloch wonders why exculpation, which I acknowledge the Given might afford, is not external constraint enough. But the external constraint that threatens to go missing is the warranting external constraint that empiricists want. My talk of exculpation is an attempt to make vivid the fact that the idea of the Given does not give them what they want, not an invitation to consider a different candidate for the required external constraint.

I take it to be intuitively obvious – if only philosophy did not distort our thinking – that empiricists are right to want what they do. And nothing McCulloch says persuades me that the thought that there must be warranting external constraint does not have that kind of status. Reasons are called for if one wants to reject it, not if one accepts it. If we could not make sense of the idea that experience discloses the world to us (which would surely be a warrant for believing it is as it appears), how could we think about the world at all? Perhaps a skepticism not based on the Cartesian Real Distinction can still refuse the title of knowledge to what perception yields, on the ground that even in a case in which experience does disclose the world, the subject cannot establish, without begging the question against the skeptic, that she is not confronted by a mere appearance. But a position on these lines does not undermine the very idea that experience can warrant belief by disclosing facts. It does not deprive us of the idea of such a position; it merely claims that we can never know for sure that we are in it. And I would urge that it is only by preserving that idea that the position manages, if it does, to exemplify the ancient skeptical outlook, in which one renounces knowledge without giving up the world.

In the discussion McCulloch exploits when he questions whether a justificatory context is sufficient for intentionality, I express a doubt about whether the supposition, or supposed supposition, that I may be a brain in a vat can be made comfortable by arguing that even if I am, my beliefs are still mostly true.[15] Perhaps the supposedly comforting thought should rather be that even if I am a brain in a vat, most of what seem to be my beliefs are indeed beliefs, and are mostly true. The idea here is not that we are to contemplate something that is definitely a brain in a vat, and consider what, if anything, it believes. I am supposed to be contemplating myself. I at least seem, at least to myself, to have beliefs. And the question is whether the phenomenology of being me, seeming to have the beliefs I seem to have, can be made to fit comfortably with the supposition, or supposed supposition, that I am a brain in a vat, by the expedient of arguing that even so I am mostly right about my environment. The supposition that I am a brain in a vat is meant to be different from the supposition that I inhabit the ordinary world, containing cats and the like. But *ex hypothesi* (if it is a hypothesis) it makes no difference to the phenomenology of being me, including my seeming beliefs, which of the two suppositions about my environment is correct. And if what I rightly take myself to be in touch with, in, say, what present themselves to me as cat beliefs, may or may not be electronic impulses (which are what I supposedly mean by "cat" if the vat-brain hypothesis is the right one), that surely undermines any idea that what present themselves to me as beliefs I have make contact with anything in particular.

McCulloch says it is not clear what drives this doubt. He puzzles over how it fits with the way I connect intentionality and justification. What disqualifies my seeming beliefs from being beliefs, on the supposition that I am a brain in a vat, cannot be that on that supposition they lack appropriate justification, since by parity of reasoning my experiences, on the same supposition, are also about my electronic environment and so capable of justifying beliefs about it. McCulloch is right about this. But why does that make trouble for my doubt? My doubt turns rather on the idea – which should be congenial to McCulloch – that the phenomenology of having a belief should not leave indeterminate what it is about. The same goes for experiences, so, as McCulloch urges, the vat-brain's supposed beliefs and experiences, supposedly about its electronic environment, stand or fall together. My suggestion is that they fall, because of the indeterminacy that is essential to the seeming supposition's seeming bite. As far as I can see, this leaves untouched the connection McCulloch puts by saying I make justification sufficient for intentionality.

Crispin Wright

I agree about the risk of diminishing returns, but there is more to say. I shall say something about Wright's Postscript, and then turn to parts of his essay that did not figure in the shorter version I responded to.[16]

The gratifying clarity I found in Wright was on the point that my problem with coherentism is transcendental, not epistemological; that it is content, not knowledge, that according to me coherentism threatens. I cannot see that his introduction of a half-way house position – what he calls "Extended Coherentism" – helped him toward this clarity. The half-way house position purports to include experience in the domain over which coherence is to extend, while leaving something still to be done to entitle us to conceive experience as enabling bits of the world to serve as rational constraints on belief-formation. Wright now disclaims any intention of reconstructing my thinking by introducing this position. In "Human Nature?", after pausing to remark that the half-way house position "may seem both dogmatic and over-simplified," he says that the position "had better be basically right if what seems to be the needed next step in McDowell's progression is to be well-motivated." That certainly sounds like a reconstruction of how I arrive where I do. In any case, my point, in the response Wright's Postscript responds to, stands: if we need a further step in a progression, whether or not it is mine, in order to get the world into the picture, it is not, by my lights, experience that the coherence relation has been extended to. This is not a position that should so much as seem to end my oscillation by giving experience its proper justificatory role. It is experience – not some mental state that can be in view even if not yet conceived as making bits of the world available to serve as rational constraints on belief-formation – that, according to me, empirical belief must be answerable to, on pain of making empirical content a mystery. Of course that is just the transcendental thought that so exasperates Wright. I cannot see that introducing the half-way house does anything to help bring it into focus.

In "Human Nature?" Wright says, about this position: "it is oversimplified ... because nothing has yet been said about the content of our *theoretical* beliefs." Not only does he now disclaim the reconstructive intention I found in his talk of "McDowell's progression." He also says, bafflingly, that I misread him when I take the charge about theoretical beliefs to be one of oversimplification. I shall come back to the substance of the charge.

I do not see why anyone should be mystified by the idea that a conception in which experience lets objective reality come into view, partly by virtue of the involvement in it of conceptual capacities, can be transcendentally helpful. If we emphasize the freedom of judgment, it can be hard to understand how what we are considering can be judgment, with its objective purport, at all. But suppose we can find conceptual capacities actualized both in free intellectual activity and in the receptivity of sensory consciousness. Partly because of the connection with judgment, the actualizations in receptivity can intelligibly be states or episodes in which reality comes into view. And partly because of the connection with experience so conceived, the actualizations in free intellectual activity can intelligibly be cases of sticking one's neck out about how things are. That, in a nutshell, is why I think a minimal empiricism, transcendentally slanted, is compelling. Of course I cannot pretend that merely describing the position in such terms, even with more elaboration, could make it compulsory to think this way. But I think there should already be enough here to make it intelligible, given minimal goodwill, that some people find it compelling.

To someone attracted by such a conception, perhaps without getting it formulated even as explicitly as in my sketch, any outlook that refuses to conceive experience in a way that would allow it to play this role will seem to miss something. That is the frame of mind I try to make vivid in the oscillation I begin with. Of course the oscillation can no more make it compulsory to embrace my minimal empiricism than a sheer description of the position could. It is obvious off-hand that my description of the oscillation can capture no discomfort felt by anyone who is happy to occupy one of its poles – Davidson, for example. Wright, however, searches my presentation for something that would aspire to *refute* coherentism, and reacts with impatience when he fails, as was inevitable, to find any such thing.

Back now to the charge of oversimplification, or, as Wright now prefers, omission about theoretical beliefs. In transcendental empiricism as I have described it, help toward finding things unmysterious goes in both directions between experience and the free intellectual activity of forming and re-forming world-views. The idea is not that we can make self-standing sense of

287

experiences as atomistically warranting "basic empirical beliefs" – thus attaining a standpoint from which we might proceed to ask hitherto unaddressed questions about theoretical beliefs. Experiences are actualizations of conceptual capacities, and an atomistic conception of the content of experiences would not cohere with a proper holism about conceptual capacities. In experience at its best one directly takes in observable facts, but that is intelligible only in the context of a whole world-view, transcending the here and now, that enters into determining the content of the conceptual capacities operative in experience. That was the point of my appeal to Sellars. Wright's distinction of Myths of the Given would be irrelevant here, even if it were a good distinction (on which see below). His charge that I short-change theoretical beliefs depends on denying me this Sellarsian holism, as if my idea had to be that objective purport is atomistically achieved by foundational empirical beliefs and spread from there to beliefs grounded on them.

Wright seems to miss the point that my distinction between *feeling pain* and *experiencing pain*, in my quasi-technical sense, is a distinction between a genus and one of its species. He thinks I am committed to supposing that the painful conditions cats, say, can be in *have nothing in common* with the painful conditions adult human beings can be in. He is right that this would do violence to common sense about cats and infants. But he is wrong about my commitments. Why can there not be two species of episodes in which a subject feels pain? They have just that in common: that in both sorts of episodes someone or something *feels pain*. The concept of a genus is not shown to be equivocal by noting that it covers more than one species. We must, and can, resist explaining the commonality by saying we have what cats have but go beyond them in conceptualizing it. (On the structurally parallel point about perception, see *Mind and World*, pp.64 and 69.) There is nothing here that threatens our ordinary responses to the sufferings of the conceptless.

Of course Wittgenstein is not in the business of finding fault with ordinary linguistic practice. But what I picked on was Wright's talk of how things are within a subject's consciousness. Such wording is not an ordinary gloss on the generic idea of, for instance, a creature's feeling pain. The image of consciousness as a realm of states of affairs goes beyond Wright's six features of ordinary thinking about sensations (with the possible exception of the second, which is surely not part of ordinary thinking about non-human animals and infants). It goes beyond the idea of an inner life, if that idea is understood – as it perhaps can be, though I do not think this is obvious – so as to fit wherever the idea of sentience fits. Wright thinks that for a creature, adult human being or not, to feel pain is for some state of affairs to obtain within its consciousness, from which it may or may not go on to an actualization of a conceptual capacity (it may not even have the relevant conceptual capacity). That, I said, is just the supposed idea of the private object, the target of Wittgenstein's devastating attack. Wright thinks this cannot be right, because he thinks it implies the "nothing in common" idea he finds in me. He is wrong about that, and on the strength of that wrong assumption he has left my claim about Wittgenstein unanswered.

Wright credits me with a quasi-inferential conception of empirical justification. I am sorry I let this activate my fear of being taken to treat experience as an intermediary between perceivers and the facts perceived. If all it means is that my view involves "content-sensitive justifiers," it is clearly correct; facts observed are just that, in my conception of perceptual knowledge.[17]

Of course the sheer obtaining of a fact, say some state of affairs on the far side of the moon, cannot justify someone in believing it obtains. But why does Wright think that makes it "inept" to say an *observed* fact can justify? He needs to exclude this in order to argue that "even McDowellian experience … is not an *unconditional* justifier." Experience at its best, on my conception, is taking in a fact. The fact is present to the subject of the experience. If a situation is appropriately describable in such terms, there is nothing perverse or mysterious about saying it constitutes an opportunity for the subject to know that the fact obtains, and in that sense a warrant for her to believe it does. False beliefs about the probability of hallucination and the like may deter a subject from taking the opportunity. Indeed it may be doxastically virtuous for her not to suppose she has a justification for the relevant belief. But it is completely unobvious that the right notion of justification or warrant, for thinking about perceptual knowledge, is one controlled by such considerations of doxastic virtue, so that our subject does not have a justification for the relevant belief – as opposed to a notion that connects with that perfectly intelligible talk of opportunities to know, which we can be prevented from taking, in unfavorable cases, by a caution dictated by doxastic virtue.[18]

In Wright's second alternative to my picture of the justification for belief that experience constitutes, the ultimate warrant for an empirical belief has to be the non-conceptual occurrence in consciousness that is said to "sustain" or "command" a particular conceptualization. That the conceptualization is so "sustained" has to be essential to its justificatory power. It makes no difference to this that the belief is supposed to be warranted only if the conceptualization "commanded" takes place. Now the Myth of the Given has many forms, as Sellars remarks at the beginning of "Empiricism and the Philosophy of Mind." But the form that concerns me is the form that mostly concerns Sellars in that work: the idea that non-conceptual occurrences in consciousness can rationally dictate, or sustain, or command, or warrant anything. It is obvious that these notions belong together. Wright's alternative is, as I said, clearly a case of the Myth of the Given in this sense. The problem is not about what he focuses on, the relation between the supposedly optional conceptualization and the belief. The problem is about the relation of "sustaining" or "commanding" that is supposed to enter into the justificatory power of the conceptualization.

This problem matches the problem that besets Wright's thinking about sensations. That problem concerns the relation between a state of affairs within a subject's consciousness, taken to be there independently of whether its subject even has the relevant conceptual capacities, and an actualization of conceptual capacities that such a state of affairs would supposedly "sustain" or "command" (the words fit here just as well). Missing what I mean to attack when I attack the Given, Wright is evidently unable to understand my suggestion (*Mind and World*, pp.18–23) that the so-called Private Language Argument just applies the insight that the Given is mythical.

The trouble here connects with Wright's distinction of Myths of the Given. In note 8 of "Human Nature?", which he cites in his Postscript, he distinguishes my Myth from the one attacked by Quine and Sellars. (He is apparently not bothered by the fact that what little I say about why my Myth is a myth is directly lifted from Sellars.) He writes:

> McDowell's Mythical Given is non-conceptual input, conceived as presented in sentience anyway, whether brought under concepts or not. By contrast, the Myth rejected by Quine is the (two-way independent) empiricist Myth of a base class of empirical judgments whose acceptability is settled just by the occurrence of episodes of sentience, independently of whatever collateral beliefs a subject may hold – a Myth of one–one mandating relations, as it were, between experience and a basic range of *synthetic* statements (in the sense of "Two Dogmas").

The Given that I reject is non-conceptual input conceived as capable of warranting (or sustaining or commanding) anything.[19] "Mandating" clearly belongs in that list. Quine's attention is on the supposedly mandated judgments, but the supposedly mandating episodes of sentience are inextricably part of the package. In one mood, Quine thinks the problem is met if one–one mandating relations are replaced by global sustaining relations between a totality of episodes of sentience and a whole world-view. In another mood, he abandons all such notions in favor of brute causation. That is better, because the problem is at least in part with the idea that episodes of sentience, present independently of a subject's conceptual capacities if any, could stand in rational relations to anything. That is what Sellars focuses on. The supposedly mandating, or sustaining, episodes of sentience are bits of the Given in the sense of what I attack. I am at a loss as to why Wright is so sure my target is different.

I shall end with a couple of remarks about things in "Human Nature?" that do not figure in Wright's Postscript. (This will still leave much unsaid.)

First, in the context of complaining about the untheoretical way in which I recommend a relaxed naturalism, Wright says: "What McDowell needs is a way of channeling the philosophical pressure that modern naturalism generates away from a direct obsession with the subject matter of normative discourses and on to their learning and practice instead." The picture here is that pressure is acknowledged, and needs to be diverted into different tracks. And now surely the diversion needs theoretical work. But the picture is wrong. My idea is that once we have been reminded that the concept of second nature is unproblematic, we see that normative discourses do not come under pressure at all from any idea of nature that is forced on us by a proper respect for the achievements of modernity.[20]

Finally, I must comment on Wright's splendid conclusion, where he drums me out of the regiment of analytic philosophers.[21] If analytic philosophy prohibits imagery except for rare special effect, and precludes letting the full import of a term (such as, perhaps, "spontaneity") emerge gradually in the course of using it, as opposed to setting down a definition at the start, I do not care if I am not an analytic philosopher. Likewise if analytic philosophy requires the kind of argument that aims to compel an audience into accepting theses. In fact I see no reason why these should be taken to be marks of the genre. Of course explicitness and clarity are another matter. But I wrote as explicitly and clearly as I knew how. As far as I can see, Wright's remarks about an extraordinary need for constructive exegesis largely reflect his point-missing and – I have to say – ill-tempered efforts to find coercive philosophy in my description of the oscillation. Wright is clearly galled by my work, perhaps particularly by my stance of not aiming to compel my readers into theses, and I think this has prevented him from seeing how straightforward my book really is.

Hilary Putnam

Of course Putnam is right that what I try to do in *Mind and World* is not simply separate from defending direct realism about perception. The conception of perceptual experience that I recommend, on transcendental grounds, in *Mind and World* enables us to see experience at its best as openness to how things are. And at one place (pp.111–113) I briefly make the point Putnam approves of from my earlier writings: non-veridical experience can be indistinguishable from veridical experience, but that does not establish that experience can reach no further than a highest common factor of the two – a conclusion that would dislodge the idea of openness.[22]

When I resisted Putnam's suggestion that I should have made more of this, my point was to keep focused on my main aim in *Mind and World*. What concerns me there is an obstacle in the path of accepting the conception of experience I recommend, and the obstacle is not the one Putnam wishes I had spent more effort on, namely the temptation to see experience as an interface – the temptation to suppose that any realism we can have is at best indirect. The obstacle that concerns me is, rather, that the plausible idea that operations of sensibility would have to be, as such, natural phenomena, in the context of a certain conception of what it is for a phenomenon to be natural, can make it seem incoherent to suppose operations of sensibility can be informed by capacities that belong to a faculty of spontaneity – a faculty whose operations, considered as such, resist subsumption under laws of nature. But that is how I urge we need to conceive experience if we are to avoid the unattractive choice

291

between coherentism and the Myth of the Given. I cannot see how giving a central place to the motivations for conceiving experience as an interface, rather than considering them merely in passing as I do, would have helped with overcoming the obstacle that is my concern. So I cannot see that it would have made my book less difficult, as Putnam argues. The difficulty Putnam finds in my book seems to me to reflect a failure to attend to what I aim to do in it. Putnam wants me to be engaged in a project more like his own in his Dewey Lectures, and he finds my execution of my somewhat different project obscure where it diverges from that expectation.

Putnam credits me with an idiosyncratic treatment of "the naturalist camp in present-day analytic philosophy." He thinks it is an oversight or tactical error that I do not discuss the distinction between reductionists and eliminativists, or the idea that functionalism and a causal or information-theoretic account of reference will accommodate mental phenomena. This reflects the same inattention to the dialectical organization of my book. I do not raise a question out of the blue about the prospects for contemporary naturalism ("the issue facing naturalism," as Putnam puts it). No doubt if I had, that would have required me to consider all the different options. But the only relevant question I raise is whether the idea of nature must be understood in terms of the realm of law. According to my diagnosis, that conception of nature underlies the worry I aim to deal with, because – along with the thought, which I aim to show how to preserve, that the space of reasons is *sui generis* – it obliterates the understanding of experience that enables us to avoid the choice between coherentism and the Myth of the Given. My purposes require no more complex classification of varieties of naturalism than the distinction between equating the idea of the natural with the idea of subsumability under law, on the one hand, and detaching the idea of the natural from the idea of law, on the other. It would not help to go into detail about different versions of the conception of nature as the realm of law, or different proposals about how that conception might be applied to mental phenomena.

Putnam thinks that when I talk of the conception of nature as the realm of law I mean a strict physicalism. So he thinks that when I consider a choice between "bald naturalism" and the relaxed naturalism I recommend, I omit a third option, in which the space of reasons is putatively accommodated as part of the subject matter of the special sciences, whose laws can have *ceteris paribus* clauses. But I deliberately give no more content to the idea of the realm of law than is conferred on it by the contrast between making phenomena intelligible by subsuming them under law and making phenomena intelligible by seeing them in terms of responsiveness to reasons.[23] And it seems obvious that subsuming occurrences under the non-strict laws of the special sciences contrasts with explaining them as exercises of rationality in just the way that subsuming occurrences under strict laws does. The point in both cases is that what we have in view is not a case of placing things in a *sui generis* space of reasons. So Putnam's third option is just a species of what I call "bald naturalism." The twofold choice is all I need; the distinction between a strict physicalism and a less restrictive, but still scientistic, naturalism is irrelevant to *irrelevant* my dialectical and therapeutic purposes.[24]

One reason why Putnam thinks I should have discussed functionalism is that he thinks Davidson's anomalous monism is central to an argument of mine that only what is conceptually shaped can justify belief. He frames this as my focusing idiosyncratically on "a minority position" in the philosophy of mind, and that makes it look plausible that I should have considered more mainstream positions as well. But this is a misunderstanding. Putnam thinks I hold that only what is conceptually shaped can justify belief because I think that what is not conceptually shaped can only be an efficient cause of belief, and – supposedly following Davidson – that an efficient cause cannot be a justification. He even says I take this last claim to be self-evident. In fact I follow Davidson in thinking it is false: reasons both efficiently cause actions *justification* and beliefs and justify them. The reason why experience as Davidson conceives it cannot justify belief is not that its relation to belief is causal, but simply that it is extra-conceptual. I do not offer an argument, any more than Davidson does, for the claim that only what is conceptually shaped can justify. *Can he say* It is one of those thoughts that, it seems to me, stands on its own feet if we *this?* can only free it from philosophy that generates the appearance that it cannot be so. Given the assumption that experience is extra-conceptual, Davidson's coherentism is excellently motivated by the insight that only what is conceptually shaped can justify, which is what unmasks the Given as a myth. That encapsulates why Davidson's thinking about experience is a useful foil for me. My exploitation of Davidson is not, as Putnam suggests, an unmotivated selection from among the positions on offer in contemporary philosophy of mind, generating an obligation, which I do not meet, to consider others as well.[25]

Putnam expresses a doubt about

> a view which wants to maintain (1) that all experiences are perceptual *and* (2) that for each perceptual experience there is either an occurrent judgment whose content is identical with the content of the experience or else a true counterfactual to the effect that the subject could have formed such a judgment *and* (3) to do justice to the "richness" of experience.

I am not sure that I am in the target area of the doubt. If I understand Putnam, he singles out perceptual experiences from experiences in general by the fact that the subject attends to their object. In my book I do not talk about attention at all, and I see nothing that commits me to accepting Putnam's (1), so understood. To get something that fits me, we might drop (1) and drop "perceptual" in (2). But I see no ground for accepting Putnam's stipulation about the concept of perception in any case, so we might drop (1) and leave (2) as it stands, without the implication about attention that Putnam attaches to it. And now, if the antecedent of the counterfactuals mentioned in (2) can include something on the lines of "if she had been attending to it," there is no obvious problem in combining (2) with (3).

Part IV Toward ethics

Charles Larmore

Larmore finds an inescapable paradox in my Wittgensteinian attitude toward philosophical problems: "how ... can showing up the mistaken assumptions underlying some philosophical problem amount to anything other than putting better views in their place?" This talk of mistaken assumptions might make Larmore's point look stronger than it is. Superstitions and confusions are not theories, to be replaced with better theories. To remind ourselves of what is obvious, or would be if it were not for philosophy, is quite different from putting forward a substantive view. It would be crazy to offer, say, "Sign-posts point the way, to those who understand them" as an interesting thesis – as if anyone, or at least anyone we need to pay attention to, might dispute it. But it can be worth saying in the context of a Wittgensteinian treatment of rule-following.

Larmore notes my acknowledgement that philosophical affliction is bound to recur. The acknowledgement qualifies the image of bringing philosophy peace. But in spite of noting the qualification, Larmore makes more fuss than is warranted about the image. It is not that philosophical activity is interminable on his conception and terminable on mine. It is rather that he and I have different ways to conceive its interminability. Interesting philosophical afflictions are deep-seated. Even after temporarily successful therapy, they re-emerge, perhaps perennially, in new forms. If the risk of re-emergence is perennial, peace is always beyond the horizon. There is no debunking of philosophy's depth and difficulty in the conception of it that Larmore so dislikes.

It is true that much of what I put forward in my own person does not sound like reminders of what is merely obvious. My diction is often that of traditional philosophy. This is a divergence from Wittgenstein, and it is not an oversight. I explicitly claim (*Mind and World*, p.155, note 30) that "moves in the language of traditional philosophy can be aimed at having the right not to worry about its problems, rather than at solving those problems." If it is feasible to do therapeutic philosophy in traditional language, there is surely something to be said for it, if only that it might help us make contact with the targets of the therapy.

Larmore thinks I should not raise the question what the conceptual contents passively received in experience are about. When experience is veridical, its contents are elements in the world, conceived as everything that is the case, and Larmore thinks I should not say they are about it. I am not convinced that this is a lapse, as he says it is. *Qua* conceptual contents, the contents of experience are thinkable. How can we disallow the question what someone who thinks them is thinking about? Case by case, the answer will specify a particular topic, say, a cabbage or a king. But if the question is asked generally, how can the answer not be "the world"?[26] Larmore thinks this would imply that experience stops short of taking in facts, but I do not see why. Anyway, I do not see why he thinks this lapse, if it is one, helps him show that my denial that I am engaged in constructive philosophy is unconvincing and obfuscating. Anyone can go astray, whatever kind of philosophy they are doing.

I also cannot see why Larmore thinks I have a problem with mistakes about what we perceive that cannot be blamed on misleading appearances. No doubt they are not mistakes in judgment about what is given to us in sense. But why can they not be mistakes in judgment, badly based on what is given to us in sense, about what is perceptually present to us?

Larmore's main claim is that, because my aim is to describe a conception of experience according to which it can give reasons for belief, I need a substantive metaphysical account of what a reason is.

He suggests someone might grant me that in experience we can be given the fact that things are thus and so, but require more in the way of argument to show that being given a fact is acquiring a reason for belief. But I cannot make sense of this separation. How could being given the fact that things are thus and so not equip one with a warrant for believing that things are thus and so? The idea that manifest facts might conceivably not have a rational bearing on the course of our thinking, so that argument is needed to show that they do, seems bizarre.

When I say reasons are there anyway, it is a way of saying that, for instance, visible smoke is a reason for believing that there is fire in the vicinity, independently of anyone's belief or fiat. Claims about what is a reason for what are true or false independently of us, much like claims about the spatial arrangements or chemical compositions of things. Some of them are true. Of course Larmore is right that retrieving this as how things obviously are requires dislodging a conception, prevalent in philosophy, of what can be simply true. If one is dazzled by the natural sciences into thinking genuine truth is restricted to what can be validated by their methods, one will suppose that claims about what is a reason for what have to be treated differently, as projections of attitudes or of score-keeping practices or whatever. As Larmore acknowledges, I work at discouraging this dazzlement by science. Why need I do more? If someone asks how claims about reasons can be simply true, our first response should be to ask why it should seem that they cannot. If the question how claims about reasons can be simply true is to be pressing, there needs to be a determinate difficulty about how it can be so. If the supposed difficulty results from a scientistic conception of reality, it lapses when we see that scientism is a superstition, not a stance required by a proper respect for the achievements of the natural sciences.

that Larmore explains why, once we have freed ourselves from
ealism about reasons still poses a problem about their metaphysical

bring the supposed problem into view by invoking the idea that
reasons is to be moved by a certain kind of cause. But of course
"Reasons can be causes" is only a slogan. The thought it sloganizes would be
more accurately expressed by saying that *someone's having a reason* can be
causally relevant, for instance to their acting or to their forming a belief. I think
this renders irrelevant Larmore's worries about how the non-spatial and non-
temporal things that reasons themselves would have to be can be causally
efficacious.

Rüdiger Bubner

Bubner notes helpfully that the modern concept of *Bildung*, which I approach
through Aristotle's conception of the molding of ethical character, pertains not
merely to the inculcation of an approximation to "a socially fixed and pre-given
ideal of virtue," as in Aristotle, but also to the acquisition of an individual
personality. The modern concept coheres with valuing a critical individuality,
whereas the Aristotelian ideal is rather that particular human beings should be
unreflectively excellent occupants of fixed social roles.

But Bubner puts this point by saying: "With 'second nature' we consciously
step back behind the level of reflection of a modern *Bildung*." This seems to
suggest that the very idea of second nature excludes reflective individuality and
points toward a uniform socialization. I find it preferable not to relegate the idea
of second nature to the status of an archaism, as this suggests, but to keep the
phrase "second nature" as suitable to express a modification of Aristotle's
picture, one that makes a proper place for reflectiveness in the personal constitution that results from being brought up into a human community. (See *Mind
and World*, pp.81–83.) With second nature so understood, we do not step back
into a pre-modern outlook. Talk of second nature can invoke everything
implied by the modern concept of *Bildung*, including what permits us to value
distinctive personality – an idea that makes sense only against the background
of cultural formation.

I do not understand why Bubner suggests there is an opposition between
"Gadamer's hermeneutic conception" and "the standard conviction of the
analytic school, that is, of the basic explanatory power of language." Michael
Dummett defines analytic philosophy in terms of the thesis that the philosophy
of thought should be a philosophy of language. I do not object to the thesis, as
Bubner implies. I object to the way Dummett recommends it, which focuses on
the role of language as instrument of communication and as vehicle of
thought, but does not consider its role as repository of tradition, which I think
is more fundamental than either of those. (See *Mind and World*, pp.124–126.)
The upshot is a somewhat Gadamerian vindication of what Dummett

identifies as the basic tenet of analytic philosophy. Indeed, a conviction of the basic explanatory power of language seems appropriately attributable to the author of Part Three of *Truth and Method*.[27] It is Gadamer who says "man's relation to the world is absolutely and fundamentally verbal in nature" (pp.475–476).

Bubner's brief essay is rich in insightful formulations. I single out in particular his fourth section, which sketches a way to think about the historicality of human spontaneity – a topic I point toward by invoking tradition, but, as Bubner says, do not develop further. I think it is very helpful to focus, as Bubner does, on the fact that the forms of life within which we come to be human individuals at all – the forms of life that constitute what, in coming to understand anything at all, we come to find self-evident – are both products of drawn-out historical evolution and dependent for their continuation on continuing whole-hearted participation by mature individuals, those who have acquired the faculty of spontaneity. Stressing the "always already articulated" character of understanding is a useful corrective to a conception of human autonomy that leaves out, or gives insufficient weight to, the necessary moment of receptivity (to echo my response to Pippin). These considerations point, as Bubner suggests in his last section, toward a Hegelian rejection of the unsituatedness that Kant makes essential to the reason that is supposed to characterize the moral agent.

J.M. Bernstein

Bernstein starts by mischaracterizing the dialectical structure of my book. He represents the position I call "bald naturalism" as the opposite pole to coherentism, in the oscillation I start from – that is, he puts it in the place that actually belongs to the Myth of the Given, which is not necessarily a naturalistic conception at all, though of course there are naturalistic varieties of it. Bald naturalism figures elsewhere in my thinking. I trace the oscillation between coherentism and the Myth of the Given to an inability to see how anything natural, as operations of sensibility would have to be, could be shaped by conceptual capacities conceived as *sui generis*, in the sense that their actualizations, so described, resist subsumption under the laws of the natural sciences. This conception of the natural appears not only in bald naturalism but also in the inclination to suppose responsiveness to reasons as such would have to be supernatural. Bald naturalism is not to be equated with a scientistic conception of the natural. Bald naturalism is the conviction – well motivated, so long as a scientistic conception of the natural is in force – that conceptualizations of things as natural, in that sense, exhaust the conceptualizations of things that stand a chance of truth. If that is what naturalness is, the only way to avoid the oscillation is to give up the idea that conceptual capacities are *sui generis*.

Bernstein finds a divergence between Adorno and me over the possibilities for a re-enchantment of nature. The re-enchantment Adorno envisages would require a transformation of society and politics, and from this standpoint my merely intellectual move looks utopian. I think this contrast is at best over-drawn. Certainly Adorno has a much richer account than I do of what gives the scientistic conception of the natural its dominant position in modern culture: not just the intellectual prominence of the natural sciences, which is all I consider, but institutional mechanisms of capitalism, bureaucratic understand-ings of practical reason, and so forth. Bernstein sometimes forgets that my story includes part of this etiology, the rise of the natural sciences to intellectual prominence – as when he describes me as "focusing on the epistemological upshot rather than the cause of disenchantment," and as "bypassing ... the sources of transcendental anxiety." I do focus on a cause; I do diagnose a source for the transcendental anxiety I consider. And in fact my focus on scientism is enough for what I try to do. It would surely be absurd to suggest that unmasking a scientistic conception of the natural as a prejudice, at least to the satisfaction of some people, is not a sensible project until, say, capitalism has been over-thrown. But that unmasking is all that the re-enchantment of nature comes to for my purposes. No doubt loosening the cultural grip of that conception of the natural in a general way (as opposed to persuading occasional intellectuals that they need not swim with the currents of their time) and undoing all its delete-rious effects on modern life (as opposed to showing why a certain sort of activity is not an obligation for philosophers) would require social change, and presum-ably something on those lines is Adorno's point. But my purposes do not require such ambitions.

Adorno attacks a rationalization of reason, one manifestation of which is an inability, as Bernstein puts it, to "acknowledge or account for the *normative dependence* of experiences on the objects they are about." He says I am "not alert" to this. Later he suggests that in my anxiety to insist on normativity all the way out, I fail to cater for the equally pressing requirement that there be dependence on objects all the way in. I find this puzzling. I aim to integrate receptivity with responsiveness to reason, in the conception of experience that I recommend, precisely in order to vindicate the idea that in experience the world itself exerts an authority over empirical thought. Dependence all the way in is a straightforward corollary.[28]

Equally puzzlingly, Bernstein accuses me of inconsistently failing to histori-cize my position. As Rüdiger Bubner points out in his contribution to this volume, I do not elaborate the historicizing implications of my Gadamerian insistence that initiation into the space of reasons is initiation into tradition, but they are certainly there.

Officially, Bernstein is agnostic about whether his thoughts about intermedi-aries, and about the central role that circumambient nature should occupy in our reflection about what we share with the other higher animals, are a problem for me, or just "friendly refinements." Sometimes this attitude slips, as when he says – inexplicably to me – that I conceive "reason and language as dirempting us from our own animality, rationalizing it." It is precisely the point of my relaxed naturalism that this diremption must be avoided – that exercises of our capacities for reason must be understood as, precisely, part of our way of living the animal lives we live.

Much of the trouble here comes from the fact that Bernstein introduces his point about intermediaries by rehearsing some of Crispin Wright's criticisms, in particular Wright's claim that my treatment of non-human animals and children does violence to ordinary thought.[29] One would not realize it from Bernstein's rehearsal of Wright's objection, but I have no problem with the obvious facts that non-human animals can feel, for instance, pain, and see, for instance, threats to their offspring, and that these things, and many more, matter to them. (See my response to Wright in this volume.) Of course facts of this kind must figure in the genealogy of our responsiveness to reasons.

Considerations like this help bring out how we can acknowledge the *sui generis* character of responsiveness to reasons as such, without threatening our entitlement to conceive conceptual capacities as natural. This is how calling our rational capacities "second nature" helps toward understanding them as natural, to echo the question Bernstein extracts from the second of the objections he borrows from Wright. The answer to the question seems to me to be obvious. The facts of our animality are present in our habitation of the space of reasons in the transfigured form that comes with acquiring conceptual capacities. But that is perfectly consistent with agreeing that many features of our human lives instantiate concepts that are also instantiated in the lives of other higher animals – for instance, the concept of nurturing the young. It misses a point I labor in *Mind and World* (pp.64, 69–70) to suppose, as Bernstein does, that insisting on this kind of commonality between human life and the lives of other animals requires rejecting what I mean when I say receptivity does not make an even notionally separable contribution to its cooperation with spontaneity in constituting experience, in the sense in which we possessors of conceptual capacities enjoy experience.

I cannot understand why Bernstein says I "fail to see" that part of what leads Kant to his conception of the transcendental "I" is his picture of the empirical world as a law-governed totality. As far as I can see, that is just another way of saying what I say when I explain this aspect of Kant's thinking in terms of his lacking a pregnant notion of second nature.

Bernstein says: "Actual experience is always more fine-grained, complex, richer, and hence more dense than any conceptual grasping of it." There is a point in saying something on these lines, if we associate "conceptual grasping" of things with bringing them into focus – perhaps making them explicit overtly in claims or inwardly in judgments. But contrary to what Bernstein suggests, this is no problem for my claim that the whole content of experience is actualization of conceptual capacities, because I do not connect actualization of conceptual capacities with bringing things into focus. (See my response to Charles Taylor.) Why should we stipulate that conceptual capacities are operative only where there is "conceptual grasping" in that sense? As far as I can see, it is only that stipulation that makes Bernstein think my conception cannot accommodate the richness of experience.

Elaborating my exploitation of the idea that perceptual demonstrative thought and utterance essentially depends on the perceived presence of whatever is referred to, Bernstein says perceptual judgments are "not *fully* discursive, where full discursivity is fleshed out in the thought that the empirical content of a judgment is equivalent to the totality of the true inferences it licenses." (Presumably the "true inferences" may not include contents expressible only demonstratively; otherwise we still have less than full discursivity on the conception Bernstein is expressing.) This conception of full discursivity is of a piece with the conception of the predicative that underlies Bernstein's distinction between predicative and non-predicative thinking. But why should we hand over the idea of discursivity, and the idea of predication, to the proponents of a rationalized conception of rationality? Why should we accept that a necessary situatedness in lived experience makes a meaningful utterance less than fully discursive, and precludes our parsing it as predicating something of something? Discourse too, including predicating, is part of life, not something we merely approximate to in so far as we approximate to the condition of a disembodied intellect.

In his conclusion, Bernstein notes, correctly, that I take the space of reasons to be "there for appreciating and refining once we have been induced into it." He says "this ignores the way in which practices shape contents." I do not ignore the way in which practices shape contents; the Gadamerian strand in my thinking is precisely an insistence on it. Bernstein's suggestion that there is an opposition here reflects an assumption I would strongly dispute, that if one wants to insist that the very idea of a conception of what is a reason for what makes sense only in the context of practices or traditions, one is thereby perhaps saddled with relativism, and certainly precluded from simple realism, about the layout of the space of reasons.

Axel Honneth

Honneth describes *Mind and World* as giving an epistemological foundation for my meta-ethical thinking, which he represents as a rather ambitious "moral realism." I have some reservations about this characterization.

All I have aimed to do in the direction of "moral realism," in my writings about ethics, is to counter bad reasons for supposing that the idea of attaining truth – getting things right – is unavailable in the context of ethical thinking. That constitutes a limited and piecemeal defense of the thesis that truth is indeed achievable in ethics. I do not see why this should seem eccentric, even ~~~~~And I am not happy with Honneth's suggestion that we can make ~~~~~ by taking the practices that underlie our comprehension of ~~~~~ts to express independent facts about human needs, vulnerabilities, and dispositions. That seems too close to the idea that ethical truth, if there is such a thing, would have to be founded in prior extra-ethical truth, an idea that, as Honneth notes, I resist in the interpretation of Aristotle (and not only there, I add).

As for the connection with Mind and World, it is not right to say, as Honneth does, that I take my departure in the book, when I present my recommended conception of experience, from moral rather than cognitive experience. When I resist a restrictive conception of the natural, the point is not to vindicate the idea that we take in more through the senses than the facts accommodated by a scientistic world-view. The point is that the restrictive conception of the natural would prevent us from making sense of the idea of taking in *anything* through the senses – including facts that scientism has no problem with. When I appeal to the Aristotelian conception according to which virtue – a specific responsiveness to reasons – is second nature, the point is to remind ourselves that there is really no tension between the idea of responsiveness to reasons, in general, and the idea of a natural capacity. This recovers a conception that makes it intelligible how experience takes in facts in general – not ethical facts in particular. No doubt dislodging a scientistic conception of the natural has the additional effect of dislodging a supposed reason for holding that what is there to be experienced is restricted to what a scientistic world-view can countenance, so there is a convergence with the aim of my writings on ethics. But that is an incidental bonus, not something central to my project in Mind and World.

Honneth says my realism seems to hover between two alternatives, pragmatism and representationalism. I think the trouble here is that his choice is not well conceived. In particular, representationalism, as he describes it, strikes me as a straw man. I believe the concept of getting things right transcends capture in ordinarily pragmatist terms, but I resist the suggestion that that commits me to supposing our access to the world can be seen as a mere passive reception, if that means that our capacities to see things straight are intelligible independently of our being practically involved with the world. Here I am refusing to select one of Honneth's alternatives, but I do not accept that I am ambivalent between them. I am simply insisting that a sensible conception of the capacity to achieve correct representations must have more resources than Honneth allows.

Searching in my writings for a definition of moral phenomena, Honneth extracts one from my limited defense of the categorical imperative – with the surprising result that "every object perceived with the validity of an imperative is a 'moral' fact." Later he has this raise a problem about how moral thinkers might understand the very point of being reflective, starting as they do with apparently perceived practical necessities. But I do not recognize the picture of me that this depends on. I do not see why Honneth is so sure we need a definition of the moral, and I certainly would not offer a definition in terms of the categorical imperative. In so far as it matters to classify questions about what to do as moral or otherwise (which is perhaps not very far), anyone who has the idea at all can tell a moral question when she sees one. People who care about morality do not have a problem distinguishing "moral" facts from other states of affairs in the world. And it strikes me as dubious that the way to address those who do not have the idea of the moral at all is to give them a definition.

Honneth's main point is, I think, independent of everything I have commented on so far. He complains that my neo-Aristotelian conception of virtue is unhelpful when we come to think about cases where pre-reflective certainties have to be suspended. And he suggests that this traces back to an unresolved tension in my thinking, between a Gadamerian conception of the anonymous happening of tradition and a more Hegelian conception of progress toward a more adequate realization of reason.

At one point he even suggests I take for granted that the morally shaped life-worlds we find ourselves in, as a result of our upbringing, are such as never to yield the uncertainty or unclarity that necessitates ethical reflection. It is true that my talk of a standing obligation to reflect is never filled out with the sort of detail Honneth looks for, concerning what shape reflection might take. But that hardly warrants accusing me of assuming that unreflective perception always suffices to handle any ethical situation.

In my writings about Aristotle, I acknowledge that Aristotle gives insufficient weight to the requirement of reflectiveness. It is not, however, completely absent, even in Aristotle's own writings. Honneth's talk of coming to understand the web of our habituated ethical responses as the embodiment of principles has a counterpart in Aristotle's talk of arguing from the *that* to the *because*. Aristotelian practical wisdom includes a sense of how the particular practical necessities that one seems to be confronted with hang together intelligibly. Honneth is quite wrong to say that this kind of thought departs from my way of seeing things.

Honneth says that my Aristotelian conception of ethical character occupies a middle position between mere habit and rational deliberation. That sounds wrong to me. I think Aristotelian practical wisdom already embraces a capacity for rational deliberation. Such a capacity is not something one still needs to attain after one has already graduated beyond mere habit into a formed ethical character.

I sympathize with Honneth in his dissatisfaction with the merely gestural quality of my allusions to reflection. But Honneth seems to assume that the way to bring more substance to our understanding of how our reflection needs to go, when the lifeworld available to perception does not yield a clear-cut answer to the question what we should do, is to talk about a *method* for ethical reflection when everyday certainties are bracketed. Honneth's own favored method involves a drive to greater inclusiveness. Now I am not convinced by his suggested criterion for progress. It seems to me that including more claims can just as well lead to deterioration, when the claims newly included do not deserve to be respected, as to improvement. But, more importantly, I am not convinced that we should expect there to be a method, a formally describable procedure, for improving our ethical thinking.

I suspect that this methodological assumption shapes Honneth's suspicion that there is an unresolved tension in my thinking. Nothing short of including a procedure would strike him as giving due weight to the idea of a progress toward realizing reason. That is why he thinks a Gadamerian appeal to a notion that works like Aristotle's notion of practical wisdom stands in opposition to a Hegelian conception of a progress of the human spirit. If we reject Honneth's methodologism, it is not so clear that there is a tension there at all, let alone that a lack of a resolution for it debilitates my thinking.

Notes

1 See "Mental Events," in *Essays on Actions and Events* (Oxford: Clarendon Press, 1980), pp.207–225.

2 Clearly these questions would require much discussion. For a very helpful treatment of Davidson, see Jennifer Hornsby, "Agency and Causal Explanation," in *Simple Mindedness* (Cambridge, MA: Harvard University Press, 1997), pp.129–153.

3 I discuss Friedman's attempt to exploit my appeal to Gadamer, in reinforcing his claim that I cannot accommodate a common sense realism, in "Gadamer and Davidson on Understanding and Relativism," in Jeff Malpas, Ulrich Arnswald, and Jens Kertscher (eds), *Gadamer's Century: Essays in Honor of Hans-Georg Gadamer* (Cambridge, MA: MIT Press, 2002), pp.173–193.

4 Already in Kant at his best, the a priori form of our sensibility is not completely autonomous – not independent of the intellect. See *Critique of Pure Reason*, tr. Norman Kemp Smith (London: Macmillan, 1929), B160–B161n.

5 By the time second nature comes on the scene for me, it is too late for bald naturalists to feel comfortable "nodding in agreement," as Pippin engagingly imagines. The point of my appeal to second nature is to make it unthreatening to hold precisely what bald naturalists deny – that concepts of conceptual phenomena cannot be integrated into the natural as they conceive it.

6 He transmutes my *insistence* on the social character of conceptual competence into an *admission* (presumably reluctant) that the perceiving subject "cannot be detached from the languages and traditions into which the subject has been initiated."

7 See the first two papers in my *Mind, Value, and Reality* (Cambridge, MA: Harvard University Press, 1998).

8 See *Ethics: Inventing Right and Wrong* (Harmondsworth: Penguin, 1977).

9 Compare *Critique of Pure Reason*, B142, where, similarly, talk of subjective and objective validity seems to amount to a distinction between subjective and objective purport.

10 I think Robert Brandom's gloss on the self-legislating theme in terms of norms as *instituted* (see *Making It Explicit: Reasoning, Representing, and Discursive Commitment* (Cambridge, MA: Harvard University Press, 1994), pp.46–55) risks falling foul of this point.

11 *Critique of Pure Reason*, B131.

12 Robert Brandom first put them to me as a topic for discussion in this context, and I consider them in my response to his "Perception and Rational Constraint: McDowell's *Mind and World*," in Enrique Villanueva (ed.), *Perception* (*Philosophical Issues*, 7 (Ridgeview, Atascadero, 1996)), pp.241–259; see ibid., pp.296–298. See also Brandom's contribution to this volume, and my response to him.

13 In the response cited in the previous note, p.297.

14 Brandom's considerations about retreating to a safer claim do not, I think, address the question I am raising here. I am not wondering if the physicist's report is "covertly the product of a process of inference." I am wondering if its credentials as knowledgeable are essentially inferential – which is not the case with standard cases of perceptual knowledge.

15 My pretext for considering this was a report by Rorty of an off-hand remark by Davidson, but the point probably does not impinge on Davidson. See Alex Byrne, "Spin Control," in Villanueva (ed.), *Perception*, pp.261–273, and my response, at pp.288–289.

16 Interested readers should consult the earlier response that Wright cites. I shall not here repeat points from it that he does not take up in his Postscript.

17 I do think the label "quasi-inferential" is unfortunate in a context in which a key distinction is the one Sellars draws between inferential and non-inferential acquisition of knowledge. And I note that the phrase "intermediary something-that-P" is Wright's own.

18 Perhaps a sufficiently unfavorable doxastic setting can make it impossible to take in facts – that is, make it impossible to enjoy experiences in my sense. That is not what Wright claims: that there can be experiences in my sense that fail to justify because of an unfavorable doxastic setting.

19 In the sense of constituting the subject's reasons for it. There is no problem about supposing that non-conceptual input might make things reasonable in the way a cyclist's sub-threshold cues about the terrain make bodily adjustments reasonable; see *Mind and World*, pp.163–164.

20 On this part of Wright's discussion, see further note 14 (pp.428–429) of my "Reply to Commentators."

21 I owe the image to Richard Rorty, who of course often gets his epaulettes slashed off.

22 The point does not turn on the fact that indistinguishability is not transitive, as Putnam seems to suggest. Even if it were, the highest common factor conception of the reach of experience would be unwarranted.

23 See *Mind and World*, pp.70–71. I do not understand why Putnam thinks he had to guess, in order to arrive at the thought that what I mean by "the realm of law" is the domain of what can be made intelligible by the methods of the natural sciences; the point is perfectly explicit at that place in my text.

24 Putnam's pretext for this misreading of my talk of the realm of law is the claim that Sellars conceived the realm of law in a strictly physicalistic way. But I do not take the idea of placing things in the realm of law from Sellars. It is my replacement for what he, much less satisfactorily in my view, contrasts with placing things in the space of reasons, namely, "empirical description." So Sellars's views about natural law, whatever they may be, are irrelevant. And in any case, I know no basis for Putnam's claim that Sellars's reflections about laws of nature exclude the laws of the special sciences.

25 Davidson's anomalous monism is not particularly to the point here. That strand in Davidson's thinking does figure elsewhere in my book (pp.74–76), as a softening of the dualism of reason and nature which, I claim, does not succeed in breaking out of the impasse that the dualism leads to. Here too, it is not a question of selecting one position in the philosophy of mind for discussion, in a way that indicates that alternatives, such as functionalism, ought to get their share of attention too. Functionalism would belong at a quite different point in my map of the options, as a specific story about how the mental can be embraced within nature conceived as the realm of law – a specific version of bald naturalism. As I have explained, the fact that there are different ways of being a bald naturalist is irrelevant to my purposes.

26 "About" shifts, harmlessly so long as we keep track of it, between, say, "thinking about NN" and "thinking about how things are with NN." For the world to be what the contents of experience are about, we need "about" in the second of these uses.

27 Hans-Georg Gadamer, *Truth and Method*, tr. revised by Joel Weinsheimer and Donald G. Marshall (New York: Crossroad, 1992).

28 Compare Richard Rorty's reaction to my book: "The Very Idea of Human Answerability to the World: John McDowell's Version of Empiricism," in Richard Rorty, *Truth and Progress: Philosophical Papers*, vol. 3 (Cambridge: Cambridge University Press, 1998), pp.138–152. Rorty accuses me of putting the world in a secular counterpart to the position of an authoritarian deity. What annoys Rorty is the centrality to my thinking of the very thing Bernstein thinks I am not alert to – my insistence that experience mediates an authority objects themselves have over empirical thought.

29 I bypass what Bernstein represents as Wright's first pass at this point. Whatever Wright intends (see his Postscript and my response), I certainly insist on a disanalogy between inferentially and non-inferentially acquired beliefs. There is not the threat Bernstein fears to the specificity of sensory experience.

INDEX